The Mini Oxford Encyclopaedic Dictionary

VOLUME 1

A–bohea

The Leisure Circle

Oxford is a trade mark of Oxford University Press

This edition published 1986 by
The Leisure Circle Ltd
by arrangement with Oxford University Press

Line-drawings by M.G. Croft

Printed and bound in Great Britain by
Cox & Wyman Ltd, Reading

PREFACE

ACCORDING to the distinction used by H. W. Fowler in the preface to the *Concise Oxford Dictionary*, a dictionary normally takes the uses of words and phrases as such for its subject-matter and is concerned with giving information about the things for which these words and phrases stand only so far as correct use of the words depends upon knowledge of the things. In an encyclopaedia, on the other hand, the emphasis will be much more on the nature of the things for which the words and phrases stand.

This book attempts to combine in a form that can be handled conveniently the essential features of dictionary and encyclopaedia. Where things are more easily explained by pictures or diagrams than by words, illustration has been used to help out definition.

VOCABULARY

The general reader for whom the book is intended may not always have another dictionary or encyclopaedia at his ready disposal and so the vocabulary has been chosen with an eye to the needs of one who may require either type of information. Information about words, however, is more often sought by the average user of a reference book than information about things and the vocabulary has therefore been based on that of the *Concise Oxford Dictionary* and the definitions retain its historical ordering. Familiar words are less fully treated, however, and the phrases illustrating such words have been more sparingly used so as to obtain a wider scope for the treatment of things.

The vocabulary should thus be adequate for the reader who consults the book for ordinary dictionary purposes. But it also contains terms in everyday use which would be excluded from an ordinary dictionary because of their technical and scientific character or which would be very briefly dealt with; familiar words in semi-technical use (e.g. *vertical trust*, *combine*, etc.); the names of famous people (e.g. statesmen, explorers, inventors, artists, and writers), historical, contemporary, or fictitious; and the names of important places and events.

Special pains have been taken to ensure that scientific and technical terms are accurate in definition and at the same time intelligible to the user, but the present pace of development in science and technology is so swift that no reference book which deals with them in even the most general way can ever be completely up to date: between the time the book is compiled and its publication new words and senses will have acquired fresh shades of meaning or become obsolescent.

In order to keep the book within reasonable compass obsolete words and phrases have been omitted except for a few which some special interest has made it desirable to retain.

ABBREVIATIONS

Abbreviations in current use appear in their alphabetical place in the body of the text to save a separate alphabet. But there is a separate list of those abbreviations used in the dictionary itself.

ETYMOLOGY

For the sake of space derivations have been omitted with a few exceptions. These occur where the etymology is especially interesting or unexpected (e.g. *penicillin*, *derrick*), or when a thing has been named after its inventor or place of origin (e.g. *Fortin barometer*, *Borstal*). In these cases the etymology is given in square brackets at the end of the entry.

CROSS-REFERENCES

Where a word is given in small capitals in a definition, this indicates that reference to the word in its alphabetical place will provide further information (e.g. INSULIN in the entry for *pancreas*) or discuss the term which is given in comparison or contradistinction (e.g. NOBLE or PRECIOUS metals as opposed to *base* metals).

PRONUNCIATION

The pronunciation indicated represents the standard speech of southern England.

1. **Accent.** The accentuation mark ′ is placed after the vowel or vowel sound in the stressed syllable.

2. **Phonetic system.** Where the pronunciation of a word or part of a word cannot be shown by the ordinary spelling and markings, a phonetic spelling is given in round brackets immediately after the black-type word. The phonetic scheme is as follows:

CONSONANTS: b; ch (ch*in*); d; dh (dh*e* = the); f; g (g*o*); h; j; k; l; m; n; ng (*si*ng); ngg (*f*ing*er*); p; r; s (*sip*); sh (sh*ip*); t; th (th*in*); v; w; y; z; zh (*vi*zh*on* = vision).

ṅ indicates French nasalization of preceding vowel.

The symbol χ represents the ch in *Ba*ch, *lo*ch, pronounced as a guttural sound or as k.

VOWEL COMBINATIONS:

ā ē ī ō ū o͞o (mate mete mite mote mute moot)
ă ĕ ĭ ŏ ŭ o͝o (rack reck rick rock ruck rook)
ār ēr īr ūr (mare mere mire mure)
âr êr ôr (part pert port)
ah aw oi oor ow (bah bawl boil boor brow)

Vowels and combinations (as *er*) printed in italic within the brackets indicate vague sounds frequently indistinguishable from each other.

Vowels marked ˘̄ may be pronounced either way, e.g. **pă′trĭot** (pā- or pă-).

3. **Pronunciation without respelling.** As far as possible pronunciation is shown without respelling by placing symbols over the words (e.g. **ā, ĕ, a̅r̅, e̅r̅, o͝o,** etc.) in the black type. Unmarked vowels in the black-type words indicate vague sounds.

(*a*) The ordinary spelling often coincides with the phonetic system described in paragraph 2.

(*b*) The following additional symbols are used in the black type:

ė = ĭ (nā′kėd, rėlȳ′, cŏ′llėge, prī′vėt)
i͡r, u͡r = **e͡r** (bi͡rth, bu͡rn)
ȳ, y̆ = ī, ĭ (ĭmplȳ′, sŭ′nny̆)
y̅r̅=i̅r̅ (ly̅r̅e)

(*c*) Final *e* when unmarked is mute, i.e. not to be pronounced. Thus **āpe** is to be pronounced āp. Where final *e* is pronounced, it is marked as in **rĕ′cĭpė**. Where *e* is mute in the headword it is mute also (unless marked) in derivatives placed in the same entry, e.g. **ba̅r̅e, ba̅r̅′ely̆, ba̅r̅′enėss.**

(*d*) A doubled consonant is pronounced as single (**sĭ′lly̆, mă′nnĭsh**) unless indicated as in **plai′nnėss** (-n-n-).

(*e*) The following letters and combinations have the usual values in English spelling which are shown alongside them:

Vowel Combinations

ae = ē (aegis)	**eu, ew** = ū (feud, few)
ai = ā (pain)	**ey** = ĭ (donkey)
air = a̅r̅ (fair)	**ie** = ē (thief)
au = aw (maul)	**ier** = e̅r̅ (pier)
ay = ā (say)	**oa** = ō (boat)
ea, ee = ē (mean, meet)	**ou** = ow (bound)
ear, eer = e̅r̅ (fear, beer)	**our** = ow*er* (flour)
ei = ē (ceiling)	**oy** = oi (boy)

Consonants

c is hard and = k (cob, cry, talc) *but*
c before **e, i, y,** is soft and = s (ice, icy, city)
dg before **e, i, y,** = j (judgement)
g before **e, i, y,** is soft and = j (age, gin, orgy), except when doubled (digger, haggis, baggy)
n before **k,** hard **c, q, x** = ng (zinc uncle, tank, banquet, minx)
ph = f (photo)
qu = kw (quit)
tch = ch (batch)
wh = w or hw (when)
x = ks (fox)

Thus in **gĕm** the pronunciation of *g* is not marked because it comes under the rule above for soft *g*, but **gĕt** is followed by (g-) to show that here exceptionally **g** before **e** is hard as in *go*.

The following combinations have the values shown:

-aġe = -ĭj (garbage)
-al, -el preceded by *d, n, t* = -l (Handel, mental)
-en, -ent preceded by *d, t,* = -n, -nt (madden, fatten, student)
-sion after vowels = -zh*o*n (division)
-sm = -zm (atheism, spasm)
-tion = -sh*o*n (salvation)
-nch when final = -nsh or -nch (trench)
-ous = *-us* (furious)
-sion after consonants = -sh*o*n (passion, tension)
-tual, -tue, -ture = -cho͞o*a*l, -cho͞o, -ch*er* as well as -tū*a*l, -tū, -tūr̄, esp. in common words

SWUNG DASH (~)

The 'swung dash' or 'tilde' is frequently used to save space in the body of the entry. It represents the headword (or a derivative of the headword printed in black type in the same entry) when this is repeated as a different part of speech or when it is used in combination with another word, either hyphenated or detached (but not when it has become part of a complete new word). For example, in the article **pitch**[1] *n.* we have ~ *v.t.* when the headword becomes a new part of speech, and ~*black* and ~*-pine* when it is in combination (but *pitchblende* as a whole word). The addition of an initial letter to the swung dash indicates a change from a small letter in the headword to a capital or vice versa (e.g. *F*~ in the article **flood** represents the Flood recorded in Genesis).

ABBREVIATIONS USED IN THE DICTIONARY

(*Abbreviations in general use have entries in the main text*)

abbrev./iation, -iated
abl./ative
abs./olute(ly)
acc./ording
accus./ative
act./ive
adj(s)., adjective(s)
adv(s)., adverb(s)
aeron./autics
AF, Anglo-French
Afr./ican
alg./ebra
allus./ive(ly)
Amer./ican
anal./ogy
anat./omy
Anglo-Ind./ian
anon./ymous
antiq./uities
anthrop./ology
app./arently
Arab./ic
Aram./aic
arbitr./ary
archaeol./ogy
archit./ecture
arith./metic
assim./ilated
assoc./iated
astrol./ogy
astron./omy
at. wt, atomic weight
attrib./utive(ly)
augment./ative
Austral./ian
av./oirdupois

b./orn
back form./ation
bibl./ical
bibliog./raphy
biochem./istry
biol./ogy
Boh./emian
bot./any
Br./itish
Braz./ilian
Bulg./arian
Burm./ese
Byz./antine

c./entury
Camb./ridge
c/irca
cap./ital
Celt./ic
cf., compare
Ch./urch
chem./istry
Chin./ese
chronol./ogy
cinemat./ography
cogn./ate
collect./ive(ly)
colloq./uial(ly)
com./mon
comb./ination
commerc./ial
comp., compar./ative
compl./ement
conch./ology
confus./ion
conj., conjunction, conjugation
conn./ected
constr./uction
contempt./uous(ly)
contr./action
cop./ulative
correl./ative
corresp./onding
corrupt./ion
cryst./allography
cu./bic

d./ied
Dan./ish
dat./ive
demonstr./ative
deriv./ative
derog./atory
dial./ect
dict./ionary
diff./erent
dim./inutive
diplom./acy
dist./inct, -inguished
distrib./utive
Du./tch
dub./ious

E., east(ern)
eccles./iastical

ecol./ogy
econ./omics
Egyptol./ogy
E. Ind., East Indian (i.e. of the East Indies)
elect./ricity
ellipt./ical
embryol./ogy
emphat./ic(ally)
eng., engin./eering
Engl., England, English
entom./ology
erron./eous(ly)
esp./ecial(ly)
ethnol./ogy
etym./ology
euphem./ism
Eur./ope(an)
exagg./eration
exc./ept
exch./ange
excl., exclamation, exclusive
expr./essing etc.

f./rom
facet./ious etc.
fam./iliar etc.
fem./inine etc.
fig./urative etc.
Fl./emish
foll./owing (word)
footb./all
fort./ification
Fr./ench
freq./uent(ly)
frequent./ative(ly)
fut./ure (tense)

Gael./ic
gen., general(ly), genitive
geog./raphy
geol./ogy
geom./etry
Ger./man
Gk, Greek
govt., government
gram./mar

Heb./rew
her./aldry
Hind./ustani
hist./orical, history
hort./iculture

i., intransitive
Icel./andic
illit./erate
imit./ative
imp., imper./ative
imperf./ect
impers./onal
improp./er(ly)
incl./uding, inclusive
Ind./ian (i.e. of the Indian sub-continent)
ind., indicative, indirect
indecl./inable
indef./inite
inf./initive
infl./uence(d)
instr./umental (case)
int./erjection
interrog./ative(ly)
intrans./itive
Ir./ish
iron./ically
irreg./ular(ly)
It., Ital./ian

Jap./anese
Jew./ish
joc./ular(ly)

L, Latin
lang./uage
l.c., lower case
LG, Low German
lit./eral(ly)
Lith./uanian
LL, late Latin

magn./etism
manuf./acture
masc./uline
math./ematics
MDu., Middle Dutch
ME, Middle English
mech./anics
med./icine
med.L, medieval Latin
metall./urgy
metaph./or(ically)
metaphys./ics
meteor./ology
Mex./ican
MG, Middle German
MHG, Middle High German
mil./itary
min./eralogy
MLG, Middle Low German
mod./ern
morphol./ogy
mus./ic
myth./ology

N., north(ern)
n./oun
N. Amer., North America(n)
nat. hist., natural history
naut./ical
nav./al
nec./essary, -essarily

neg./ative(ly)
neut./er
nom./inative
Norm./an
north./ern
Norw./egian
ns., nouns
N.T., New Testament
num./eral

obj./ect
obl./ique
obs./olete
obsolesc./ent
occas./ional(ly)
OE, Old English
OF, Old French
OHG, Old High German
OIr., Old Irish
OLG, Old Low German
ON, Old Norse
onomat./opoeic
ophthalm./ology
opp., (as) opposed (to), opposite
ord./inary, -inarily
orig./inal(ly)
ornith./ology
O.T., Old Testament

p./age
paint./ing
palaeog./raphy
palaeont./ology
parenth./etic(ally)
parl./iament(ary)
part./iciple, -icipial
pass./ive(ly)
past t./ense
path./ology
pedant./ic(ally)
perf./ect (tense)
perh./aps
Pers./ian
pers./on(al)
Peruv./ian
pharm./acy, -acology
philol./ogy
philos./ophy
phon., phonet./ics
phot., photog./raphy
phr./ase
phrr., phrases
phys./ics
phys. chem., physical chemistry
physiol./ogy
pl./ural
pluperf./ect
poet./ical
Pol./ish
pol./itics etc.
pol. econ., political economy

pop./ular(ly)
Port./uguese
poss./essive
pp., pages
pr./onounced
prec., (the) preceding (word)
pred./icate, -icative
pref./ix
prep./osition(al)
pres./ent (tense)
pret./erite
print./ing
prob./able, -ably
pron., pronoun,
pronounced, pronunciation
prop./er(ly)
pros./ody
psych., psychol./ogy
psychoanal./ysis

railw./ay
R.C., Roman Catholic
ref./erence
refl./exive(ly)
rel./ative
repr./esent
rhet./oric
Rom./an
Russ./ian

S., south(ern)
S. Afr., South African
Sansk./rit
Sax./on
Sc./ottish
Scand./inavian
sculp./ture
sent./ence
Serb./ian
sing./ular
Slav./onic
sociol./ogy
sp./elling
Span./ish
spec./ial(ly)
specif./ic(ally)
sport./ing
Stock Exch., Stock Exchange
subj., subject, subjunctive
superl./ative
surg./ery
surv./eying
Swed./ish
syn./onym

tech./nical(ly)
teleg./raphy
term./ination
Teut./onic
theatr./ical

theol./ogy
trans./itive
transf., in transferred sense
transl./ation
trig./onometry
Turk./ish
typ./ography

U.K., United Kingdom
ult./imate(ly)
unexpl./ained
Univ./ersity
Univv., Universities
U.S., United States
usu./al(ly)

v./erb
var., variant, various
varr., variants
v. aux., verb auxiliary

vbl, verbal
vbs., verbs
v.i., verb intransitive
voc./ative
v.r., verb reflexive
v.t., verb transitive
vulg./ar(ly)

W., west(ern)
w./ith
W. Afr., West African
wd, word
wds, words
W. Ind., West Indian (i.e. of the West Indies)

yr(s), year(s)

zool./ogy

A

A, a (ā). 1. 1st letter of modern English and ancient Roman alphabet, descended, through Greek and Latin, from first letter, *aleph* (א), of Hebrew and Phoenician alphabets, in English representing orig. a low-back-wide vowel sound and now a number of vowel sounds. 2. 1st in series, order, or class, esp. (alg. etc.) first known quantity. 3. *A*, (mus.) 6th note of natural scale (C major); scale or key with this note for tonic. 4. *A. 1*, applied in Lloyd's Register to ships in first-class condition in respect of both hull (designated by A) and equipment (1); hence, first-class, prime, perfect.

A *abbrev.* Adult (i.e. that may contain material unsuitable for children, of cinema film); alto; ampere(s); Australian (in $A, Australian dollars).

a, an (*a*, *a*n; emphat., ā, ăn) *adj.* (the indefinite article) One; some, any; (in, to, for) each.

Å *abbrev.* Ångström(s).

a- *prefix.* 1. On, in, at. 2. (also *an-*) Without, not.

A.A. *abbrev.* Anti-aircraft; Automobile Association; *AA*, (of cinema film) for exhibition only to persons over 14 years.

A.A.A. *abbrev.* (U.S.) Agricultural Adjustment Administration; Amateur Athletic Association; Automobile Association of America.

Aa'chen (ahχ-). (Fr. *Aix-la-Chapelle*) Ancient city of Germany near Belgian and Dutch borders, scene of coronation of German kings until 16th c.

A. and M., A. & M. *abbrev.* (Hymns) Ancient and Modern.

aar'dvârk (âr-) *n.* S. Afr. ant-eating quadruped (*Orycteropus*

afer) with long extensile tongue. [Du., = 'earth-pig']

aardwolf (âr'dwŏŏlf) *n.* (pl. *-ves*). Carnivorous mammal (*Proteles cristatus*) resembling the hyena.

Aaron (âr'*o*n). Brother of Moses and traditional founder of Jewish priesthood; *~'s beard*, (see Ps. 133: 2) any of various plants, esp. a St. John's wort (*Hypericum calycinum*); *~'s rod*, (see Numbers 17: 8) plant with tall flowering stem, esp. a mullein (*Verbascum trapsus*).

aasvogel (ah'sfōgl) *n.* Any of several large S. Afr. vultures. [Du., = 'carrion-bird']

ab-, abs- *prefix.* Off, away, from.

A.B. *abbrev.* Able seaman.

ă'ba, ă'bba, abay'a *ns.* Sack-like outer garment worn by Arabs.

abă'ck *adv.* Backwards; *taken ~*, (of ship) with square sails pressed back against the mast by the wind; (fig.) surprised, disconcerted.

ă'bacus *n.* (pl. *-cuses* or *-cī*). 1. Frame for arithmetical calculation

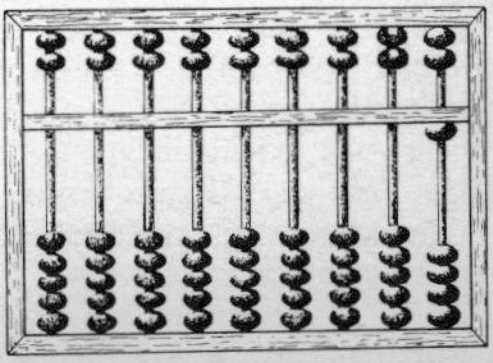

with balls sliding on wires, used before the adoption of the nine figures and zero, and still in China etc. and in elementary teaching. 2. (archit.) Upper member, often a square flat slab, of capital, supporting architrave.

Abă'ddon. Hebrew name of APOLLYON.

aba'ft (-bah-) *adv.* On or towards stern of ship. ~ *prep.* Aft of, behind.

ăbalō'nė *n.* (U.S.) Haliotis.

abă'ndon *v.t.* Give up, surrender, forsake. ~ *n.* Careless freedom. **abă'ndonment** *n.* **abă'ndoned** (-nd) *adj.* (esp.) Profligate.

abăndonee' *n.* Underwriter to whom salvage of wreck is abandoned.

abā'se *v.t.* Humiliate, lower, make base. **abā'sement** *n.*

abă'sh *v.t.* Embarrass, confound.

abā'te *v.* Diminish, make or become less; lower; deduct (part of price); (law) quash (action), end (nuisance). **abā'tement** *n.*

ă'batis, abă'ttis *n.* (mil.) Obstacle of felled trees with branches pointing outwards.

ă'battoir (-twar) *n.* Slaughterhouse.

abaya: see ABA.

A'bba[1] (ă-). Used (in '~, *Father*') in invocations to God; title of bishops in Syriac and Coptic Churches. [Aram. = 'father']

abba[2]: see ABA.

ă'bbacy̆ *n.* Office, jurisdiction, or tenure of abbot or abbess.

A'bbas[1] (ă-; *or* abah's) (566–652). Uncle of Muhammad.

A'bbas[2] (ă-; *or* abah's), 'the Great'. Shah of Persia; reigned 1587–1628.

A'bbasĭd (ă-; *or* abah'-) *n.* Member of dynasty of caliphs ruling in Baghdad 750–1258, claiming descent from ABBAS[1].

abbā'tial (-shal) *adj.* Of an abbey, abbot, or abbess.

ă'bbé (-ā) *n.* Frenchman entitled to wear ecclesiastical dress, esp. without official duties.

ă'bbėss *n.* Female superior of community of nuns, in those orders in which monks are governed by abbots.

Abbevĭ'llian (ăbv-) *adj.* & *n.* (Culture) of the earliest palaeolithic period in Europe, represented by the remains found at Abbeville, N. France (formerly called CHELLEAN).

ă'bbey *n.* Body of monks or nuns governed by an abbot or abbess; monastic buildings; church or house once an abbey or part of it.

A'bbey Thē'atre (ă-, -*er*). Irish national theatre, located since 1904 in Abbey St., Dublin.

ă'bbot *n.* Superior of community of monks (now chiefly in Benedictine and Augustinian orders), usu. elected by the monks for life or period of years, and freq. holding certain episcopal rights; ~ *of misrule*: see MISRULE. [Aram. *abba* father]

abbrē'vĭāte *v.t.* Shorten, contract (esp. word, by writing part for the whole). **abbrēvĭā'tion** *n.*

A B C *n.* Alphabet; rudiments of subject; alphabetical railway timetable.

ă'bdĭcāte *v.* Renounce, relinquish, (esp. crown) formally or by default. **ăbdĭcā'tion** *n.*

ă'bdomėn (*or* ăbdō'-) *n.* 1. (anat.) Part of body between diaphragm and floor of pelvis, containing digestive and other organs. 2. (zool.) Hinder part, not bearing walking limbs, of insects, spiders, etc. **ăbdŏ'mĭnal** *adj.* **ăbdŏ'mĭnallȳ** *adv.*

ăbdū'cent *adj.* (anat., of muscles) Drawing back.

abdŭ'ct *v.t.* Take away (esp. woman) by force or fraud; (of muscle etc.) draw limb from normal position. **abdŭ'ction, abdŭ'ctor** *ns.*

abea'm *adv.* On a line at right angles to ship's or aircraft's length; opposite the middle of ship's or aircraft's side.

ābėcėdar'ian *adj.* 1. Arranged alphabetically, as the 119th Psalm. 2. Elementary, ignorant. ~ *n.* (U.S.) Pupil learning the alphabet.

à Becket, Thomas: see BECKET[2].

abĕ'd *adv.* (archaic, poet.) In bed.

Abĕdnē'gō (ă-; *or* *a*bĕ'dnĭgō). One of three Jewish youths who came unharmed from a furnace into which they were thrown by Nebuchadnezzar (Dan. 3).

A'bel (ā-). 2nd son of Adam, killed by his brother Cain (Gen. 4: 1–16).

Abélard (ăbā-), Pierre (1079–1142). French philosopher; lecturer in the schools of Paris; advocate of rational theological inquiry and founder of scholastic theology. (See also HÉLOÏSE.)

abē'le (*or* ā'bl) *n.* White poplar, *Populus alba.*

Aberdee'n (ă-). City on E. coast of N. Scotland, former county town of Aberdeenshire, since May 1975 part of the region of Grampian; known as the 'granite city' and humorously credited with extremely parsimonious population; university, 1494; ~ *Angus*, (one of) a breed of polled black beef cattle; ~ *terrier*, Scotch terrier. **Aberdō'nian** *adj.* & *n.*

aberglaube (ah'berglowb*e*) *n.* Superstition, irrational belief. [Ger.]

ăbĕ'rrant *adj.* 1. Wandering, straying from moral standard. 2. (biol.) Diverging from normal type. **ăbĕ'rrance** *n.*

ăberrā'tion *n.* 1. Mental or moral slip or error; deviation from type. 2. (optics) Non-convergence of rays to one focus. 3. (astron.; also ~ *of light*) Displacement of true position of heavenly body to observer on earth, due to earth's motion and non-instantaneous transmission of light; *planetary* ~, aberration due to motion of the planet itself.

abĕ't *v.t.* Help or encourage, esp. in wrongdoing. **abĕ'tter, abĕ'ttor** *ns.*

ăb ĕ'xtra. From outside. [L]

abey'ance (-bā-) *n.* State of suspension, dormant condition (of rights etc.).

ABERDEEN

abhŏr' *v.t.* Regard with disgust and hatred. **abhŏ'rrent** *adj.* Inspiring disgust, repugnant, detestable. **abhŏ'rrentlў** *adv.* **abhŏ'rrence** *n.*

abī'de *v.* (past t. and past part. *abōde*, occas. *abided*). Remain; continue; dwell (archaic); wait for (archaic); (with neg.) tolerate; ~ *by*, remain faithful to.

A'bĭgail (ă-). 1. Wife of Nabal

and subsequently of David (1 Sam. 25). 2. In Beaumont and Fletcher's 'Scornful Lady', the 'waiting gentlewoman' (cf. 1 Sam. 25: 24–31); hence (*a*~), waiting-woman, lady's-maid.

abĭ'lĭtȳ *n.* Sufficient power, capacity (*to* do); legal competency (to act); cleverness, talent, mental power.

Abĭ'mėlĕch (-k). 1. Son of Gideon, one of the judges of Israel: see Judges 8, 9. 2. King of Gerar, southern Palestine: see Gen. 20, 26.

ăb ĭnĭ'tio (-shĭō) From the beginning (abbrev. *ab init.*). [L]

ābīōgĕ'nėsĭs *n.* T. H. Huxley's term for spontaneous generation (opp. BIOGENESIS).

ă'bjĕct *adj.* Brought low, miserable, craven, degraded. **ă'bjĕctlȳ** *adv.*

abjur'e (-oor) *v.t.* Renounce on oath. **ăbjurā'tion** *n.*

abl. *abbrev.* Ablative.

ăblā'tion *n.* 1. Removal (esp. in surgery, of part of body). 2. (geol.) Wastage of a glacier by evaporation and melting.

ă'blatĭve *adj.* (gram.) Of the case denoting direction from a place, also time and source, agent, or instrument. ~ *n.* (Word in) ablative case; ~ *absolute*, Latin construction of noun and participle (both in ablative case), expressing time, occasion, or circumstances.

ă'blaut (-owt) *n.* (philol.) Systematic vowel permutation (not due to influence of contiguous sounds) in root of word in derivation, as in s*i*ng, s*a*ng, s*u*ng.

ablā'ze *adv.* Blazing; on fire.

ā'ble *adj.* Having the power or ability; talented, clever; ~*-bodied*, physically fit, robust; ~ *seaman*, (abbrev. A.B.) rating in Royal Navy above *ordinary seaman*.

ablū'tion (*or* -ōō-) *n.* Ceremonial washing; water or wine used in this; (pl.) process of washing oneself.

ă'bnėgāte *v.t.* Deny oneself (thing), renounce (right, belief). **ăbnėgā'tion** *n.*

abnôr'mal *adj.* Deviating from type, exceptional, irregular. **ăbnôr'mallȳ** *adv.* **ăbnôrmă'lĭtȳ** *n.*

abnôr'mĭtȳ *n.* Irregularity; monstrosity.

A'bō (ă-), **ă'bō** *n.* (Austral. slang) Aboriginal.

Åbo (aw'bōō). Swedish name of TURKU, Finland.

aboar'd (-ôrd) *adv.* & *prep.* On board (ship, railway train, etc.)

abō'de *n.* Dwelling-place.

abŏ'lĭsh *v.t.* Put an end to.

ăbolĭ'tion *n.* Action or fact of abolishing; in 18th and 19th centuries esp. movement against slavery. **ăbolĭ'tionĭsm** *n.* **ăbolĭ'tionĭst** *n.* One advocating abolition, esp. of slavery or capital punishment.

ăbomā'sum *n.* Fourth stomach of ruminant.

A-bŏmb (-m) *abbrev.* Atom(ic) bomb.

abŏ'mĭnable *adj.* Morally or physically loathsome, detestable, odious, revolting; *A*~ *Snowman*, YETI. **abŏ'mĭnablȳ** *adv.*

abŏ'mĭnāte *v.t.* Loathe, dislike strongly.

abŏmĭnā'tion. *n.* Loathing; object or practice deserving of aversion or disgust; ~ *of desolation*, desecration of the Temple at Jerusalem: see Dan. 9: 27, Matt. 24: 15.

ăborĭ'gĭnal *adj.* Indigenous, existing or present at dawn of history or before arrival of colonists or invaders. ~ *n.* Aboriginal inhabitant. **ăborĭ'gĭnēs** (-z) *n.pl.* (also sing. *-ine*) Aboriginal inhabitants, plants, etc.

abôr't *v.* 1. (Cause to) miscarry; (biol.) become sterile, remain undeveloped. 2. Fail, cease prematurely. 3. (aeronaut., U.S.) Terminate (space-flight) prematurely. ~ *n.* (aeronaut., U.S.) Premature termination of space-flight.

abôrtĭfā'cient (-shent) *adj.* & *n.* (Drug etc.) causing abortion.

abôr'tion *n.* 1. Expulsion of foetus from uterus before 28th week of pregnancy, either spontaneous or induced (in law, expulsion at any time before the full term); (pop.) operation etc. inducing this. 2. Foetus expelled in abortion. 3. Misshapen creature.

abŏr'tionĭst *n.* One who performs abortion.

abŏr'tĭve *adj.* Premature; fruitless; rudimentary. **abŏr'tĭvelў** *adv.* **abŏr'tĭvenėss** *n.*

Aboukir Bay (*a*boo͞'kēr): see NILE.

abou'lĭa, abū'lĭa *n.* (psychol.) Loss of will-power.

abou'nd *v.i.* Be plentiful; be rich *in*, teem or be infested *with*.

abou't *adv.* On every side; near; somewhere round; here and there; astir; almost; (naut.) on or to the opposite tack (so *come, put,* ~, = TACK *v.*²); *be* ~ *to* (do), be on the point of doing; *come* ~, happen; *put* ~, distracted, annoyed; ~ *turn!* (mil. etc.) turn so as to face in opposite direction. ~ *prep.* 1. On every side of; near; with. 2. Concerning. 3. Occupied with. 4. Here and there in, on, etc.

abo've (-ŭv) *adv.* Higher up, overhead; upstream; earlier in a book etc. ~ *prep.* Over, higher than, of higher rank, etc., than; in addition to; ~*-board*, without concealment; fair, open, honest.

ăb ō'vō. From the (very) beginning. [L]

Abp *abbrev.* Archbishop.

ăbracadă'bra *n.* Cabbalistic word formerly used as charm, orig. by Gnostics, and believed to have power of curing agues etc. when written in triangular arrangement and worn as amulet; (now) spell, mysterious formula, gibberish.

abrā'de *v.t.* Scrape off, wear away, injure, by rubbing.

A'brahăm (ā-). Hebrew patriarch, from whom all Jews trace their descent (Gen. 11: 27–25: 10); ~*'s bosom*, heavenly abode of the blessed dead (Luke 16: 22); *Plains of* ~, plateau near Quebec, scaled from St. Lawrence River by English army under WOLFE (1759) and scene of subsequent battle with French under Montcalm which decided fate of Canada.

ăbrā'sion *n.* Rubbing or scraping off; rough or sore place on skin caused by this; (geol.) wearing away of earth's surface by windborne particles of rock or sand (cf. EROSION).

abrā'sĭve *adj.* Tending to produce abrasion. ~ *n.* Any substance, as emery, carborundum, etc., used for grinding or polishing.

ăbrėă'ction *n.* (psychiatry) Removal, by revival and expression, of the emotion associated with an event which has undergone repression in memory.

abrea'st (-ĕst) *adv.* Side by side and facing the same way; ~ *of*, keeping up with, not behind (times etc.).

abrĭ'dge *v.t.* Condense, shorten, curtail. **abrĭ'dgement, -gment** *n.* Curtailment; epitome, abstract.

abroa'd (-awd) *adv.* In or to foreign lands; broadly, in different directions; (of rumour etc.) current; *from* ~, from foreign countries.

ă'brogāte *v.t.* Repeal, cancel. **ăbrogā'tion** *n.*

abrŭ'pt *adj.* Sudden, hasty; brusque; disconnected; steep; (bot.) truncated. **abrŭ'ptlў** *adv.* **abrŭ'ptnėss** *n.*

abs-: see AB-.

A'bsalom (ă-). 3rd and favourite son of DAVID, killed while leading rebellion against his father (2 Sam. 13–19).

ă'bscėss *n.* Local inflammation of body tissues with deep suppuration caused by bacteria which destroy the cells in the centre of the area and leave a cavity filled with pus.

abscĭ'ssa *n.* (pl. *-s* or *-ae*). (geom.) Part of line between fixed point on it and ordinate to it from any other point.

abscĭ'ssion *n.* Cutting off; (bot.) separation.

abscŏ'nd *v.i.* Go away secretly, fly from the law.

ă'bseil (-sāl) *n.* (mountaineering) Descent using a rope doubled over a projection. ~ *v.i.* Use abseil.

ă'bsence *n.* Being away or

absent; non-existence, want (*of*); abstracted state.

ă'bsent *adj.* Not present; not existing; abstracted in mind: ~-*minded*, abstracted, preoccupied, whence ~-*mindedly*, ~-*mindedness*. **absĕ'nt** *v.t.* Keep (oneself) away, withdraw (oneself).

ăbsentee' *n.* Person not present, one who absents himself from his duties etc.; person (esp. landlord) habitually living away from property. **ăbsentee'ism** *n.*

ă'bsinth, -the *n.* Wormwood, the plant or its essence; strong greenish-grey liqueur flavoured with wormwood and aniseed.

ă'bsĭt ō'mĕn. May no ominous significance attach to the words. [L]

ă'bsolute (-ūt *or* -ōōt) *adj.* Complete, perfect, pure; unrestricted, independent; despotic, ruling arbitrarily; not in (the usual) grammatical relation with other words; real, not relative or comparative; unqualified; self-existent and conceivable without relation to other things; ~ *alcohol*, containing at least 99% pure alcohol by weight; ~ DROUGHT, ~ HUMIDITY: see these words; ~ *magnitude*, magnitude of a star as it would appear at a distance of 10 parsecs; ~ *music*, self-dependent instrumental music without literary or other extraneous suggestions (opp. PROGRAMME music); ~ *pitch*, ability to recognize or reproduce pitch of notes, (also) pitch of a note defined scientifically in terms of vibrations per second; ~ *temperature*, temperature measured on a Centigrade (Celsius) scale which has its zero at absolute zero; ~ *zero*: see ZERO. **ă'bsolutelȳ** *adv.* Completely, independently; (colloq., *absolu'tely*) yes, quite so.

ăbsolu'tion (-ū- *or* -ōō-) *n.* Formal forgiveness, esp. ecclesiastical declaration of forgiveness of sins; remission of penance.

ă'bsolutĭsm (-ū- *or* -ōō-) *n.* 1. (theol.) Dogma that God acts absolutely in matter of salvation. 2. (pol.) Principle of absolute government, despotism. **ă'bsolutĭst** *n.* Supporter of absolute government; (metaphys.) one who maintains absolute identity of subject and object.

absŏ'lve (*or* -z-) *v.t.* Set or pronounce free from blame etc.; acquit.

absôr'b (*or* -z-) *v.t.* Swallow up, incorporate; engross the attention of; suck in (liquid); take in (heat, light, etc.). **absôr'bable** *adj.* That can be absorbed.

absôr'bent (*or* -z-) *adj.* Having a tendency to absorb; ~ *cotton*, (U.S.) = COTTON[1] wool. ~ *n.* Absorbent substance.

absôr'ption (*or* -z-) *n.* Action of absorbing, fact of being absorbed; natural or medicinal removal of tissues or deposits.

abstai'n *v.i.* Keep oneself *from* doing something, esp. from drinking alcohol. **abstai'ner** *n.*

abstē'mĭous *adj.* Sparing or moderate in food, drink, etc. **abstē'mĭouslȳ** *adv.* **abstē'mĭousnėss** *n.*

abstĕ'ntion *n.* Refraining or holding back; (parl. etc.) not using one's vote.

ă'bstĭnence *n.* Abstaining from food, pleasure, etc.: *total* ~, abstaining from alcohol. **ă'bstĭnent** *adj.* Practising abstinence.

ă'bstrăct *adj.* Not concrete; theoretical, not practical; (of art etc.) concerned with pure form and pattern, free from representational qualities. ~ *n.* 1. *the* ~, ideal or theoretical way of regarding things. 2. Epitome, summary. 3. Abstraction, abstract term. **abstră'ct** *v.t.* Deduct, remove; steal; disengage (attention etc.); summarize; *abstra'cted*, withdrawn in thought, not attending.

abstră'ction *n.* Withdrawal, removal; abstract idea; absent-mindedness; abstract art.

abstru'se (-ōōs) *adj.* Hard to understand, profound. **abstru'selȳ** *adv.* **abstru'senėss** *n.*

absûr'd *adj.* Incongruous, unreasonable, ridiculous. **absûr'dlȳ** *adv.* **absûr'dĭtȳ** *n.*

abŭ'ndance *n.* Plenty, more than enough; affluence; call in solo whist (see SOLO); (phys.) amount present. **abŭ'ndant** *adj.* Plentiful, rich, in abundance. **abŭ'ndantlў** *adv.*

abū'se (-z) *v.t.* Make bad use of, misuse; speak insultingly to or about. ~ (-s) *n.* Misuse, perversion; unjust or corrupt practice; insulting speech. **abū'sĭve** *adj.* **abū'sĭvelў** *adv.* **abū'sĭvenėss** *n.*

abŭ't *v.* Have common boundary with; border (*on*); end *on*, lean *against*. **abŭ'tment** *n.* (archit.) Support from which arch, vault, etc., springs, and which receives the lateral thrust. **abŭ'tter** *n.* (law) Owner of adjoining property.

Abў'dŏs. 1. Ancient city on the Hellespont, home of LEANDER. 2. Ancient ruined city of Upper Egypt.

abў'sm *n.* (poet.) Abyss.

abў'smal (-z-) *adj.* Bottomless (esp. fig.). **abў'smallў** *adv.*

abў'ss *n.* Primal chaos; bottomless chasm; deep gorge.

abў'ssal *adj.* Of lowest depths of ocean.

Abўssĭ'nĭa (ă-) *n.* Former name of Ethiopia. **Abўssĭ'nĭan** *adj.* & *n.*

A.C. *abbrev.* Aircraftman (also A/C); Alpine Club; alternating current (also a.c.); *ante Christum* (L, = 'before Christ').

a/c *abbrev.* Account.

A.C.A. *abbrev.* Associate of the Institute of Chartered Accountants.

acā'cia (-sha) *n.* 1. Leguminous shrub or tree of genus *A~* (subfamily Mimoseae), found in warmer regions of Old World and Australia, some species of which yield gum arabic, catechu, etc. 2. N.-Amer. locust-tree (*Robinia pseud-Acacia*, false ~), with sweet-scented pea-like flowers, freq. grown as ornamental tree in England etc.

ă'cadēme *n.* (properly) = ACADEMUS; (used by mistake in poet. style for) the Greek ACADEMY, hence, college, university. [Gk; mistake perh. caused by Milton's 'grove of Academe', i.e. Academus]

ăcadĕ'mĭc *adj.* 1. Of an academy or academician; of a university or college. 2. Of the philosophic school of Plato, sceptical. 3. Scholarly; abstract, cold, merely logical; unpractical; theoretical, conventional. ~ *n.* Member of university; (pl.) academic arguments.

ăcadĕ'mĭcal *adj.* Of a college or university. **ăcadĕ'mĭcallў** *adv.* **ăcadĕ'mĭcals** (-z) *n.pl.* Academical robes, college or university costume.

acădemĭ'cian (-shan) *n.* Member of academy, esp. of Académie française or Royal Academy of Arts.

Académie française (ăkădāmē frahṅsāz). French literary academy, founded by Richelieu (1635); membership, limited to 40, is considered the highest distinction for men of letters; among its functions are the compilation and periodical revision of a dictionary of the French language (1st ed. 1694), and of a grammar (1st ed. 1932).

Acadē'mus (ă-). (Gk legend) Hero who revealed hiding-place of their sister Helen to the Dioscuri when they invaded Attica.

acă'demў *n.* 1. *A~*, pleasure-garden near Athens (said to have belonged to ACADEMUS) in which Plato taught; Plato's followers, the philosophical school founded by him. 2. A secondary or high school (esp. private). 3. Place of training in a special art. 4. Society for cultivating literature, art, etc.; *the A~*, (esp.) the Royal Academy of Arts; one of its annual exhibitions.

Acā'dĭa. Name given by French to district in what is now known as Nova Scotia, first settled by them at end of 16th c. **Acā'dĭan** *adj.* & *n.* (Native, inhabitant) of Acadia; (descendant) of Acadians.

acănthŏpterў'gĭan *adj.* & *n.* (Fish) of group Acanthopterygii, usu. with hard spiny rays in dorsal and anal fins.

acă'nthus *n.* 1. Herbaceous plant of genus *A~* with large, deeply-cut, hairy, shining leaves, native of southern Europe, Asia, and Africa. 2. (archit.) Conventionalized leaf of *A. mollis* or *A. spinosus* (with narrower spiny-toothed leaves) used as ornament, esp. on the Corinthian and Composite capitals.

ă'carĭd *n.* Arachnid of family Acaridae, a mite or tick.

acătalĕ'ctĭc *n.* & *adj.* (pros.) (Line) that is not catalectic.

acc. *abbrev.* Account; accusative.

Accad, Accadian: see AKKAD.

accē'de (*a*ks-) *v.i.* Consent, agree (*to*); (also ~ *to*) enter upon office or dignity, join party.

accĕlerā'ndō (aks- *or* ach-) *adv.*, *adj.*, & *n.* (pl. *-os*). (mus.) (Passage performed) with gradual increase of speed. [It.]

accĕ'lerāte (*a*ks-) *v.* Make, become, quicker; cause to happen earlier; put on pace; *accelerated particle*, (phys.) one subjected to acceleration, esp. by electrical or magnetic means.

accĕlerā'tion (*a*ks-) *n.* Accelerating; vehicle's power to accelerate; (phys.) rate of increase in velocity of moving body (written, e.g., 10 ft per sec./sec. if body moves 10 ft per second faster in every second).

accĕ'lerative (*a*ks-) *adj.* Tending to increase speed.

accĕ'lerātor (*a*ks-) *n.* Thing that increases anything's speed; pedal which operates throttle of internal combustion engine; substance added to mixture to reduce time taken by chemical reaction; electrical or magnetic apparatus giving high velocities to free electrons or other atomic particles; ~ *nerve*, any of the cardiac sympathetic nerves, discharges from which quicken and strengthen the heart-beats.

ă'ccent (ăks-) *n.* Prominence given to syllable by stress or pitch; mark used to indicate syllabic pitch, vowel quality, etc. (see ACUTE, CIRCUMFLEX, GRAVE², ~); individual, local, or national mode of pronunciation; (pl.) speech; (pros.) rhythmical stress; (mus.) stress recurring at intervals; (fig.) distinctive character; emphasis *on*.

accĕ'nt *v.t.* Pronounce with accent or stress, emphasize; mark with (written) accents; intensify, make conspicuous.

accĕ'ntor (*a*ks-) *n.* Bird of family Prunellidae, including the DUNNOCK (*hedge* ~).

accĕ'ntūal (*a*ks-) *adj.* Of accent; (esp. of verse) in which metre or rhythm results from alternation of strong and weak (not long and short) syllables.

accĕ'ntuallỹ *adv.*

accĕ'ntūāte (*a*ks-) *v.t.* Accent (esp. in fig. senses). **accĕntūā'tion** *n.*

accĕ'pt (*a*ks-) *v.t.* Consent to receive; answer (invitation etc.) affirmatively; receive as adequate or true; tolerate; agree to meet (bill of exchange); undertake (office). **accĕ'ptance, accĕ'ptor** *ns.*

accĕ'ptable (*a*ks-) *adj.* Worth accepting, welcome, pleasing. **accĕ'ptablỹ** *adv.* **accĕptabĭ'lĭtỹ** *n.*

acceptā'tion (ăks-) *n.* Particular sense given to word or phrase; generally recognized meaning.

accĕ'ptėd (*a*ks-) *adj.* Generally recognized or believed in.

ă'ccĕss (ăks-) *n.* 1. Approach; addition; right or means of approach; being approached. 2. Attack or outburst.

accessary: see ACCESSORY *n.*

accĕ'ssĭble (*a*ks-) *adj.* Able to be reached or entered; open to influence (of). **accĕ'ssĭblỹ** *adv.* **accĕssĭbĭ'lĭtỹ** *n.*

accĕ'ssion (*a*ks-) *n.* Acceding or attaining (esp. to throne or manhood); joining, addition; (law) addition to property by natural growth or artificial improvement.

accĕ'ssorỹ (*a*ks-) *adj.* Additional, subordinately contributive, adventitious. ~ *n.* 1. (correctly spelt *accessary* but *-ory* is now more usual) Person who is privy *to* an (esp. criminal) act or helps in it but is not the chief actor. 2. Accompaniment, adjunct; (pl., commerc.) smaller articles of (esp. woman's) dress, as shoes, gloves, etc.; minor fittings for motor-car, camera, etc.

acciaccatura (*a*chahk*a*toor'*a*) *n.*

(mus.) Grace-note performed quickly before an essential note of a melody.

ă'ccidence (ăks-) *n.* Part of grammar dealing with inflexions, i.e. with the accidents or non-essentials of words; book, or part of one, on this subject.

ă'ccident (ăks-) *n.* 1. Event without apparent cause, the unexpected; unintentional act, chance misfortune, mishap. 2. Property or quality not essential to our conception of a substance, attribute; mere accessory. **ăccidĕ'ntal** *adj.* **ăccidĕ'ntallȳ** *adv.* **ăccidĕ'ntal** *n.* (mus.) Sharp ♯, flat ♭, or natural ♮ sign occurring not in key signature but before particular note.

accidie (ă'ksĭdĭ) *n.* Sloth; laziness or indifference.

acclai'm *v.t.* Welcome or applaud loudly, hail. ~ *n.* Shout of applause or welcome.

ăcclamā'tion *n.* Loud and eager assent; (pl.) shouting in person's honour.

acclī'mate (*or* ă'klĭmāt) *v.* (U.S.) = ACCLIMATIZE. **ăcclĭmā'tion** *n.*

acclī'matīze *v.t.* Habituate to new climate or surroundings. **acclīmatīzā'tion** *n.* Fact, process, of acclimatizing, esp. (biol.) in ref. to transference of plants or animals to a new environment.

acclĭ'vĭtȳ *n.* Upward slope.

ăccolā'de (*or* -ahd) *n.* 1. Ceremony of conferring knighthood, usu. by stroke on shoulder with flat of sword. 2. Expression of approval. 3. (mus.) Vertical line or brace coupling staves.

accŏ'mmodāte *v.t.* 1. Adapt (*to*); harmonize; reconcile, settle differences between; compose (quarrel). 2. Equip, supply (*with*); oblige, confer favour on; find lodging for. **accŏ'mmodāting** *adj.* Obliging.

accommodā'tion *n.* 1. Adaptation, adjustment; (of eye) adjustment of shape of lens to bring light rays from various distances to focus upon retina; (of sense organs) property which causes the nervous discharges initiated by a stimulus of constant activity to diminish or die out. 2. Settlement, compromise. 3. Serviceable thing, convenience. 4. Lodgings. 5. Money loan. 6. ~ *address*, address where letters are sent for person who has no permanent address or wishes to conceal it; ~ *bill*, bill of exchange given not for value received but for purpose of raising money on credit; ~ *ladder*, ladder up ship's side for entering or leaving small boat.

acco'mpanĭment (-ŭm-) *n.* Accompanying thing; appendage; (mus.) subsidiary part, gen. instrumental, supporting a solo instrument or voice, choir, etc.

acco'mpanĭst, -ȳist (-ŭm-) *n.* Performer of accompaniment.

acco'mpanȳ (-ŭm-) *v.t.* Go with, escort, attend; coexist with; (mus.) support (player, singer, chorus, etc.) by performing subsidiary part.

accŏ'mplĭce (*or* -ŭm-) *n.* Associate, usu. subordinate, in guilt or crime.

accŏ'mplĭsh (*or* -ŭm-) *v.t.* Perform, carry out, succeed in doing. **acco'mplĭshed** (-sht) *adj.* Having accomplishments. **acco'mplĭshment** *n.* Achievement, fulfilment; social attainment.

accor'd *v.* 1. Agree, be consistent (*with*). 2. Grant (indulgence, request, etc.). ~ *n.* Consent; mutual agreement; harmonious correspondence in colour, tone, etc.; volition (as *of one's own* ~).

accor'dance *n.* Conformity, agreement. **accor'dant** *adj.*

accor'dĭng *adv.* ~ *as*, in proportion as, in a manner depending on which of certain alternatives is true; ~ *to*, in a manner consistent with; on the authority of. **accor'dĭnglȳ** *adv.* Correspondingly; in accordance with what might be expected; in due course; therefore.

accor'dĭon *n.* Small portable musical instrument with bellows and keyboard admitting wind to metal reeds when keys are depressed; ~ *door*, ~ *pleat*(*ing*), door, pleat(ing), having a series of folds like the bellows of an accordion.

accŏ′st *v.t.* Approach and address (esp. boldly); (of prostitute) solicit.

accouchement (ăkōōshmahṅ) *n.* Lying-in, delivery. ***accoucheur*** (ăkōōshẽr) *n.* Man-midwife. ***accoucheuse*** (-ẽrz) *n.* Midwife. [Fr.]

accou′nt *n.* 1. Counting, reckoning; *money of* ~, denominations of money used in reckoning. 2. Amount of money deposited with a bank; credit facilities allowed by shop etc. to customer; statement of money received and expended, with balance; statement of discharge of responsibilities generally, answering for conduct; final account at judgement-seat of God (esp. in *sent, gone, to one's* ~); *balance, square* ~*s* (*with*), settle account by payment of money due (freq. fig.); *for* ~ *of*, to be sold on behalf of; *give* (*good*) ~ *of oneself*, be successful, give favourable impression; *keep* ~*s*, keep statement of expenditure and receipts; *on* ~, as interim payment; *on* ~ *of*, in consideration of, because of; *on no* ~, not for any reason, certainly not; *on one's own* ~, for one's own purposes and at one's own risk. 3. Reckoning in one's favour, profit, advantage; *turn to* ~, make useful. 4. Estimation; *make* ~ *of*, value, esteem; *take into, leave out of*, ~, (fail to) take into consideration. 5. Narration, report, description (*of*). ~ *v.* 1. Consider, regard as. 2. ~ *for*, give reckoning for; answer for; explain cause of, serve as explanation of.

accou′ntable *adj.* 1. Bound to give account, responsible, liable. 2. Explicable. **accountabĭ′lĭtў** *n.*

accou′ntancў *n.* Profession or duties of accountant.

accou′ntant *n.* Professional keeper or inspector of accounts; *chartered* ~: see CHARTER *v.t.*

accou′tre (-ōōter) *v.t.* Attire, equip, esp. with special costume (chiefly in past part. *accoutred*). **accou′trement** (-ōōtre-) *n.* (usu. in pl.) Equipment, trappings.

Accra (*a*krah′). W.-Afr. seaport on Gulf of Guinea, capital of Ghana.

accrĕ′dĭt *v.t.* Gain credit for, dispose one to believe; send out with credentials; attribute *to*. **accrĕ′dĭtėd** *adj.* Officially recognized; generally accepted.

accrē′te *v.* Grow together or into one; form round or on *to*; attract (such additions). **accrē′tion** *n.* Growth by organic enlargement; increase by external additions; adhesion of extraneous matter; matter so added, extraneous addition.

accru′e (-ōō) *v.i.* Fall (*to* one) as a natural growth, advantage or result (esp. of interest on invested money).

accū′mūlāte *v.* Heap up, amass, make money; grow numerous, form increasing mass or heap. **accūmūlā′tion** *n.* **accū′mūlatĭve** *adj.*

accū′mūlātor *n.* 1. One who collects. 2. Electric cell (or group of these connected in series) in which the chemical action which produces the current can be reversed by passing an electric current through it in the opposite direction, and which thus constitutes a means of storing electric energy in the form of chemical energy; storage battery. 3. Bet in which the amount won on one event is staked on a subsequent event.

ă′ccūrate *adj.* Precise, exact, correct. **ă′ccūratelў** *adv.* **ă′ccūracў** *n.*

accûr′sėd, accûr′st *adj.* Lying under a curse; execrable, detestable.

ăccūsā′tion (-z-) *n.* Accusing, being accused; indictment.

accū′satĭve (-z-) *adj.* (gram.) Of the case chiefly denoting the direct object of a verb or used following certain prepositions. ~ *n.* (Word in) accusative case. **accū′satĭvelў** *adv.*

accūsatôr′ial (-z-) *adj.* ~ *procedure* etc., that in which prosecutor and judge are not the same (opp. *inquisitorial*).

accū′satorў (-z-) *adj.* Conveying or implying accusation.

accū′se (-z) *v.t.* Charge with

fault, indict; blame, lay fault on.

accŭ'stom *v.t.* Familiarize by habit or custom. **accŭ'stomed** (-md) *adj.* Customary, usual; wonted, used.

āce *n.* 1. Card, die-face, etc., with one pip; one point at rackets etc. 2. Distinguished airman (orig., one who has brought down ten enemy aircraft); person excelling in any sport or skill; (tennis etc.) unreturnable stroke, esp. a service; point thus scored.

acē'dia *n.* = ACCIDIE.

Acĕ'ldama (*or* ak-). Field near Jerusalem purchased for cemetery with blood-money received by Judas Iscariot (see Matt. 27: 8; Acts 1: 19); scene of slaughter or bloodshed. [Aram. = 'field of blood']

acĕ'phalous *adj.* Headless; (zool.) having no part of body specially organized as head; (bot.) with head aborted or cut off; (pros.) lacking the regular first syllable.

acer'bĭtȳ *n.* Astringent sourness; bitterness of speech, manner, or temper.

ă'cėtal *n.* Colourless pleasant-smelling liquid formed by slow oxidation of alcohol; class of complex ethers, derivatives of aldehyde, of which this is the type.

ăcetă'ldėhȳde *n.* Aldehyde.

ăcėtă'nĭlīde *n.* White crystalline solid made by action of acetic acid on aniline and used as febrifuge and analgesic.

ă'cėtāte *n.* Salt of acetic acid; synthetic material in the manufacture of which acetic acid is used; ~ *fibre*, textile fibre made from cellulose acetate.

acē'tĭc *adj.* Of, producing, vinegar; ~ *acid*, colourless pungent biting organic acid (CH_3COOH) which gives vinegar its characteristic taste.

acē'tifȳ *v.* Turn into vinegar, make or become sour. **acētĭfĭcā'tion** *n.*

aceto-, acet- *prefix.* (chem.) Derived from, connected with, acetic acid or acetyl.

ă'cėtōne *n.* Colourless fragrant inflammable liquid ketone (CH_3COCH_3) widely used as an organic solvent and in making chloroform etc.

ă'cėtous (*or* asē'-) *adj.* Of, producing, vinegar; sour, acid.

ă'cėtȳl *n.* Monovalent radical (CH_3CO) of acetic acid. **acĕtȳlā'tion** *n.* Introduction of acetyl group(s) into (a compound) by means of a chemical reaction. **acĕ'tȳlāte** *v.* **acĕ'tȳlātėd, acĕ'tȳlating** *adjs.*

acĕ'tȳlēne *n.* Colourless, nearly odourless (when pure), highly inflammable gaseous hydrocarbon, usu. prepared by adding water to calcium carbide (impurities in which produce the characteristic unpleasant smell), and used for lighting, for welding and cutting metals, etc.

A.C.F. *abbrev.* Army Cadet Force.

Achaea (*a*kē'*a*). 1. District of ancient Greece along S. shore of Gulf of Corinth. 2. Roman province comprising all the southern part of Greece. **Achae'an** *adj.* & *n.* 1. In Homer, apparently = Greek; hence, (one) of the early Greeks; of the early Greek civilization. 2. In classical times, (inhabitant) of Achaea.

Achates (*a*kā'tēz). (Gk & Rom. legend) Friend of Aeneas, usu. called *fidus* (faithful) ~; hence, *fidus* ~, faithful friend.

ache (āk) *v.i.* & *n.* (Suffer, be a source of) continuous dull pain.

ă'chēne (-k-; *or* -kē'n) *n.* (bot.) Small dry one-seeded fruit which does not open to liberate seed.

A'cheron (ăk-). (Gk myth.) One of the rivers of Hades, over which the dead were carried by Charon's ferry.

A'chėson (ăch-), Edward Goodrich (1856–1931). American inventor of carborundum and artificially prepared graphite.

Acheu'lian (*a*shōō-) *adj.* & *n.* (Of) the palaeolithic period succeeding the Abbevillian. [*St. Acheul*, Amiens, France]

achie've *v.t.* Accomplish;

acquire; reach (an end). **achie′vement** *n.* 1. Completion, accomplishment; thing accomplished. 2. (her.) Escutcheon or ensign armorial commemorating distinguished feat, hatchment.

Achilles (*a*kĭ′lēz). (Gk legend) Hero of the Trojan war, son of Peleus and Thetis; was killed by Paris with a poisoned arrow that pierced his heel where his mother had held him in infancy when she plunged him into the Styx to make him invulnerable; hence, *Achilles' heel*, vulnerable part; ~ *tendon*, tendon in heel by which calf-muscles extend foot.

ăchromă′tĭc (-k-) *adj.* Colourless; transmitting light without dispersing it into its constituent colours; ~ *lens*, pair of lenses, e.g. one of crown glass and the other of flint glass, the dispersion of one correcting the dispersion of the other. **achrōmatĭsm** *n.* Achromatic quality. **achrō′matize** *v.t.*

acĭ′cūlar *adj.* Like a small needle or bristle.

ă′cĭd *adj.* 1. Sour, sharp to taste; (fig.) biting, severe. 2. Having properties of an acid. ~ *n.* One of a class of chemical compounds in which hydrogen may be replaced by metals to form salts, neutralizing alkalis, usu. corroding or dissolving metals, and having sour taste; ~ *drop*, sweet made of sugar strongly flavoured with tartaric acid; ~ *salt*, a salt derived from an acid having more than one replaceable hydrogen atom, one at least of which has not been replaced by a metal; ~ *test*, testing for gold by means of aqua fortis; (fig.) crucial test. **acĭ′dĭfȳ** *v.*

acĭ′dĭc *adj.* Acid; acid-forming.

ăcĭ′dĭtȳ *n.* Acid property.

ăcidō′sis *n.* (path.) Acid condition of blood and body tissues.

acĭ′dūlātėd, acĭ′dūlous *adjs.* Made slightly acid.

ACHILLES

A'cĭs (ā-). (Gk myth.) Lover of GALATEA².

ăck-ăck *adj.* & *n.* Anti-aircraft (gun etc.). [from letter A in signallers' former phonetic alphabet]

ăck ĕ'mma. 1. *Ante meridiem.* 2. Air mechanic. [names in signallers' former phonetic alphabet of letters A, M]

acknow'lėdge (-nŏl-) *v.t.* Admit the truth of, admit, own; announce receipt of; express appreciation of. **acknow'ledg(e)ment** *n.* Acknowledging; thing given or done in return for service etc.

aclĭ'nĭc *adj.* ~ *line*, magnetic equator, line on which magnetic needle has no dip.

ă'cmė *n.* Highest point or pitch, culmination; (fig.) point of perfection.

ă'cnė *n.* Skin eruption due to inflammation of sebaceous glands, common in adolescence, and characterized by red pimples esp. on face.

ă'colȳte *n.* Officer of one of the two 'ministries' which replaced minor orders in R.C. Church in 1973, attending priests and deacons, lighting and carrying candles, etc.; attendant, esp. at altar; assistant.

Aconcagua (ăkŏnkah'gwa). Extinct volcano and highest peak (7035 m.; 23,080 ft) in Andes, near boundary between Argentina and Chile.

ă'conīte *n.* Plant of poisonous ranunculaceous genus *Aconitum*, with five blue or yellow sepals, of which one is helmet-shaped; esp. the common European *A. napellus*, monkshood, or *A. lycoctonum*, wolfsbane; dried root of this plant used in pharmacy and as poison.

acŏ'nĭtīne (*or* -ēn) *n.* Bitter white crystalline highly poisonous alkaloid, essential principle of aconite.

ā'cōrn *n.* Fruit of oak, oval nut growing in shallow woody cup; ~ *barnacle*, sessile barnacle, of many genera.

acŏtȳlē'don *n.* (bot.) Plant with no distinct cotyledons or seed-leaves, as fern, moss, etc. **acŏtȳlē'donous** *adj.*

acou'stĭc (-ōō- *or* -ow-) *adj.* Of the sense of hearing; of sound, of acoustics; (of building material) sound-absorbent; ~ *mine*, underwater mine designed to be detonated by sound-waves proceeding from ship's propellers. **acou'stĭcs** *n.* Science of sound; properties of building, room, etc., in respect of audibility of sounds. **acou'stĭcal** *adj.* **acou'stĭcallȳ** *adv.*

acquai'nt *v.t.* Make aware or familiar, inform; *be acquainted with*, have personal knowledge of. **acquai'ntance** *n.* Personal knowledge; person with whom one is acquainted but not intimate. **acquai'ntanceshĭp** *n.*

ăcquĭĕ'sce *v.i.* Agree, esp. tacitly; not object. **ăcquĭĕ'scence** *n.* **ăcquĭĕ'scent** *adj.*

acquīr'e *v.t.* Gain, get, come to have; *acquired characteristic*, characteristic gained through influence of environment, and not inherited from parents; *acquired taste*, (object of) liking gained by experience. **acquīr'ement** *n.* Acquiring; (pl.) mental attainments.

ăcquĭsĭ'tion (-z-) *n.* Acquiring; thing acquired, useful or pleasant addition.

acquĭ'sĭtĭve (-z-) *adj.* Desirous of, given to, acquiring and retaining. **acquĭ'sĭtĭvelȳ** *adv.* **acquĭ'sĭtĭvenėss** *n.*

acquĭ't *v.t.* Pay (debt); declare not guilty, free from blame; ~ *oneself* (*well*, *ill*, etc.), perform one's part or duty.

acquĭ'ttal *n.* Discharge from debt; performance (of duty); deliverance from a charge by verdict etc.

acquĭ'ttance *n.* Payment of or release from debt; receipt in full.

acre¹ (ā'ker) *n.* Land-measure, legally 4840 sq. yds (4047 sq. m), but varying in some districts, (pl.) lands, fields; *county* (*land*) *of broad* ~*s*, Yorkshire. **acreage** (ā'kerĭj) *n.* Amount of acres, acres collectively.

Acre² (ā'ker). (also *St. Jean d'Acre*; Arab. *'Akkā*) Seaport of Israel; captured by Christians in 3rd Crusade, 1191; recaptured, the last Christian stronghold in the Holy Land, 1291.

ă'crĭd *adj.* Bitterly pungent, irritating; of bitter temper or manner. **ă'crĭdlȳ** *adv.* **acrĭ'dĭtȳ** *n.*

ăcrĭflā'vĭne (*or* -ēn) *n.* Orange-red powder used as antiseptic for wounds etc.

ăcrĭmō'nĭous *adj.* Marked by acrimony. **ăcrĭmō'nĭouslȳ** *adv.* **ăcrĭmō'nĭousnėss** *n.*

ă'crĭmonȳ *n.* Bitterness of temper or manner.

ă'crobăt *n.* Performer of daring and spectacular gymnastic feats, rope-dancer. **ăcrobă'tĭc** *adj.* **ăcrobă'tĭcallȳ** *adv.* **ăcrobă'tĭcs** *n.*

ăcromĕ'galȳ *n.* Disease due to over-activity of pituitary gland, resulting in overgrowth of bones esp. of extremities and skull.

ă'cronȳm *n.* Word formed from initial letters of other words (e.g. *Ernie*, *Nato*).

ăcrophō'bĭa *n.* (psych.) Dread of high places.

acrŏ'polĭs *n.* Citadel or upper fortified part of ancient Greek city, esp. (*A*~) that of Athens, situated on a hill about 250 ft high and richly adorned, esp. in 5th c. B.C., with architecture and sculpture.

acrŏ'ss *prep.* & *adv.* From side to side (of), to or on the other side (of), forming a cross with.

acrŏ'stĭc *n.* Poem etc. in which first or first and last letters of lines form word(s), the alphabet, etc.; puzzle so made.

ăcroter̄'ion *n.* (pl. *-ia*). (archit.) Pedestal for statue or ornament on angle of classical pediment.

acrȳ'lĭc *adj.* ~ *acid*, monobasic acid (CH_2:CH . COOH); ~ *fibre*, *resin*, synthetic substance prepared from acrylic acid or its derivatives. ~ *n.* Acrylic fibre, resin, etc.

ăct *n.* 1. Thing done, deed; process of doing something. 2. Decree passed by legislative body, court of justice, etc.; statute; (law) instrument in writing to verify facts. 3. Each of main divisions of dramatic work, in which definite part of whole action is completed. 4. Variety or circus turn. 5. *Acts* (*of the Apostles*), book of N.T. immediately following Gospels, relating early history of Christian Church and dealing largely with the lives and work of the Apostles Peter and Paul; traditionally ascribed to St. Luke. ~ *v.* 1. Represent in mimic action, perform (play); personate, play part of (on stage or fig. in real life); perform on stage. 2. Perform actions, do things; perform special functions; (of things) work, fulfil functions; ~ *as*, perform in character of, serve as; ~ *on*, influence, affect; regulate one's conduct by, put into practice.

A.C.T. *abbrev.* Australian Capital Territory.

Actae'on (ă-). (Gk myth.) Hunter who, because he accidentally saw Artemis bathing, was changed into a stag and killed by his own hounds.

ă'ctĭng *adj.* (esp., prefixed to title) Temporarily doing duties of; doing alone duties nominally shared with others.

ăctĭ'nĭc *adj.* Of actinism; ~ *rays*, rays possessing actinism, as the green, blue, violet, and ultra-violet rays of sunlight, which have a marked photochemical effect.

ă'ctĭnīde *n.* Element with atomic number between 89 (actinium) and 103.

ă'ctĭnĭsm *n.* That property of radiant energy, found esp. in the shorter wavelengths of the spectrum, by which chemical changes are produced, as in photography.

ăctĭ'nĭum *n.* (chem.) Radioactive element, found in pitchblende; symbol Ac, at. no. 89, principal isotope at. wt 227.

ăctĭnŏ'mėter *n.* Instrument for measuring heat radiation.

ăctĭnomōr'phĭc *adj.* (biol.) Radially symmetrical. **ăctĭnomōr'phĭsm** *n.*

ăctĭnomȳcē'tēs (-z) *n.pl.* Group of minute organisms of the order Actinomycetales, commonly held to be filamentous bacteria.

ăctĭnozō′an *adj.* & *n.* = ANTHOZOAN.

ă′ction *n.* 1. Process of acting, exertion of energy or influence; *out of* ~, not functioning; ~ *committee*, one chosen to take active steps; ~ *painting*, form of abstract art in which paint is applied by spontaneous or random action of artist. 2. Thing done. 3. Series of events represented (in drama). 4. Mode of acting; mechanism of instruments etc. 5. Legal process; *take* ~, institute legal proceedings; take steps in regard to any matter. 6. Battle, engagement between opposing forces. ~ *v.t.* Bring legal action against. **ă′ctionable** *adj.* Affording ground for action at law.

A′ctium (ă-). Promontory of W. coast of Greece (opposite modern Preveza on Gulf of Amurakia), near which, in 31 B.C., the fleets of Mark Antony and Cleopatra were decisively defeated by Octavian (Augustus).

ă′ctĭvāte *v.t.* Make active, esp. (phys.) radioactive; render (molecules) capable of reacting chemically. **ăctĭvā′tion** *n.*

ă′ctive *adj.* 1. Working, acting, operative; consisting in or marked by action; energetic, diligent; (of volcano) liable to erupt; ~ *list*, list of officers who are on active service or available for it; ~ *service*, full-time service in one of the armed forces. 2. (gram.) Applied to a voice of the verb comprising all forms of intransitive verbs, and those forms of transitive verbs that attribute the verbal action to the person or thing whence it proceeds; (loosely, of verb) in which the subject acts on or affects something else. 3. Radioactive. ~ *n.* Active voice or form of verb. **ă′ctivelȳ** *adv.*

ă′ctĭvĭst *n.* One who advocates taking action.

ăctĭ′vĭtȳ *n.* Exertion of energy; state or quality of being active, energy, diligence, liveliness; active force or operation; (phys.) radioactivity.

ă′ctor *n.* (fem. *a′ctrėss*) Dramatic performer; ~-*manager*, actor who is also manager of theatre or company.

ă′ctūal *adj.* Existing, real, present, current. **ă′ctūallȳ** *adv.* In actual fact, really; even, as a matter of fact.

ăctūă′lĭtȳ *n.* Reality, realism.

ă′ctūalīze *v.t.* Realize in action, treat realistically.

ă′ctūarȳ *n.* Expert on insurance who calculates risks and premiums. **ăctūar′ĭal** *adj.*

ă′ctūāte *v.t.* Serve as motive to; communicate motion to. **ăctūā′tion** *n.*

acū′ĭtȳ *n.* Sharpness, acuteness.

acū′lėate *adj.* 1. (zool.) Having a sting. 2. (bot.) Prickly, pointed.

acū′mĕn (*or* ă-) *n.* Keen discernment, penetration.

acū′mĭnate *adj.* (biol.) Tapering to a point.

ăcūpŭ′ncture *n.* 1. Chinese practice of pricking areas of skin with needles for therapeutic purposes. 2. (med.) Pricking of tissue with a needle for drainage etc.

acu′shla (-ōō-) *n.* Darling. [Ir. *ā cuisle* O pulse (of my heart)!]

acū′te *adj.* 1. Sharp, keen, penetrating; clever. 2. (of disease) Coming sharply to a crisis, not chronic. 3. (of sound) Sharp, shrill; having acute accent. 4. (fig.) Severe, crucial. 5. ~ *accent*, accent ′, originally indicating a high or rising pitch on the vowel so marked; ~ *angle*: see ANGLE[1]. **acū′telȳ** *adv.* **acū′tenėss** *n.*

A.C.W. *abbrev.* Aircraftwoman.

ă′cȳl *n.* (chem.) Acid radical.

ăd *n.* (colloq.) Advertisement; advertising.

ad- *prefix.* To, with sense of motion or direction to, reduction or change into, addition, adherence, increase, or intensification.

A.D. *abbrev.* Anno Domini.

ă′dage *n.* Traditional maxim, proverb.

adagio (adahj′yō) *adv.*, *adj.*, *n.* (pl. *-os*). (mus. & dancing) Leisurely (passage or movement). [It.]

A′dalbĕrt (ă-), St. (*c* 955–97). Missionary in N. Germany and Poland, called 'apostle of the

ADAM AND EVE

Prussians'; martyred in Bremen, commemorated 23 April.

A'dam[1] (ă-). (in Hebrew tradition) The first man (see Gen. 2: 4, 3: 24), who lived with his wife Eve in the Garden of Eden, but was driven from it for eating the fruit (traditionally an apple) of 'the tree of the knowledge of good and evil'; *the old* ~, person's innate sinful nature; ~*'s ale*, water; ~*'s apple*, projection formed by the THYROID cartilage, particularly prominent in males; ~*'s Peak*, mountain in Ceylon with a hollow on the summit which is said by Muslims to be Adam's footprint and by Buddhists to be Buddha's. [Heb., = 'man']

A'dam[2] (ă-), Robert (1728–92). The best known of a family of Scottish architects; introduced into Britain a neo-Classical style of decoration, furniture, etc., based on ancient Roman and Italian Renaissance designs; *James* ~ (1730–94), architect, his brother.

ă'damant *n.* Thing impenetrably hard; stubborn or unyielding person; fabulous mineral with properties of hardness and attraction. **ădamă'ntīne** *adj.* **ă'damant** *adj.* Unshakeable, inflexible. **ă'damantlȳ** *adv.*

A'damīte (ă-) *n.* 1. Child of Adam, human being; unclothed man. 2. Member of heretical sect in N. Africa (2nd and 3rd centuries), who believed that they enjoyed Adam's original state of innocency, and wore no clothes.

A'dams[1] (ă-, -z), John (1735–1826). 2nd president of U.S. 1797–1801; member of committee formed to draft Declaration of Independence.

A'dams[2] (ă-, -z), John (*c* 1760–1829) alias Alexander Smith. English seaman, one of the *Bounty*[2] mutineers; founded settlement on Pitcairn Island.

A'dams[3] (ă-, -z), John Couch (1819–92). English astronomer, discoverer of the planet Neptune.

A'dams[4] (ă-, -z), John Quincy (1767–1848). Son of John ADAMS[1]; 6th president of U.S. 1825–9.

Adanson (ădahṅsawṅ), Michel (1727–1806). French botanist; first exponent of classification of plants into natural orders.

adă'pt *v.* Suit, make suitable, fit (*to*, *for*); alter, modify, so as to make suitable for new surroundings, purpose, etc. **adăptabĭ'lĭtȳ** *n.* **adă'ptable** *adj.*

ădaptā'tion *n.* (esp. biol.) Process, characteristic of living matter, by which organism or species becomes adjusted to its environment; that which is so adapted.

A.D.C. *abbrev.* Aide-de-camp.

ădd *v.* Join by way of increase or supplement; perform arithmetical process of addition; ~ *up*, find sum of; make desired total (also fig.); *adding machine*, machine that performs arithmetical processes.

ă'ddăx *n.* Large light-coloured antelope (*Addax nasomaculatus*) of N.-Afr. deserts, with spiral horns.

addĕ'ndum *n.* (pl. *-da*). Something to be added, addition, appendix.

ă'dder *n.* Small venomous snake, viper (*Vipera berus*), only poisonous snake found in England; *death* ~, *horned* ~, *puff* ~, highly poisonous African and Australian species of Viperidae; ~*'s tongue*,

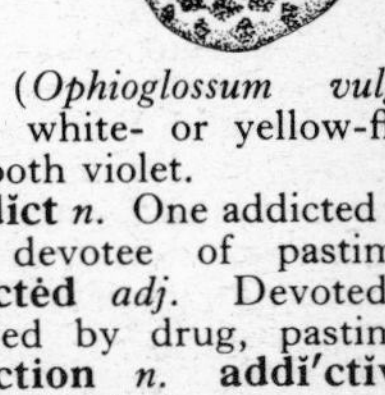

fern (*Ophioglossum vulgatum*); Amer. white- or yellow-flowered dog-tooth violet.

ă'ddict *n.* One addicted to drug etc.; devotee of pastime etc. **addĭ'ctėd** *adj.* Devoted *to* or enslaved by drug, pastime, etc. **addĭ'ction** *n.* **addĭ'ctĭve** *adj.* Causing addiction.

A'ddĭson[1] (ă-), Joseph (1672–1719). English essayist and poet; contributor to 'Tatler' and joint-author (with Steele) of 'Spectator'.

A'ddĭson[2] (ă-), Thomas (1793–1860). English physician; first to recognize ~'s *disease*, disease connected with defective functioning of suprarenal glands and freq. characterized by bronzy pigmentation of skin.

addĭ'tion *n.* Adding; arithmetical process of putting together two or more numbers or amounts to form a total; thing added; *in* ~, as an added thing etc. (*to*); ~ *reaction*, (chem.) one in which two univalent atoms or radicals are taken up by an unsaturated molecule, the double bond being converted into a single bond. **addĭ'tional** *adj.* **addĭ'tionallў** *adv.*

ă'ddĭtĭve *adj.* Of addition; to be added; ~ *process*, process of colour reproduction in which the primary colours are superimposed one upon another. ~ *n.* Substance added to mixture or alloy in order to impart specific qualities to the resulting product.

ă'ddle *v.* Make or become addled. ~ *adj.* ~*-headed*, ~*-pated*, confused in mind. **ă'ddled** (-ld) *adj.* (of egg) Rotten, producing no chicken; muddled, crazy; *A~ Parliament*, that summoned in April 1614 and dissolved in June, without having passed a Bill.

addrĕ'ss *n.* 1. Readiness, skill, adroitness. 2. Superscription of letter etc.; place to which letters etc. are directed; place of residence. 3. Manner, bearing, in conversation; way of addressing person. 4. Discourse delivered to audience; esp., parliamentary reply to Royal Speech at opening of Parliament. 5. (pl.) Courteous approach, courtship. ~ *v.t.* 1. Direct in speech or writing; speak to; send as written message (*to*); write address on outside of (letter etc.). 2. Apply *oneself*, direct one's skill or energies (*to*). 3. (golf) ~ *the ball*, take aim, prepare to make stroke.

ăddrĕssee' *n.* Person to whom letter etc. is addressed.

addrĕ'ssogrăph (*or* -ahf) *n.* Machine for addressing letters. [trade-name]

addū'ce *v.t.* Cite as proof or instance.

addū'cent *adj.* (anat., of muscles) Drawing together certain parts of the body.

addŭ'ct *v.t.* Draw to a common centre or towards median line or long axis of body. **addŭ'ction, addŭ'ctor** *ns.*

A'dėlaide (ă-). Seaport and capital of South Australia.

Adélie Lănd (*a*dā'lē). French territory in coastal region of Antarctica, south of Australia.

A'den (ā-). Seaport and coaling-station in SW. Arabia near entrance to Red Sea; capital city of the People's Democratic Republic of Yemen; until 1967 part of a British protectorate.

ă'dėnoids (-z) *n.pl.* Pathological enlargement of lymphoid tissue between back of nose and throat, occurring usu. in children and often obstructing breathing. **ădėnoi'dal** *adj.* **ădėnoi'dallў** *adv.*

ădėnō'ma *n.* (pl. *-ata*, *-as*) (med.) Benign tumour in or resembling glandular tissue.

ă'dĕpt (*or* *a*dĕ'pt) *adj.* Thoroughly proficient (*in*). **ă'dept** *n.* Adept person.

ă'dėquate *adj.* Proportionate *to* what is necessary; sufficient. **ă'dėquatelў** *adv.* **ă'dėquacў** *n.*

ăd fīnĕm (*or* fē-). Towards the end (abbrev. *ad fin.*). [L]

adhēr'e *v.i.* Stick fast, cleave (*to*).

adhēr'ent *adj.* Sticking; connected with (*to*). ~ *n.* Supporter (*of* party etc.). **adhēr'ence** *n.*

adhē'sion *n.* Adhering; (chem.) molecular force of attraction between different kinds of molecules (opp. COHESION); (med.) abnormal union of tissue as a result of inflammation.

adhē'sĭve (*or* -z-) *adj.* & *n.* Adhering, sticky (substance). **adhē'sĭvelў** *adv.*

ăd hŏc. Arranged for this purpose; special(ly). [L]

ădĭabă'tĭc *adj.* (of physical change) Involving neither loss nor gain of heat.

adieu (*a*dū') *int.* & *n.* (pl. -*s*, -*x*, pr. -z) Goodbye; *make, take, one's* ~, say good-bye. [Fr. *à Dieu* to God]

ăd infīnī'tum. Without limit, for ever. [L]

ăd inĭ'tium (-shĭum). At the beginning (abbrev. *ad init.*). [L]

ăd ĭ'nterĭm. For the meantime. [L]

ă'dĭpocēre *n.* Greyish fatty or saponaceous substance, chiefly fatty acids with minor qualities of mineral salts, etc., formed in dead animal bodies by decomposition of body fats when exposed to moisture.

ă'dĭpōse *adj.* Of fat, fatty; ~ *tissue*, connective tissue cells in animal body containing large globules of fat. **ădĭpŏ'sĭtў** *n.*

Adĭrŏ'ndăck Mou'ntains (ă-, -tĭnz). (also *Adirondacks*) Group of mountains in New York State, U.S., a holiday resort.

ă'dĭt *n.* Horizontal entrance to, or passage in, mine.

A'dĭtĭ (ah-). (in Veda) Personification of infinity or of all-embracing nature; (Hinduism) mother of the gods.

Adj. *abbrev.* Adjutant.

adjā'cent (*a*j-) *adj.* Lying near *to*, contiguous. **adjā'cencў** *n.*

ă'djėctĭve (ăj-) *adj.* Additional, not standing by itself, dependent; ~ *law*, subsidiary part of law, procedure. ~ *n.* (gram.) Name of attribute added to name of thing to describe thing more fully or definitely. **ădjėctī'val** *adj.* **ădjėctī'vallў** *adv.*

adjoi'n (*a*j-) *v.t.* Be contiguous with.

adjourn (*a*jẽr'n) *v.* Put off, postpone; break off; (of persons met together) suspend proceedings and separate; move *to* another place. **adjour'nment** *n.*(esp.) *move the* ~ (in House of Commons), bring motion that the House shall adjourn, esp. in order to discuss a specified matter (which, if the motion is carried, is discussed the same evening).

Adjt *abbrev.* Adjutant.

adjŭ'dge (*a*j-) *v.t.* Adjudicate upon; pronounce or award judicially; condemn.

adju'dĭcāte (*a*jōō-) *v.* Decide upon; pronounce; sit in judgement and pronounce sentence; award prizes etc. in competition. **adjudĭcā'tion, adju'dĭcātor** *ns.*

ă'djŭnct (ăj-) *n.* Subordinate or incidental thing, accompaniment; (gram.) amplification of the predicate, subject, etc.; (logic) non-essential attribute. **adjŭ'nctĭve** *adj.* **adjŭ'nctĭvelў** *adv.*

adjure (*a*joor') *v.t.* Charge under oath or penalty of curse *to* do; request earnestly. **ădjurā'tion** *n.*

adjŭ'st (*a*j-) *v.* Arrange, put in order; harmonize; adapt (*to*). **adjŭ'stment** *n.* **adjŭ'stable** *adj.*

ă'djutant (ăjōō-) *n.* 1. (army etc.) Officer assisting commanding officer by communicating orders, conducting correspondence, etc.; *A~-General*, second executive officer of British General Staff of Army, whose duties are concerned with recruiting, training, etc. 2. (also ~ *bird*) Large stork of genus *Leptoptilus*, esp. Indian *L. dubius*, walking with stiff-legged gait.

A'dler (ă-), Alfred (1870–1937). Austrian psychologist; put forward theory of inferiority complex.

ad lib. *abbrev.* *Ad libitum.*

ă'dlĭ'b *v.* (colloq., orig. U.S.) Improvise (words, music, etc.) in acting etc.

ăd lĭ'bĭtum. To the extent etc. desired. [L]

Adm. *abbrev.* Admiral.

Admē'tus (ă-). (Gk legend) Husband of ALCESTIS.

admĭ'nĭster *v.* 1. Manage (affairs, estate, etc.); dispense (justice, sacraments, etc.); act as administrator. 2. Formally present (oath to be sworn) *to*. 3. Furnish, give; apply (remedies). 4. Contribute *to* (one's comfort etc.)

admĭnĭstrā'tion *n.* 1. Administering; management; management of public affairs, government; (law) management of deceased person's estate; *letters of* ~, authority to administer intestate estate. 2. Body of administrators; ministry, Government. **admĭ'nĭstrāte** *v.* Administer. **admĭ'nĭstratĭve** *adj.* Of administration; executive. **admĭ'nĭstrātor** *n.* **admĭ'nĭstrātrĭx** *n.* (pl. *-trīcēs*).

Female administrator (in legal sense).

ă'dmĭrable *adj.* Worthy of admiration; estimable, excellent. **ă'dmĭrablў** *adv.*

ă'dmiral *n.* 1. Naval officer commanding fleet or subdivision of fleet; (hist.) commander-in-chief of navy; *A~ of the Fleet*, highest rank of British naval officers. 2. Privileged commander of fishing or merchant fleet. 3. (hist.) Ship that carries the admiral, flagship. 4. *red ~, white ~*, two European species of butterfly (*Vanessa atalanta, Limenitis sibylla*). [Arab. *'amīr* commander]

ă'dmiraltў *n.* 1. Office, rank, of admiral; (rhet.) command of the seas. 2. *A~ Board*, department of Ministry of Defence superintending Royal Navy; (*High*) *Court of A~*, part of High Court of Justice concerned with maritime questions and offences.

A'dmiraltў I'slands (ă-, īlandz). Group of small islands of Bismarck Archipelago, under Australian administration.

admīr'e *v.t.* Regard with pleased surprise or approval; (colloq.) express admiration of. **ădmĭrā'tion** *n.* **admīr'er** *n.* One who admires; (archaic) lover.

admĭ'ssion *n.* Admitting, being admitted, fee for this; acknowledgement that something is true.

admĭ't *v.* 1. Allow entrance or access (*to*). 2. Allow, permit; accept as valid or true; acknowledge; *~ of*, be capable of or compatible with; leave room for. **admĭ'ttance** *n.* **admĭ'ttėdlў** *adv.*

admĭ'x *n.* Add as an ingredient, mingle *with*. **admĭ'xture** *n.*

admŏ'nĭsh *v.t.* Urge; give advice; warn; remind, inform. **admŏ'nĭshment** *n.*

ădmonĭ'tion *n.* Admonishing; warning, reproof. **admŏn'ĭtorў** *adj.*

ăd nau'sėăm (*or* -z-). To a disgusting extent. [L]

ado' (-o͞o) *n.* Fuss; difficulty.

adō'bė (*or* -ō'b) *n.* Sun-dried clay used for building by Indians in Mexico etc.; house made of such clay bricks. [Span., f. *adobar* daub, plaster]

ădolĕ'scent *adj.* & *n.* (Person) between childhood and maturity; between the ages (roughly) of 14 and 20. **ădolĕ'scence** *n.*

Adōnā'ī (*or* -ah'ī). 1. Hebrew title of reverence for God, pronounced as substitute for the tetragrammaton. 2. (liturgy) Appellation of Christ. [Heb., = 'my lord(s)']

Adō'nĭs. (Gk myth.) Beautiful youth loved by Aphrodite; he was killed by a boar but restored to life by Persephone; Zeus decreed that he should spend part of each year with her and the rest on earth with Aphrodite; hence, handsome young man; *~ blue*, kind of butterfly, *Lysandra bellargus*.

adŏ'pt *v.t.* Take into relationship not previously occupied, esp. take as one's own child, assume rights and duties of parent towards; take (idea etc.) from another and use as one's own; take up, choose; assume responsibility for (road etc.); approve (accounts, report). **adŏ'ption** *n.* *~ society*, organization which arranges adoption of orphaned or unwanted infants. **adŏ'ptĭve** *adj.*

adōr'e *v.t.* Regard with very deep respect and affection; worship as a deity; like very much; (R.C. Ch.) offer form of reverence to. **adōr'able** *adj.* **adōr'ablў** *adv.* **ădorā'tion** *n.*

adōr'er *n.* Worshipper; ardent admirer, lover.

adōr'n *v.t.* Add beauty or lustre to; furnish with ornament(s). **adōr'nment** *n.*

Adră'stus. (Gk myth.) King of Argos and leader of expeditions against Thebes.

ăd rĕm. To the point; to the purpose. [L]

adrē'nal *adj.* At or near kidney; *~ gland*, suprarenal gland, one of two yellowish-brown ductless glands lying on upper anterior surface of kidneys. *~ n.* Adrenal gland.

adrĕ'nalĭn *n.* Hormone secreted by adrenal glands and affecting circulation and muscular action;

this obtained from these glands in animals or prepared synthetically, used in medicine as a stimulant.

A'drian (ā-). Name of six popes: *Adrian I*, pope 772–95; *Adrian II*, pope 867–72; *Adrian III*, pope 884–5; *Adrian IV* (Nicholas Breakspear), pope 1154–9, only English pope; *Adrian V*, pope in 1276; *Adrian VI*, pope 1522–3, most recent non-Italian pope, born at Utrecht.

Adrianō'ple (ā-). Former name of Edirne; scene of a battle (A.D. 378) in which Romans were defeated by Visigoths. [f. the emperor HADRIAN]

Adriă'tic (ā-) *adj.* ~ *Sea*, arm of Mediterranean lying between Italy and Balkan peninsula. ~ *n.* Adriatic Sea; *Marriage of the* ~, (hist.) annual Ascension-Day ceremony symbolizing the sea-power of Venice, during which the Doge dropped a ring into the water from his state barge.

adrĭ'ft *adj.* Drifting; at mercy of wind and tide or of circumstances; (colloq.) not at one's post; deficient in knowledge, training, etc.

adroi't *adj.* Dextrous, deft. **adroi'tlў** *adv.* **adroi'tnėss** *n.*

ădscĭtĭ'tious (-shus) *adj.* Adopted from without; supplemental.

adsŏr'b *v.t.* Act as adsorbent of. **adsŏr'bent** *adj.* & *n.* (Substance) producing adsorption.

adsŏr'ption *n.* Process by which specific gases, vapours, or substances in solution adhere to exposed surfaces of certain, usu. solid, materials. **adsŏr'ptĭve** *adj.*

ă'dsŭm (*or* -sōōm) *int.* I am here, as answer in roll-call etc. [L]

ă'dūlāte *v.t.* Flatter basely. **ădūlā'tion** *n.* **ă'dūlātorў** *adj.*

Adŭ'llam. Cave where all who were distressed, in debt, or discontented came to join David when he fled from Saul (see 1 Sam. 22: 1–2); applied by John Bright to Liberal M.P.s who voted with Conservatives against Reform Bill of 1866. **Adŭ'llamīte** *n.* Member of any dissident political group.

ă'dult (*or* adŭ'lt) *adj.* Fully grown, mature. ~ *n.* Adult person, animal, plant, etc.; ~ *education*, courses etc. provided by local authorities for persons over school age.

adŭ'lterant *adj.* & *n.* (Thing) employed in adulterating.

adŭ'lterāte[1] *v.t.* Falsify, corrupt, debase, esp. by admixture of baser ingredients. **adŭlterā'tion** *n.*

adŭ'lterate[2] *adj.* Defiled by adultery; spurious, counterfeit.

adŭ'lterer *n.* (fem. *adŭ'lterėss*) Person guilty of adultery.

adŭ'lterīne *adj.* Of, born of, adultery; adulterated, counterfeit; illegal, unlicensed.

adŭ'lterў *n.* Voluntary sexual intercourse of married person with one who is not his or her spouse. **adŭ'lterous** *adj.* **adŭ'lterouslў** *adv.*

ă'dumbrāte (*or* adŭ'm-) *v.t.* Represent in outline; faintly indicate; typify, foreshadow; overshadow. **ădumbrā'tion** *n.*

ăd valōr'ĕm. (of taxes or duties) In proportion to (estimated) value of goods. [L]

adva'nce (-vah-) *n.* 1. Going forward, progress. 2. Personal approach, overture; (pl.) amorous approaches. 3. Rise in price. 4. Payment beforehand; loan. 5. *in* ~, in front, ahead; beforehand; ~ *copy*, copy of book etc., supplied before publication; ~ *guard*, guard before main body of army. ~ *v.* Move or put forward; bring forward (claims etc.); accelerate (events); pay (money) before it is due; lend; help on, promote; make progress; raise (price), rise (in price). **adva'nced** (-st) *adj.* Far on in progress; ahead of times, others, etc. **adva'ncement** *n.* (esp.) Promotion, preferment; furtherance, improvement.

adva'ntage (-vah-) *n.* Better position, precedence, superiority; favourable circumstance; (lawn tennis) next point won after deuce (~ *in*, ~ *out*, advantage to server, striker); *mechanical* ~: see MECHANICAL; *take* ~ *of*, use (circumstance) profitably; exploit (person) unfairly. ~ *v.t.* Be beneficial to;

be an advantage to; further, promote. **ădvantā'ġeous** (-jus) *adj.* **ădvantā'ġeouslў** *adv.*

ă'dvent *n.* 1. Arrival, esp. important one. 2. *A~*, season before Christmas, beginning on 4th Sunday before it; coming of Christ; (also *Second A~*) second coming of Christ.

A'dventĭst (ă-) *n.* (also *Second ~*) Member of one of various sects believing in imminence of second coming of Christ.

ădventĭ'tious (-shus) *adj.* Coming from without, accidental, casual; (bot.) in an unusual position, sporadic (~ *root!*); (law, of inheritance) coming from a stranger or by collateral succession. **ădventĭ'tiouslў** *adv.*

advĕ'nture *n.* Unexpected or exciting experience; daring enterprise, hazardous activity. ~ *v.* 1. (rhet.) Hazard, imperil; incur risk. 2. Dare to go or come *into*, dare to enter *on*.

advĕ'nturer (-cher-) *n.* (fem. *advĕ'nturėss*) One who seeks adventure; speculator; one who lives by his wits.

advĕ'nturous (-cher-) *adj.* Venturesome, enterprising. **advĕ'nturouslў** *adv.*

ă'dvĕrb *n.* (gram.) Word expressing any relation of place, time, circumstance, causality, manner, or degree, or modifying or limiting attribute or predicate. **ădvĕr'bial** *adj.* **advĕr'biallў** *adv.*

ă'dversarў *n.* Opponent, enemy; *the A~*, the Devil.

advĕr'satĭve *adj.* (of words etc.) Expressing opposition or antithesis. **advĕr'satĭvelў** *adv.*

ă'dvĕrse *adj.* Contrary, hostile *to*; hurtful, injurious. **ă'dverselў** *adv.*

advĕr'sĭtў *n.* Condition of adverse fortune; misfortune.

advĕr't[1] *v.i.* Refer *to.*

ă'dvert[2] *n.* (colloq.) Advertisement.

ă'dvertīse (-z) *v.* Notify, warn, inform; make generally or publicly known; proclaim merits of; esp., try to encourage sales of (product) by public announcement; ~ *for*, ask for by public notice. **ă'dvertīser** *n.*

advĕr'tĭsement (-sm-) *n.* Advertising; public announcement (in newspaper, by posters, etc.).

advī'ce *n.* Opinion given or offered as to action; information given, news; (pl.) communications from a distance; (commerc.) formal notice of transactions.

advī'sable (-z-) *adj.* To be recommended; expedient. **advīsabĭ'lĭtў** *n.*

advī'se (-z) *v.* Offer advice (to); recommend; (commerc.) announce.

advī'sed (-zd) *adj.* Deliberate, considered; judicious. **advī'sėdlў** *adv.*

advī'ser (-z-) *n.* Counsellor, esp. person habitually consulted; *legal ~*, solicitor.

advī'sorў (-z-) *adj.* Giving advice; consisting in giving advice.

ă'dvocacў *n.* Function of advocate; pleading in support *of*.

ă'dvocate *n.* Professional pleader in court of justice, counsel (technical title in Roman law courts and in countries retaining Roman law, as Scotland, France, etc.); one who pleads for another; one who speaks for cause etc.; *Faculty of Advocates*, Scottish bar; *Lord A~*, principal law-officer of Crown in Scotland; *Advocates' Library*, library in Edinburgh opened 1689 and presented to nation by Faculty of Advocates, 1924; since 1925 the National Library of Scotland. **ă'dvocāte** *v.t.* Plead for, support (policy etc.).

ădvocā'tus dĭă'bolī (*or* -aht-, -lē). Devil's advocate (see DEVIL). [L]

advow'son (-z-) *n.* (law) Right of presentation to benefice.

advt. *abbrev.* Advertisement.

ă'dўtum *n.* (pl. *-ta*). Innermost part of temple; private chamber, sanctum. [Gk *aduton* not to be entered (*duō* enter)]

ădze *n.* Carpenter's tool for cutting away surface of wood, like axe with arched blade at right angles to handle. ~ *v.t.* Dress or cut with adze.

A.E. Pseudonym of G. W. RUSSELL[2].

ae'dīle *n.* (Rom. hist.) Magistrate who superintended public buildings, games, shows, etc.

Aegē'an (ĭj-) *adj.* ~ *Sea*, arm of Mediterranean between Greece and Asia Minor; ~ *Civilization*, Bronze Age civilization of the coasts and islands of the Aegean Sea, the MINOAN and MYCENAEAN civilizations. ~ *n.* Aegean Sea.

Aegir (ē'jẽr). (Scand. myth.) Chief of the sea-giants, representing the peaceful ocean.

ae'gis *n.* (Gk myth.) Shield of Zeus or Athene; *under the* ~ *of*, under the protection or sponsorship of.

Aegi'sthus (ĭg- *or* ĭj-). (Gk legend) Nephew of Atreus, whom he murdered, and lover of CLYTEMNESTRA, who helped him murder her husband Agamemnon.

ae'grotăt *n.* (Degree awarded on) certificate that candidate is ill. [L, = 'he is sick']

Æ'lfric (ăl-) (*c* 955–1020). English monk and writer, chiefly of homilies and lives of saints.

Aenē'as (ĭn-) (Gk & Rom. legend) Trojan hero; son of Anchises and Aphrodite; escaped after fall of Troy and after long wandering reached the Tiber; regarded by Romans as founder of their State.

Aenē'id (ĭn-; *or* ē'nĭĭd). Epic poem by Virgil in twelve books of Latin hexameters relating story of Aeneas after fall of Troy.

Aeō'lian *adj.* 1. Of Aeolis. 2. Of Aeolus; caused by, relating to, wind; ~ *deposit*, substance deposited on earth by wind, as desert sand; ~ *harp*, musical instrument consisting of rectangular box on or in which are stretched strings or wires producing musical sounds as the wind passes across them; ~ *Islands*, ancient name of Lipari Islands; ~ *mode*, (mus.) ancient Greek mode; 9th of ecclesiastical modes, with A as final and E as dominant.

Ae'olis. Coastal district of NW. Asia Minor colonized by Greeks at very early date.

Ae'olus. (Gk myth.) God of the winds.

ae'on, ē'on *n.* An age of the universe; immeasurable period; eternity.

aepyor'nis *n.* Gigantic flightless extinct bird of genus *A* ~, resembling moa and known from remains found in Madagascar.

ā'erāte (*or* ār-) *v.t.* Expose to mechanical or chemical action of air; charge with carbon dioxide; *aerated waters*, sweetened flavoured beverages charged with carbon dioxide. **aerā'tion, aer'ātor** *ns.*

aer'ial (ār-) *adj.* Of air, gaseous; ethereal; immaterial, imaginary; atmospheric; existing, moving, happening, in the air; conducted by aircraft. ~ *n.* Radiating or receiving wire(s) or rod used in radio communication. **aer'ialist** *n.* Performer on high wire or trapeze.

aer'ie, aer'ȳ (*or* ārĭ) *n.* Varr. of EYRIE.

aer'iform (ār-) *adj.* Of the form of air, gaseous; unsubstantial.

aero-, aer- (ār-) *prefix.* Air-; of aircraft.

aerobă'tics (ār-) *n.pl.* Feats of expert and often spectacular aviation. **aerobă'tic** *adj.*

ā'erōbe (*or* ār'-) *n.* Micro-organism capable of living only in the presence of atmospheric oxygen; opp. ANAEROBE. **āerŏ'bic** *adj.*

aerobiŏ'logy (ār-) *n.* Study of airborne micro-organisms esp. as agents of infection.

aer'odrōme *n.* Airfield.

aerodȳnă'mics (ār-) *n.* Branch of dynamics dealing with the effects produced in air by the motion of solid bodies through it and the effects produced on such bodies by the air through which they pass. **aerodȳnă'mic, -ical** *adjs.* **aerodȳnă'mically** *adv.* **aerodȳnă'micist** *n.*

aer'odȳne (ār-) *n.* Heavier-than-air aircraft.

aer'ofoil (ār-) *n.* Any or all of the lift-producing surfaces of an aircraft, as wings, ailerons, tail-plane, fins, etc.

aer'olīte, -līth (ār-) *n.* Meteorite.

aer'onaut (ār-) *n.* (obs.) Navigator or pilot of airship or aeroplane. **aeronaut'ic, -ical** *adjs.* Of, pertaining to, aeronautics.

aeronau′tĭcs *n.pl.* Science or practice of flight; aerial navigation.

aer′oplāne (ār-) *n.* Heavier-than-air powered flying machine with wings. (*Illustration, p. 12.*)

aer′osŏl (ār-) *n.* System of colloidal particles dispersed in a gas, as mist, fog, etc.; (container

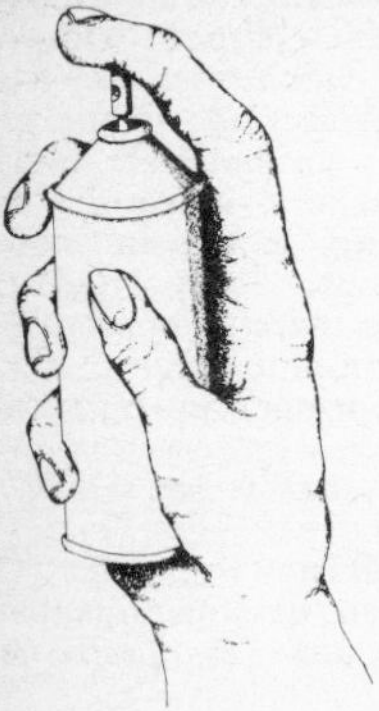

holding) substance packed under pressure with spraying device.

aer′ospāce (ār-) *n.* Earth's atmosphere and outer space; (*attrib.*) of (industry concerned with) aircraft etc. for operation in aerospace.

aerostă′tĭcs (ār-) *n.* Physics of gases in equilibrium; science of air navigation. **aerostăt′ĭc, -ĭcal** *adjs.*

Ae′schȳlus (ēsk-) (525–456 B.C.). Athenian poet regarded as founder of Greek tragic drama; of his many tragedies only seven are extant: 'The Persians', 'The Seven against Thebes', 'Prometheus Bound', 'The Suppliants', and the Orestes trilogy, 'Agamemnon', 'Choephori', and 'Eumenides'.

Aescūlā′pĭus. (Rom. myth.) = ASCLEPIUS.

Æ′sir (ă-). (Scand. myth.) Collective name of the gods.

Ae′sŏp (6th c. B.C.). Semi-legendary Phrygian teller of fables about animals, said to have been a slave in Samos; the fables attributed to him are prob. compiled from various sources.

ae′sthēte *n.* Professed lover of beauty.

aesthĕ′tĭc *adj.* Of appreciation of the beautiful; having such appreciation; in accordance with principles of good taste; *A~ Movement*, movement in late 19th-c. England advocating 'art for art's sake'. **aesthĕ′tĭcallȳ** *adv.* **aesthĕ′tĭcism** *n.* **aesthĕ′tĭc, -ĭcs** *ns.* Philosophy of the beautiful; philosophy of art.

ae′stĭval *adj.* Of summer.

ae′stĭvāte *v.i.* Spend the summer, esp. (zool.) in state of torpor.

aestĭvā′tion *n.* (zool.) Aestivating; (bot.) arrangement of petals in flower-bud before expansion.

aeta′tĭs (ītah-). Of or at the age of (abbrev. *aet.*, *ae′tăt.*). [L]

Æthelred: see ETHELRED.

Æthelstan: see ATHELSTAN.

aetĭŏ′logȳ *n.* Assignment of a cause; philosophy of causation; (med.) science of causes of disease. **aetĭolŏ′gĭcal** *adj.* **aetĭolŏ′gĭcallȳ** *adv.*

Aëtius (āĕ′tĭŭs) (d. 454). Roman general who, with Theodoric, defeated Attila at Châlons, 451.

A.F. *abbrev.* Admiral of the Fleet; audio FREQUENCY.

A.F.A. *abbrev.* Amateur Football Alliance.

afar′ *adv.* At, to, a distance; *from ~*, from a distance.

A′fars and I′ssas (ăfarz, ĭ-), Territory of the. Small French territory on NE. coast of Africa; formerly Somaliland, independent since 1977; capital, Jibouti.

A.F.A.S. *abbrev.* Associate of the Faculty of Architects and Surveyors.

A.F.C. *abbrev.* Air Force Cross.

ă′ffable *adj.* Easy of address, courteous, complaisant. **ă′ffablȳ** *adv.* **affabĭ′lĭtȳ** *n.*

affair′ *n.* Business, concern; (colloq.) thing; love affair; (pl.) ordinary pursuits of life; (pl.) public, commercial or professional business or transactions.

ăffaire *n.* Love affair. [Fr.]

affĕ′ct[1] *v.t.* Practise, use; assume (character); pretend to have or feel; pretend (*to* do). **affĕ′ctėd**

adj. Artificially assumed or displayed; full of affectation. **affĕ'ctėdlў** *adv.*

affĕ'ct² *v.t.* Attack (as disease); move, touch; produce (material effect on). **affĕ'ctĭng** *adj.* Emotionally moving. **affĕ'ctĭnglў** *adv.*

ă'ffĕct³ *n.* (psychol.) Emotion, feeling, as antecedent of action.

ăffėctā'tion *n.* Studied display *of*; artificiality of manner; pretence.

affĕ'ction *n.* 1. Affecting, being affected. 2. Mental state, emotion; kindly feeling, love. 3. Bodily state due to any influence; (esp.) malady, disease. 4. Temporary or non-essential state, relation, etc.; property, attribute. **affĕ'ctionate** *adj.* Loving, fond; showing love or tenderness. **affĕ'ctionatelў** *adv.*

affĕ'ctĭve *adj.* Of the affections, emotional.

ă'fferent *adj.* (of blood- and lymph-vessels, nerves, etc.) Bringing, conducting, inwards or towards.

affī'ance *v.t.* Promise solemnly in marriage.

ăffĭdā'vĭt *n.* Written statement, confirmed by oath, to be used as judicial proof. [L, = 'has stated on oath']

affĭ'lĭāte *v.t.* 1. (of institution) Adopt (persons as members, societies as branches); attach *to*, connect *with* (a society). 2. (law) Fix paternity of (illegitimate child) for purpose of maintenance; father (thing) *upon*, trace *to*. **affĭlĭā'tion** *n.* ~ *order*, (law) magistrate's order requiring payment of maintenance by man for his illegitimate child.

affĭ'nĭtў *n.* Relationship, relations, by marriage or in general; structural resemblance; similarity of character suggesting relationship; liking, attraction; (chem.) tendency of substances to combine with others.

affĭr'm *v.* Assert strongly; make formal declaration or affirmation; state in the affirmative; ratify (judgement). **ăffirmā'tion** *n.* Affirming, esp. (law) solemn declaration by person who conscientiously declines taking oath.

affĭr'matĭve *adj.* Affirming, expressing assent; (logic) expressing agreement of the two terms of a proposition. ~ *n.* Affirmative answer. **affĭr'matĭvelў** *adv.*

affĭ'x *v.t.* Fasten, append, attach. **ă'ffĭx** *n.* Appendage, addition; (gram.) prefix or suffix.

afflā'tus *n.* Divine impulse; inspiration.

afflĭ'ct *v.t.* Distress with bodily or mental suffering. **afflĭ'ction** *n.* Misery, distress; pain, calamity.

ă'ffluent (-lōō-) *adj.* Flowing freely; abounding; wealthy. ~ *n.* Tributary stream. **ă'ffluence** *n.* Wealth, abundance.

ă'fflŭx *n.* Flow towards a point; accession.

affôr'd *v.t.* (with *can*) Have the means, be rich enough, manage to spare (time etc.); furnish; bestow; yield supply of.

affŏ'rėst *v.t.* Convert into a forest; plant with trees. **affŏrėstā'tion** *n.*

affră'nchīse (-z) *v.t.* Free from servitude or obligation.

affray' *n.* Breach of peace caused by fighting or rioting in public place.

affrī'ght (-īt) *v.t.* (archaic) Frighten. ~ *n.* Alarm, terror.

affro'nt (-ŭnt) *v.t.* Insult openly; face defiantly. **affro'ntėd** *adj.* (her.) Guardant; also face to face.

affro'nt *n.* Open insult.

affū'sion *n.* Pouring on, esp. of water in baptism.

Afghan (ă'fgăn) *adj.* Of Afghanistan or its people; (strictly) of the Duranni tribe of Pathans who inhabit E. Afghanistan and speak Pashtu; of the Pashtu language; ~ *hound*, hunting dog of ancient breed with long silky hair and tuft on head; ~ *Wars*, three campaigns (1839–42, 1879–80, 1919) fought by the British in Afghanistan in order to secure the NW. frontier of India. ~ *n.* 1. Afghan person or language. 2. (*a*~) knitted or crocheted woollen coverlet.

ăfghă'nĭ (ăfg-) *n.* Principal monetary unit of Afghanistan, = 100 puls.

Afghă'nĭstăn (ăfg-). Inland republic of SW. Asia bounded on

W. by Iran, on S. and E. by Pakistan and on N. by U.S.S.R.; founded in 18th c. by Durrani tribe of Pathans who broke away from Mogul Empire; later under British protection but declared a sovereign state in 1921; inhabited by various chiefly Muslim peoples, including Afghans and Tajiks, speaking several languages of which the principal are Pashtu and Persian (the official language); capital, Kabul.

afĭciona'do (-syonahdō) *n.* Devotee of bullfighting (or other sport or pastime). [Sp.]

afie'ld *adv.* On, in, or to the field; away, at a distance.

afīr'e *adv.* & *pred. adj.* On fire.

A.F.L. *abbrev.* American Federation of Labor.

aflā'me *adv.* & *pred. adj.* In flames; in a glow of light.

afloa't *adv.* & *pred. adj.* Floating; at sea, on board ship; full of water; out of debt, paying one's way.

A.F.M. *abbrev.* Air Force Medal.

afoo't *adv.* & *pred. adj.* On one's feet; astir; in operation or employment.

afor'e *adv.* & *prep.* (naut.) In front (of); (archaic, dial.) before, previously.

afore- *prefix.* Before, previously.

ā fortĭor'ī. With stronger reason. [L]

afrai'd *pred. adj.* Alarmed, frightened; sorry to say or suspect.

ă'freet, -rit, rite (-rēt) *n.* (Muslim myth.) Evil demon.

afrĕ'sh *adv.* Anew, with fresh beginning.

A'frĭca (ă-). Continent, largest southward projection of the landmass which constitutes the Old World, surrounded by sea except where Isthmus of Suez joins it to Asia, and extending nearly as far southward of equator as northward; its indigenous inhabitants are dark-skinned peoples varying in colour from light copper in N. to black in equatorial and southern parts; it was visited by Portuguese from 15th c. onwards but remained largely unknown, except for limited colonization by the Dutch and British in the Cape region and by the French in Algeria, until mid-19th c.; in the 'scramble for Africa' of the 1880s the leading European nations competed for colonies and the continent was divided between them, Liberia and Ethiopia alone remaining under native rule; since 1946 many former colonies have secured political independence.

A'frĭcan (ă-) *adj.* Of Africa or its people. ~ *n.* African person, esp. dark-skinned person as dist. from European or Asiatic settlers or their descendants. **A'frĭcanĭsm** *n.* (esp.) African nationalism. **A'frĭcanĭst** *adj.* & *n.* **A'frĭcanīze** *v.t.* Subject to rule of African Negroes. **Afrĭcanīzā'tion** *n.*

Afri'dĭ (-rē-) *n.* (Member of) a Pathan people of the mountainous region between Afghanistan and Pakistan.

Afrĭkaa'ns (ă-, -ahns) *n.* Language, derived from Dutch, used in the Republic of South Africa as one of its two official languages, the other being English. ~ *adj.* Of Afrikaans or its speakers.

Afrĭkă'nder (ă-) *n.* 1. (hist.) Afrikaner. 2. (One of) a breed of red beef cattle.

Afrĭka'ner (ă-, -kah-) *n.* Person born in South Africa of European stock (now usu. one descended from Dutch, not British, settlers).

Afro- (ă-) *prefix.* African; African and —.

ăfrormō'sĭa *n.* N. and W. African tree of genus *A*~; its timber.

A.F.S. *abbrev.* Army Fire Service; Auxiliary Fire Service.

aft (ah-) *adv.* In, to, or towards stern of ship or tail of aircraft.

a'fter (ah-) *adv.* Behind; later. ~ *prep.* Behind; in pursuit of; following in point of time; in view of; next in importance to; according to; in imitation of; ~ *all*, in spite of everything that has happened, been said, done, etc. ~ *conj.* In or at a time subsequent to that when. ~ *adj.* Later, following; nearer stern of ship or tail of aircraft; *a'fterbirth*, placenta and membrane enveloping foetus in womb, extruded after the child; ~-*care*, attention bestowed on person(s) after period of treatment or training, e.g. after discharge from hospital or prison; *a'fterdamp*, mixture of gases containing lethal amount of carbon monoxide, found in coal-mine after explosion of fire-damp; ~-*effect*, delayed effect; effect following after an interval; *a'fterglow*, glow in west after sunset; (phys.) glow persisting after cessation of electric current; ~-*grass*, grass that grows after the first crop has been mown for hay, or among stubble after harvest; ~-*image*, image retained by retina and producing visual sensation after the eyes are turned away or closed; ~-*life*, life after death; later period of person's life; *a'ftermath*, after-grass; (fig.) results, consequences; ~-*pains*, pains caused by uterine contraction after childbirth; ~-*taste*, taste remaining or recurring after eating or drinking (freq. fig.); *a'fterthought*, reflection after the act; later expedient or explanation.

a'ftermōst (ah-) *adj.* (naut.) Farthest aft.

afternōō'n (ah-) *n.* Time between noon and evening.

a'fters (ah-, -z) *n.pl.* (colloq.) Course which follows main course of meal.

a'fterwards (ah-, -z) *adv.* Later, subsequently.

A.F.V. *abbrev.* Armoured fighting vehicle.

A.G. *abbrev.* Adjutant-General; air gunner.

a'ga (ah-) *n.* Commander or chief officer in Ottoman Empire; *Aga Khan*, title given to Hasan Ali Shah (1800–81), when he fled from Persia and settled in Bombay under British protection, and subsequently held by his successors; as direct descendant of Muhammad's son-in-law Ali, the Aga Khan is spiritual leader (Imam) of the Ismaili sect of Muslims. [Turk. *aghā* master, *khan* ruler, king]

A'găg (ā-). King of Amalekites, spared by Saul but killed by Samuel: see 1 Sam. 15: 7–33.

agai'n (*or* -ĕn) *adv.* Another time, once more; further, besides; on the other hand; in return, in response; ~ *and* ~, repeatedly; *as much* ~, twice as much; *half as much* ~, one-and-a-half times as much.

agai'nst (*or* -ĕnst) *prep.* In opposition to; in contrast to; in anticipation of; into collision with; opposite to (usu. *over* ~). ~ *conj.* (archaic) By the time that.

aga'l (-ahl) *n.* Cord wound round keffiyeh, keeping it in position. [Arab. *ʻiqāl* rope]

Agamĕ'mnon (ă-). (Gk legend) King of Argos, brother of Menelaus, and commander of the Greek host which besieged Troy; murdered on his return from Troy by his wife Clytemnestra and her lover Aegisthus.

Aganĭ'ppė (ă-). (Gk antiq.) Fountain on Mt. Helicon sacred to the Muses.

ăgapă'nthus *n.* African LILY.

agā'pe[1] *adv.* & *pred. adj.* Gaping.

ă'gapē[2] *n.* 1. Love-feast held by early Christians in connection with Lord's Supper. 2. Spiritual love (opp. EROS[1]). [Gk, = 'brotherly love']

Agapĕ'monė (ă-) *n.* (= 'abode of love') Institution founded in Somerset (1845) by Henry James Prince (1811–99), where he and his followers lived with property in common, professed certain religious doctrines, and were believed to practise free love. **Agapĕ'monīte** *adj.* & *n.* (Member) of the Agapemone.

ā'gar-ā'gar *n.* Gelatinous substance obtained from various seaweeds and used as laxative, as solidifying agent in culture media for bacteria etc., and in East as food. [Malay]

ă'garĭc *n.* Fungus of family Agaricaceae, including common mushroom, with central stalk and umbrella-like cap with radiating gills on lower side.

ă'gate *n.* 1. Any of various semi-precious stones, semi-pellucid and variegated, usu. having a banded appearance and consisting largely of silica. 2. (U.S., print.) = RUBY *n.* 3.

agā'vė *n.* Plant of genus *A~* (family Agavaceae), including American aloe, with large rosette of spiny leaves and, after a number of years, a gigantic terminal inflorescence bearing numerous flowers once in the plant's life.

āge *n.* 1. Length of life or of existence; a generation; (colloq., esp. in pl.) long time. 2. Particular length of life qualifying one for a purpose; *come of ~*, (Engl. law) attain age of 18 (formerly 21) years, assume rights and responsibilities of adult; *under ~*, not of full age; of less than age required. 3. Latter part of life (also *old ~*). 4. Great period, as *Ice A~*, *Patriarchal A~*. ~ *v.* 1. (Cause to) grow old. 2. Become mature. 3. Fix colours and mordants in (printed cloth etc.) by exposing to steam or to warm moist atmosphere. **ā'g(e)ing** *n.* (esp.) Change of properties occurring in some metals after heat treatment or cold working. **aged** *adj.* 1. (ājd) Of the age of; (of horses) more than 6 years old. 2. (ā'jĭd) Old. **ā'gelėss** *adj.* Never becoming old or outmoded. **ā'gelėssnėss** *n.*

ā'gency̆ *n.* Active operation, action; instrumentality; action personified; office of agent; agent's business establishment.

agĕ'nda *n.pl.* (freq. as sing.) Things to be done, items of business to be considered at a meeting.

ā'gent *n.* One who, thing that, exerts power or produces effect; one acting for another in business, law, politics, etc.; natural force acting on matter.

agent prŏvŏcateur (ahzhahṅ, -tẽr). Person employed to detect suspected offenders by tempting them to overt action. [Fr.]

Agēsĭlā'us (444–360 B.C.). King of Sparta, leader of successful campaign against Persians; killed in war against Thebes.

agglŏ'merāte[1] *v.* Collect into a mass. **agglŏmerā'tion** *n.* **agglŏ'merative** *adj.*

agglŏ'merate[2] *adj.* Collected into a mass. ~ *n.* Mass; (geol.) aggregate of angular fragments of rock (of any or of several kinds) that has been shattered by volcanic action and subsequently consolidated into a mass.

agglu'tĭnāte (-lōō-) *v.* 1. Unite as with glue; combine simple words to express compound ideas without important change of form or loss of meaning. 2. Turn into glue. **agglutĭnā'tion** *n.* **agglu'tĭnative** *adj.* (of languages) Characterized by the joining of simple roots to express compound ideas without material change of form or loss of meaning.

ă'ggrandīze *v.t.* Increase the power, rank, wealth, etc., of; exaggerate. **aggră'ndĭzement** *n.*

ă'ggravāte *v.t.* Increase the gravity of; (colloq.) exasperate. **ăggravā'tion** *n.*

ă'ggrėgāte[1] *v.* Collect together; unite; amount to. **ăggrėgā'tion** *n.*

ă'ggrėgate[2] *adj.* Collected into one body; collective, total; (law) composed of associated individuals; (bot., of fruit) formed from carpels of one flower (as raspberry). ~ *n.* Total; assemblage, collection; (phys.) mass formed by union of homogeneous particles; (geol.) mass of minerals formed into one rock; (building) material mixed with lime, cement, bitumen, etc., to make concrete.

aggrĕ'ssion *n.* Beginning of quarrel; unprovoked attack. **aggrĕ'ssor** *n.*

aggrĕ'ssĭve *adj.* Of attack, offensive; disposed to attack; self-assertive. **aggrĕ'ssĭvely̆** *adv.* **aggrĕ'ssĭvenėss** *n.*

aggrie'ved (-vd) *pred. adj.* Distressed, oppressed; injured, having a grievance.

agha'st (*a*gah-) *adj.* Terrified; struck with amazement.

ă'gīle *adj.* Quick-moving; nimble, active. **ă'gīlely̆** (-l-lĭ) *adv.* **agĭ'lĭty̆** *n.*

A'gĭncourt (ăj-, -kõrt). Village of NW. France, scene of victory (1415) of Henry V of England over French.

BATTLE OF AGINCOURT

ă'giō *n.* Percentage charged for changing paper money into cash, or one currency into another more valuable; excess value of one currency over another. **ă'giotage** *n.* Exchange business; speculation in stocks; stock-jobbing.

agi'stment *n.* (law) Contract for feeding cattle etc. on pasture-land for money payment; profit from this.

ă'gitāte *v.* 1. Shake, move; disturb, excite. 2. Revolve mentally, discuss, debate; keep up an agitation (*for*).

ăgitā'tion *n.* 1. Shaking. 2. Commotion, disturbance. 3. Debate, discussion; keeping of matter constantly before public; public excitement.

ăgita'tō (-tah-) *adv.* (mus.) In an agitated manner. [It.]

ă'gitātor *n.* 1. Person who creates excitement or disturbance, esp. for political ends. 2. Mechanical device for keeping liquid etc. in motion.

Aglā'ia (-y*a*). (Gk myth.) One of the three Graces (see GRACE *n.* 3).

ă'glėt *n.* Metal tag of a lace; tag or spangle as dress-ornament, esp. (now written *aiguillette*) tagged braid or cord hanging from shoulder in some military or naval uniforms; catkin of hazel, birch, etc.

A.G.M. *abbrev.* Annual general meeting.

ă'gnail *n.* Torn skin at root of finger-nail; resulting soreness.

ă'gnāte *adj.* Descended from the same male ancestor; of same clan or nation. ~ *n.* Agnate person or animal.

A'gnės (ă-), St. (4th c.). Patron saint of virgins, martyred in the persecution of Diocletian and commemorated 21 Jan.

A'gni (ă-). (Vedic myth.) God of fire.

ăgnō′mĕn *n.* Additional name, esp. (Rom. antiq.) fourth name occas. assumed by Romans.

ăgnŏ′stĭc *n.* One who holds that nothing is known, or likely to be known, of the existence of God or gods or of anything beyond material phenomena. ~ *adj.* Pertaining to agnostics or agnosticism. **ăgnŏ′stĭcism** *n.* [Gk *agnōstos* (*theos*) unknown (god); taken by T. H. Huxley f. Acts 17: 23]

Agnus Dei (ăg′nōōs dā′ē). Part of the Mass beginning with these words; figure of lamb as emblem of Christ bearing cross or banner; small disc of wax stamped with this figure and blessed by pope. [L, = 'lamb of God']

agō′ *adv.* Past, gone by; since.

agŏ′g *adv.* & *pred. adj.* Eager(ly), expectant(ly).

agŏ′nĭc *adj.* Making no angle; ~ *line*, line joining places where magnetic compass points to true north.

ă′gonīze *v.* Torture; suffer agony, writhe in anguish; wrestle; make desperate efforts for effect.

ă′gonȳ *n.* Extreme bodily or mental suffering, esp. the last sufferings of Jesus Christ before the Crucifixion; *death* ~, *last* ~, death pangs; ~ *column*, in newspaper, column of personal advertisements (for missing friends etc.).

ăgora′ (-ah) *n.* (pl. *-rōt*) $\frac{1}{100}$ of an Israeli pound.

ăgoraphō′bĭa *n.* Morbid dread of open spaces.

ăgou′tĭ (-ōō-) *n.* Rodent (several species in genus *Dasyprocta*) of Central America and W. Indies, related to guinea-pig, nocturnal in habit and destructive to sugar-plantations etc.

Agra (ah′-). City on river Jumna in Uttar Pradesh, capital of Mogul emperors from early 16th c. to mid-17th c.; site of the TAJ MAHAL.

agrār′ĭan *adj.* Of landed property or cultivated land. **agrār′ĭanism** *n.*

agree′ *v.* Consent (*to*); be in accord, harmonize in opinion etc. (*with*); (gram.) have same number, gender, case, or person.

agree′able (-rĭa-) *adj.* Pleasing (*to*); (colloq.) well-disposed (*to, to do*); **agree′ablȳ** *adv.*

agree′ment *n.* Mutual understanding, covenant; (law) contract legally binding on parties; accordance in opinion; (gram.) concord in number, case, gender, person.

agrĕ′stĭc *adj.* Rural, rustic.

Agrĭ′cola, Gnaeus Julius (A.D. 40–93). Roman general; governor of Britain for several years from 78.

ă′grĭcŭlture *n.* Cultivation of the soil. **ăgrĭcŭ′ltural** *adj.* (-cher-) **ăgrĭcŭ′lturĭst, -turalĭst** *ns.*

ă′grĭmonȳ *n.* Perennial plant of the rose family, esp. *Agrimonia eupatoria*, which has yellow flowers and hooked clinging fruit; *hemp* ~, see HEMP.

Agrĭ′ppa, Marcus Vipsanius (*c* 63–12 B.C.). Roman general, son-in-law of the Emperor Augustus.

agrŏ′nomȳ *n.* Rural economy, husbandry. **ăgronŏ′mĭc, -ĭcal** *adjs.* **ăgronŏ′mĭcs, agrŏ′nomĭst** *ns.*

agrou′nd *adv.* & *pred. adj.* On the bottom of shallow water.

ā′gūe *n.* Malarial fever; cold shivering stage of this; shivering fit.

ah *int.* Exclamation of joy, sorrow, surprise, entreaty, etc.

A.H. *abbrev.* *Anno Hegirae* (L, = in the year of the HEGIRA).

aha (ah-hah′) *int.* Exclamation of surprise, triumph, mockery.

A′hăb (ā-). King of Israel (see 1 Kings 16–22).

Ahasūēr′us (*a*hăz-). Persian king (see Esther *passim*, Ezra 4: 6, Dan. 9: 1); generally supposed to be XERXES.

A′hăz (ā-). King of Judah (see 2 Kings 16).

ahead (*a*hĕ′d) *adv.* & *pred. adj.* In advance *of*, in a direct line forward.

ahoy′ *int.* (naut.) Call used in hailing.

Ah′rĭman. Principle of evil in the Zoroastrian system.

Ahura-Mă'zda (*a*hoor'*a*). = ORMAZD.

ai (ah'-ĭ) *n.* Three-toed sloth (*Bradypus tridactylus*) of S. America. [f. its cry]

A.I. *abbrev.* Artificial insemination (*A.I.D.* by donor, *A.I.H.* by husband).

aid *v.t.* Help, assist, promote. ~ *n.* Help, assistance; (hist.) grant of subsidy or tax to king, exchequer loan; helper; material source of help.

Ai'dan, St. (d. 651). Monk of Iona, apostle to Northumbria and first bishop of Lindisfarne.

aide n. Aide-de-camp; assistant.

aide-de-camp (ā'd*e*kahṅ) *n.* (pl. *aides-de-camp*). (orig. mil.) Officer acting as confidential assistant to senior officer. [Fr.]

aide-mémoire (ādmāmwar̂) *n.* Manual of formulae etc. to serve as aid to the memory; in diplomatic use, memorandum. [Fr.]

ai'grĕtte *n.* = EGRET; long white plume grown by this in breeding-season; tuft of feathers or hair; spray of gems etc.

aiguille (ā'gwēl) *n.* Sharp peak of rock.

aiguillette (āgwĭlĕ't): see AGLET.

ail *v.* Trouble, afflict; be ill.

ai'lment *n.* Illness, esp. slight one.

ai'leron *n.* Hinged flap on trailing edge of aircraft wing, near the tip, providing variation of lift on either side and used to execute the movement known as 'banking'. [Fr. 'little wing, fin', dim. of *aile* wing]

ailūrophō'bĭa (īl-) *n.* Morbid fear of cats. **ailūr'ophōbe** *n.*

aim *v.* Direct *at*; point (gun etc.); deliver blow, discharge missile (*at*); take aim; form designs. ~ *n.* Direction of or act of directing a missile or weapon towards an object; design, purpose, object. **ai'mlėss** *adj.* **ai'mlėsslў** *adv.* **ai'mlėssnėss** *n.*

Ai'nū (īn-) *n.* (Member of) a Caucasoid people in Japan and U.S.S.R. with hairy bodies; their language.

air *n.* 1. Invisible, odourless, and tasteless mixture of gases enveloping the Earth, consisting chiefly of oxygen and nitrogen, with some carbon dioxide and traces of other gases, and breathed by all land animals; atmosphere; unconfined space; breeze; *on the* ~, broadcast(ing) by radio transmission. 2. Appearance; mien; affected manner. 3. (mus.) Melody, tune, aria. 4. (attrib.) Of aircraft or flying. 5. ~ *ball, -balloon, -bladder, -jacket,* etc., containing air or inflated by air; *air'borne,* transported by air or aircraft; (of aircraft) having left the ground; in flight; ~*-brake,* brake operated by piston driven by compressed air; also, brake consisting of flaps or other movable surfaces, normally lying parallel to air-flow, turned through 90° to retard progress of aircraft or car; ~ *brick,* ventilating brick; *air'brush,* fine spray for paint used in commercial art and for retouching photographs; *Air Chief Marshal,* title, rank, of officer in R.A.F., ranking next below a Marshal and above an Air Marshal; *Air Commodore,* title, rank, of officer in R.A.F. immediately above Group Captain; ~ *-conditioning,* process of cleaning air and controlling its temperature and humidity before it enters a room, building, etc., and in certain manufacturing processes; ~*-cooled* (*adj.*) cooled by exposure to stream of air; *air'craft,* (pl. same) any kind of flying machine, including aeroplanes, airships, helicopters, etc.; these collectively; *aircraft carrier,* ship designed to carry aeroplanes, with special deck for taking-off and landing; *air'craftman, air'craftwoman,* lowest rank in R.A.F., W.R.A.F.; ~*-cushion,* cushion inflated by air; body of air serving to provide support, esp. in ~*-cushion vehicle,* hovercraft; *air'field,* area of land where aircraft are accommodated and maintained and may take off or land; ~ *force,* branch of armed forces using aircraft in fighting (in U.K., Royal Air Force) *air'graph,* photographic reproduction of letter etc. conveyed by air mail in form of microfilm to save weight; *~-gun*, gun from which missile is discharged by compressed air; ~ *hostess*, stewardess in passenger aircraft; ~ *letter*, folding form for air mail letters; *~-lift*, transportation of supplies by air to area cut off from normal communications; (*v.t.*) transport thus; *air'line*, line of aircraft for public service; *air'liner*, large passenger aeroplane; ~ *-lock*, stoppage of flow of liquid in pump or pipe by bubble of air; also, see LOCK² *n.* 2; ~ *mail*, mail carried by aircraft; *air'man*, member of crew of aircraft; member of air force; *Air Marshal*, title, rank, of officer in R.A.F., equivalent to Lieutenant-General in the army; *~-minded* (*adj.*) interested in, or enthusiastic for, use and development of aircraft; *air'plane*, (orig. U.S.) aeroplane; ~ *pocket*, local condition of atmosphere, as a down current or sudden change of wind velocity, which causes aircraft to lose height suddenly; *air'port*, aerodrome for transport of passengers and goods by air; *~-power*, power of offensive and defensive action dependent upon a supply of aircraft; *~-pump*, pump for exhausting vessel etc. of its air; (also) compressor; ~ *raid*, attack by aircraft; *air'screw*, aircraft propeller; *~-sea rescue*, applied to the branch of the R.A.F. whose task is to rescue airmen and passengers from the sea, and to such operations; ~ *-shaft*, passage for ventilating mine or tunnel; *air'ship*, flying machine lighter than air; dirigible balloon; *~-sickness*, kind of nausea sometimes affecting persons in an aircraft; *~-space*, space containing air; air lying over a particular territory and considered subject to its jurisdiction; ~ *speed*, speed of aircraft in relation to the air, as dist. from *ground speed*; *air'strip*, strip of land prepared for the taking off and landing of aircraft, often for temporary use; ~ *terminal*, town office of airline equipped for reception of passengers; *air'tight*, impermeable to air; *A~ Training Corps*, organization for the training of cadets for the R.A.F.; *air'way*, ventilating passage in mine; route regularly followed by aircraft; (device to secure) passage for air into lungs; *air'worthy*, (of aircraft) in fit condition to be flown. ~ *v.* Expose to open air, ventilate; finish drying (clothes etc.) by warmth; parade (grievances, opinions, etc.).

Air'edāle (ārd-) *n.* One of a breed of large terriers with rough reddish-brown coats. [Valley of river Aire, West Yorkshire]

air'lèss *adj.* Stuffy; breezeless, still. **air'lèssnèss** *n.*

air'ȳ *adj.* Breezy; light, thin; immaterial; sprightly, graceful, delicate; superficial, flippant. **air'ilȳ** *adv.*

aisle (īl) *n.* Division of church,

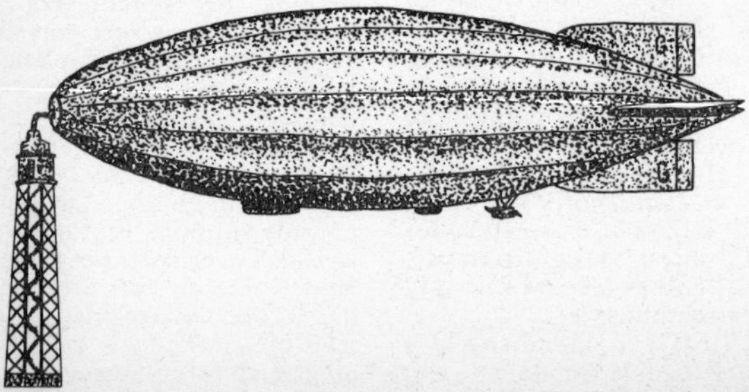

AIRSHIP

esp. parallel to nave, choir, or transept, and divided from it by pillars; passage between rows of seats, in church, theatre, etc. [L *ala* wing]

ait *n.* Small isle, esp. one in a river.

aitch *n.* Letter H, h.

ai'tchbōne *n.* Rump bone, cut of beef over this bone.

Aix-la-Chăpĕlle (-lah-sh-). French name of AACHEN.

Aja'nta (*a*jŭ-). Village in S. central India with caves containing Buddhist frescoes and sculptures.

aja͡r' *adv.* (of a door) Slightly open.

A'jăx (ā-). (Gk legend) 1. Greek hero of the Trojan war, son of Telamon king of Salamis. 2. Another Greek, son of Oileus king of Locris, who was killed after a shipwreck on his homeward journey after the fall of Troy.

A'kba͡r (ă-). Jalaludin Muhammad (1542–1605), Mogul emperor; enlarged the Mogul Empire in India to its greatest extent.

à Kempis, Thomas: see THOMAS À KEMPIS.

Akhna'ten (ăknah-). Name (lit. 'glory of the sun') taken by Amenhotep IV, king of Egypt of 18th dynasty (14th c. B.C.), who tried to replace the worship of Ammon by that of Ra, and built a new capital at Tell el Amarna, away from Thebes where the old priesthood was established.

akĭ'mbō *adv.* & *adj.* (of arms) With hands on hips and elbows out.

akĭ'n *pred. adj.* Related by blood; (fig.) of similar character.

A'kkăd, A'cc- (ă-). Northern part of ancient Babylonia; also, the city (Agade) founded by Sargon *c* 2300 B.C. **Akkā'dĭan, Acc-** *adj.* & *n.* (Native or inhabitant) of Akkad; (of) the language of this people, the oldest known Semitic language.

a.l. *abbrev.* Autograph letter.

à la (*ah lah*). After the manner of. [Fr]

Ala. *abbrev.* Alabama.

A.L.A. *abbrev.* American Library Association.

Alabama (ăl*a*bah'm*a*, U.S. -ă'm*a*). State in south-eastern U.S., admitted to the Union in 1819; capital, Montgomery.

ă'labaster (-bah-) *n.* Translucent granular gypsum rock of white, pink, or yellowish colour, used for statues etc. ~ *adj.* Of alabaster; resembling it in whiteness or smoothness.

à la carte (ah lah ka͡rt). (of meal) Ordered by separate items from the bill of fare (opp. *table d'hôte*). [Fr.]

ală'crĭtў *n.* Briskness, cheerful readiness.

Ală'ddĭn. Hero of a story in 'Arabian Nights', who acquired a lamp the rubbing of which brought a genie to do the will of the owner.

A'lamein (ă-, -ăn), El. Place near the NE. coast of Egypt, where German forces advancing on Egypt were checked and defeated in 1942.

à la mode (ah lah mōd). In the fashion, fashionable; *beef* ~, a kind of beef stew. [Fr.]

Å'land I'slands (aw-, īl*a*ndz). Group of islands in the Gulf of Bothnia constituting a department of Finland.

ā'lar *adj.* Pertaining to wings; wing-shaped, wing-like; axillary.

Alarcón (ălarkō'n), Pedro Antonio de (1833–91). Spanish poet, dramatist, and prose writer.

Alarcón y Mendoza (ălarkō'n ĭ mĕndō'th*a*), Juan Ruiz de (*c* 1581–1639). Mexican-Spanish dramatist.

A'laric (ă-) (*c* 370–410). A Visigoth, the first Germanic conqueror of Rome (A.D. 410).

alar'm *n.* Call to arms; warning sound giving notice of danger; warning; frightened anticipation of danger; sudden uneasiness; mechanism that sounds alarm; ~ *clock*, clock with apparatus that can be set to ring at predetermined time; ~*s and excursions*, (joc.) noise and bustle. ~ *v.t.* Arouse to sense of danger; disturb, agitate. **alar'ming** *adj.* **alar'mingly** *adv.* [It. *all' arme* to arms]

alar'mist *n.* One who raises alarm on slight grounds; panic-monger.

alar'um *n.* (archaic) Alarm.

ală's (*or* -ahs) *int.* Exclamation of grief, pity, concern.

Ală'ska. State of the U.S. in the extreme NW. of N. America, with coasts in Arctic Ocean, Bering Sea, and North Pacific; discovered by Russian explorers (under Vitus Bering) in 1741, and further explored by Cook, Vancouver, and others during the last quarter of 18th c.; the territory was purchased from Russia in 1867 and admitted to the Union in 1959; capital, Juneau. **Ală'skan** *adj.* & *n.*

ălb *n.* Vestment reaching to feet, worn by celebrant at Eucharist over the cassock and by some consecrated kings.

Alba, Duke of: see ALVA.

ă'lbacore *n.* Large species of fish of N. Amer. E. and W. coasts (*Thunnus alalunga*) allied to tunny; other fish of the same genus. [Arab. *al* the, *bakr* young camel]

A'lban (awl-), St. (d. *c* 304). First British martyr, commemorated on 22 June; martyred at Verulamium, which was afterwards named St. Albans.

Alban. *abbrev.* (Bishop) of St. Albans (replacing surname in his signature).

Albā'nia (ă-). Balkan State between Greece and Yugoslavia; under Turkish rule from 16th c. until 1912, when disputes arising from the demand for Albanian autonomy nearly caused a European war; in Jan. 1925 the country was proclaimed a republic, which continued until 1928 when it was changed into a monarchy; again proclaimed a republic in 1946; capital, Tirana. **Albā'nian** *adj.* & *n.* (Native, inhabitant, language) of Albania.

A'lbany[1] (awl-). Ancient poetic name, of Gaelic origin, for the N. part of Britain.

A'lbany[2] (awl-). House near Piccadilly, London, formerly belonging to Frederick, Duke of York and Albany, converted *c* 1803 into sets of chambers where many famous men of letters have resided.

ă'lbatross *n.* Very long-winged oceanic bird (genus *Diomedea*), allied to petrel, found chiefly in the S. hemisphere; *wandering* ~, one of the largest sea-birds (*D. exulans*), white when adult, with dark wings and hooked beak. [f. obs. *alcatras* frigate-bird, f. Span. and Port., f. Arab. *al-qadus* the bucket (name for the pelican, from its supposed water-carrying habit)]

albē'it (awl-) *conj.* Though.

Albéniz (ălbānē'th), Isaac (1860–1909). Spanish pianist and composer, famous chiefly for works based on the rhythm of Spanish popular music.

A'lberich (ă-, -ĭχ). (Scand. myth.) King of the elves, guardian of the treasure of the Nibelungs, stolen from him by Siegfried.

A'lbert[1] (ă-), Prince (1819–1861). Prince of Saxe-Coburg-Gotha; cousin and consort (1840) of Queen Victoria; *Lake* ~, large shallow lake in Uganda, discovered in 1864, re-named *Lake Mobutu Sese Seko*,

1973; *Royal* ~ *Hall*, large concert and exhibition hall erected (1867–71) in Kensington, London; ~ *Medal*, (abbrev. A.M.) awarded since 1866 for 'gallantry in saving life at sea or on land'; ~ *Memorial*, an elaborate monument, designed by Sir Gilbert Scott, erected (1872–6) in Hyde Park, London.

A'lbert[2] (ă-) (1875–1934). King of the Belgians (1909–34), commander-in-chief of the Belgian army during the war of 1914–18.

ă'lbert[3] *n.* (archaic) Watch-chain, with cross-bar for insertion in button-hole of waistcoat, named after Prince ALBERT[1].

Alber̃'ta (ă-). Western prairie province of Canada, bounded on the south by the U.S.A., and on the west by the Rocky Mountains; capital, Edmonton.

Alberti (ălbar̄'tĭ), Leon Battista degli (1404–72). Italian architect, painter, writer on art, poet, and musician.

Alber̃'tus Mă'gnus (ă-) (1193 or 1206–1280). Swabian Dominican monk, one of the great scholastic philosophers; known as 'Doctor Universalis'.

ălbĕ'scent *adj.* Growing white, fading into white.

Albĭgĕ'nsēs (ă-, -z) *n.pl.* Members of a heretical sect preaching a form of Manichaean dualism in S. France, 11th–13th c. **Albĭgĕ'nsĭan** *adj.* & *n.* [L, f. town of *Albi*]

ălbi'nō (-bē-) *n.* Animal or human being marked by congenital absence of pigment in skin and hair, which is white, and eyes, which are pink or very pale blue and unduly sensitive to light; plant lacking normal colouring. **ălbĭnŏ'tĭc** *adj.* **ă'lbĭnĭsm** *n.*

Albī'nus (ă-). = ALCUIN.

A'lbĭon (ă-). Ancient poetical name for Britain.

Alboin (ălbwăn) (d. 573). King of the Lombards, conqueror and settler of northern Italy (568).

Albuera (ălbwar̄'*a*). Small village in Spain, scene (1811) of a combined English, Portuguese, and Spanish victory over the French under Marshal Soult.

ă'lbum *n.* Blank book for insertion of autographs, photographs, etc.; long-playing record or set of records.

ă'lbūmėn (*or* -bū'-) *n.* White of egg; a constituent of animal cells, milk, etc., found nearly pure in white of egg; (bot.) substance found between skin and embryo of many seeds, usu. the edible part. **ălbū'mėnīze** *v.t.* Coat (paper) with an albuminous solution. **ălbū'mĭnōse, ălbū'mĭnous** *adjs.*

ălbū'mĭn *n.* Any of a class of water-soluble proteins.

ălbū'mĭnoid *n.* Any of a class of organic compounds forming chief parts of organs and tissues of animals and plants; protein. **ălbūmĭnoi'dal** *adj.*

ălbūmĭnūr̃'ĭa *n.* (med.) Condition in which the urine contains proteins, sometimes a symptom of kidney disease.

A'lbūquerque (ă-, -kẽrk), Afonso d' (1453–1515). Portuguese navigator, founder of Portuguese power in India.

ălbur̃'num *n.* Recently formed wood in trees, sap-wood.

Alcae'us (ălsē-) (b. *c* 620 B.C.). Greek lyric poet of Mitylene in Lesbos. **ălcā'ĭc** *adj.* (esp.) Of a metre invented by Alcaeus, a stanza of four lines:

— — ⏑ — — | — ⏑ ⏑ — ⏑ ⏓
— — ⏑ · — | — ⏑ ⏑ — ⏑ ⏓
— — ⏑ — — — ⏑ — —
— ⏑ ⏑ — ⏑ ⏑ — ⏑ — ⏑

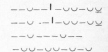

A'lcatrăz (ă-). Island in San Francisco Bay, California; former site of U.S. federal prison.

Alcĕ'stĭs (ă-). (Gk legend) Wife of Admetus, whose life she saved by giving her own; she was brought back from Hades by Hercules.

ă'lchėmy (-k-) *n.* Medieval forerunner of chemistry, primarily the attempt to transmute base metals into gold or silver. **ălchĕ'mĭc, -ĭcal** *adjs.* **ă'lchėmist** *n.* [Arab. *al-kimia*; f. *al* the, Gk *khēmeia* transmutation of metals]

Alcĭbī'adēs (ă-, -z) (*c* 450–404

B.C.). Athenian general and politician to whose irresponsibility the defeat of Athens in the Peloponnesian War was partly due.

Alcĭ'nōus (ă-). (Gk legend) King of Phaeacia and father of Nausicaa; entertained Ulysses during his journey home from Troy.

A'lcman (ă-). (7th c. B.C.). Principal lyric poet of Sparta, a native of Lydia, brought to Sparta as a slave.

Alcmē'nė (ă-). (Gk myth.) Wife of Amphitryon and mother of Hercules by Zeus.

A'lcŏck (awl-), Sir John William (1892–1919). English aviator; with A. W. BROWN[2] made first non-stop flight across the Atlantic, 1919 (Newfoundland to Ireland, 16 hrs 12 m.).

ă'lcohŏl *n.* 1. Colourless volatile inflammable liquid, also called *ethyl* ~ (C_2H_5OH), formed by fermentation of sugars and contained in wine ('spirit of wine'), beer, whisky, etc., of which it is the intoxicating principle, also used in medicine and industry as a solvent for fats, oils, etc., and as a fuel. 2. Any liquor containing alcohol. 3. (chem.) Any of a class of compounds analogous to alcohol in constitution and derived from hydrocarbons by the replacement of hydrogen atoms by hydroxyl groups. [Arab. *al* the, *koh'l* powder (for staining eyelids)]

ălcohŏ'lĭc *adj.* Pertaining to, containing, alcohol. ~ *n.* Person suffering from alcoholism.

ă'lcoholĭsm *n.* Diseased condition caused by excessive consumption of alcoholic liquors.

ălcoholŏ'mėter *n.* Instrument for measuring alcoholic content of liquids.

A'lcŏtt (awl-), Louisa May (1832–88). Amer. author of 'Little Women' and other books for girls.

ă'lcōve *n.* Vaulted recess in room-wall; recess in garden-wall or hedge; summer-house. [Arab. *al-qobbah* the vault]

Alcuin (ă'lkwĭn) (735–804). English theologian and man of letters, Charlemagne's coadjutor in educational reforms, and finally abbot of Tours.

Alcȳ'onė (ă-). (Gk legend) Wife of Ceyx; threw herself into the sea after finding the body of her shipwrecked husband on the shore; the gods changed both into kingfishers, and the sea is said to be calm while they are nesting; hence the expression 'halcyon days'.

Ald. *abbrev.* Alderman.

Aldĕ'baran (ă-). Bright, reddish star in the constellation Taurus. [Arab., = 'the following' (because it follows the Pleiades)]

ă'ldėhȳde *n.* Any of a class of organic compounds containing the group CHO— in their structures, esp. acetaldehyde, CH_3CHO. [abbrev. of L. *al*cohol *dehyd*rogenatum (deprived of hydrogen)]

a'lder (awl-) *n.* Tree (genus *Alnus*) of birch family, esp. *A. glutinosa*, growing by lakes and streams and in marshy ground; ~ *buckthorn*, shrub (*Rhamnus frangula*) of buckthorn family growing in damp peaty soils.

a'lderman (awl-) *n.* (hist.) Co-opted member of an English county or borough council, next in dignity to mayor; as an Anglo-Saxon title, a noble or person of high rank. **aldermă'nĭc** *adj.* **a'ldermanshĭp** *n.* **a'ldermanrȳ** *n.* (hist.) Ward, district of a borough having its own alderman; rank of alderman.

A'lderney (awl-). One of the four larger Channel Islands. ~ *n.* One of the dairy cattle bred in the Channel Islands, now including Jersey and Guernsey breeds.

A'ldershŏt (awl-). Town in Hampshire having a permanent military camp and training centre.

A'ldhĕlm (ă-), St. (*c* 640–709). English churchman and scholar, 1st bishop of Sherborne; author of Latin works in verse and prose.

A'ldīne (awl-) *adj.* & *n.* (Edition) printed by Aldus Manutius.

A'ldĭs lămp (awl-). Signalling lamp, used esp. in navy and air force, in which Morse signs are transmitted by rotating a mirror at whose focus the light is located. [inventor, A. C. W. *Aldis*]

A'ldus Manū'tius (awl-, -shĭus) (1450–1515). Aldo Manuzio, Italian printer whose press at Venice

issued the first printed editions of many Greek authors, and introduced italics into typography.

āle *n.* Liquor made from an infusion of malt by fermentation, flavoured with hops etc.; beer; ~*-house*, (hist.) house selling ale.

Alĕ'ctō. (Gk myth.) One of the Furies (see FURY).

alee' *adv.* & *pred. adj.* On the lee side of a ship, to leeward.

Aleman (ălĭmah'n), Mateo (*c* 1550–1614). Spanish picaresque novelist.

Alembert (ălahṅbar̄), Jean le Rond d' (1717–83). French encyclopaedist, philosopher, and mathematician.

alĕ'mbĭc *n.* (hist.) Apparatus used by alchemists for distilling. [Arab. *alanbig* still, f. Gk *ambix -ikos* cup, cap of a still]

Alençon (ălahṅsawṅ). Town in NW. France, famous for the manufacture of needlepoint lace (*point d'Alençon*), orig. copied from Venetian lace.

Alĕ'ppō. Ancient city in Syria, twice besieged (though not taken) during the Crusades.

alẽr't *adj.* Watchful, vigilant; lively, nimble. ~ *n.* Warning-call, alarm; warning of air-raid etc., period of warning; *on the* ~, on the look-out. **alẽr'tlÿ** *adv.* **alẽr'tnėss** *n.* **alẽr't** *v.t.* Make alert, warn. [It. *all' erta* to the watch-tower]

Aleu'tian I'slands (-shan īlandz). (also *Aleutians*) Group of islands in U.S. possession extending SW. from Alaska.

Alexa'nder[1] (ălĭgzah-) (356–323 B.C.), 'the Great'. King of Macedon; son of Philip II of Macedon; educated by Aristotle;

became king 336 B.C.; was nominated by the Greek states to conduct the war against Persia, in which he was victorious; he extended his conquests to Egypt (where he founded Alexandria) and India.

Alexa'nder[2] (ălĭgzah-). Name of three kings of Scotland: *Alexander I* (*c* 1078–1124), reigned 1107–24; *Alexander II* (1198–1249), reigned 1214–49; *Alexander III* (1241–85), reigned 1249–85.

Alexa'nder[3] (ălĭgzah-). Name of eight popes: *Alexander VI*, see BORGIA, Rodrigo.

Alexa'nder[4] (ălĭgzah-). Name of three emperors of Russia: *Alexander I* (1777–1825), emperor 1801–25 during the Napoleonic Wars; sponsor of the Holy Alliance; *Alexander II* (1818–81), emperor 1855–81, assassinated in St. Petersburg; *Alexander III* (1845–94), emperor 1881–94.

Alexa'nder Nĕ'vskĭ (ălĭgzah-; nĕf-) (1220–63). Russian saint and national hero, called 'Nevski' from the river Neva, on the banks of which he defeated the Swedes.

Alexa′ndra (ălĭgzah-) (1844–1925). Wife of Edward VII and queen of Gt Britain, daughter of Christian IX of Denmark.

Alexa′ndrĭa (ălĭgzah-). City and seaport of Egypt, founded by Alexander the Great 332 B.C.; capital of Egypt under the Ptolemies; until the Roman conquest of Egypt it was a centre of Greek culture, and possessed a famous library, part of which was accidentally burnt when Julius Caesar was besieged in the city.

Alexa′ndrĭan *adj.* Of Alexandria; ~ *period*, period of Hellenistic literature with Alexandria as its chief centre from end of the time of Alexander the Great to the Roman conquest of Greece, 300–146 B.C.

ălexă′ndrīne (-ĭgz-) *adj.* & *n.* (pros.) (Line) of six iambic feet, or twelve syllables, the French heroic verse. [so called because it was used in early poems on the subject of Alexander the Great]

ălfă′lfa *n.* = LUCERNE[1].

Alfieri (ălfyār′ĭ), Vittorio, Count (1749–1803). Italian dramatist; author of tragedies on classical and other subjects, satirical comedies, and political works.

Alfŏ′nsō (ă-). Name of several kings of Spain, the last of whom, *Alfonso XIII* (1886–1941), was deposed in 1931 when Spain became a republic.

A′lfrėd (ă-) (849–899), 'the Great'. King of the West Saxons 871; drove the Danes from his territories; built a navy; composed

a code of laws; encouraged the revival of letters in the W. of England, himself translating Latin works into English.

ălfrĕ′scō *adv.* In the open air. ~ *adj.* Open-air.

ă′lga *n.* (pl. *-gae*). One of the Algae, a division of primitive

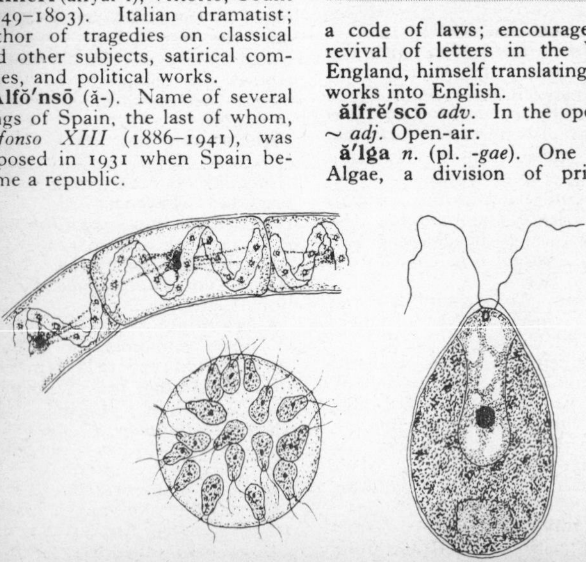

ALGAE

cryptogamic plants including green, brown, and red seaweeds, pond-scums, and many microscopic water-plants showing immense diversity of structure.

ă'lgėbra *n.* Branch of mathematics dealing with relations and properties of numbers by means of letters and other general symbols. **ălgėbrā'ic, -ical** *adjs.* **ălgėbrā'ically** *adv.* **ă'lgėbrāist** *n.* [Arab. *al-jebr* the reunion of fragments]

Alger'ia (ă-). Republic in N. Africa; under French rule until 1962; capital, Algiers. **Alger'ian** *adj.* & *n.*

ălgi'nic *adj.* ~ *acid*, colloidal acid ($C_6H_8O_6$) obtained from certain algae.

A'lgŏl[1] (ă-). Eclipsing binary star in the constellation Perseus. [Arab. *al-gul* the destruction]

A'lgŏl[2], **ALGOL** (ă-) *n.* International algebraic language for use in programming computers. [*algo*rithmic *l*anguage]

Algŏ'nquian (ă-) *n.* & *adj.* (One) of a widely-spread group of N.-Amer. Indian languages; Algonquin.

Algŏ'nquin, -kin (ă-) *n.* & *adj.* (Member) of a group of N.-Amer. Indian tribes formerly living near the Ottawa River in Canada; (of) their language; Algonquian.

ă'lgorism *n.* Arabic system of notation. [med. L *algorismus*, f. Arab. *al-Khowarazmi* the man of Khiva, surname of a 9th-c. Muslim mathematician]

ă'lgorithm *n.* 1. = ALGORISM. 2. Process or rules, usu. expressed algebraically, for (esp. machine) calculation etc. **ălgori'thmic** *adj.*

Alhă'mbra (ă-). Palace of the Moorish kings at Granada, built in 13th c. [Arab. *al* the *ḥamrā'* red: thought to refer to the colour of the bricks or the name of the founder]

A'lĭ (ă-). Cousin and son-in-law of Muhammad; regarded by some Muslims as the first caliph, his three predecessors being considered interlopers.

ā'lias *adv.* & *n.* (Name by which one is or has been called) on other occasions.

A'lĭ Ba'ba (ă-, bah-). Hero of a story supposed to be from the 'Arabian Nights'; discovered the magic formula ('Open Sesame!') which opened the cave in which forty robbers kept the treasures they had accumulated.

ă'libī *n.* Plea that when an alleged act took place one was elsewhere; (colloq., orig. U.S.) excuse. ~ *v.t.* (colloq.) Provide with an alibi.

Alică'ntė (ă-) *n.* Red wine made in Alicante, a province of SE. Spain.

A'lice (ă-). Heroine of 'Alice's Adventures in Wonderland' and 'Through the Looking-Glass' by Lewis Carroll; ~ *band*, type of hair-band worn by Alice in Tenniel's illustrations to the latter.

ă'lidāde *n.* Movable arm of quadrant etc. carrying the sights and indicating degrees cut off on the arc. [Arab *al'idadah* the revolving radius (upper arm)]

ā'lien *adj.* Not one's own; foreign; differing in nature (*from*); repugnant (*to*). ~ *n.* Stranger, foreigner. ~ *v.t.* (law) Transfer ownership of. **ā'lienable** *adj.* **ālienabi'lity** *n.*

ā'lienāte *v.t.* Estrange, transfer ownership of; divert (*from*). **ālienā'tion** *n.* Estrangement; transference of ownership; diversion to different purpose.

ā'lienist *n.* (formerly) Psychiatrist.

Alighieri: see DANTE.

ali'ght[1] (-īt) *v.i.* Dismount, descend (*from*); settle, come to earth (from the air).

ali'ght[2] (-īt) *pred. adj.* Kindled, on fire, lighted up.

ali'gn (-īn) *v.* Place, lay, in a line; bring into line; form a line. **ali'gnment** *n.* Act of aligning; formation in a straight line, esp. of soldiers.

alī'ke *pred. adj.* Similar, like. ~ *adv.* In like manner.

ă'liment *n.* Food; mental sustenance. **ălimĕ'ntal** *adj.* **ălimĕ'ntally** *adv.*

ălĭmĕ'ntarȳ *adj.* Nourishing; performing functions of nutrition; providing maintenance; ~ *canal,*

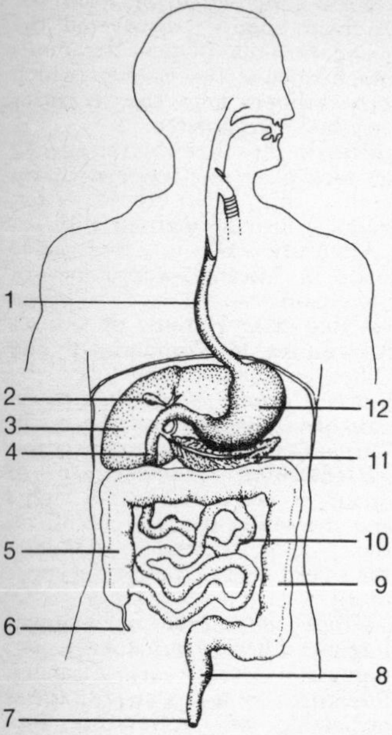

1. Oesophagus 2. Gall bladder 3. Liver 4. Duodenum 5. Caecum 6. Appendix 7. Anus 8. Rectum 9. Colon 10. Small intestine 11. Pancreas 12. Stomach

ALIMENTARY CANAL

channel in animal body through which food passes, including whole length from mouth, through the intestines to the anus.

ălĭmentā'tion *n.* Nourishment; maintenance.

ă'lĭmonȳ *n.* Maintenance allowance made to woman from (former) husband after legal separation or divorce.

ălĭphă'tic *adj.* (chem.) Fatty; belonging to the group of organic compounds in which the carbon atoms are linked in open chains as opposed to rings.

ă'lĭquŏt *adj.* & *n.* (Part) contained by the whole an integral number of times, thus, 6 is an aliquot part of 18.

alī've *pred. adj.* Living; active, brisk; fully susceptible *to*; swarming *with*.

alĭ'zarĭn *n.* Red colouring matter of madder. [prob. f. Arab. *al* the, *'uṣāra* juice, extract]

ă'lkalī *n.* (pl. *-is*). (chem.) Any of a number of substances having strongly basic properties and including the carbonates and hydroxides of the alkali metals of ammonium and the hydroxides of some other reactive metals; ~ *metal*, any of a group of highly reactive metallic elements including lithium, sodium and potassium. **ă'lkalīne** *adj.* **ălkalĭ'nĭtȳ** *n.* [Arab. *al* the, *qily* cinders, lye]

ă'lkaloid *n.* Any of a large group of nitrogenous organic substances of vegetable origin having basic or alkaline properties, many, as morphine, strychnine, cocaine, etc., being used as drugs.

ă'lkāne *n.* Any member of the paraffin series of hydrocarbons.

ă'lkēne *n.* Any member of the ethylene series of hydrocarbons; olefine.

ă'lkȳl *adj.* Derived from, or related to, the paraffin series of hydrocarbons; ~ *radical*, any of the series of radicals derived from paraffin hydrocarbons by removal of a hydrogen atom, e.g. methyl (CH_3), ethyl (C_2H_5).

all (awl) *adj.* The entire; the greatest possible; the entire number of; ~ *clear*, signal giving information that there is no danger; esp., signal that hostile aircraft have left the neighbourhood; *A~ Fools' Day*, 1 April (the celebration of which is probably a survival of ancient festivities held at spring equinox) when the unsuspecting are made victims of practical jokes or sent on fools' errands; *A~ Hallows*, (archaic) All Saints' Day; *~-Hallows Eve*, Hallowe'en, 31 Oct., the last day of the year in the old Celtic calendar, and the night of all the witches; *A~ Saints' Day*, 1 Nov., day on which there is a general celebration of all Christian saints; *A~ Souls' Day*, 2 Nov., day on which prayers are offered for the souls of all the faithful deceased. ~ *n.* All men; the whole, every one, everything; *at* ~, in any way; in any degree; of any kind; ~*-in*, inclusive; (of wrestling) with no restrictions; ~ *one*, just the same. ~ *adv.* Wholly, quite; ~ *in*, (colloq.) quite exhausted; ~ *out*, using or involving all resources; fully extended; at top speed; ~ *over*, (colloq.) displaying great affection towards; in characteristic behaviour; ~ *right*, safe and sound, in good state; satisfactorily; (as sentence) I consent; all is well; ~*-round*, having ability and skill of all kinds, esp. in a game; ~*-rounder* (*n.*); ~ *there*, (colloq.) having all one's wits about one; ~ *the same*, in spite of this, notwithstanding.

Allah (ă'la). Muslim name of God. [Arab., f. *al* the, *ilah* god, cf. Heb. *eloah*]

Allăhăbă'd (ă-). Indian city at the confluence of the Jumna with the Ganges; capital of Uttar Pradesh; a place of Hindu pilgrimage.

ă'lla prī'ma (*or* -ē-) *adv.* & *n. phr.* (Using) the direct method of painting without underpainting.

allay' *v.t.* Put down, repress; alleviate; diminish.

ăllėgā'tion *n.* Alleging; assertion (esp. one not proved).

allĕ'ge *v.t.* Affirm, advance as argument or excuse.

Allėghe'nў Mou'ntains (ă-, -gā-; -tinz). (also *Alleghenies*) Ranges of the Appalachian system in eastern U.S.

allē'giance (-jans) *n.* Duty of subject to sovereign or government; loyalty.

ă'llėgorīze *v.* Treat as an allegory, make allegories.

ă'llėgorў *n.* Narrative description of subject under guise of another suggestively similar; figurative story. **ăllėgŏ'ric, -ical** *adjs.* **ăllėgŏ'ricallў** *adv.*

ăllėgrĕ'ttō *adv.*, *adj.*, & *n.* (pl. *-os*). (mus.) (Passage or movement played) somewhat briskly. [It.]

alle'grō (-lā-) *adj.*, *adv.*, & *n.* (pl. *-os*). (mus.) Lively, gay (passage or movement), in brisk time. [It.]

allē'le, allē'lomŏrph *ns.* Gene which occupies the same relative position on homologous chromosomes.

ăllėlu'ia (-lōōya) *n.* Song of praise to God. [Heb. *hallĕlū-yāh* praise ye the Lord]

allemande (ă'lmahnd) *n.* (Music for) dance in quadruple time and moderately quick. [Fr., ='German (dance)']

A'llenbў (ă-), Edmund Henry Hynman, Viscount (1861–1936). Commander of British forces in Egypt and Palestine, 1917–18; High Commissioner for Egypt and Sudan, 1919–25.

ăllergĕ'nic *adj.* Causing allergic reaction.

ă'llergў *n.* Hypersensitivity of body tissues esp. to the action of some particular foreign material, as certain foods, pollens, microorganisms, etc.; (fig.) antipathy. **allĕr'gic** *adj.* Of, possessing, allergy; susceptible *to* (also fig.).

allē'viāte *v.t.* Make less burdensome or severe. **allēviā'tion** *n.* **allē'viative, allē'viatorў** *adjs.*

ă'lley *n.* Narrow street; walk, passage; (U.S.) back street; enclosure for skittles etc.

Alleyn (alā'n), Edward (1566–1626). English actor; built with Henslowe the Fortune Theatre in Cripplegate, London; built and endowed Dulwich College. **Alley'nian** *n.* Member of Dulwich College.

allī'ance *n.* Act, state, of allying or being allied; union by marriage; relationship; confederation, league (esp. between States); *Holy A*~: see HOLY; *Triple* ~: see TRIPLE.

ă'llied (-īd) *adj.* Combined, united (*to*, *with*); *the A*~ *Powers*, the Allies.

ă'lligātor *n.* Crocodilian (genera *Alligator* and *Cayman*) of New World and China, having certain teeth in lower jaw which fit into pits, not into notches as in crocodiles proper; ~*-pear*, AVOCADO. [Span. *el lagarto*, f. L *lacerta* lizard]

allĭterā'tion *n.* Commencement of two or more words in close connection with the same letter or sound, esp. as a device in verse. **allĭ'terāte** *v.i.* (Contain words that) begin with the same sound. **allĭ'terătive** *adj.* **allĭ'terativelў** *adv.*

ă'llocāte *v.t.* Assign (*to*); locate. **ăllocā'tion** *n.* Apportionment.

allō'dium *n.* (hist.) Estate held absolutely, without acknowledgement to an overlord. **allō'dial** *adj.* **allō'diallў** *adv.*

allŏ'pathў *n.* Traditional medical practice which aims at curing disease by remedies having opposite effect to that caused by the disease (opp. HOMOEOPATHY). **ăllopă'thic** *adj.* **ăllopă'thicallў** *adv.* **allŏ'pathist** *n.*

allŏ't *v.t.* Give as due share.

allŏ'tment *n.* Apportioning; lot in life; share allotted to one; portion of land let out for cultivation, esp. small plot where occupier produces vegetables and fruit crops for home consumption.

ă'llotrōpe *n.* One form of an element, differing from another or others in crystal form, or in chemical properties, or in molecular complexity, or in all three (as oxygen and ozone; yellow and red phosphorus; graphite and diamond). **ăllotrŏ'pic** *adj.* **ă'llotropў** (*or* alŏ'-) *n.* Existence of elements in allotropic form.

allow' *v.* Admit; (U.S.) form the opinion (*that*); permit; admit *of*; give (limited periodical sum); add, deduct, in consideration of something; ~ *for*, take into consideration. **allow'able** *adj.*

allow'ance *n.* 1. Permission; tolerance. 2. Limited portion, esp. yearly income; addition to salary to cover special expenses, as *entertainment* ~, *foreign service* ~; *family* ~, allowance paid by State or employer to parent of family. 3. Deduction, discount; *make* ~(*s*) *for*, allow for. ~ *v.t.* Make allowance to (person).

allow'ėdlў *adv.* Admittedly.

ă'lloy (*or* aloi') *n.* 1. Metal consisting of a metallic element with admixture of another metal or non-metals, usu. having more useful properties than its constituents (e.g. brass is an alloy of copper and zinc, type-metal an alloy of lead and tin and antimony). 2. (archaic) Base metal mixed esp. with gold or silver. **alloy'** *v.t.* 1. Form an alloy (of). 2. Debase.

a'llspīce (awl-) *n.* Pimento, supposed to combine flavour of cinnamon, nutmeg, and cloves.

A'llston (awl-), Washington (1779–1843). American Romantic painter.

allū'de (*or* -ōōd) *v.i.* Make indirect or passing reference *to*.

allūr'e *v.t.* Tempt, entice; fascinate, charm. ~ *n.* Personal charm. **allūr'ement** *n.*

allū'sion (*or* -ōō-) *n.* Indirect or passing reference.

allū'sĭve (*or* -ōō-) *adj.* Containing an allusion, full of allusions. **allū'sĭvelў** *adv.* **allū'sĭvenėss** *n.*

allū'vĭon (*or* -ōō-) *n.* Wash of sea against shore or of river against banks; flood; (esp.) alluvium; (law) formation of new land by action of water.

allū'vĭum (*or* -ōō-) *n.* (pl. *-via*, *-viums*). Deposit of earth, sand, etc., left by flood esp. in river valleys and deltas. **allū'vĭal** *adj.* ~ *cone, fan*, deposit left by swift stream entering a valley or plain. **allū'vĭallў** *adv.*

allȳ'[1] *v.t.* Combine, unite, for special object. **ă'llȳ** (*or* ălī') *n.* Person, State, etc., allied with another; *the Allies*, members of the Triple Entente and those who joined them in the 1914–18 war; nations opposed to the Axis Powers in the 1939–45 war.

ă'llў[2] *n.* Choice playing-marble of marble, alabaster, or glass.

A'lma (ă-). River in the Crimea, scene of first battle in the Crimean War, 1854, in which the French and British defeated the Russians.

almacantar: see ALMUCANTAR.

A'lmăck (awl- *or* ŏl-), William (d. 1781). Founder of ~'*s Assembly Rooms* in St. James's, London, celebrated in the 18th and early 19th centuries as the scene of social functions, and of a gaming-club.

A'lmagĕst (ă-). 1. Arabic version of Ptolemy's astronomical treatise. 2. (in the Middle Ages; also *a*~) Any of various other celebrated textbooks of astrology and alchemy. [Arab. *al* the, Gk *megistē* (*suntaxis*) great (system)]

A'lma Mā'ter (ă-; *or* mah-). Title used in reference to one's university or school. [L, = 'fostering mother']

a'lmanăc, -ck (awl- *or* ŏl-) *n.* Annual calendar of months and days with astronomical and other data.

A'lmanăch de Gō'tha (awl- *or* ŏl-; -k, -t*a*). Annual publication giving information about European royalty, nobility, and diplomats.

Alma-Tă'dėma (ăl-), Sir Lawrence (1836–1912). Painter of classical subjects; born in Holland, naturalized as an Englishman.

almighty (awlmī'tĭ) *adj.* All-powerful; *the A*~, God.

a'lmond (ahm-) *n.* Kernel of stone-fruit of two varieties of *Prunus amygdalus* (*sweet, bitter* ~), allied to plum and peach; the tree; anything almond-shaped.

ă'lmoner (*or* ahm-) *n.* 1. Official distributor of alms. 2. Medical social worker, usu. woman at hospital or clinic, with duty of helping patients to carry out doctor's advice esp. after discharge from hospital (formerly also responsible for collecting fees).

ă'lmonrў (*or* ahm-) *n.* (hist.) Place where alms were distributed; almoner's residence.

a'lmōst (awl-) *adv.* Very nearly.

alms (ahmz) *n.* Charitable relief of the poor; donation; *a'lms-house*, one founded by charity for reception of poor, usu. old, people; *a'lmsman*, one supported by alms.

ălmūcă'ntar, -mac- *n.* Line of constant altitude above the horizon. [Arab. *al-mukanṭar*, f. *kanṭara* to bridge]

ă'lōe *n.* Liliaceous plant of genus *A*~, with erect spikes of flowers, rosettes of fleshy leaves (often spiny), and bitter juice; (pl.) purgative drug procured from juice of aloes; *American* ~, kind of agave. **ălōĕ'tĭc** *adj.* (med.) Containing aloes.

alŏ'ft *adv.* & *pred. adj.* High up; upward; esp. in(to) the upper parts of a ship's rigging.

alō'ne *pred. adj.* Not with others, solitary. ~ *adv.* Only, exclusively.

alŏ'ng *prep.* From end to end of, through any part of the length of; *alo'ngside*, close to side of ship; *alongside of*, side by side with. ~ *adv.* In company or conjunction *with*; *all* ~, all the time.

alōō'f *adv.* & *pred. adj.* Away, apart.

ălōpē'cĭa *n.* (med.) Baldness; (pop. used for) ~ *areata*, affection of scalp causing temporary bald patches. [Gk *alopekia* fox-mange f. *alopex* fox]

alou'd *adv.* Audibly, not in a whisper; (archaic) loudly.

ălp *n.* Mountain-peak; green pasture-land on (Swiss) mountain-side.

ălpă'ca *n.* S. Amer. domesticated camel-like hoofed mammal, bred in Andes for its long woolly hair; its fleece; fabric of alpaca hair mixed with cotton; any of various silk, cotton or rayon fabrics more or less resembling this. [Arab *al* the, Peruvian name *paco*]

ă'lpėnstŏck *n.* Staff with iron point used in mountain climbing.

ă'lpha *n.* 1st letter of Greek alphabet (Α, α), corresponding to *a*, used in enumerations etc.; examiner's first-class mark; (astron.) chief star of constellation; ~ *and omega*, first and last letters of Greek alphabet; hence, beginning and end (see Rev. 1 : 8); ~ *particles*, *rays*, first of three types of radiation emitted by radioactive substances, consisting of positively charged particles; ~ *plus*, superlatively good.

ă'lphabĕt *n.* Set of letters (in customary order) used in a language; first rudiments; symbols representing speech sounds (*phonetic* ~); *deaf-and-dumb* ~: see DEAF. **ălphabĕ'tical** *adj.* Of the alphabet; esp. in ~ *order*. **ălpha-**

bĕ'ticallÿ *adv.* [Gk *alpha, beta,* first two letters of alphabet]

ă'lpīne *adj.* Of the Alps or other lofty mountains; (geol.) of a European episode of mountain formation during the Tertiary era. *~ climate,* (geog.) that of regions above coniferous forests and below line of permanent snow; *~ plant,* plant native to these regions, or (loosely) to mountain districts, or suited to similar conditions. **ă'lpĭnist** *n.* Alpine climber.

Alps (ă-). Mountain range extending from Ligurian Sea and Rhône valley through Switzerland to the western Hungarian plain.

already (awlrĕ'dĭ) *adv.* Beforehand; by this time, thus early.

a.l.s. *abbrev.* Autograph letter signed.

A'lsăce (ă-; *or* -săs'). French province W. of the Rhine; inhabited by mixed German and Latin stocks; annexed with part of Lorraine (the annexed territory was known as Alsace-Lorraine) by Germany after the Franco-Prussian war of 1870; restored to France after the 1914–18 war.

Alsā'tia (ă-, -sh*a*). 1. Old name of Alsace. 2. Former cant name of precinct of Whitefriars, London, which, until its privileges (orig. those enjoyed by the Carmelites) were abolished in 1697, was a sanctuary for debtors and law-breakers. **Alsā'tian** *adj.* & *n.* (Native, inhabitant) of Alsace; (also *~ wolf-dog*) German shepherd dog.

a'lsō (awl- *or* ŏl-) *adv.* In addition; *~-ran,* horse not among first three in a race; (fig.) person etc. not distinguished in contest.

ălt *n.* (mus.) High note; *in ~,* in the octave (beginning with G) above the treble stave.

Altā'ic (ă-) *adj.* & *n.* (Of) a family of languages comprising Turkish, Mongol, and Tungus.

a'ltar (awl- *or* ŏl-) *n.* Flat-topped block for offerings to deity; Communion table; *lead to the ~,* marry (a woman); *~-cloth,* linen cloth used at Communion or Mass; silk frontal and super-frontal; *a'ltarpiece,* painting or sculpture above back of altar.

a'lter (awl- *or* ŏl-) *v.* Change in character, position, etc.; *altered rock,* (geol.) rock which has been metamorphosed by pressure or heat. **alterā'tion** *n.*

a'lterative (awl- *or* ŏl-) *adj.* Tending to alter. *~ n.* Treatment, medicine, that alters processes of nutrition.

a'ltercāte (awl- *or* ŏl-) *v.i.* Dispute hotly, wrangle. **altercā'tion** *n.*

ă'lter ĕ'gō. One's other self, intimate friend. [L]

altẽr'nate (awl- *or* ŏl-) *adj.* (of things of two kinds) Coming each after one of the other kind; placed on alternate sides (of line, stem, etc.). **altẽr'natelÿ** *adv.* **a'lternāte** *v.* Arrange, perform, alternately; interchange (one thing) alternately *with,* by another; succeed each other by turns; consist of alternate things; *alternating current,* (abbrev. A.C. or a.c.) electric current whose direction is regularly reversed; *alternating generations,* (biol.) reproductive cycle in which the offspring differ in structure and habits from their parents but resemble their grandparents; (also, erron.) cycle in which sexual reproduction is preceded and followed by asexual. **alternā'tion** *n.*

altẽr'native (awl- *or* ŏl-) *adj.* Available in place of another (thing); (of two things) mutually exclusive. *~ n.* Permission to choose between two things; either of two possible courses; one of more than two possibilities. **altẽr'nativelÿ** *adv.*

a'lternātor (awl- *or* ŏl-) *n.* Dynamo producing alternating current.

ă'lthôrn (-t-h-) *n.* Alto saxhorn.

although (awl-dhō') *conj.* Though.

ă'ltĭmēter *n.* Aneroid barometer indicating altitude reached, as in aviation.

ă'ltĭtūde *n.* 1. Height. 2. (geom.) Length of perpendicular from vertex to base. 3. (geog.) Height above mean sea-level. 4.

(astron., of heavenly body) Angular distance above horizon. 5. High place, (fig.) eminence.

ă'ltō *n.* (pl. *-os*). Highest adult male voice (ill. VOICE); female voice of similar range, contralto; singer with alto voice; musical part for this. ~ *adj.* (of instrument) Tenor; ~ *clef*: see CLEF.

ăltocū'mūlus *n.* (meteor.) Type of cloud, of medium height, in form of thin patches often very close together or almost joined.

altogĕ'ther (awl-, -dh-) *adv.* Totally; on the whole. ~ *n. in the* ~, completely naked.

ă'lto-rèlie'vo (-lē-) *n.* (Sculpture in) high relief. [It. *alto-rilievo*]

ăltostrā'tus *n.* (meteor.) Continuous veil of cloud, thin or thick, of medium height.

ă'ltruism (-rōō-) *n.* Regard for others as a principle of action. **ăltruĭ'stic** *adj.* **ăltruĭ'stically** *adv.*

ă'lum *n.* One of series of double sulphates, esp. that of potassium and aluminium, used industrially, esp. in paper-making and leather tanning.

alū'mina *n.* Aluminium oxide (Al_2O_3), which occurs as ruby, sapphire, etc., and as bauxite from which aluminium is obtained. **alū'mināte** *n.* Compound of alumina with one of the stronger bases.

ălūmĭ'nium *n.* (chem.) Light silvery white metallic element (symbol Al, at. no. 13, at. wt. 26·9815), not found naturally but widely distributed in the form of compounds, obtained by electrolysis and widely used esp. in alloys for construction of aircraft etc.

ălū'minize *v.t.* Coat with aluminium. **ălūminīzā'tion** *n.*

ălū'minous *adj.* Of the nature of alum or alumina; containing aluminium.

ălū'minum *n.* (U.S.) = ALUMINIUM.

alŭ'mnus *n.* (pl. *-nī*). (Former) pupil of a school or university. [L, = 'foster-child']

A'lva, A'lba (ă-), Fernando Alvarez de Toledo, Duke of (1508–82). Spanish general, Stadholder of the Netherlands, 1567–73.

ălvē'olar (*or* -vĭō'-) *adj.* Of an alveolus; ~ *consonant*, one formed with point of tongue behind the upper teeth. ~ *n.* Alveolar sound or consonant.

ă'lvėolate *adj.* Honey-combed, pitted with small cavities.

alvē'olus (*or* -vĭō'-) *n.* (pl. *-lī*). Small cavity, socket of a tooth; terminal air-sac of lung in which exchange of gases between lung and blood takes place; cell of honeycomb; conical chamber of belemnite.

always (aw'lwāz) *adv.* At all times, on all occasions, in all circumstances.

ăm. 1st pers. sing. pres. of BE.

a.m. *abbrev. Anno mundi* (L, = in the year of the world); *ante meridiem.*

A.M. *abbrev.* Albert Medal.

A'madis of Gaul (ăm-). Hero of a Spanish (or Portuguese) 15th-c. romance of chivalry.

amai'n *adv.* (archaic) Vehemently; in all haste.

Amă'lėkīte *adj.* & *n.* (Member) of a nomadic people descended from Esau (Gen. 36: 12), proverbial for treachery.

amă'lgam *n.* Alloy of a metal or metals, with mercury, freq. plastic and used, e.g., in dentistry.

amă'lgamāte *v.* Combine, unite (esp. of business firms); mix; (of metals) alloy with mercury. **amălgamā'tion** *n.*

amănūĕ'nsis *n.* (pl. *-ses*). One who writes from dictation, or copies; literary assistant.

ă'marănth *n.* Imaginary unfading flower; plant of genus *Amaranthus*, including love-lies-bleeding; purple colour. **ămarăʹnthine** *adj.* (poet.) Unfading; purple.

Amar'na, Tell el. Site of Akhetaten, city of ancient Egypt built by AKHNATEN; ~ *letters, tablets*, cuneiform tablets of 14th c. B.C. found there, containing letters from neighbouring governors etc.

ămarȳ'llis *n.* Autumn-flowering bulbous plant of genus *A~* comprising only one species, *A. belladonna* from Cape of Good Hope, also called belladonna lily. [Gk *Amarullis* name of a country girl in Theocritus and Virgil]

amă'ss *v.t.* Heap together; accumulate.

ă'mateur (-tėr *or* -tūr) n. One who is fond *of*; one who practises a thing, esp. an art or game, as a pastime (freq. opp. *professional*). **ămateu'rĭsh** (*or* ă'-) *adj.* Like an amateur; imperfect in execution, unskilful. **ămateu'rĭshlȳ** *adv.* **ămateu'rĭshnėss, ămateu'rĭsm** *ns.*

Ama'tĭ (-ah-). Name of a family of violin-makers of Cremona, flourishing *c* 1550–*c* 1700: *Nicola ~* (1596–1684) taught Antonio Stradivari.

ă'matĭve *adj.* Disposed to loving. **ă'matĭvenėss** *n.*

ă'matŏl *n.* High explosive, a mixture of ammonium nitrate and trinitrotoluene. [irreg. f. *am*(monia) + (trinitro)*tol*(uol)]

ă'matorȳ *adj.* Pertaining to a lover or sexual love.

amā'ze *v.t.* Overwhelm with wonder. ~ *n.* (poet.) Amazement. **amā'zėdlȳ, amā'zĭnglȳ** *advs.* **amā'zement** *n.*

A'mazon[1] (ă-). (Gk myth.) One of a race of female warriors alleged by Herodotus to exist in Scythia; hence, female warrior; tall strong or athletic woman.

A'mazon[2] (ă-). Great river of S. America, flowing into the southern Atlantic on N. coast of Brazil; it bore various names after its discovery in 1500 and was finally named because of a legend that a tribe of female warriors lived somewhere on its banks.

Amazō'nĭan (ă-) *adj.* Of the Amazons; of the Amazon river.

ămbă'ssador *n.* Minister sent by one sovereign or State on mission to another; minister permanently representing sovereign or State at foreign court or government; official messenger. **ămbăssadôr'ĭal** *adj.* **ămbă'ssadrėss** *n.* Female ambassador; ambassador's wife.

ă'mber *n.* & *adj.* (Made of, coloured like) yellow translucent fossil resin found chiefly on S. shore of Baltic and valued as ornament; (of) cautionary traffic light between red (= stop) and green (= go). [Fr. *ambre*, f. Arab. *'anbar* ambergris, to which the name originally belonged]

ă'mbergris (-ēs) *n.* Wax-like grey or blackish substance found floating in tropical seas, and in intestines of sperm-whale, odoriferous and used in perfumery. [Fr. *ambre gris* grey amber]

ămbĭdĕ'xtrous *adj.* Able to use left hand as readily as right; double-dealing. **ămbĭdĕ'xtrouslȳ** *adv.* **ămbĭdĕ'xtrousnėss** *n.*

ă'mbĭent *adj.* Surrounding. **ă'mbĭence** *n.* Environment, surroundings; atmosphere.

ămbĭ'gūous *adj.* Obscure; of double meaning; of doubtful classification; of uncertain issue. **ămbĭ'gūouslȳ** *adv.* **ămbĭ'gūousnėss** *n.* **ămbĭgū'ĭtȳ** *n.* Double meaning; expression capable of more than one meaning.

ă'mbĭt *n.* Precincts; bounds; compass, extent.

ămbĭ'tion *n.* Ardent desire for distinction; aspiration *to* (be or do); object of such desire.

ămbĭ'tious (sh*us*) *adj.* Full of or showing ambition; strongly desirous. **ămbĭ'tiouslȳ** *adv.* **ămbĭ'tiousnėss** *n.* [L *ambitio* canvassing for votes, f. *ambire* go round]

ămbĭ'valence *n.* State of having either or both of two contrary values or qualities; co-existence in one person of contradictory emotions (as love and hatred) towards the same person or thing. **ămbĭ'valent** *adj.*

ă'mble *v.i.* (of horse etc.) Move by lifting two feet on one side together; ride, move, at an easy pace. ~ *n.* Pace of an ambling horse; easy pace.

ămblȳō'pia *n.* Dimness of vision without discernible change in the eye. **ămblўŏ'pĭc** *adj.* **ămblўŏ'pĭcallў** *adv.*

ă'mbō *n.* (pl. *-bōs, -bō'nēs*) Pulpit in early Christian churches.

Amboi'na (ă-), **ăm-** *n.* Very hard ornamental wood (*Pterocarpus indicus*) exported from the Moluccas. [town and island of the Moluccas]

A'mbrōse (ă-, -z), St. (*c* 340–97). Bishop of Milan; Doctor of the Church; commemorated 7 Dec. (in B.C.P. calendar 4 April). **Ambrō'sĭan** *adj.* Of St. Ambrose; ~ *chant*, mode of chanting reputedly developed by St. Ambrose.

ămbrō'sĭa (-z-) *n.* (myth.) Food of the gods; anything delightful to taste or smell; beebread. **ămbrō'sĭal** *adj.* **ămbrō'sĭallў** *adv.* [L, f. Gk, f. *ambrotos* immortal].

ă'mbrў *n.* Var. of AUMBRY.

ă'mbūlance *n.* Vehicle for conveyance of sick or injured persons.

ă'mbūlant *adj.* (med.) Walking, not confined to bed.

ă'mbūlatorў *adj.* Pertaining to, adapted for, walking, movable; not permanent. ~ *n.* Place for walking; arcade, cloister; esp., aisle round apse at east end of church.

ămbuscā'de *n.* Ambush. ~ *v.* Lie, conceal, in ambush.

ă'mbush (-ŏŏ-) *n.* Concealment of troops, troops concealed, in a wood, etc.; lying in wait. ~ *v.* Lie in wait (for); *ambushed*, (of troops) concealed.

A.M.D.G. *abbrev.* *Ad majorem Dei gloriam* (L, = 'to the greater glory of God').

âme damnée (ahm dahnā). Devoted adherent, tool. [Fr., = 'damned soul']

ameer' *n.* Var. of EMIR.

amē'lĭorāte *v.* (Cause to) become better. **amēlĭorā'tion** *n.* **amē'lĭoratĭve** *adj.* **amē'lĭoratĭvelў** *adv.*

āmĕ'n[1] (*or* ah-) *int.* So be it (used at end of prayer etc.). ~ *n.* Utterance of 'amen'; expression of assent. [Heb. *'āmēn* certainly, truly]

Amen[2]: see AMMON.

amē'nable. *adj.* Responsible; liable *to*; capable of being tested by (*to*); responsive, tractable. **amē'nablenėss, amēnabĭ'lĭtў** *ns.* **amē'nablў** *adv.*

amĕ'nd *v.* Abandon evil ways; correct an error in (document), make professed improvements in (measure before Parliament, proposal, etc.); make better. **amĕ'ndment** *n.*

amende honorable (ămahnd ŏnŏrahbl). Public apology and reparation. [Fr.]

amĕ'nds (-z) *n.* Reparation, restitution, compensation.

Amĕnhō'tĕp (ah-). Name of four pharaohs of the 18th dynasty in Egypt; ~ *IV*: see AKHNATEN.

amĕ'nĭtў *n.* Quality of being pleasant, agreeable; (characteristic of) situation, climate, disposition, etc., that is agreeable or pleasant (often pl.); ~ *bed*, accommodation for which a charge is made in a National Health Service hospital, for patient desiring privacy.

Amĕnō'phĭs (ah-). = AMENHOTEP.

āmĕnorrhoe'a (-rē*a*) *n.* (physiol.) Absence of menstruation.

amĕ'ntum *n.* (pl. *-ta*). Catkin. **ămĕntā'ceous** (-sh*u*s), **ămentĭ'ferous** *adjs.*

amer'ce *v.t.* Fine; punish. **amer'cĭable** *adj.* **amer'cement, amer'cĭament** *ns.*

Amĕ'rĭca. Continent of the New World or western hemisphere, consisting of two great land-masses, *North* ~ and *South* ~, joined by the narrow isthmus of *Central* ~; N. America comprises Canada, the United States, and Mexico; Central and S. America are divided into a number of independent States. N. America was prob. visited by Norse seamen in 8th or 9th c., but for the modern world the continent was discovered by Christopher Columbus, who reached the W. Indies in 1492 and the S. American mainland in 1498. [named after *Amerigo* VESPUCCI]

Amĕ'rĭcan *adj.* Of America or its people; of the United States of

America; ~ *Civil War*, war (1861–5) between eleven Southern (Confederate) States and the rest of the Union, arising from the secession of the Southern States who disagreed esp. with the Northern (Federal) States' policy of freeing the Negro slaves imported from Africa to work in the plantations, and ending in their defeat; ~ *cloth*, flexible cotton cloth treated with cellulose nitrates to make it resemble shiny leather; ~ *English*: see ENGLISH; (*North-*) ~ *Indian*, one of the aboriginal inhabitants of N. America, chiefly nomadic tribes of hunters and warriors with red skins and black smooth hair; ~ *organ*, instrument resembling harmonium but sucking wind inward through reeds instead of expelling it; ~ *Revolution*, ~ *War of Independence*, revolt (1775–83) of the English colonies in N. America which subsequently formed the United States. ~ *n.* 1. American person. 2. Citizen of the U.S. 3. American English.

Amĕ'rĭcanĭsm *n.* 1. Word or phrase peculiar to or borrowed from U.S. 2. Attachment to, sympathy with, U.S.

Amĕ'rĭcanīze *v.* Naturalize as an American; make, become, American in character. **Amĕ'rĭcanīzātion** *n.*

Amĕ'rĭca's Cŭp (-z). Yachting trophy orig. presented by the R.Y.S. for a race round the Isle of Wight (1851), and won by the American schooner *America*; offered as a challenge trophy for a race between English and American yachts, but in spite of many attempts not subsequently regained by an English yacht.

ămerĭ'cium (*or* -shĭ-) *n.* (chem.) Metallic radioactive transuranic element; symbol Am, at. no. 95, principal isotope at. wt 241. [f. *America* (first made at Berkeley, California)]

ă'mėthȳst *n.* Purple or violet precious stone, a variety of quartz coloured by manganese. **ămėthȳ'stīne** *adj.* [Gk *amethustos* not drunken (*methu* wine), because the stone was supposed to have the power of preventing intoxication]

Amhă'rĭc (ă-) *adj.* & *n.* (Of) the official and court language of Ethiopia, a Semitic language related to ancient Ethiopic.

ā'mĭable *adj.* Feeling and inspiring friendship; lovable. **āmĭabĭ'lĭtȳ** *n.* **ā'mĭablȳ** *adv.*

ă'mĭcable *adj.* Friendly. **ămĭcabĭ'lĭtȳ** *n.* **ă'mĭcablȳ** *adv.*

ă'mĭce[1] *n.* Square of white linen worn by celebrant priest about the neck and shoulders (formerly on head).

ă'mĭce[2] *n.* Cap, hood, cape, of religious orders; badge worn by French canons on left arm.

A.M.I.C.E. *abbrev.* Associate Member of the Institution of Civil Engineers.

amī'cus cūr'ĭae. Disinterested adviser. [L, = 'friend of the court']

amĭ'd *prep.* In the middle of; in the course of.

ā'mĭde *n.* Compound formed from ammonia by replacement of one or more hydrogen atoms by a metal or acid radical.

amĭ'dshĭps *adv.* In the middle of ship.

amĭ'dst *prep.* (poet.) Amid.

A.M.I.E.E. *abbrev.* Associate Member of the Institution of Electrical Engineers.

A.M.I.Mech.E. *abbrev.* Associate Member of the Institution of Mechanical Engineers.

Amĭndi'vĭ I'slands (ŭm-, -dē-, īlandz): see LACCADIVE ISLANDS.

ā'mīne *n.* (chem.) Compound derived from ammonia by replacing one or more of the hydrogen atoms by certain aliphatic or aromatic radicals.

amīno- *prefix* (chem.) Pertaining to, or containing the group NH_2, as ~*-acid*.

amir' (-ēr) *n.* Var. of EMIR.

amĭ'ss *adv.* & *pred. adj.* Out of order; wrong(ly); untoward(ly).

ămĭtō'sĭs *n.* (pl. *-sēs*). (biol.) Direct division of a nucleus or cell without mitosis. **ămĭtŏ'tĭc** *adj.*

ă'mĭtȳ *n.* Friendship, friendly relations.

ă'mmėter *n.* Instrument for

measuring electric currents. [AM(PERE) + METER]

ă'mmō *n.* (colloq.) Ammunition.

A'mmon¹, A'men² (ă-). Supreme god of the ancient Egyptians in the Theban religion; his worship spread to Greece, where he was identified with Zeus, and to Rome, where he was known as Jupiter Ammon.

A'mmon² (ă-). Ancient country of the Ammonites, in S. Transjordan. **A'mmonīte²** *adj.* & *n.* (Member) of a Semitic people traditionally descended from Lot (Gen. 19: 38), living in Ammon.

ammō'nĭa *n.* Colourless gas (NH_3) with pungent smell, very soluble in water, giving alkaline solution; aqueous solution of this gas. [f. Jupiter AMMON¹, near whose temple sal ammoniac is said to have been prepared]

ammō'nĭăc *adj.* Of the nature of ammonia; *sal* ~, ammonium chloride (NH_4Cl), a hard white crystalline salt used in pharmacy, electric batteries, etc. **ămmonī'acal** *adj.* Of or resembling ammonia.

ammō'nĭātėd *adj.* Combined with ammonia.

ă'mmonīte¹ *n.* Member of an extinct group of cephalopods with chambered shell coiled in a flat

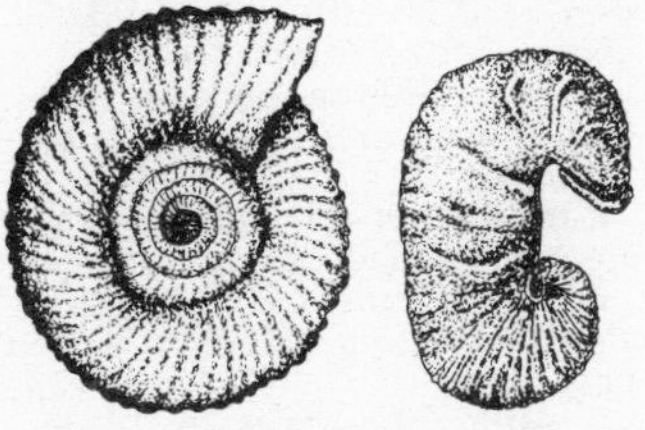

AMMONITE

spiral, freq. found fossilized in some Mesozoic rocks. [L *cornu Ammonis* horn of AMMON]

Ammonite²: see AMMON².

ammō'nĭum *n.* (chem.) Radical (NH_4), which has not been isolated, whose compounds resemble those of the alkali metals.

ămmūnĭ'tion *n.* Military stores (now only of projectiles with their necessary propellants, detonators, fuses, etc.); also fig.

ămnē'sĭa (-z- *or* -zh*a*) *n.* Loss of memory.

ă'mnėstȳ *n.* Pardon granted by sovereign or State for an offence, esp. one of a political character. ~ *v.t.* Give amnesty to.

ă'mnĭŏn *n.* (zool., physiol.) Membrane enclosing embryo or foetus. **ămnĭŏ'tic** *adj.* Of the amnion; ~ *fluid*, fluid filling amniotic sac; ~ *sac*, cavity enclosed by amnion.

amoe'ba (*amēba*) *n.* Primitive single-celled animalcule perpetually changing shape by pro-

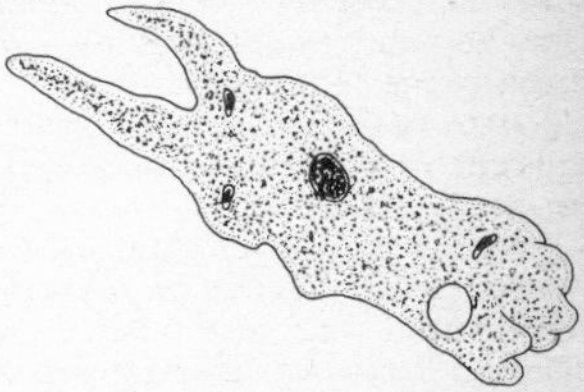

truding portions of its body (pseudopods) and reproducing by fission. **amoe'bic, amoe'boid** *adjs.*

amŏ'k, amŭ'ck *adv.* *run* ~, run about in murderous frenzy; get out of control. [Malay *amok* rushing in frenzy]

amo'ng, amo'ngst (-mŭ-) *prep.* In the assemblage or number of; surrounded by, within the limits of; by joint action of; between; ~ *themselves*, with one another.

Amŏntĭlla'dō, a- (-ah-) *n.* One of the principal types of dry sherry, with nutty flavour. [Span., = 'made like (the wine of) *Montilla*' (place in Cordova)]

āmŏ'ral *adj.* Non-moral; outside the sphere of morals.

A'morīte (ă-) *adj.* & *n.* (Member) of an ancient Semitic people of the Middle East.

ă'morous *adj.* Inclined to love; in love; of or pertaining to love. **ă'morouslȳ** *adv.* **ă'morousnėss** *n.*

amor'phous *adj.* Shapeless; (chem., min.) not crystalline. **amor'phism** *n.* **amor'phouslȳ** *adv.* **amor'phousnėss** *n.*

amŏr′tīze *v.t.* Alienate in mortmain; extinguish (debt, usu. by sinking-fund); gradually write off initial cost of (asset). **amŏrtīzā′tion** *n.*

A′mŏs (ā-) (*c* 760 B.C.). Hebrew minor prophet; book of O.T. containing his prophecies.

amou′nt *v.i.* Be equivalent *to*; add up *to*. ~ *n.* Total, quantity.

amour′ (-oor). Love affair, intrigue.

amour prŏpre (ămoor prŏpr). Self-esteem. [Fr.]

ămp *n.* = AMPERE.

ămpėlŏ′psĭs *n.* (pl. *-sēs*). Climbing plant allied to vine, esp. virginia creeper. [Gk, = 'looking like a vine' (*ampelos* vine, *opsis* appearance)]

ă′mperage *n.* Strength of current of electricity measured in amperes.

Ampère (ahṅpār), Andre-Marie (1775–1836). French physicist and mathematician; established the relation between magnetism and electricity.

ă′mpēre (*or* -ār) *n.* Fundamental unit of electric current, that which if maintained in two straight parallel conductors 1 metre apart would produce between these a force equal to 2×10^{-7} newton per metre of length (abbrev. A); ~ *turn*, magnetomotive force produced by one ampere passing through one complete turn of a conducting coil. [f. AMPÈRE]

ă′mpersănd *n.* The sign '&' (= *and*). [f. phrase 'and *per se* (= by itself) and']

ămphĕ′tamīne *n.* Powerful synthetic drug which stimulates the heart and respiration, constricts blood-vessels, and induces sleeplessness.

ămphĭ-, ămph- *prefix.* Both, of both kinds, on both sides, around.

ămphĭ′bĭan *adj.* & *n.* 1. (Animal) living both on land and in water; (animal) of the Amphibia, a class of vertebrates intermediate between reptiles and fishes and including anurans, caecilians, and urodeles. 2. (Aeroplane, tank, etc.) able to operate both on land and water. [Gk *amphibios* leading a double life]

ămphĭ′bĭous *adj.* Living both on land and in water, connected with both; (mil.) amphibian; involving both land and sea forces.

ă′mphĭbrach (-ăk) *n.* Metrical foot of three syllables, one long between two short, or one accented between two unaccented (◡ – ◡).

ămphĭŏ′xus *n.* Lancelet of genus *Branchiostoma*.

ămphĭ′prostȳle *adj.* & *n.* (Building) with portico at both ends.

ămphĭsbae′na *n.* 1. Fabulous serpent with head at each end. 2. (zool.) Worm-like lizard of genus *A*~. [Gk *amphis* both ways, *baino* go]

ă′mphĭtheatre (-ĭater) *n.* Oval or circular building or arena with seats rising in tiers round a central open space; natural formation resembling this; semicircular gallery in theatre; (fig.) scene of a contest.

Amphĭtrī′tė (ă-). (Gk myth.) Sea-goddess, the wife of Poseidon.

Amphĭ′trȳon (ă-). (Gk myth.) Husband of Alcmene; while he was absent Zeus impersonated him and became the father of Hercules by Alcmene. In Moliere's comedy 'Amphitryon' (iii. 5) a servant, perplexed by the impersonation, exclaims 'Le véritable Amphitryon est l'Amphitryon où l'on dine'; hence, a generous host or a gastronome.

ă′mphora *n.* (pl. *-rae*). Greek or Roman two-handled vase.

ămphotĕ′rĭc *adj.* (chem.) Capable of reacting as either acid or base.

ă′mple *adj.* Spacious, extensive; abundant; quite enough. **ă′mplȳ** *adv.*

ă′mplĭfȳ *v.* Enlarge; increase strength of (electric current, signal, etc.); add details. **ămplĭfĭcā′tion** *n.* **ă′mplĭfīer** *n.* (esp.) Appliance for increasing strength of electrical signals.

ă′mplĭtūde *n.* 1. Breadth; abundance; wide range. 2. (astron.) Distance from due east or

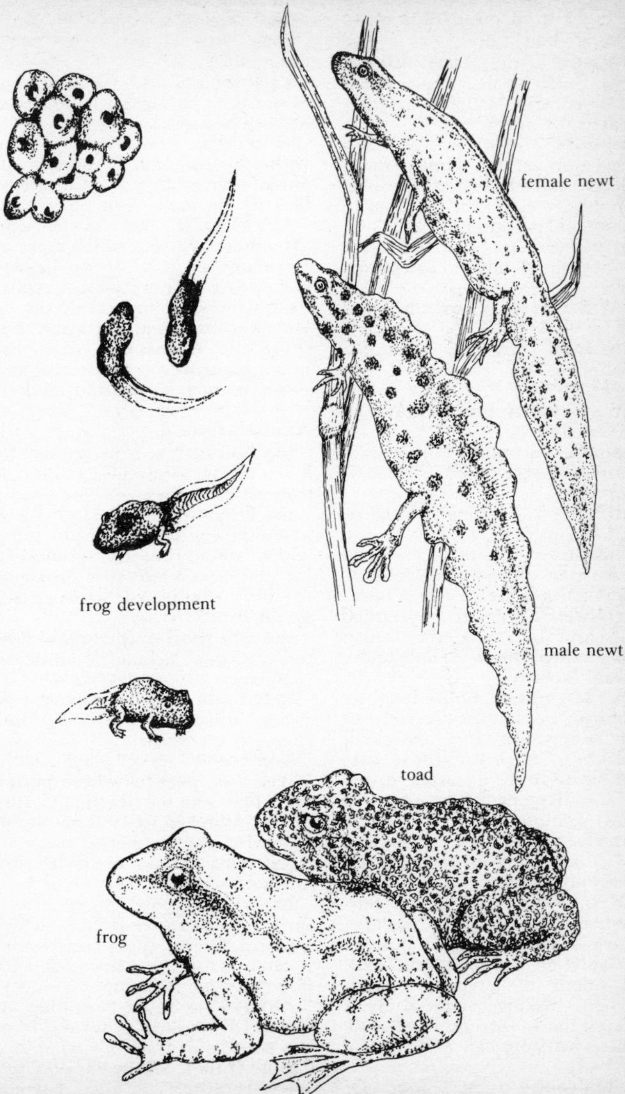

AMPHIBIANS

west at which celestial body rises or sets. 3. (phys.) Maximum displacement from mean position of vibrating body etc.

ă'mpoule (-ōōl), **ă'mpūle** *n.* (med.) Small sealed glass vessel used for storing sterilized materials prepared for injection.

ămpu'lla (-ŏŏla) *n.* (pl. *-ae*). Roman globular two-handled flask; medieval pilgrim's bottle; vessel for holding chrism or oil used in ceremonial anointing.

ă'mpūtāte *v.t.* Cut off (esp. part of animal body). **ămpūtā'tion** *n.*

A.M.S. *abbrev.* Army Medical Staff (*or* Service).

A.M.S.E. *abbrev.* Associate Member of the Society of Engineers.

Am'sterdă'm (ă-). Capital of the Netherlands.

amuck: see AMOK.

Amu Da'rȳa (ahmōō' dah-): see OXUS.

ă'mūlėt *n.* Thing worn as charm against evil.

A'mundsen (ămŏŏ-), Roald (1872–1928). Norwegian explorer; explored North-west Passage 1903–6; reached S. Pole 1911; perished in attempt to rescue the Italian airship expedition to N. Pole under General Nobile.

amū'se (-z) *v.t.* Cause laughter or smiles; be or find diversion or light occupation for; entertain. **amū'sĭng** *adj.* **amū'sĭnglȳ** *adv.* **amū'sement** *n.* Pleasant diversion; excitement of laughter or smiles; pastime.

ă'mȳl *n.* (chem.) Radical (C_5H_{11}) occurring in the structure of various isomeric alcohols (~ *alcohols*), some of which are constituents of fusel-oil; ~ *acetate*, colourless volatile liquid derived from amyl alcohol and acetic acid, with odour of jargonelle pears, used in making artificial fruit essences and as solvent of cellulose acetate. **amȳ'lĭc** *adj.* [Gk *amulon* fine meal]

ămȳlā'ceous (-shus) *adj.* Of starch, starchy.

ă'mȳloid *adj.* & *n.* Starchy (food).

an[1] *adj.*: see A.

ăn[2] *conj.* (archaic) If.

an-[1]: see A-, 2.

ăna-, an-[2] *prefix.* Up, back, again, anew.

ā'na *n.* (pl. *-s*). Collection of person's sayings; anecdotes, literary gossip, about a person.

-āna *suffix.* Appended to a name with the meaning: sayings of, anecdotes about, publications bearing on, persons or places.

Anabă'ptĭst (ă-) *n.* & *adj.* (Member) of a sect which arose in Germany in 1521, was heavily persecuted by both Catholics and Protestants, and suppressed (lit. = 'one who baptizes over again' because the Anabaptists held that infant baptism was ineffectual and some of them rebaptized adults); also (opprobriously) = BAPTIST. **Anabă'ptĭsm** *n.*

ănă'bolĭsm *n.* Synthesis by living things of complex molecules from simpler ones.

ană'chronĭsm (-kr-) *n.* Error in computing time; event or thing which would be incongruous in the period in which it is supposed to have happened or existed. **anăchronĭ'stĭc** *adj.*

ănacolū'thon *n.* (pl. *-tha*). Sentence, words, lacking grammatical sequence.

ănacŏ'nda *n.* Tropical S. Amer. aquatic and arboreal boa (*Eunectes murinus*).

Ană'crėon (*c* 563–478 B.C.). Greek lyric poet, of whose poems very few genuine fragments survive. **anăcrėŏ'ntĭc** *adj.* & *n.* (Poem) in the manner or metre of Anacreon's lyrics; convivial and amatory.

ănacru'sĭs (-ōō-) *n.* (pl. *-sēs*). (pros.) Unstressed syllable at beginning of verse; (mus.) unstressed note(s) before the first bar-line. [Gk *anakrouō* strike up]

Anadȳŏ'menė (ă-) Epithet of Venus (Aphrodite) as sprung from the sea-foam. [Gk, = 'rising']

anae'mĭa *n.* Deficiency of red blood-corpuscles or their haemoglobin, often causing paleness. **anae'mĭc** *adj.* (freq. fig.).

anā'erōbe (*or* anār-) *n.* Micro-organism which can live and reproduce in the absence of atmospheric oxygen. **anaerō′bĭc** *adj.*

ănaesthē′sia (ănĭs-, -zĭa) *n.* Loss of sensation; insensibility, esp. to pain, induced by certain drugs; *general* ~, anaesthesia of the whole body; *local* ~, anaesthesia induced in a limited area of the body.

ănaesthĕ′tĭc (ănĭs-) *adj.* & *n.* (Drug) inducing local or general anaesthesia, used esp. in surgical operations.

anae′sthėtĭst *n.* One who administers anaesthetics during surgical operation.

anae′sthėtīze *v.t.* Render insensible; administer anaesthetics to.

ă′naglȳph *n.* Embossed ornament in low relief; (photog.) composite stereoscopic picture printed in superimposed complementary colours.

ă′nagrăm *n.* Word or phrase formed by transposing letters of another.

ā′nal *adj.* Of the anus.

ă′nalĕcts, analĕ′cta *ns.pl.* Literary gleanings.

ănălgē′sĭa (-z-) *n.* Absence of pain; relief of pain. **ănălgē′tĭc, ănălgĕ′sĭc** *adjs.* & *ns.* (Drug) giving analgesia.

ănalŏ′gĭc *adj.* Of analogy. **ănalŏ′gĭcal** *adj.* According to analogy; expressing an analogy. **ănalŏ′gĭcallȳ** *adv.*

ană′logous *adj.* Similar, parallel (to); (biol., of limb or organ) similar in function but not necessarily in structure or position (cf. HOMOLOGOUS). **ană′logouslȳ** *adv.*

ă′nalogue (-ŏg) *n.* Analogous word or thing; ~ *computer*: see COMPUTER.

ană′logȳ *n.* Agreement, similarity; analogue; (math.) proportion; (logic) process of reasoning from parallel cases; (gram.) process whereby words and grammatical forms are built up on the model of others.

ă′nalȳse (-z) *v.t.* Examine minutely the constitution of; PSYCHOANALYSE; (chem.) ascertain the elements present in a compound or the constituents of a mixture, sample of food, etc.: (gram.) resolve into grammatical elements.

ană′lȳsĭs *n.* (pl. *-sēs*). Resolution into simple elements; PSYCHOANALYSIS; (math.) branch of mathematics using algebraic and calculus methods; (philos.) clarification of concepts and knowledge; (cricket, also *bowling, bowler's* ~) statement of number of balls bowled, wickets taken, runs made, etc.; *chemical* ~, determination of composition of substances; *qualitative* ~, identification of elements or compounds present; *quantitative* ~, determination of precise amounts of elements etc. present. **ă′nalȳst** *n.* One skilled in (chemical) analysis; PSYCHOANALYST. **ănalȳ′tĭc** *adj.* Pertaining to analysis; **ănalȳ′tĭcal** *adj.* Employing the method of analysis; (of language) using separate words instead of inflexions; ~ *psychology*: see PSYCHOLOGY. **ănalȳ′tĭcallȳ** *adv.*

anā′nas (*or* anahn-) *n.* Pineapple.

Ananī′as (ă-). 1. Jewish high priest before whom Paul was brought (Acts 23). 2. Husband of Sapphira, struck dead because he 'lied unto God' (Acts 5).

ă′napaest *n.* Metrical foot of three syllables, the first two short and the last long (◡◡—). **ănapae′stĭc** *adj.*

ană′phora *n.* 1. (also *A*~) Part of Eucharistic service in the Greek Orthodox Church; (R.C. Ch.) Canon of the Mass. 2. Repetition of words or phrases at beginning of a succession of clauses.

ănaphȳlă′xĭs *n.* (med.) Extreme sensitivity of tissues to the re-introduction of an antigen. **ănaphȳlă′ctĭc** *adj.*

ă′narchĭst (-k-) *n.* Advocate of **ă′narchĭsm,** system or theory which conceives of society without government.

ă′narchȳ (-k-) *n.* Absence of government; disorder, political and social confusion. **anar′chĭc, -ĭcal** *adjs.* Lawless. **anar′chĭcallȳ** *adv.*

anăstĭgmă'tĭc *adj.* Free from astigmatism (used esp. of photographic lenses in which this error is corrected).

anăstomō'sĭs *n.* (pl. *-ōsēs*). Cross-connection of arteries, rivers, etc.

ană'thėma *n.* Accursed thing; curse of God; curse of the Church, excommunication; imprecation. **ană'thėmatīze** *v.* Curse. [Gk *anathema* thing devoted, (later) accursed thing]

Anatō'lĭa (ă-). Asiatic part of Turkey; (in ancient usage) Asia Minor. **Anatŏ'lĭc** *adj.* **Anatō'-lĭan** *adj.* & *n.*

ănatŏ'mĭcal *adj.* Belonging to anatomy; structural. **ănatŏ'mĭcallȳ** *adv.*

ană'tomĭst *n.* Dissecter of bodies; one skilled in anatomy. **ană'tomīze** *v.* Dissect; (fig.) analyse.

ană'tomȳ *n.* (Science of) bodily structure; dissection; analysis.

Anăxă'gorăs (ă-) (5th c. B.C.). Greek philosopher and scientist; acc. to his explanation of the universe, the permanent elements of which it is constituted are unlimited in number, and are combined in bodies in changing proportions, as the result of a system of circulation directed by Spirit or Intelligence, a supreme independent force; he also explained solar eclipses.

ă'ncėstor *n.* (fem. *ă'ncėstrėss*) Any of those from whom one's father or mother is descended, progenitor.

ăncĕ'stral *adj.* Belonging to, inherited from, ancestors.

ă'ncėstrȳ *n.* Ancestral lineage; ancient descent; ancestors.

Anchises (ăngkī'sēz). (Rom. myth.) Father of Aeneas by Venus.

ă'nchor (-k-) *n.* Heavy implement consisting usu. of long shank and two (curved) barbed arms, used for mooring ship to bottom of sea etc.; anchor-plate; (also ~ *man*) last man of relay team; (fig.) source of confidence; BOWER[2]-~, KEDGE-~, SHEET-ANCHOR: see these words; *~-plate*, heavy piece of metal or timber as point of support, e.g. for cables of suspension-bridge. ~ *v.* Secure (ship) with anchor; (fig.) fix firmly; cast anchor, come to anchor.

ă'nchorage (-k-) *n.* Anchoring; lying at anchor; anchoring-ground; (fig.) thing to depend upon.

ă'nchorīte (-k-) *n.* (fem. *ă'nchorėss*) Hermit, recluse. **ănchorĕ'tĭc** *adj.*

ă'nchovȳ (*or* ănchō'-) *n.* Small fish of herring family, esp. the Mediterranean *Engraulis encrasicholus*, esteemed for its rich pungent flavour and used in sauces.

ănchu'sa (-chōō- *or* -kū-) *n.* Plant of borage family of genus *A~*, with blue or purple trumpet-shaped flowers.

ancien régime (ahṅsyăṅ rāzhēm). System of government in France before the Revolution; (transf.) former regime. [Fr., = 'old rule']

ā'ncient[1] (-shent) *adj.* Belonging to times long past; having existed, lived, long; ~ *history*; see HISTORY; so ~ *historian*; ~ *lights*: see LIGHT[1] 6; ~ *monument*, structure scheduled by the Department of the Environment as being of historical or architectural interest. ~ *n. the A~ of Days*, God (Dan. 7: 9); *the ~s*, civilized people of antiquity. **ă'ncientlȳ** *adv.* **ā'ncientnėss** *n.*

ă'ncient[2] (-shent) *n.* (obs.) = ENSIGN.

ăncĭ'llarȳ (*or* ă'-) *adj.* Subservient, subordinate.

ă'ncon *n.* 1. (physiol.) Elbow; *A~ sheep*, breed of sheep with long bodies and short legs, the forelegs crooked. 2. (archit.) Console usu. consisting of two reversed volutes.

and (*a*nd; emphat., ănd) *conj.* Particle connecting words, clauses, and sentences.

Andalusia (ănd*a*lōō'zĭa). Ancient province of S. Spain. **Andalu'sĭan** *adj.* & *n.*

A'ndaman I'slands (ă-, īl*a*ndz). Large group of islands in Bay of Bengal; administered (with Nicobar Islands) by the Republic of India; chief city, Port Blair.

ăndă'ntė *adv.* & *n.* (mus.) (Movement) in moderately slow time. ***ăndănti'nō*** (-tē-) *adv.* & *n.* (pl. *-os*). (Movement) slightly quicker (orig. slower) than *andante.* [It.]

A'ndersen (ă-), Hans Christian (1805–75). Danish poet and dramatist, best known for his fairy-tales.

A'nderson (ă-), Mrs Elizabeth Garrett (1836–1917). English physician, a pioneer of the professional education of women.

A'ndēs (ă-, -z). Mountain range running from N. to S. along the whole of the Pacific coast of S. America.

Andhra Prade'sh (ah'ndra, -dāsh). State of SE. India; chief city, Hyderabad.

ă'ndiron (-īrn) *n.* Stand for supporting logs on hearth, fire-dog.

Andŏ'rra (ă-). Semi-independent State (generally regarded as an autonomous republic) in the Pyrenees, on the border between France and Spain; under the joint suzerainty of France and the Spanish bishop of Urgel; capital, Andorra la Vella. **Andŏ'rran** *adj.* & *n.*

A'ndrėa dĕl Sâr'tō (ă-) (1486–1531). Florentine painter.

Andrea Ferrara: see FERRARA.

Andreev (ăndrā'ĕf), Leonid Nikolaevich (1871–1919). Russian novelist and playwright.

A'ndrew (ă-, -rōō), St. Apostle and patron saint of Scotland, commemorated 30 Nov.; *St. ~'s Ambulance Association*, organization, founded 1882, responsible for Red Cross work in Scotland; *St. ~'s cross*, cross shaped like the letter X, saltire; (her.) white saltire on blue ground, used as national cross of Scotland.

A'ndrewes (ă-, -rōōz), Lancelot (1555–1626). English bishop, one of the translators of the Authorized Version of the Bible.

A'ndroclēs (ă-, -z). Runaway slave in story by Aulus Gellius (2nd c. A.D.) who extracted a thorn from the paw of a lion which later recognized and refrained from attacking him in the arena.

ăndroe'cium (-rēs-) *n.* (bot.) Stamens collectively.

ă'ndrogėn *n.* Any organic compound which promotes development of masculine characteristics. **ăndrogĕ'nĭc** *adj.*

ăndrŏ'gy̆nous (*or* -g-) *adj.* Hermaphrodite; (bot.) with both staminate and pistillate flowers in a cluster. **ăndrŏ'gy̆ny̆** *n.*

Andrŏ'machė (ă-, -k-). (Gk legend) Wife of HECTOR[1].

Andrŏ'mėda (ă-). 1. (Gk legend) Daughter of Cassiopeia; was rescued by Perseus from a sea-monster for whom she was fastened to a rock. 2. (astron.) Constellation, conspicuous for its great spiral nebula. **Andrŏ'mėdēs, Andrŏ'mėdĭds** (-z) *ns. pl.* (astron.) System of meteors appearing to radiate from a point in Andromeda and usu. seen in November.

ă'nėcdōte *n.* Narrative of detached incident. **ă'nėcdōtage** *n.* Anecdotes; (joc.) garrulous old age. **ă'nėcdōtĭst** *n.* **ănėcdō'tal, ănėcdŏ'tĭc, -ĭcal** *adjs.*

anē'le *v.t.* Anoint; give extreme unction to.

anĕ'mogrăph (*or* -ahf) *n.* Anemometer equipped with recording apparatus (usu. pen and rotating drum). **anĕ'mogrăm** *n.* Record traced by this.

ănėmŏ'mėter *n.* Instrument for measuring speed (sometimes also direction) of wind. **ănėmomĕ'trĭc** *adj.* **ănėmŏ'mėtry̆** *n.*

anĕ'monė *n.* Plant of the buttercup family of genus *A~*, with flowers of various colours. [Gk, = 'wind-flower']

ănėmŏ'phĭlous *adj.* (bot.) Pollinated by wind.

anĕ'nt *prep.* (archaic) Concerning.

ă'neroid *adj.* & *n.* (Barometer) that measures air-pressure by its action on the flexible lid of a metal box nearly exhausted of air, not by height of fluid column.

ă'neurȳsm, -ĭsm (-ūr-) *n.* (path.) Localized dilatation of an artery caused by a weakening in its wall.

anew' *adv.* Again; in a different way.

ă'ngarȳ (ăngg-) *n.* (law) Belligerent's right (subject to compensation) of seizing or destroying neutral property under stress of military necessity.

ā'ngel (-j-) *n.* 1. Divine messenger; *orders of ~s*, three hierarchies, each consisting of three orders, to which angels were held to belong by Dionysius the Pseudo-Areopagite, namely: seraphim, cherubim, thrones; dominations, virtues, powers; principalities, archangels, angels. 2. Lovely or innocent being; loving or obliging person. 3. (also *~-noble*) Old English gold coin showing the archangel Michael piercing a dragon. 4. (U.S.) Financial backer, esp. of theatrical production. 5. (pl., colloq.) Height (of aircraft from ground), specif. 1,000 ft. 6. *~ cake*, very light sponge-cake; *~-fish*, (esp.) S. Amer. freshwater fish (various species of *Pterophyllum*), laterally flattened, with bars of black and silver; *~s on horseback*, savoury dish of oysters wrapped in slices of bacon. [Gk *aggelos* messenger]

ănġĕ'lĭc (-j-) *adj.* Like an angel; *A~ Doctor*, St. Thomas Aquinas.

ănġĕ'lĭca (-j-) *n.* Aromatic umbelliferous plant used in cooking and medicine; candied stalk of this.

Anġĕ'lĭco (ănj-), Fra. Name given after his death to a Dominican friar, Fra Giovanni da Fiesole (1387–1455), painter of religious subjects, active in Florence and Rome.

ānġėlŏ'logȳ (-j-) *n.* Doctrine concerning angels.

ă'nġėlus (-j-) *n.* (R.C. Ch.) Devotional exercise (beginning *Angelus domini*; L, = 'the angel of the Lord') commemorating the Incarnation, said at morning, noon, and evening, at sound of bell; bell for this.

ă'nger (-ngg-) *n.* Hot displeasure, rage. *~ v.t.* Make angry, enrage. [ON *angr* affliction]

ANGELICO Annunciation

A'ngėvin (ănj-) *adj.* Of Anjou or its ruling house; ~ *kings*, PLANTAGENET kings of England. ~ *n.* Native or inhabitant of Anjou; member of its ruling house.

ăngī'na (-j-) *n.* Constrictive sensation or pain; (in full ~ *pectoris*) intense pain in chest, accompanied by sense of suffocation, caused by insufficient blood-supply to heart during sudden exertion.

ă'ngiosperm (-j-) *n.* Flowering plant, i.e. one which has ovules enclosed in an ovary (opp. GYMNOSPERM).

angle[1] (ă'nggl) *n.* Space between two meeting lines or planes; inclination of two lines to each other (*acute* ~, angle smaller than 90°; *obtuse* ~, greater than 90°; *reflex* ~, greater than 180°; *right* ~, angle of 90°); corner, sharp projection; (colloq.) point of view; ~-*iron*, metal plate of L-shaped section. **ă'ngled** (-ld) *adj.* ~ *deck*, flight deck on aircraft-carrier with landing path inclined to ship's fore-and-aft axis.

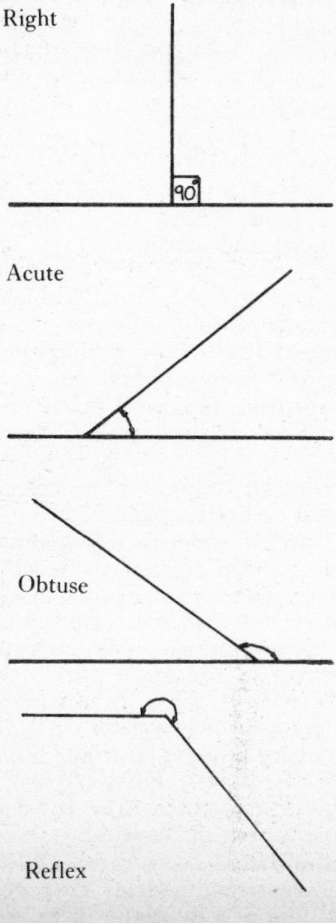

ANGLES

angle[2] (ă'nggl) *v.i.* Fish with hook and bait; (fig.) use artifice, hints, etc., to obtain something. **ă'ngler** *n.* 1. Fisherman. 2. (zool.) Fish (esp. *Lophius piscatorius*) that preys on smaller fish, attracting them by filaments attached to its head and mouth.

Angles, A'nglī (ă'ngglz, ăngg-) *ns.pl.* People of Angul (Angel), a district of Holstein; one of the Germanic tribes that settled in Britain, where they formed the kingdoms of Northumbria, Mercia, and East Anglia, and finally gave their name to England and the English.

Anglesey (ă'ngglsĭ). Island of NW. Wales across the Menai Strait; former county of Wales, since April 1974 part of Gwynedd.

A'nglican (ăngg-) *adj.* Of the reformed Church of England or any Church in the Anglican Communion; ~ *chant*, short harmonized melody in two or more phrases each beginning with a reciting note, for singing to unmetrical words, as psalms, canticles; ~ *Communion*, Churches in communion with, and recognizing the leadership of, the see of Canterbury. ~ *n.* Member of Anglican Church. **A'nglicanism** *n.*

ă'nglicė (ăngg-) *adv.* In English. [L]

ă'nglicize (ăngg-) *v.* Make, become, English in form or character. **ă'nglicism** *n.* English idiom; preference for what is English.

Anglo- (ăngg-) *prefix.* English; English and —, as ~-*German*.

A'nglo-Că'tholic (ăngg-) *adj.* & *n.* (Adherent) of the section of the Church of England which emphasizes both the continuity of the Reformed Church with the medieval Church and its status as the national branch of the Catholic Church.

A'nglo-I'ndĭan (ăngg-, ĭ-) *adj.* & *n.* 1. (Person) of British birth having lived long in India. 2. (in Eurasian use) = EURASIAN. 3. (English vocabulary) adopted from Indian language.

A'nglo-Nŏr'man (ăngg-) *adj.* & *n.* (Of) the variety of the Norman dialect of Old French spoken in England after the Norman Conquest.

A'nglophīle, -phĭl, A'nglophōbe (ăngg-) *ns.* One who loves, hates, the English. **Anglophō'bĭa** *n.*

A'nglo-Să'xon (ăngg-) *adj.* & *n.* English Saxon (as dist. from Old Saxon); Old English (person, language) before the Norman Conquest; (person) of English descent; (U.S.) (plain, forthright) English language.

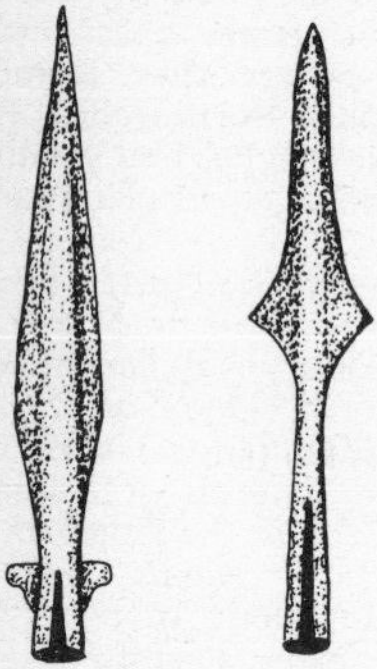

Spearheads

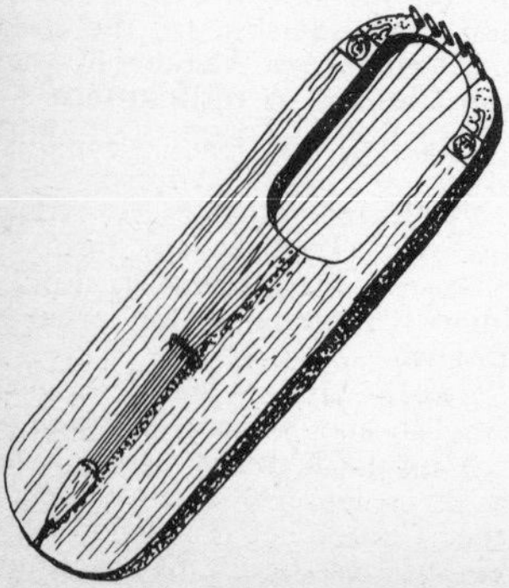

Lyre

Angō'la (ăngg-). Former Portuguese province of W. Africa, N. of SW. Africa; independent 1975.

Angŏr'a (ăngg-). Former name of ANKARA; fabric made from fleece of Angora goat, mohair; (also ~ *wool*) sheep's wool mixed with hair of Angora rabbit; ~ *cat, goat, rabbit*, varieties of these animals with long silky hair.

Angostūr'a (ăngg-). Former name of Ciudad Bolivar, town in Venezuela on Orinoco; *a~* (*bark*), aromatic bark formerly used as tonic and febrifuge, obtained from S. Amer. tree of family Rutaceae.

ă'ngrȳ (ăngg-) *adj.* Enraged, resentful; irritable, passionate; (of wound etc.) inflamed, painful. **ă'ngrĭlȳ** *adv.*

angst (ah-) *n.* Anxiety; remorse. [Ger.]

Ångström[1] (aw'ngstrẽrm), Anders Jonas (1814–74). Swedish physicist and astronomer; ~ *unit*, unit used in measuring the wavelengths of light, one hundred-millionth of a centimetre.

ångström[2] (aw'ngstrẽrm) *n.* Ångström unit (abbrev. Å).

Anguĭ'lla (ănggw-). Island in the West Indies, under British rule.

ă'nguĭsh (ănggw-) *n.* Severe mental or bodily pain.

ă'ngūlar (ăngg-) *adj.* Having angles; sharp-cornered; placed in, at, an angle; wanting plumpness or suavity; ~ *distance*, (math.) distance between two points measured in terms of the angle which they make with a third (in astronomy the point of observation).

A'ngus (ăngg-). Former county of E. Scotland, lying N. of the Tay estuary, since May 1975 part of the region of Tayside.

ănhē'dral *adj.* 1. (aeron.) Having negative dihedral. 2. (cryst.) Not bounded by plane faces. ~ *n.* Negative dihedral.

Anhwei (ah'nhwā'). Province of China on the Yangtze Kiang.

ănhȳ'drīde *n.* Substance formed by removal of water from a compound; substance which combines with water to form an acid or base.

ănhȳ'drous *adj.* (chem.) Having no water; deprived of water of crystallization.

ănicŏ'nĭc *adj.* (Gk antiq.; of idols and symbols) Not shaped in human or animal form.

ă'nĭlīne *n.* Phenylamine ($C_6H_5NH_2$), an oily liquid with characteristic smell, made by reduction of nitro-benzene and used in the manufacture of many chemicals, dye-stuffs, drugs, etc. ~ *adj.* Derived from aniline; ~ *dye*, (pop.) any synthetic dye-stuff. [formerly got from *anil*, the shrub indigo]

ă'nĭma *n.* (psychol.) Inner aspect of personality, esp. its unconscious facets. [L, = 'breath', 'soul']

ănĭmadvĕr'sion *n.* Criticism, censure. **ănĭmadvĕr't** *v.i.* Pass criticism or censure *on*.

ă'nĭmal *n.* Organized being endowed with life, sensation, and voluntary motion; animal other than man; quadruped; brutish man. ~ *adj.* Pertaining to the functions of animals; pertaining to animals as opp. to vegetables; carnal; ~ *magnetism*, (formerly) mesmerism; ~ *spirits*, natural buoyancy. [L *anima*, breath]

ănĭmă'lcūle *n.* Microscopic animal.

ă'nĭmalĭsm *n.* Animal activity; sensuality; doctrine that men are mere animals.

ă'nĭmalīze *v.t.* Convert into animal substance, sensualize.

ă'nĭmate *adj.* Living, lively. **ă'nĭmāte** *v.t.* Give life to; make lively; encourage; *animated cartoon*: see CARTOON, 3. **ănĭmā'tion** *n.* **ă'nĭmātėdlȳ** *adv.*

ă'nĭmĭsm *n.* Attribution of living soul to inanimate objects and natural phenomena. **ă'nĭmĭst** *n.* **ănĭmĭ'stĭc** *adj.*

ănĭmŏ'sĭtȳ *n.* Active enmity.

ă'nĭmus *n.* Animating spirit; animosity.

ă'nĭŏn *n.*: see ION. **ănīŏ'nĭc** *adj.* Of anions; having an active anion. (Gk *ana* up, +ION]

ă'nĭse *n.* Umbelliferous plant (*Pimpinella anisum*) with aromatic fruits.

ă'nĭseed *n.* Fruits of anise, used as carminative and for flavouring.

ănĭsĕ'tte (-z-) *n.* Colourless sweet liqueur flavoured with aniseed.

Anjou (ahṅzhōō). Old French province on the Loire, W. of Touraine; Henry II of England, as a Plantagenet, was count of Anjou, but it was lost to the English Crown by King John (1204).

A'nkara (ă-). Capital city of Turkey since 1923.

ă'nkle *n.* Joint connecting foot with leg; slender part between this and calf. **ă'nklėt** *n.* Fetter or ornamental band round ankle.

ănkylō'sĭs *n.* (pl. *-osēs*). Formation of stiff joint by consolidation of articulating surfaces. **ă'nkȳlōse** (-z) *v.* (of joints, bones) Stiffen, unite.

ă'nna *n.* Former coin of India and Pakistan, $\frac{1}{16}$ of rupee.

ă'nnals (-z) *n.pl.* Narrative of events year by year; historical records. **ă'nnalĭst** *n.* Writer of annals.

A'nnăm (ă-). Formerly, eastern coastal portion of Indo-China, since 1946 part of Vietnam. **Annamē'se** (-z) *adj.* & *n.*

Annă'polis (*a*-). Capital of Maryland, U.S., site of the U.S. Naval Academy.

ă'nnātes (-ts) *n.pl.* (R.C. Ch.) First year's revenue of see or benefice, formerly paid to pope.

Anne[1] (ăn) (1665–1714). Queen of Gt. Britain 1702–14; 2nd daughter of James II; succeeded William, husband of her sister Mary, in 1702, and died with no surviving issue; *Queen* ~, (archit.) applied to a style of red-brick and stone houses of *c* 1660–*c* 1720; *Queen ~'s Bounty*, Crown revenues from tithes and first-fruits (formerly paid to the pope, and appropriated by the Crown in

1534), granted by her to the Church of England.

Anne[2] (ăn), St. Mother of the Virgin Mary; commemorated 26 July.

annea'l *v.t.* Toughen (glass or metals) by heating and then cooling; temper.

Anne Boleyn: see BOLEYN.

ă'nnėlĭd *n.* One of the phylum Annelida, segmented worms (including earth-worms, leeches, etc.)

Anne of Cleves (ăn, ŏv, klēvz) (1515–57). Daughter of John, Duke of Cleves, and 4th wife of Henry VIII of England; the marriage (1540) was annulled after a few months.

annĕ'x *v.t.* Add as subordinate (part); append; take possession of (territory); attach as an attribute, addition, or consequence. **ănnėxā'tion** *n.* **ă'nnĕxe, -ĕx** *n.* Addition to document; building added to larger one, esp. to provide extra accommodation.

annī'hĭlāte (-nīi-) *v.t.* Demolish, destroy utterly. **annīhĭlā'tion** *n.* Utter destruction; (theol.) destruction of soul as well as body.

ănnivẽr'sarȳ *n.* Yearly return of a date, celebration of this.

ă'nnō aeta'tĭs su'ae (ītah-, soōī). In the (specified) year of his or her age. [L]

A'nnō Dŏ'mĭnī (ă-). In the year of our Lord, of the Christian era (abbrev. A.D.); (as *n.*, colloq.) advancing age. [L]

ă'nnotāte *v.t.* Furnish with notes. **ănnotā'tion, ă'nnotātor** *ns.*

annou'nce *v.t.* Declare, make publicly known; intimate the approach of. **annou'ncement** *n.* **annou'ncer** *n.* (esp.) Broadcasting official who announces programme, reads news items, etc.

annoy' *v.t.* Irritate; molest, harass. **annoy'ance** *n.* Molestation; vexation; disgust.

ă'nnūal *adj.* Reckoned by the year; recurring yearly; lasting for one year; that lives only for a year; published in yearly numbers. ~ *n.* Plant that lives for one year; book etc. published in yearly numbers. **ă'nnūallȳ** *adv.*

annū'ĭtȳ *n.* Sum payable in respect of a particular year; yearly grant; investment of money entitling investor to series of equal annual sums. **annū'ĭtant** *n.* One who holds an annuity.

annŭ'l *v.t.* Abolish, cancel; declare invalid. **annŭ'lment** *n.*

ă'nnūlar *adj.* Ring-like; ~ *eclipse*, partial eclipse of sun, during which a ring of the sun's surface can be seen outside the moon's disc, occurring when the distance of the moon from the earth in relation to the distance of the sun from the earth is too great for the eclipse to be total.

ă'nnūlate, -ātėd *adjs.* Furnished, marked, with rings; formed of rings.

ă'nnūlėt *n.* Little ring; (her.) small circle; (archit.) fillet or moulded band encirculing a column.

ă'nnūlus *n.* (pl. *-lī*). Ring, ring-like body, esp. (bot.) ring of cells round sporangia in ferns.

annŭ'nciāte (*or* -shĭ-) *v.t.* Announce.

ănnŭnciā'tion *n.* Announcement; *the A~*, the announcement of the Incarnation made by the angel Gabriel to the Virgin Mary (Luke 1: 26–38); festival commemorating this, Lady Day, 25 March.

Annunzio (*a*noo'ntsĭō), Gabriele d' (1863–1938). Italian poet, airman, and politician.

ă'nōde *n.* (elect.) Positive pole or terminal.

ă'nodal, ănŏ'dĭc *adjs.* **ă'nodīze** *v.t.* Cover (metal) with a protective film by electrolysis in which the metal acts as the anode. [Gk *anodos* way up]

ă'nodȳne *adj.* & *n.* (Medicine, drug) able to assuage pain; (anything) mentally soothing.

anoi'nt *v.t.* Apply ointment, oil, to, esp. as religious ceremony at baptism or on consecration as priest or king; *the Lord's Anointed*, Christ; king by divine right.

anŏ'malous *adj.* Irregular, abnormal. **anŏ'malouslȳ** *adv.* **anŏ'malousnėss** *n.*

anŏ'malȳ *n.* Irregularity; (astron.) angular distance of planet or satellite from its last perihelion or perigee. **anŏmalĭ'stĭc** *adj.* (astron.) ~ *year*, time (365 days, 6 hrs, 13 m., 53·1 sec.) earth takes to pass from perihelion to perihelion; ~ *month*, time (27 days, 13 hrs, 18 m., 33·1 sec.) moon takes to pass from perigee to perigee.

anŏ'n *adv.* (archaic) Soon, presently.

anon. *abbrev.* Anonymous.

ă'nŏnȳm *n.* Person whose name is not revealed; pseudonym. **ănonȳ'mĭtȳ** *n.*

anŏ'nȳmous *adj.* Not named; not bearing author's, painter's, etc., name. **anŏ'nȳmouslȳ** *adv.*

anŏ'phelēs (-z) *n.* Mosquito of genus *A*~, comprising numerous species, many of which are carriers of malaria. [Gk, = 'hurtful']

ă'norăk *n.* Long hooded jacket of skin or cloth worn esp. in Arctic regions; weather-proof jacket of similar style for sports wear etc. [Eskimo *anoraq*]

ănorĕ'xĭa *n.* (path.) Loss of appetite.

anŏ'smĭa (-z-) *n.* Lack of the sense of smell.

ano'ther (-ŭdh-) *adj.* Additional, different; a similar (one). ~ *pron.* Additional one; unnamed additional party to legal action; different one.

anŏ'xĭa *n.* (med.) Lack of oxygen, caused by asphyxiation or high altitude (*direct* ~), or by various diseases which render the blood incapable of conveying enough oxygen to the tissues (*indirect* ~).

Anschluss (ă'nshlo͞os) *n.* Annexation, esp. of Austria to Germany. [Ger. = 'union']

A'nsĕlm (ă-), St. (1033–1109). Italian monk, a pupil of Lanfranc; became abbot of Bec in Normandy and later (1093) archbishop of Canterbury; commemorated 21 April.

ă'nserīne *adj.* Of, like, a goose; silly.

answer (ah'nser) *v.* Give answer; reply to (charge); be responsible *for*; fulfil (purpose); suffice; correspond *to* (description etc.); act or operate in response (*to*); ~ *back*, reply (esp. to rebuke) impertinently. ~ *n.* Something said or done in response to a question, accusation, etc.; defence; solution; (mus.) repetition of theme by another voice or instrument, esp. in fugue. **a'nswerable** *adj.* Responsible.

ănt *n.* Small hymenopterous insect of superfamily Formicoidea, with complex instincts and social system, proverbial for industry; ~*-eater*, any of various mammals

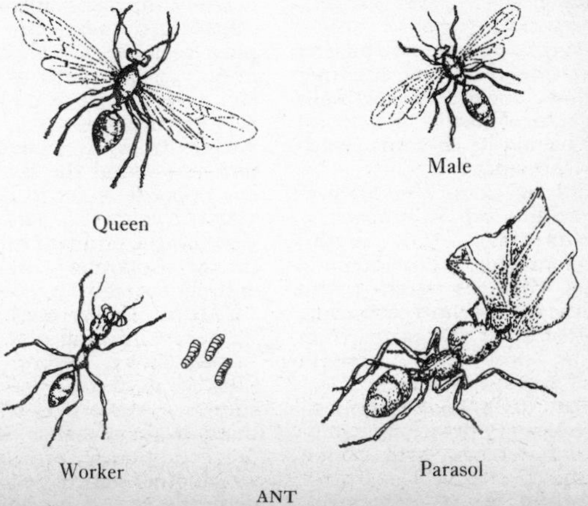

Queen Male Worker Parasol

ANT

ANT-EATERS

living on ants; *~-heap*, *~-hill*, mound over ants' nest; (loosely) conical nest of termites; (fig.) crowded dwelling(s) swarming with people.

ant-: see ANTI-

ă'nta *n.* (pl. *-tae*). Square pilaster on either side of door or at corner of buildings; one of two short walls forming sides of portico; *in antis*, (of portico) having its columns standing between antae.

ăntă'cĭd *adj.* & *n.* (Agent) preventing acidity, esp. in stomach.

Antae'us (ă-). (Gk myth.) Libyan giant, son of Poseidon and Ge; when Hercules wrestled with him, Antaeus was only overcome when lifted from the earth, from which he drew new strength whenever he touched it.

ăntă'gonĭsm *n.* Active opposition; opposing principle; (biochem.) interference with action or growth.

ăntă'gonĭst *n.* 1. Opponent. 2. (physiol.) Counteracting muscle. **ăntăgonĭ'stĭc** *adj.*

ăntă'gonīze *v.* Counteract, tend to neutralize (force etc.); evoke hostility in, make into an enemy.

ăntâr'ctĭc *adj.* Of the south polar regions; *A~ Circle*, parallel of 66° 33′ S., south of which the sun does not rise at mid-winter or set at midsummer.

Antâr'ctĭc *n.* Regions (both land and sea) round the S. Pole. [Gk *anti* opposite + ARCTIC]

Antâr'ctĭca (ă-). (also *Antarctic Continent*) Continent mainly within the Antarctic Circle, almost entirely covered by ice-sheet.

ă'ntė *n.* (poker etc.) Stake put up before drawing new cards.

ăntė- *prefix*. Before.

ăntėcē'dent *adj.* Previous; presumptive, *a priori*. *~ n.* Preceding thing or circumstance; (logic) part of conditional proposition on which other part depends; (gram.) noun, clause, etc., to which following (relative) pronoun or adverb refers; (math.) first term of ratio; (geog., of river) one which has maintained its course in spite of changes in land formation; (pl.) past history.

ă'ntėchāmber *n.* Room leading to chief apartment.

ă'ntėchăpel *n.* Outer part at west end of chapel.

ăntėdā'te *v.t.* Affix, assign, an earlier than the true date to; precede; anticipate.

āntėdĭlū'vĭan (*or* -ōō-) *adj.* Belonging, referring, appropriate, to the time before the Flood; very old, old-fashioned. ~ *n.* Antediluvian person.

ă'ntėfix *n.* Ornament above cornice of classical building concealing joint between tiles.
ăntėfĭ'xal *adj.*

ă'ntėlōpe *n.* Any of several cloven-hoofed ruminants (related to deer, goats, and cattle) including the chamois, gazelle, and gnu.

ă'ntė merĭ'dĭĕm. (abbrev. a.m.) Between midnight and noon. **ă'ntė-merĭ'dĭan** *adj.* [L]

ăntėnā'tal *adj.* Previous to birth or childbirth; relating to the care of pregnant women.

ăntĕ'nna *n.* (pl. *-nae*). 1. Sensory organ found in pairs on heads of insects and crustacea, usually long slender projections like horns, sometimes knobbed.
2. Aerial. [L, = 'sail-yard']

ăntĕ'nnūle *n.* (zool.) Minute organ resembling antenna.

ăntėpĕ'ndĭum *n.* (pl. *-dia*). Veil, hanging, for front of altar; frontal.

ăntėpėnŭ'lt, ăntėpėnŭ'ltĭmate *adjs.* & *ns.* (Syllable) last but two.

ăntēr'ĭor *adj.* More to the front; prior *to*.

ă'ntėrōōm *n.* Room leading to another, antechamber.

ănthē'lĭon *n.* Luminous ring

ANTELOPES

projected on cloud or fog-bank opposite the sun.

ă'nthėm *n.* Composition for church use sung antiphonally; any non-metrical setting of sacred words as non-essential item in service; song of praise.

ănthē'mĭon *n.* (pl. *-ia*). (archit.) Ancient Greek ornament of radiating plant forms.

ă'nther *n.* Terminal part of stamen containing pollen in pollen sacs.

ănthŏ'logy̆ *n.* Collection of small choice poems; literary collection; collection of paintings, songs, etc.; *Greek A~*, large collection of epigrams and short poems from Greek writers of 5th c. B.C.–6th c. A.D. **ănthŏ'logīze** *v.* Make an anthology *from.* [Gk *anthologia*, f. *anthos* flower, *-logia* collection (*legō* gather)]

A'nthony̆[1], **A'ntony̆**[2] (ănto-), St. (*c* 251–356). Born in Egypt, the first Christian monk; ~ *pig*, smallest pig of litter, named after St. Anthony as patron saint of swine-herds; *St. ~'s cross*, T-shaped cross; *St. ~'s fire*, any of various inflammatory or gangrenous skin diseases, as erysipelas, ergotism, popularly supposed in the Middle Ages to be cured by the intercession of St. Anthony.

A'nthony̆[2], **A'ntony̆**[3] (ănto-) of Padua, St. (1195–1231). Portuguese Franciscan monk, patron saint of Portugal.

ănthozō'an *adj.* & *n.* (Aquatic animal) of the class Anthozoa, including corals, sea-anemones, etc. [Gk *anthos* flower, *zōon* animal]

ă'nthracēne *n.* (chem.) Aromatic hydrocarbon ($C_{14}H_{10}$) obtained by distillation of coal-tar and used in manufacture of alizarin and other dyes.

ă'nthracīte *n.* Glossy variety of coal containing much carbon and low percentage of volatile matter, burning with hot smokeless flame and leaving little ash. **ănthracĭ'tĭc** *adj.*

ă'nthrăx *n.* Disease of sheep and cattle, transmitted to man by infected wool, bristles, etc., and characterized by inflammatory skin lesions, caused by a bacillus (*B. anthracis*).

ă'nthropoid *adj.* Resembling man; ~ *ape*, one of the primates most nearly related to man, i.e. chimpanzees, gibbons, orang-utans, and gorillas. ~ *n.* Anthropoid ape.

ănthropŏ'logy̆ *n.* Science of man; study of man as an animal (*physical* ~) and of human, esp. primitive, societies (*social* ~). **ănthropolŏ'gĭcal** *adj.* **ănthropolŏ'gĭcally̆** *adv.* **ănthropŏ'logĭst** *n.*

ănthropŏ'mėtry̆ *n.* Measurement of human body. **ănthropomĕ'trĭc** *adj.*

ănthropomor'phĭsm *n.* Ascription of human form and attributes to God, or of human attributes to something irrational or impersonal. **ănthropomor'phĭc** *adj.*

ănthropomor'phous *adj.* Having human form. **ănthropomor'phīze** *v.* Regard as anthropomorphous.

ănti-, ănt- *prefix.* Opposite, against; (in the arts, literature, etc.) unlike the conventional form.

ănti-air'craft (-ahft) *adj.* & *n.* (Force) for shooting down, or for defence against, hostile aircraft (abbrev. A.A.).

ă'ntiar *n.* Upas tree of Java; poison obtained from it.

ăntĭbīō'sĭs *n.* Condition of antagonism between organisms, esp. micro-organisms (opp. SYMBIOSIS).

ăntĭbīŏ'tĭc *adj.* & *n.* (Substance, drug, as penicillin, streptomycin) obtained from a mould, fungus, or other micro-organism, or prepared synthetically, and having the power to inhibit the growth of other micro-organisms, e.g. bacteria.

ă'ntĭbŏdy̆ *n.* (physiol.) Protein formed within the body to inactivate other compounds (esp. bacterial toxins and viruses) which are foreign to it, and found in blood-plasma.

ă'ntĭc *n.* (often pl.) Grotesque posture or trick.

A'ntĭchrīst (ă-, -k-). Great personal opponent of Christ expected by early Christians to appear before the end of the world; person hostile to Christ and his teaching.

ăntĭchrĭ'stian (-k-) *adj.* Opposed to Christianity.

ăntĭ'cĭpāte *v.t.* Look forward to, expect; perform action before (another person or event), (of event) happen before (another event); satisfy (wish), obey (command), before it is expressed; use in advance. **ăntĭ'cĭpatĭve, ăntĭ'cĭpātorў̆** *adjs.* **ăntĭ'cĭpatĭvelў̆** *adv.* **ăntĭcĭpā'tion** *n.* (esp., mus.) Sounding of single note of chord before chord itself.

ăntĭclĕ'rical *adj.* & *n.* (Person) opposed to undue influence of clergy, esp. in politics, or to existence of organized clerical hierarchy. **ăntĭclĕ'rĭcalĭsm** *n.*

ăntĭclī'măx *n.* Lame end to anything promising a climax.

ă'ntĭclīne *n.* (geol.) Arch-like fold in bed(s) of rock (opp. SYNCLINE). **ăntĭclī'nal** *adj.*

ăntĭ-clŏ'ckwīse (-z) *adj.* & *adv.* (Moving) in opposite direction to hands of a clock, in curve from right to left as seen from centre.

ăntĭcȳ'clōne *n.* Atmospheric system in which barometric pressure is high, and from centre of which air tends to flow spirally outward (clockwise in N. hemisphere, anti-clockwise in S. hemisphere).

ă'ntĭdōte *n.* Medicine etc. used to counteract disease or poison.

ă'ntĭ-free'ze *n.* Chemical agent (usu. ethylene glycol) added to water to lower its freezing-point.

ă'ntĭgėn *n.* Substance that stimulates production of an antibody when introduced into a living organism.

Antĭ'gonė (ă-). (Gk legend) Daughter of Oedipus; she buried the body of her brother Polynices by night, against the order of King Creon; he condemned her to death but she took her own life.

Antĭ'gūa (ă-; *or* -tē'gwa). One of the Leeward Islands, in the West Indies, discovered in 1493 by Columbus and settled by English in 1632; independent since 1967; capital, St. John's.

ă'ntĭ-hēr'ō *n.* Hero of unconventional type in novel etc.

ăntĭhĭ'stamine (-ēn) *adj.* & *n.* (Drug) that counteracts the effect of histamine, used esp. in treatment of allergic conditions.

Antĭ-Jă'cobĭn (ă-) *adj.* & *n.* (Person) opposed to the Jacobins, or to the French Revolution; see JACOBIN², 2.

ă'ntĭ-knŏck (-ĭ-n-) *n.* Substance added to fuel to reduce pinking in engines (see PINK⁵).

Antĭ'llēs (ă-, -z). Group of West Indian islands; *Greater* ~, Cuba, Jamaica, Hispaniola (Haiti and the Dominican Republic), and Puerto Rico; *Lesser* ~, group of smaller islands to the SE.

ă'ntĭlŏg, ăntĭlŏ'garĭthm (-dhm) *ns.* Number to which a logarithm belongs (100 is the ~ of 2 to the base 10).

ăntĭmacă'ssar *n.* Covering on chair-back to protect it from hair-grease or as ornament. [f. *Macassar oil*, pop. as hair-oil in 19th c.]

ă'ntĭmonў̆ *n.* (chem.) Brittle metallic element, bluish-white, of flaky crystalline texture, used in alloys esp. with lead, and in medicine; symbol Sb, at. no. 51, at. wt 121·75.

ă'ntĭng *n.* Rubbing or placing of ants in their plumage by birds, apparently to kill parasites.

ăntĭnō'mĭan *adj.* & *n.* (Person) holding that the moral law is not binding on Christians on the ground that faith alone is sufficient to salvation. **ăntĭnō'mĭanĭsm** *n.*

ăntĭ'nomў̆ *n.* Contradiction in a law, or between laws, principles, etc.

Antĭ'nōus (ă-). Bithynian youth, favourite of the Emperor Hadrian, represented in art as the ideal type of youthful beauty.

A'ntĭŏch (ă-, -k). Name of several ancient cities of the Near East, esp. (1) the capital of Syria under the Seleucid kings (now Antakya in Turkey near the Syrian border); (2) 'Antioch towards Pisidia' in the Roman province of Galatia (near the present Yalvac in SW. Anatolia, Turkey).

ă'ntipar̄ticle *n.* (phys.) One of a pair of particles of equal mass but with opposite electrical charge (e.g. electron and positron) or direction of magnetic moment.

Anti'pater (ă-) (*c* 398–319 B.C.). Macedonian general; succeeded Alexander as ruler of Macedonia.

ănti'pathў *n.* Constitutional or settled aversion (*to, against, between*). **ăntipathĕ'tic, ăntipă'thic** *adjs.*

ănti-per̄sonnĕ'l *adj.* (of bombs) Designed to kill or injure persons.

ăntiper̄'spirant *n.* Substance applied to the skin to reduce perspiration.

ă'ntiphon *n.* Verse of psalm or other traditional scriptural passage sung during divine service, freq. one sung responsively by alternating choirs.

ănti'phonal *adj.* Sung alternately. ~ *n.* Collection of antiphons.

ănti'phonarў *n.* Antiphonal.

ănti'phonў *n.* Antiphon; antiphonal singing.

Anti'podēs (ă-, -z) *n.pl.* Places on opposite sides of the earth; esp. Australasia as region diametrically opposite to Europe. **ănti'podal** *adj.* **ăntipodē'an** *adj.* & *n.* [Gk, 'having the feet opposite']

ă'ntipōpe *n.* Pope in opposition to one (held to be) canonically chosen.

ăntipȳrĕ'tic *adj.* & *n.* (Drug) allaying or preventing fever.

ă'ntiquarў *n.* Student or collector of antiques or antiquities. **ăntiquār'ian** *adj.* & *n.* **ăntiquār'ianism** *n.*

ă'ntiquātėd *adj.* Out of date; antique.

ănti'que (-ēk) *adj.* Of or existing from old times; old-fashioned; of the ancients. ~ *n.* Relic of ancient art or of old times; piece of old furniture, work of art, etc., regarded as valuable esp. by collectors.

ănti'quitў *n.* Ancientness; ancient times, esp. (*classical* ~) the period of the ancient Greek and Roman civilizations; (pl.) customs, practices, etc., of ancient times, objects surviving from them.

ăntirrhī'num (-rī-) *n.* Plant of genus *A*~, with pouched flowers that can be made to gape; snapdragon. [Gk *anti* counterfeiting + *rhinos* nose]

ăntiscor̄bū'tic *adj.* & *n.* (Medicine etc.) preventing or curing scurvy.

ănti-Sĕ'mīte *adj.* & *n.* (Person) hostile to Jews. **ănti-Sėmi'tic** *adj.* **ănti-Sĕ'mitism** *n.*

ăntisĕ'psis *n.* (med.) Antiseptic treatment or condition.

ăntisĕ'ptic *adj.* & *n.* (Agent) counteracting sepsis. **ăntisĕ'ptically** *adv.*

ă'ntiser̄um *n.* (pl. *-a*) Antitoxic serum; serum containing antibodies, esp. one used therapeutically.

ăntisō'cial (-shl) *adj.* Opposed to principles on which society is based. **ăntisō'ciallў** *adv.*

ăntistă'tic *adj.* Counteracting the effect of static electricity.

Anti'sthenēs (ă-, -z) (5th c. B.C.). Athenian philosopher, pupil of Socrates and founder of the Cynic school of philosophy.

ănti'strophė *n.* (Lines recited during) returning movement from left to right in ancient Greek choruses. **ăntistrŏ'phic** *adj.* [Gk, = 'turning about']

ănti'thėsis *n.* (pl. *-esēs*). Contrast of ideas marked by parallelism of strongly contrasted words; direct opposite. **ăntithĕ'tic, -ical** *adj.*

ăntitŏx'in *n.* Serum or principle serving to neutralize a toxin. **ăntitŏ'xic** *adj.*

ă'nti-trāde *adj.* & *n.* 1. (Wind) blowing in opposite direction to trade wind in the upper air of the same region. 2. (Wind) blowing in opposite direction to trade wind, but in different region, and on the surface.

ă'ntitȳpe *n.* That which a type or symbol represents; see TYPE *n.* 4. **ăntitў'pical** *adj.*

ă'ntler *n.* Whole or any branch of either horn of deer.

A'ntonīne (ă-) *adj.* Of Antoninus Pius or Marcus Aurelius Antoninus; ~ *Wall*, wall built during the reign of the former from Forth to Clyde.

Antonī'nus Pī'us (ă-) (A.D. 86–161). Roman emperor 138–161.

ăntŏnomā'sia (-z-) *n.* Substitution of epithet etc. for proper name; use of proper name to express general idea (e.g. *a Solomon*).

A'ntonў¹ (ă-), Mark. Marcus Antonius (*c* 83–30 B.C.), Roman general and consul; member of 2nd triumvirate; became enthralled by Cleopatra; was deprived of his powers (32 B.C.) by the senate and defeated at battle of Actium.

Antony²,³, St.: see ANTHONY¹,².

ă'ntonўm *n.* Word of contrary meaning to another.

A'ntrĭm (ă-). Town and county of Northern Ireland.

ă'ntrum *n.* (pl. *-tra*). Cavity in the body, esp. one in the upper jaw-bone.

A'ntwērp (ă-). (Fl. *Antwerpen*, Fr. *Anvers*) Belgian city-port.

Anū'bĭs. (Egyptian myth.) Jackal-headed deity, ruler of the dead, whom he conducts to the shades.

anūr'an *adj.* & *n.* (Member) of the Anura, an order of the Amphibia comprising frogs and toads, the adult forms of which have no tails or gills but have strong hind legs for leaping and swimming.

ā'nus *n.* Opening, at end of alimentary canal, through which solid matter is excreted.

ă'nvĭl *n.* Block (usu. of iron) on which metal is worked by smith; thing resembling this, esp. the INCUS.

anxī'ėtў (ăngz-) *n.* Uneasiness, concern; solicitous desire; neurotic fear. **ă'nxious** (-kshus) *adj.* Troubled, uneasy; earnestly desirous; causing anxiety. **ă'nxiouslў** *adv.*

a'nў (ĕ-) *adj.* & *pron.* One or some but no matter which; whichever is chosen; ~ *amount of*, a great deal of. ~ *adv.* At all, in some degree.

a'nўbŏdў (ĕ-) *n.* & *pron.* Any person; important person.

a'nўhow (ĕ-) *adv.* Anyway; in any case.

a'nўone (ĕ-, -wŭn) *n.* & *pron.* Anybody.

a'nўthing (ĕ-) *n.* & *pron.* Whatever thing; a thing, no matter which.

a'nўway (ĕ-) *adv.* In any way whatever; anyhow.

a'nўwhere (ĕ-, -ār) *adv.* & *pron.* (In to) any place.

A'nzăc (ă-) *n.* Member of the Australian and New Zealand Army Corps; Australian or New Zealand serviceman. [initials of name]

A.O.C.(-in-C.) *abbrev.* Air Officer Commanding(-in-Chief).

ā'orĭst *adj.* (Gk & Sansk. gram., of tense) Denoting in the indicative mood a simple past tense, in other moods occurrence, without limitations as to continuance etc. ~ *n.* Aorist tense or form.

āor'ta *n.* Great artery issuing from left ventricle of heart, carrying blood through its branches to all other parts of body.

à outrance (ah ōōtrahṅs). To the death. [Fr.]

A.P. *abbrev.* Associated Press.

apā'ce *adv.* Swiftly.

Apache *n.* & *adj.* 1. (*a*pă'chĭ) (Member) of tribe of N. Amer.

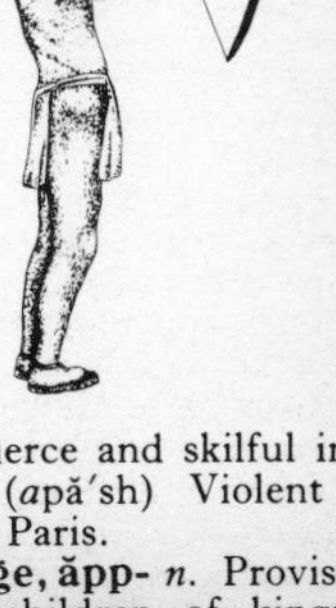

Indians fierce and skilful in raiding. 2. (*a*pă'sh) Violent street ruffian in Paris.

ă'panage, ăpp- *n.* Provision for younger children of kings etc.; dependency; perquisite.

apâr't *adv.* Aside, separately; into pieces; to or at a distance.

apâr'theid (-hāt) *n.* Policy of racial segregation in S. Africa; similar policy elsewhere. [Afrikaans]

apâr'tment *n.* Single room of a house; (pl. *or* sing.) set of rooms; (sing., chiefly U.S.) flat.

ă'pathy̆ *n.* Insensibility to suffering; indifference; mental indolence. **ăpathĕ'tĭc** *adj.* **ăpathĕ'tĭcally̆** *adv.*

ă'patīte *n.* Crystallized phosphate of lime.

āpe *n.* Anthropoid ape (see ANTHROPOID); (pop.) monkey; *great ~s*, gorilla, chimpanzee, orang-utan; *~-man*, pithecanthrope. ~ *v.t.* Imitate, mimic.

orang-utan

chimpanzee

APE

Apĕ'llēs (-z) (4th c. B.C.). Greek painter.

A'pĕnnīnes (ă-, -nz). Mountain range running down the length of Italy.

aperçu (ahpārsōō) *n.* Summary exposition, conspectus; an insight. [Fr.]

apēr'ĭent *adj.* & *n.* Laxative.

apĕ'rĭtif, apéritif (-ĕrĭtēf) *n.* Alcoholic drink taken before meal to stimulate appetite; appetizer.

apĕ'rĭtĭve *adj.* & *n.* Laxative.

ă'perture *n.* Opening, gap; space through which light passes in camera or other optical instrument.

āpĕ'talous *adj.* Without petals.

ā'pĕx *n.* (pl. *ā'pĭcēs*, *ā'pĕxes*). Tip, top; vertex (of cone, triangle).

aphā'sĭa (-z-) *n.* Loss of speech, partial or total, or loss of power to understand written or spoken language as result of damage to the brain.

aphē'lĭon *n.* (pl. *-lĭa*). Point of planet's or comet's orbit farthest from sun.

ă'phĭd *n.* Aphis. **aphĭ'dĭan** *adj.*

ā'phĭs *n.* (pl. *-idēs*). Small soft-bodied insect of family Aphididae, infesting leaves and stems of plants.

aphō'nĭa *n.* Absence or loss of the power of speech, due to congenital defect or organic disease or functional disturbance.

ă'phorĭsm *n.* Short pithy statement or maxim. **ăphorĭ'stĭc** *adj.*

ăphrodĭ'sĭăc (-z-) *adj.* & *n.* (Drug, food, etc.) provoking sexual desire. [f. APHRODITE]

Aphrodī'tė (ă-). (Gk myth.) Goddess of love (esp. sensual), beauty, and fertility, born of the sea-foam; identified by the Romans with Venus; her cult was of eastern origin, and she was identified with Astarte, Ishtar, etc.

ā'pĭary̆ *n.* Place where bees are kept. **ā'pĭarĭst** *n.* Bee-keeper.

ă'pĭcal *adj.* Belonging to an apex; placed at the tip; (phon., of sound) articulated with tip of tongue.

ā'pĭcŭlture *n.* Bee-keeping.

apie'ce *adv.* Severally, each.

A'pĭs (ah- *or* ā-). (Egyptian myth.) God, the incarnation as a bull of the sun-god Ptah, represented as a bull with the disc of the sun between his horns.

ā'pĭsh *adj.* Like an ape.

aplŏ'mb (-m) *n.* Self-possession.

Apŏ'calўpse *n.* Revelation, esp. that made to St. John in the island of Patmos; book of N.T. ('Revelation of St. John the Divine') recording this. **apŏcalў'ptĭc** *adj.* & *n.* (Teaching, literature) involving revelation. **apŏcalў'ptĭcal** *adj.* **apŏcalў'ptĭcallў** *adv.*

ăpocar'pous *adj.* (bot.) Having the carpels distinct.

apŏ'copė *n.* Cutting off of last sound or syllable of word.

Apocr. *abbrev.* Apocrypha.

apŏ'crўpha *n.pl.* 1. *the A~*, set of books which were included in the Septuagint but excluded from the Jewish canon, accepted as canonical by the early Church, since the Reformation not so regarded by Protestant churches but freq. included in Bibles between O.T. and N.T. 2. Other writings of doubtful authenticity. **apŏ'crўphal** *adj.* 1. Of the Apocrypha; also applied to a number of early Christian writings in similar form to the canonical books of N.T. 2. Of doubtful authenticity, spurious. [Gk *apokrupha* hidden or secret (writings), i.e. those reserved for the initiated and often falsely ascribed]

ă'podal *adj.* & *n.* (zool.) Limbless (creature); (member) of the Apoda, an order of the Amphibia containing tropical legless wormlike animals some of which have scales; (fish) with no ventral fin.

apŏ'dosĭs *n.* (pl. *-sēs*). Concluding clause of sentence; consequent clause in a conditional sentence.

ă'pogee *n.* Point in orbit of moon, planet, or artificial satellite farthest from earth; (fig.) highest point. **ăpogē'an** *adj.*

Apŏllĭnar'ius, -ar'ĭs (*c* 310–*c* 390). Bishop of Laodicea *c* 360; asserted that in Christ were to be found human body and soul but not human spirit, which was replaced by the divine Logos. **Apŏllĭnar'ian** *adj.* & *n.* (Supporter) of Apollinarius or his heresy.

Apŏ'llō. (Gk & Rom. myth.) God sometimes identified with the sun and called *Phoebus* (*Apollo*); son of Zeus and Leto and brother of Artemis; represented ideal type of manly beauty; associated esp. with music, poetry, and prophecy.

Apŏ'llyon. 'The destroyer', the angel of the bottomless pit (Rev. 9: 11).

apŏlogĕ'tĭc *adj.* Regretfully

APOLLO

acknowledging, excusing, fault or failure; of the nature of an apology. **apologĕ'tĭcallў̆** *adv.* **apologĕ'tĭcs** *n.pl.* Reasoned defence, esp. of Christianity. **apŏ'logist** *n.* One who defends by argument. **apŏ'logīze** *v.i.* Make an apology.

ăpolō'gĭa *n.* Defence or justification of conduct or opinions.

ă'pologue (-ŏg) *n.* Moral fable.

apŏ'logў̆ *n.* Regretful acknowledgement of offence; statement of regret; apologia; ~ *for*, poor or scanty specimen of.

ă'pophthegm (-*o*fthĕm; -*o*thĕm) *n.* Terse or pithy saying. **ăpophthegmă'tĭc** (-*o*fthĕg-, -*o*thĕg-) *adj.*

ă'pophȳge *n.* (archit.) Outward curve at top or bottom of a column.

ăpoplĕ'ctĭc *adj.* Pertaining to, causing, apoplexy; liable to, suffering from, apoplexy. **ăpoplĕ'ctically** *adv.*

ă'poplĕxў̆ *n.* Seizure caused by blockage or rupture of an artery in the brain.

ăposīopē'sĭs *n.* (pl. *-pēsēs*). (rhet.) Breaking off short for effect.

apŏ'stasў̆ *n.* Renunciation of religious vows, faith, party, etc.

apŏ'state *n.* & *adj.* (One) guilty of apostasy. **apŏ'statīze** *v.i.* Become an apostate.

ā pŏstĕrĭor'ī. (Reasoning) from effects to causes. [L, = 'from what comes after']

apŏ'stle (-sl) *n.* Messenger, esp. (*A*~) any of the twelve sent forth by Christ to preach Gospel (Matt. 10: 2); first successful Christian missionary in a country; leader of reform; ~ *spoon*, one with figure of one of the Apostles on the handle; *Apostles' Creed*, simplest and prob. oldest of the Christian creeds, ascribed by tradition to the Apostles. **apostŏ'lĭc** *adj.* Of the Apostles; of the character of an Apostle; of the pope, esp. as successor of St. Peter.

apŏ'strophė *n.* Exclamatory address, esp. to absent person or to inanimate object; sign (') of omission of letter(s) or of possessive case. **apŏ'strophīze** *v.t.*

apŏ'thėcarў̆ *n.* (archaic) Druggist, pharmaceutical chemist. [Gk *apothēkē* store-house]

ăpothē'cĭum *n.* (pl. *-cĭa*). (bot.) Cup-shaped fruit body containing asci, freq. brightly coloured, produced by some fungi.

apŏthėō'sĭs *n.* (pl. *-ōsēs*). Deification; transformation; deified ideal. **apŏ'thėosīze** *v.t.*

ăpotropā'ĭc *adj.* Having or reputed to have the power of averting evil influence or ill luck. **ăpotropā'ĭcallў̆** *adv.*

app. *abbrev.* Appendix; apparent(ly).

appa'l (-awl) *v.t.* Dismay, terrify. **appa'llĭng** *adj.* Horrifying; (colloq.) very bad.

Appalā'chĭan Mou'ntains (ă-, -tĭnz). (also *Appalachians*) Mountain system of eastern N. America, which in early days of settlement in America confined English settlers to the eastern coastal belt.

appanage: see APANAGE.

ăpparā'tus *n.* Mechanical requisites, an appliance, for doing something, esp. for scientific experiment; ~ *crĭ'tĭcus*, materials for critical study of document; variant readings of manuscripts or early editions, usu. printed below text.

appă'rel *v.t.* Dress, attire. ~ *n.* 1. Dress, clothing. 2. (eccles.) Embroidered panel on dalmatic or tunicle.

appă'rent (*or* -ār-) *adj.* Manifest; seeming; *heir* ~, one who cannot be superseded by birth of nearer heir (cf. PRESUMPTIVE). **appă'rentlў̆** *adv.*

ăpparĭ'tion *n.* Appearance, esp. of startling kind; thing thought to be seen but having no material existence.

appea'l *v.i.* Call *to* higher tribunal for alteration of decision of lower; call (*to* witness) for corroboration, (*to* person) for assistance etc.; make earnest request; call upon umpire for decision; ~ *to*, be, prove, attractive to. ~ *n.* Act or right of appealing; quality that appeals; *Court of A*~, one hearing cases previously tried in inferior court.

appear' *v.i.* Become visible;

present oneself; act as counsel; be published; seem; be manifest. **appear'ance** *n.* Appearing; look, aspect; (pl.) outward show (of prosperity etc.); apparition.

appea'se (-z) *v.t.* Pacify, soothe; satisfy. **appea'sement** *n.* (esp.) Policy (orig. that of ·Neville Chamberlain in 1938–9) of making concessions to an aggressor.

appĕ'llant *adj.* Appealing; concerned with appeals. ~ *n.* One who appeals to higher court. **appĕ'llate** *adj.* Taking cognizance of appeals.

ăppellā'tion *n.* Name, title.

appĕ'llative *adj.* (of words) Designating a class (not an individual). ~ *n.* Common noun.

appĕ'nd *v.t.* Attach as an accessory; add, esp. in writing. **appĕ'ndage** *n.*

appĕndĭcĕ'ctomȳ *n.* (surg.) Excision of appendix.

appĕndĭcī'tis *n.* Inflammation of vermiform appendix.

appĕ'ndĭx *n.* (pl. *-icēs*, *-ixes*). 1. Subsidiary addition (*to* book etc.) 2. Small process developed from organ, esp. vermiform appendix of the intestine.

ăppertai'n *v.i.* Belong, be appropriate, relate, *to*.

ă'ppėtīte *n.* Desire, inclination (*for* food, pleasure, etc.); relish. **ă'ppėtīzer** *n.* Anything taken to give appetite for a meal. **ă'ppėtīzĭng** *adj.* Rousing appetite.

A'ppĭan Way (ă-). Roman highway running SE. from Rome to Brundisium (Brindisi), begun by the censor Appius Claudius Caecus, 312 B.C.

applau'd *v.* Express approval (of), esp. by hand-clapping; praise.

applau'se (-z) *n.* Approbation loudly expressed.

ă'pple *n.* Firm fleshy edible fruit of a rosaceous tree of genus *Malus; upset person's ~-cart*, spoil plans; *a'pplejack*, (U.S.) spirit distilled from cider; apple brandy; ~ *of the eye*, pupil, treasured object; *~-pie bed*, one with sheets folded (as a joke) so as to prevent a person from stretching at full length between them; *~-pie*

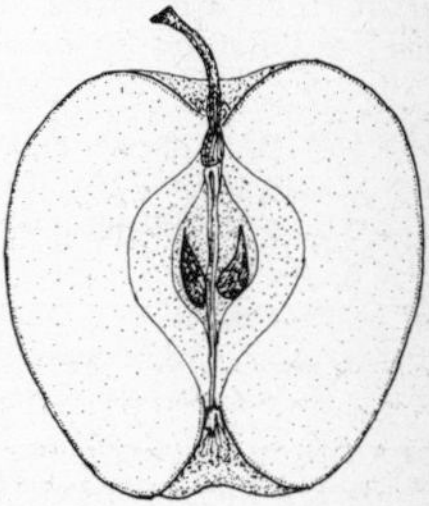

order, extreme neatness; ~ *of discord*, (Gk myth.) golden apple, inscribed 'For the fairest', contended for by Hera, Athene, and Aphrodite; hence, cause, subject, of dispute; ~ *of Sodom*, fruit which, acc. to ancient writers, dissolved into smoke and ashes when plucked, Dead Sea apple.

A'ppleton (ăplt-), Sir Edward Victor (1892–1965). British physicist; Nobel Prize for physics 1947; ~ *layer*, F^2-layer of the ionosphere.

applī'ance *n.* Applying; device, piece of equipment.

ă'pplĭcable *adj.* Capable of being applied. **ăpplĭcabĭ'lĭtȳ** *n.*

ă'pplĭcant *n.* One who applies.

ăpplĭcā'tion *n.* Applying; thing applied; request; relevancy, diligence.

ă'pplĭcātor *n.* Device for applying substance.

appliqué (-ē'kā) *n.* & *adj.* (Needlework) consisting of pieces of material cut out and sewn to the surface of other material of different colour or texture; material so applied. ~ *v.t.* Sew (material) to another as appliqué.

applȳ' *v.* Put close *to*, put in

contact; administer (remedy); devote (*to*); refer (*to*); address oneself (*for* help etc.) *to*; make application (*for*); make use of; *applied*, put to practical use.

appoggiatura (-ŏjatoor'a) *n.* (mus.) Grace-note consisting of momentary delay of melodic note into following chord of which it does not properly form a part, eventually moving one degree to the note it has displaced. [It.]

appoi'nt *v.t.* Fix (time etc.); prescribe, ordain; assign *to* office; *well, badly, appointed*, so equipped.

appoi'ntment *n.* Act of appointing; agreement to meet at specific time; office assigned; (pl.) fitments.

appŏr't (*or* ă'-) *n.* Material thing produced, professedly by occult means, at spiritualist séance.

appŏr'tion *v.t.* Give as due share; portion out. **appŏr'tionment** *n.*

ă'pposĭte (-z-) *adj.* Well put; appropriate. **ăpposĭ'tion** *n.* Placing side by side; *in* ~, (gram.) syntactically parallel; in same case etc.

apprai'se (-z) *v.t.* Fix price for; estimate. **apprai'sal, apprai'sement** *ns.*

apprē'ciable (-sha-) *adj.* Capable of being estimated; perceptible. **apprē'ciablў** *adv.*

apprē'cĭāte (*or* -shĭ-) *v.* Estimate rightly; recognize, understand; be sensitive to; esteem highly; raise, rise, in value. **apprēcĭā'tion** *n.* **apprē'cĭatĭve** *adj.*

ăpprėhĕ'nd *v.t.* Seize, arrest; understand; anticipate with fear.

ăpprėhĕ'nsĭble *adj.* Perceptible to senses.

ăpprėhĕ'nsion *n.* 1. Arrest. 2. Understanding. 3. Uneasiness.

ăpprėhĕ'nsĭve *adj.* Relating to sensuous perception, or intellectual understanding; uneasy in mind. **ăpprėhĕ'nsĭvelў** *adv.* **ăpprėhĕ'nsĭvenėss** *n.*

apprĕ'ntĭce *n.* Learner of a craft, bound to serve, and entitled to instruction from, his employer for a specified term. ~ *v.t.* Bind as apprentice (*to*). **apprĕ'ntĭceshĭp** *n.*

apprī'se (-z) *v.t.* Give notice *of*, inform.

ă'pprō *n.* (colloq.) Approval (*on* ~).

approa'ch *v.* Come near or nearer (to); set about (task); make overtures to. ~ *n.* Approaching; access, passage; (golf) shot which is intended to reach green. **approa'chable** *adj.* Easy of access; welcoming, friendly to advances.

ă'pprobāte *v.t.* (U.S.) Approve formally, sanction.

ăpprobā'tion *n.* Sanction, approval. **ă'pprobātĭve, ă'pprobātorў** *adjs.*

apprō'prĭate *adj.* Suitable, proper. **apprō'prĭatelў** *adv.* **apprō'prĭāte** *v.t.* Take possession of; devote to special purposes. **apprōprĭā'tion** *n.*

appro've (-oov) *v.* Confirm, sanction, commend; ~ *of*, pronounce or consider good; *approved school*: see COMMUNITY home. **appro'val** *n.* Approving; *on* ~, (of goods supplied) to be returned if not satisfactory.

apprŏ'xĭmate *adj.* Very near; fairly correct. **apprŏ'xĭmatelў** *adv.* **apprŏ'xĭmāte** *v.* Bring or come near (*to*). **apprŏxĭmā'tion** *n.*

appûr'tėnance *n.* Appendage; accessory; belonging. **appûr'tėnant** *adj.* Belonging, appertaining.

Apr. *abbrev.* April.

après-ski (ă'prĕ skĭ *or* shĭ) *n.* & *adj.* (Of, suitable for) time after a day's skiing.

ā'prĭcŏt *n.* Succulent orange-pink fruit, with smooth stone, of the rosaceous tree *Prunus armeniaca*; this tree; colour of the fruit.

A'prĭl (ā-). 4th month of Gregorian (2nd of Julian) calendar, with 30 days; ~ *Fool*, one hoaxed on ~ *Fool's Day*, All Fools' Day. [L *Aprīlis*]

ā priōr'ī *adv.* & *adj. phr.* (Reasoning) from cause to effect; deductive(ly). [L, = 'from what is before']

ā'pron *n.* 1. Garment worn in front of body to protect clothes; *tied to ~-strings of* (mother, wife, etc.), unduly dependent on. 2. Part of ceremonial dress (of bishops, freemasons, etc.). 3. (theatr.) Advanced strip of stage for playing scenes before proscenium arch; ~ *stage*, stage equipped with this. 4. Part of lathe carrying gears and controls. 5. Area near hangars of airfield for accommodation of aircraft manœuvring on ground. 6. Broad strip on inner side of boat's bow strengthening the stem.

ăpropo's (-pō) *adv.* To the purpose; in respect *of.* ~ *adj.* Pertinent.

ăpse *n.* Semicircular or polygonal recess, usu. with vaulted roof, in church or other building.

ă'psĭdal *adj.* 1. Of the form of an apse. 2. Of the apsides (see foll.)

ă'psĭs *n.* (pl. *ă'psĭdēs, apsī'dēs*). Aphelion or perihelion of planet; apogee or perigee of moon.

ăpt *adj.* Suitable, appropriate: quick, ready; inclined (*to*). **ă'ptlȳ** *adv.* **ă'ptnėss** *n.*

ă'pterous *adj.* Wingless.

ă'pterȳx *n.* = KIWI, 1. [Gk *a-* not, *pterux* wing]

ă'ptĭtūde *n.* Fitness; natural propensity; ability; (psychol.) capacity to acquire skill in a particular field of bodily or mental performance.

Apuleius (ăpūlē'*u*s), Lucius (b. *c* A.D. 123). Platonic philosopher, of Madaura in N. Africa; author of the satire known as 'The Golden Ass'.

Apū'lĭa. Ancient country and modern region (It. *Puglia*) forming the 'heel' of SE. Italy. **Apū'lĭan** *adj.* & *n.*

ă'qua fōr'tĭs. (obs.) Nitric acid; *aqua forti* or *a.f.* (on prints), etched by (so-and-so). [L, = 'strong water']

ă'qualŭng *n.* & *v.i.* (Use) diver's portable breathing apparatus, consisting of cylinders of compressed air with valve and mouthpiece.

ăquamari'ne (-ēn) *n.* Bluish-green transparent beryl; colour of this. [L *aqua marina* sea-water]

ă'quaplāne *n.* Board towed behind speed-boat, carrying a rider. ~ *v.i.* 1. Ride on aquaplane. 2. (of vehicle travelling on wet surface) Lose contact with surface through build-up of water beneath tyres.

ă'qua rē'gĭa. Mixture of concentrated nitric and hydrochloric acids, able to dissolve gold and platinum, which are not attacked by the unmixed acids. [L, = 'royal water']

ăquarĕ'lle *n.* (Painting in) transparent water-colour.

aquār'ĭum *n.* (pl. *-s*, *-ia*). Artificial pond or tank for keeping live aquatic plants, fishes, or animals; place containing such tanks.

Aquār'ĭus. The Water-carrier, a constellation; 11th sign (♒) of the zodiac, which the sun enters about 21 Jan. **Aquār'ĭan** *adj.* & *n.*

aquă'tĭc (*or* -ŏt-) *adj.* Living in or frequenting water; (of sports) conducted in or on water. ~ *n.* Aquatic plant or animal; (pl.) aquatic sports.

ă'quatĭnt *n.* (Colour-)print with finely grained transparent effect, produced by coating a copper plate (or plates) with a porous resin ground, painting the design on it with varnish, immersing it in nitric acid, and inking it, when the protected parts, being less corroded by the acid, will take up less ink; this process. ~ *v.* Work in aquatint; reproduce by this means.

ăquavi't (-vēt) *n.* Colourless or yellowish alcoholic spirit distilled from potatoes or other starch-containing plant; schnapps.

ă'qua vi'tae (vētī). (obs.) Brandy or other alcoholic spirit. [L, = 'water of life']

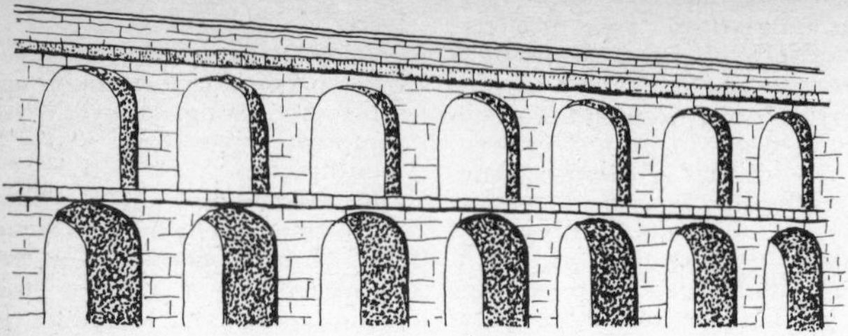

AQUEDUCT

ă'quėdŭct *n.* Artificial channel, esp. elevated structure of masonry across valley etc. for conveyance of water.

ā'quėous *adj.* Of water, watery; (geol.) produced by the action of water; ~ *humour*: see HUMOUR *n.* 3.

ăquĭlē'gĭa *n.* Plant of genus *A*~; columbine.

ă'quĭlīne *adj.* Of an eagle; eagle-like; curved like eagle's beak.

Aquī'nas, St. Thomas (*c* 1225–

74). Italian philosopher, a Dominican friar, whose writings, notably his 'Summa Totius Theologiae', represent the culmination of scholastic philosophy.

Aquĭtai'ne (ă-). Ancient province of SW. France, comprising at some periods the whole country from the Loire to the Pyrenees; by the marriage of Eleanor of Aquitaine to Henry II it became one of the English possessions in France.

A.R.A. *abbrev.* Associate of the Royal Academy.

A'rab (ă-) *n.* 1. One of an orig. Semitic people inhabiting Saudi Arabia and neighbouring countries. 2. Arab horse of a breed noted for its graceful build and speed. 3. *street a*~, homeless child. ~ *adj.*

ărabĕ'sque (-sk) *adj.* Arabian; Moorish, esp. in design; fantastic. ~ *n.* 1. Decoration of fancifully twisted scroll-work, leaves, etc., orig. devised by Muslim artists owing to ban on images. 2. Musical composition suggestive of this decoration. 3. (ballet) Pose in which dancer stands on one foot with one arm extended in front and the other arm and leg extended behind.

Arā bĭa. Peninsula of SW. Asia, largely desert, lying between the Red Sea and the Persian Gulf and bounded on the north by Jordan and Iraq; SAUDI ~: see entry; ~ *Deserta*, ancient name for the Syrian desert and parts of the Arabian peninsula; ~ *Felix*, ancient name for the more fertile SW. mountainous coastal regions of Arabia (see YEMEN); ~ *Petraea*, ancient name for the Sinai peninsula, including PETRA.

Arā'bĭan *adj.* Of Arabia or the Arabs; ~ *camel*, one-humped camel (*Camelus dromedarius*); ~ *Nights'* (*Entertainments*), also called the 'Thousand and One Nights', a collection of fairy-stories and fantastic romances written in Arabic, linked together by a framework of Persian origin, though the tales themselves, which were probably collected in Egypt at some time in the 14th–16th centuries, are for the most part not Persian but Arabian in character; ~ *Sea*, NW. part of Indian Ocean, between Arabia and India. ~ *n.* Arab.

A'răbĭc (ă-) *adj.* Arabian; *gum a~*, gum exuded from various kinds of acacia and used in the manufacture of adhesives, confectionery, and in textile printing, pharmacy, etc.; ~ *numerals*, those (1, 2, 3, etc.) now in common use in all western countries, most of which were first used in India and were introduced into the west by the Arabs. ~ *n.* Semitic language, orig. that of the Arabs, but now spoken in a large part of N. Africa, Syria, and neighbouring countries.

Ara'bĭ Pă'sha (-ah-) (*c* 1839–1911). Egyptian soldier and politician of anti-European sympathies.

A'rabĭst (ă-) *n.* Student of Arabic or of Arab civilization etc.

ă'rable *adj.* & *n.* Ploughed or ploughable land.

A'rabȳ (ă-). (poet.) Arabia.

arā'ceous (-sh*u*s) *adj.* Of the Araceae or arum family of plants.

Ară'chnė (-k-). (Gk legend) Skilful weaver who challenged Athene to a contest; Athene tore the work up and when Arachne hanged herself changed her into a spider.

ară'chnĭd (-k-) *n.* (zool.) Member of the Arachnida, a class of wingless arthropods including spiders, scorpions, mites, king crabs, and others, and distinguished from insects esp. by having eight or more legs and no antennae.

ară'chnoid (-k-) *adj.* 1. Of the arachnids. 2. (anat.) Of the three membranes surrounding the brain and supporting the blood-vessels. ~ *n.* Arachnoid membrane.

A'ragon (ă-). Region of Spain, bounded on N. by the Pyrenees and on E. by Catalonia and Valencia.

A'ral Sea (ă-). Inland sea of U.S.S.R., E. of Caspian Sea.

A'răm (ă-). Biblical name of Syria. **Aramae'an** *adj.* & *n.*

A.R.A.M. *abbrev.* Associate of the Royal Academy of Music.

Aramā'ĭc (ă-) *adj.* & *n.* (Of) the NW. Semitic language, closely related to Hebrew, spoken in SW. Asia in the later Babylonian Empire and until *c* 7th c. A.D.

A'ran I'slands (ă-, il*a*ndz). Group of three islands off W. coast of Ireland, lying across mouth of Galway Bay. **A'ran** *adj.* Of a type of patterned knitwear.

A'ranȳ (ah-), János (1817–82). Hungarian national epic poet.

A'rarăt (ă-). Either of two peaks of the Armenian plateau, in which region Noah's ark is said (Gen. 8: 4) to have rested after the Flood (*Great* ~, 5165 m, 16,945 ft).

ăraucār'ia *n.* Coniferous tree of genus *A*~ including monkey puzzle. [*Arauco* district in Chile]

ar'balĕst *n.* Crossbow with special mechanism for drawing it.

ar'bĭter *n.* Judge; one appointed by two parties to settle dispute, umpire; one with entire control *of*; *elegantiae* ~: see PETRONIUS ARBITER.

arbĭ'trament *n.* Decision of dispute by arbiter; authoritative decision.

ar'bĭtrarȳ *adj.* Derived from mere opinion, capricious; despotic; (law) discretionary. **ar'bĭtrarĭlȳ** *adv.*

ar'bĭtrāte *v.* Decide by arbitration. **arbĭtrā'tion** *n.* Settlement of dispute by an arbiter.

ar'bĭtrātor *n.* One appointed to settle dispute.

ar'bor *n.* Main support of machine; axle or spindle on which wheel revolves.

arborā'ceous (-sh*u*s) *adj.* Tree-like; wooded.

Ar'bor Day (ar-). Day set apart annually in U.S., S. Australia, and elsewhere for public tree-planting.

arbor'ėal *adj.* Of, living in, trees.

arbor'ėous *adj.* Wooded; arboreal; arborescent.

arborĕ'scent *adj.* Tree-like; branching. **arborĕ'scence** *n.*

arborē'tŭm *n.* (pl. *-ta*). Tree-garden.

ar'boriculture *n.* Cultivation of trees and shrubs. **arboricu'ltural** (-cher-) *adj.* **arboricu'lturist** *n.*

ar'bor vi'tae (vētī). Coniferous evergreen shrub of genus *Thuja.*

ar'bour (*-er*) *n.* Shady retreat with sides and roof of trees or climbing plants.

Ar'buthnot (ar-), John (1667–1735). Scottish physician and writer of political pamphlets and medical works.

arbū'tus *n.* Evergreen plant of genus *A*~ of the heather family including strawberry tree.

arc *n.* 1. Part of circumference of circle or other curve. 2. (elect.) Intense electrical discharge in gas or vapour, a luminous bridge of conducting gas formed between two separate electrical poles; ~ *lamp*, ~ *light*, lamp using this; ~ *welding*: see WELD².

A.R.C.A. *abbrev.* Associate of the Royal College of Art.

arcā'de *n.* 1. Passage arched over; any covered walk, esp. one with shops etc. at side(s). 2. (archit.) Series of arches supporting, or attached to, a wall.

Arcā'dia (ar-). Mountainous district in the Peloponnese, taken as an ideal region of rustic contentment (in this sense also *Ar'cady*). **Arcā'dian** *adj.* & *n.* (Native, inhabitant) of Arcadia; ideal(ly) rustic.

arcā'ne *adj.* Mysterious, secret.

arcā'num *n.* (usu. in pl. *-na*). Mystery, secret.

arch¹ *n.* Structure, usu. curved, consisting of wedge-shaped pieces so arranged as to support one another by mutual pressure, and used to carry weight of roof, wall, etc., or as ornament; any curved structure resembling this in form and function; curve; vault; (anat.) curve on inner side of foot; *Court of Arches*, ecclesiastical court of the province of Canterbury, orig. held in church of St. Mary-le-Bow (or 'of the Arches'); ~ *bridge*, bridge supported on arches; *ar'chway*, arched passage or entrance. **ar'chwise** (-z)

adv. **arch** *v.* Furnish with, form into, form, an arch; span.

arch² *adj.* Making hints or allusions in a jocose affected manner. **ar'chly** *adv.* **ar'chness** *n.*

arch- *prefix.* Chief, superior; leading; extreme; first.

archaeŏ'logy (-ki-) *n.* Study of ancient cultures through their material remains; *industrial* ~, study of machinery etc. formerly used in industry. **archaeolŏ'gical** *adj.* **archaeolŏ'gically** *adv.* **archaeŏ'logist** *n.*

archā'ic (-k-) *adj.* Primitive, antiquated; no longer in common use. **archā'ically** *adv.*

ar'chāism (-k-) *n.* Obsolete word or phrase; retention or imitation of the old or obsolete (esp.

in language and art). **ar′chāize** *v.*
ar′chāngel[1] (-k-, -j-) *n.* Angel of highest rank (see ANGEL). **archăngĕ′lic** *adj.*
Ar′chāngel[2] (ark-, -j-). (Russ. *Ar′khange′lsk*) Port of northern U.S.S.R., on White Sea.
archbi′shop *n.* Chief bishop. **archbi′shopric** *n.*
archdea′con *n.* Ecclesiastical dignitary next below bishop, superintending rural deans and holding ecclesiastical court. **archdea′conry** *n.*
archdī′ocėse *n.* Archbishop's see.
ar′chdūke *n.* Prince of former imperial house of Austria. **archdū′cal** *adj.* **archdŭ′chėss, archdŭ′chy** *ns.*
archėgō′nium (-k-) *n.* Female organ in cryptogams, corresponding to pistil in flowering plants.
arch-ĕ′nemy *n.* Chief enemy; *the* ~, Satan.
ar′cher *n.* One who shoots with bow and arrows. **ar′chery** *n.*
ar′chėtype (-k-) *n.* 1. Original model, prototype. 2. (Jungian psychol.) Universal symbol; mental image given by inheritance.
ar′chfie′nd *n.* Satan.
archidiā′conal (-ki-) *adj.* Of an archdeacon.
archiėpi′scopal (-ki-) *adj.* Of an archbishop.
Archi′lochus (-kil′*o*k*u*s) (*fl.* 648 B.C.). Greek poet of Paros, celebrated for satirical iambic verse.
archimă′ndrīte (-k-) *n.* Superior of monastery of Orthodox Church, equivalent to abbot in Western Churches.
Archimē′dēs (ark-, -z) (*c* 287–212 B.C.). Greek mathematician of Syracuse; said to have made many mechanical inventions, including the screw (named after him) for raising water; *principle of* ~, (phys.) principle that when a body is partly or completely immersed in a fluid the apparent loss of weight is equal to the weight of the fluid displaced. **Archimē′dėan** *adj.*
archipĕ′lagō (-k-) *n.* (pl. -*os*). Sea with many islands; group of islands; *the A*~, the Aegean Sea.
ar′chitĕct (-k-) *n.* 1. Designer of buildings who prepares plans and superintends execution. 2. Designer of ship. 3. (fig.) Designer.
architĕctŏ′nic (-k-) *adj.* 1. Of architecture. 2. Of the systematization of knowledge.
ar′chitĕcture (-k-) *n.* Science of building; thing built; style of building; construction. **architĕ′ctural** (-kch*e*r-) *adj.* **architĕ′cturally** *adv.*
ar′chitrāve (-k-) *n.* 1. Main beam resting immediately on two or more columns; lowest part of entablature. 2. Moulded frame round doorway, window, or arch.
ar′chīve (-k-) *n.* (usu. pl.). Public records; place in which these are kept. **ar′chivist** *n.* Keeper of archives.
ar′chivōlt (-k-) *n.* Under-curve of arch; mouldings decorating this.
ar′chon (-k-) *n.* One of 9 chief magistrates in ancient Athens; chief magistrate of other ancient Greek cities; ruler, president. **ar′chonship** *n.*
A.R.C.M., A.R.C.O., A.R.C.S. *abbrevs.* Associate of the Royal College of Music, of Organists, of Science.
ar′ctic *adj.* Of the North Pole; northern; intensely cold; *A*~ *Circle*, parallel of 66° 32′ N., north of which the sun does not rise at midwinter or set at midsummer; *A* ~ *Ocean*, ocean N. of the Arctic Circle. **Ar′ctic** *n.* Regions (both land and sea) round the North Pole. [Gk *arktos* bear, Ursa Major]
Arctūr′us (ar-). (astron.) Brightest star in the constellation Boötes. [Gk *arktos* bear, *ouros* guardian, because of its position in a line with the tail of Ursa Major]
Ar′den (ar-). Woodland district of N. Warwickshire, part of an ancient forest formerly covering a great part of the Midlands and W. England.
Ardennes (ardĕ′n *or* -ĕ′nz). Ancient forest district including

parts of Belgium, Luxemburg, and N. France.

ar'dent *adj.* Eager, zealous, fervent; burning. **ar'dentlў** *adv.*

ar'dour (-*er*) *n.* Zeal; warmth,

ar'dūous *adj.* Hard, laborious; strenuous. **ar'dūouslў** *adv.* **ar'dūousnėss** *n.*

are[1] *n.* Unit of square measure, = 100 square metres.

are[2]**.** 1st, 2nd, and 3rd pers. pl. pres. of BE.

ar'ėa *n.* Extent of surface; region; space intended for specific use, as *dining*, *parking*, ~; scope, range; sunk court or yard before basement of house.

ă'rėca (*or* arē'ka) *n.* Tropical Asiatic palm of genus *A*~, bearing pungent astringent fruit; ~ *nut*, astringent seed of a species of areca; betel.

arē'na *n.* Central part of amphitheatre, in which combats took place ; central part of stadium; scene of conflict or action.

ărėnā'ceous (-sh*u*s) *adj.* Sandy; sand-like.

Arėŏ'pagus (ă-). Hill at Athens where (in antiquity) highest judicial court met; hence, this court. **Arėŏ'pagīte** (-g-) *n.* Member of court of Areopagus. [Gk *Areios pagus* hill of Ares]

Ares (ar'ēz). (Gk myth.) God of war, son of Zeus and Hera; identified with the Roman MARS.

Ar'ĭan[1] *adj.* & *n.*

arête (-ā't) *n.* Sharp ridge of mountain. [Fr.]

Arėthū'sa (ă-, -*za*). (Gk legend) Water-nymph who fled from Greece to Ortygia in Sicily, pursued by the river-god Alpheus; the waters of the river Alpheus (in the Peloponnese) were believed to flow unmixed through the sea and emerge mingled with the fountain of Arethusa at Ortygia.

Arėti'nō (ă-, -ēnō), Pietro (1492–1556). Italian author of comedies, satires, and licentious poems.

ar'gali *n.* Large Asiatic wild sheep, *Ovis ammon*.

Argand (argahṅ), Aimé (*c* 1750–1803). Swiss inventor of the ~ *lamp* (ar'gand), with a tubular wick, which allows air to reach both inner and outer surfaces of the flame; ~ *burner*, gas-burner constructed on the same principle.

ar'gent *n.* & *adj.* Silver (colour, esp. in heraldry).

argentĭ'ferous *adj.* Yielding silver.

Ar'gentīne[1] (ar-). Republic occupying most of S. part of S. America E. of the Andes; first settled by Spaniards (1526 onwards); remained a Spanish colony until a revolt, beginning in 1810, led to the declaration in 1816 of the independence of the *Provincias Unidas del Rio de la Plata* ('United Provinces of the Silver River'); capital, Buenos Aires. **Argentĭ'nian** *adj.* & *n.* [L *argentum* silver, because the Rio de la Plata district exported it]

ar'gentīne[2] *adj.* Of silver; silvery.

ar'gil *n.* (Potter's) clay. **argillā'ceous** (-sh*u*s) *adj.*

Ar'gīve (arg-) *adj.* & *n.* (Native, inhabitant) of ARGOS or Argolis; Greek.

Ar'gō (ar-): see ARGONAUTS.

ar'gŏl *n.* Crude tartar; grey or red substance deposited from fermented wines.

Ar'golis (ar-): see ARGOS.

ar'gŏn *n.* (chem.) Inert gaseous element, present to extent of about 1 % in the air, discovered *c* 1894 by Lord Rayleigh and Sir William Ramsay, used in gas-filled electric light bulbs etc.; symbol Ar, at. no. 18, at. wt 39·948.

Ar'gonauts (ar-) *n.pl.* (Gk legend) Heroes who accompanied Jason on board the ship *Argo* on the quest for the Golden Fleece.

Ar'gŏs (ar-). Ancient Greek town of the E. Peloponnese, from which the peninsula of Argolis derived its name.

ar'gosў *n.* (hist., poet.) Large vessel (orig. of Ragusa or Venice) carrying rich merchandise; (poet.) ship. [prob. from It. *Ragusea* (*nave*) (ship) of Ragusa]

ar'got (-ō) *n.* Jargon, slang, of a class or group, formerly esp. of thieves.

ar'gue *n.* Maintain by reasoning; reason; prove, indicate; raise objections, dispute. **ar'guable** *adj.*

ar'gufy *v.i.* (colloq.) Dispute excessively.

ar'gument *n.* Reason advanced; debate; summary of subject-matter of book etc. **argumentā'tion** *n.* Methodical reasoning; debate.

argumĕ'ntative *adj.* Logical; fond of arguing. **argumĕ'ntatively** *adv.* **argumĕ'ntativeness** *n.*

Ar'gus[1] (ar-). 1. (Gk myth.) Fabulous person with 100 eyes, slain by Hermes; after his death Hera transferred his eyes to the tail of the peacock. 2. (Gk legend) Dog of Ulysses, who recognized his master on his return from Troy after an absence of 20 years.

ar'gus[2] *n.* Pheasant of genus *Argusianus*, natives of Asia. [f. ARGUS[1]]

Argy'llshire (arg-). Former county on W. coast of Scotland, since May 1975 part of the region of Strathclyde.

ar'ia *n.* Long accompanied song for one voice in opera and oratorio; song-like movement in instrumental composition. [It.]

Ariă'dnė (ă-). (Gk myth.) Daughter of Minos, king of Crete; helped Theseus to escape from the labyrinth of the Minotaur by providing him with a clue of thread; then became his wife, but he deserted her in the island of Naxos, where she was found and married by Dionysus.

Arian[1] **:** see ARES.

Arian[2]**, Arianism :** see ARIUS.

A.R.I.B.A. *abbrev.* Associate of the Royal Institute of British Architects.

ă'rid *adj.* Dry, parched; (geog., of climate or region) having insufficient water to support vegetation. **ari'dity** *n.*

Ar'iel (ar-). In Shakespeare's 'The Tempest', a spirit released by the magician Prospero from imprisonment by a witch, Sycorax.

Aries (ar'ēz). The Ram, a constellation; 1st sign (♈) of the zodiac, which the sun enters at the vernal equinox.

ari'ght (-īt) *adv.* Rightly.

ă'ril *n.* (bot.) Extra seed-covering, freq. brightly coloured (e.g. yew, spindle).

Arimathē'a (ă-): see JOSEPH[1], 3.

Arī'on (7th c. B.C.). Greek poet and musician of Lesbos; said to have perfected the dithyramb; acc. to legend, sailors on a ship resolved to murder him, but he begged first to play a tune, did so, and leapt overboard; dolphins were attracted by the music, and one bore him on its back to land.

Ariŏ'stō (ă-), Lodovico (1474–1533). Italian poet, author of the romantic epic 'Orlando Furioso'.

arī'se (-z) *v.i.* (past t. *arō'se*, past part. *arisen* pr. -ĭzn). Appear, spring up, occur, get up, rise. **arī'sings** (-z) *n.pl.* Secondary or waste products; remains.

Aristar'chus[1] (ă-, -k-) of Samos (3rd c. B.C.). Astronomer and mathematician; maintained that the earth revolved round the sun, though he thought that its orbit was a circle (not an ellipse).

Aristar'chus[2] (ă-, -k-) of Samothrace (*c* 217–*c* 145 B.C.). Librarian at Alexandria; edited the Greek classics; regarded as the originator of scientific scholarship.

Aristī'dēs (ă-, -z) (d. *c* 466 B.C.). Athenian general and statesman, called 'the Just'; commanded his tribe at the battle of Marathon; was archon in 489, but was later ostracized and died in poverty.

Aristi'ppus (ă-). Name of two Greek philosophers: the elder (late 5th c. B.C.), a native of Cyrene and friend of Socrates, is freq. called the founder of the Cyrenaic school, prob. by confusion with the younger, his grandson (fl. *c* 400–365), who taught that immediate pleasure is the only end of action.

ăristŏ'cracy *n.* The nobility; supremacy of privileged order; government by nobles.

ă'ristocrăt *n.* Member of aristocracy. **ăristocră'tic** *adj.* Belonging to the aristocracy; having distinguished bearing and manners. **ăristocră'tically** *adv.*

Aristŏ′phanēs (ă-, -z) (*c* 445–*c* 385 B.C.) Athenian comic dramatist; author of comedies (the 'Birds', 'Frogs', 'Wasps', etc.) caricaturing his contemporaries and their attitude to public affairs.

A′ristŏtle (ă-) (384–322 B.C.). Greek philosopher; pupil of Plato at Athens; became tutor to the young Alexander of Macedon; returned to Athens in 335; there conducted the PERIPATETIC school; wrote the 'Ethics', 'Politics', and 'Poetics', and works of zoology, physics, metaphysics, logic (which he invented), and rhetoric. **Aristotē′lian** *adj.* & *n.*

arĭ′thmėtic *n.* Science of numbers; computation. **ărithmĕ′tical** *adj.* **ărithmĕ′ticallў** *adv.* **ărithmėtĭ′cian** (-shan) *n.*

Ar′ĭus (ãr-) (*c* 250–*c* 336). Priest of Alexandria; denied the true Divinity of Christ. **Ar′ian**[2] *adj.* & *n.* (Supporter) of Arius or his heresy. **Ar′ianism** *n.*

Ariz. *abbrev.* Arizona.

Arizō′na (ă-). State in south-western U.S., admitted to the Union in 1912; capital, Phoenix.

ârk *n.* 1. Chest, box; *A~ of the Covenant, of Testimony*, wooden coffer containing tables of Jewish law, the most sacred religious symbol of early Israel; *~ of the Law*; chest or cupboard in Jewish synagogue containing scrolls of the Law. 2. Covered floating vessel in which NOAH was saved at the Deluge.

Ark. *abbrev.* Arkansas.

Arkansas (ãr′kansaw). State in south-central U.S., admitted to the Union in 1836; capital, Little Rock.

Arkwright (ãr′krīt), Sir Richard (1732–92). English engineer, inventor of the spinning-frame.

Arles (ãrl). Town of S. France, on the river Rhône, on the site of a Roman city (*Arelate*), the chief residence of Constantine.

ârm[1] *n.* Upper limb of human body; sleeve; branch; arm-like thing; *armchair*, chair with supports for arms; (fig.) applied to persons who theorize without actively participating; *ar′mpit*, hollow under arm at shoulder. **âr′mful** *n.* **âr′mlėss** *adj.*

ârm[2] *n.* 1. Particular kind of weapon; (pl.) weapons. 2. Each

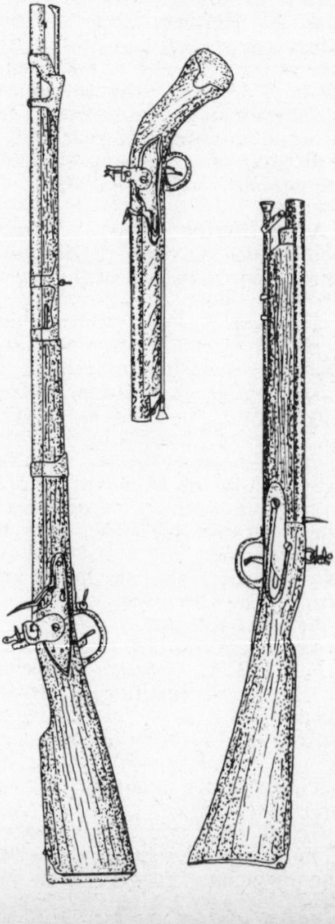

FIREARMS

kind of force, as *air* ~, *infantry* ~. 3. (pl.) Heraldic devices; *coat of* ~s: see COAT; *King of Arms:* see KING. ~ *v.* Furnish with arms; take up arms; provide, furnish, *with.*

Armada (ârmah'da). (also *Spanish* ~) Fleet sent by Philip II of Spain against England in 1588; it was defeated in the Channel and dispersed by the English fleet under Lord Howard of Effingham and such captains as Drake, Frobisher, and Hawkins; many of the ships were lost in attempting to return round the N. of Scotland.

ârmadĭ'llō *n.* (pl. *-os*). Burrowing, usu. nocturnal, S.-Amer. mammal, protected by bony plates resembling armour. [Span. dim. of *armado* armed creature]

Armagĕ'ddon (âr-, -g-). Place where the kings of the earth are to be gathered together for 'the battle of that great day of God Almighty' (Rev. 16: 14–16).

Armagh (ârmah'). County and county town of Northern Ireland.

âr'mament *n.* Force equipped for war; military weapons and munitions; process of equipping for war.

âr'mature *n.* 1. Arms, armour, defensive covering of animals or plants. 2. Piece of soft iron placed in contact with poles of a magnet to preserve the intensity of magnetization or to support a load; core of laminated iron wound round by coils of insulated copper-wire, that part of a dynamo which rotates in the magnetic field. 3. Framework of wire, wood, etc., round which sculptor builds clay or plaster model.

Armē'nĭa (âr-). Constituent republic of U.S.S.R., lying S. of the Caucasus, part of the former kingdom of Armenia, most of which was under Turkish rule from the 16th c.; capital, Erivan.

Armē'nĭan *adj.* Of Armenia or its people or language. ~ *n.* Armenian person or language.

âr'mĭger *n.* One entitled to bear heraldic arms.

ârmĭ'llarȳ *adj.* Pertaining to bracelets; ~ *sphere,* skeleton celestial globe consisting of metal rings representing the equator, ecliptic, tropics, etc., revolving on an axis.

Armĭ'nĭus[1] (âr-) (18 B.C.–A.D. 19). Latinized form of Hermann, chief of the German tribe of the Cherusci, leader of the insurrection against the Romans under Varus, who were defeated at the battle of the Teutoburg forest (A.D. 8).

Armĭ'nĭus[2] (âr-), Jacobus (d. 1609). Latinized form of Harmensen, a Dutch Protestant theologian, with views opposed to those of CALVIN esp. on predestination. **Armĭ'nĭan** *adj.* & *n.* **Armĭ'nĭanĭsm** *n.*

âr'mĭstice *n.* Cessation of hostilities by agreement between belligerents; short truce; *A~ Day,* 11 Nov., formerly kept as anniversary of the armistice that ended hostilities in the war of 1914–18 (since war of 1939–45 celebrated on Remembrance Sunday). [L *arma* arms + *-stitium* stopping]

âr'mlėt *n.* Band worn round arm.

ârmŏr'ĭal *adj.* Of heraldic arms.

âr'morȳ *n.* Heraldry.

Armŏ'rĭcan (âr-) *adj.* = HERCYNIAN.

âr'mour (-mer) *n.* 1. (hist.) Defensive covering for body worn in fighting. 2. (also ~ *plate*) Steel plates etc. protecting ship, tank, car, etc., from projectiles etc. (so ~*-plated*); tanks and other fighting vehicles equipped with such armour. ~ *v.t.* Furnish with such protective covering; *armoured car, train,* one supplied with protective armour and (usu.) guns; *armoured column, division,* etc., one equipped with armoured cars, tanks, etc.

âr'mourer (-mer-) *n.* Manufacturer of arms; one in charge of ship's or regiment's small arms.

âr'mourȳ (-mer-) *n.* Place where small arms are kept; armourer's workshop.

âr'mȳ *n.* Organized body of persons armed for fighting on land; vast host; ~ *corps,* main subdivision of an army in the field

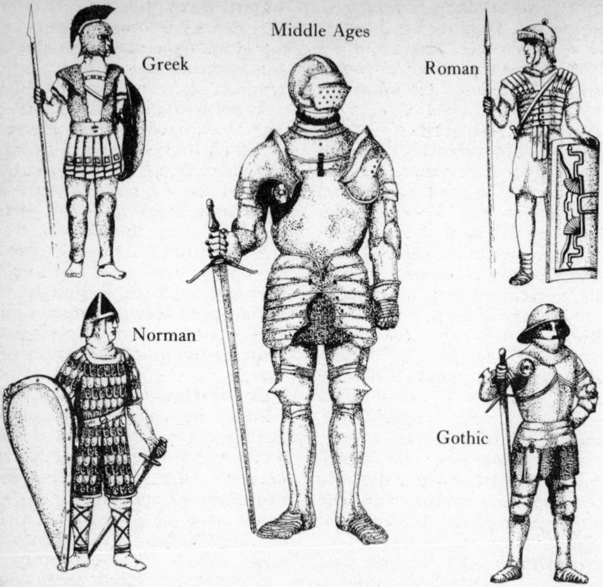

ARMOUR

consisting of two or more divisions and certain technical and administrative units; ~ *list*, official list of commissioned officers.

Arne (ar̂n), Thomas (1710–78). English composer of operas, masques (including 'Alfred' which contains 'Rule, Britannia!'), and songs.

ar̂'nĭca *n.* Composite plant of genus *A~*, largely American, including mountain tobacco; tincture, prepared from root and rhizome of mountain tobacco and used for bruises, sprains, etc.

Ar'nō (ar̂-). River of N. Italy, flowing through Florence and Pisa.

Ar'nold[1] (ar̂-) of Brescia (d. 1155). Italian Augustinian, an ascetic who vigorously condemned the temporal power and abuses of the clergy and the papacy; executed by Adrian IV.

Ar'nold[2] (ar̂-), Matthew (1822–88). English poet and critic; son of Thomas ARNOLD[3].

Ar'nold[3] (ar̂-), Thomas (1795–1842). Headmaster of Rugby (1828–42) which he raised to the rank of a great public school.

ar̄'oid *adj.* & *n.* Araceous (plant).

arō'ma *n.* Fragrance; subtle pervasive quality.

ăromă'tic *adj.* 1. Fragrant, spicy. 2. (chem.) Of the group of organic compounds in which the carbon atoms are arranged in 6-membered rings (as in benzene).

arou'nd *adv.* On every side; round; here and there. ~ *prep.* All round; about; enveloping; approximately.

arou'se (-z) *v.t.* Awaken; stir up into activity.

A.R.P. *abbrev.* Air-raid precautions.

ar̂pĕ'ggĭō (-ĕjĭō) *n.* (pl. *-os*). Chord of which notes are not played simultaneously but 'harpwise', i.e. in succession. [It. *arpa* harp]

arquebus: see HARQUEBUS.

arr. *abbrev.* Arrives, arriving, etc.

ă'rrack (*or* *a*ră'k) *n.* Alcoholic spirit manufactured in the East, esp. from coco-palm or rice. [Arab. *'araḳ* sweat, alcoholic spirit made from grapes or dates]

arrai'gn (-ān) *v.t.* Indict, accuse; call in question. **arrai'gnment** *n.*

A'rran (ă-). Scottish island at mouth of Firth of Clyde.

arrā'nge (-j) *v.* Put in order; settle; settle beforehand order etc. of; form plans, take steps; adapt. **arrā'ngement** *n.*

ă'rrant *adj.* Downright, notorious.

ă'rras[1] *n.* Rich tapestry; hangings of this round walls of room. [f. ARRAS[2]]

Arras[2] (ărah). Town in NE. France famous in 13th–16th centuries for tapestry weaving.

array' *v.t.* Dress, esp. with display; marshal (forces). ~ *n.* Dress; imposing series; martial order; (math.) arrangement of numbers etc. in rows or columns; (radio) assembly of aerials.

arrear' *n.* That which is behind; (pl.) outstanding debts; work etc. in which one is behindhand; *in* ~(*s*), behindhand. **arrear'age** *n.* Arrear.

arrĕ'st *v.t.* Stop; (law) ~ *judgement*, stay proceedings after verdict; seize (person) esp. by legal authority; catch (attention); catch attention of. ~ *n.* Legal apprehension; stoppage; seizure. **arrĕ'stable** *adj.* (esp.) ~ *disease*, one that can be prevented from getting worse; ~ *offence*, (law) offence for which person can be arrested without a warrant.

arrĕ'ster *n.* (mech.) Attachment for bringing an object to a stop.

Arrhe'nius (ărān-), Svante August (1859–1927). Swedish physical chemist, awarded Nobel Prize in 1903 for his work on the physical chemistry of electrolytes.

arrière-pensée (ărĭār pahṅsā) *n.* Ulterior motive; mental reservation. [Fr.]

ă'rrĭs *n.* 1. (archit.) Sharp edge where two planes or curved surfaces meet; ~ *gutter*, V-shapped gutter; ~ *rail*, rail made by cutting a square section of timber across its diagonal. 2. (eng.) Raised circle of material left on surface of metal plate when hole is drilled through it.

arrī've *v.i.* Come to destination or end of journey; be brought; come; establish one's reputation or position. **arrī'val** *n.*

arriviste (ărēvēst) *n.* Person determined to 'arrive' or succeed. [Fr.]

ă'rrogant *adj.* Overbearing, presumptuous. **ă'rrogantlў** *adv.* **ă'rrogance** *n.*

ă'rrogāte *v.t.* Claim unduly. **ărrogā'tion** *n.*

arrondissement (*a*rawṅdēsmahṅ) *n.* Administrative subdivision of French department. [Fr.]

ă'rrow (-ō) *n.* Missile shot from bow, usu. consisting of straight slender wooden shaft with sharp point or head of stone or metal, and feathers fastened to the butt; mark like an arrow or arrowhead, often used as indication of direction etc.; *a'rrowhead*, water-plant, *Sagittaria sagittifolia*, with arrow-shaped leaves, growing in ponds and slow streams; *a'rrowroot*, tropical plant *Maranta arundinacea*; starch obtained from its rhizomes, used as food esp. for invalids.

ar̂se *n.* (vulg.) Buttocks, rump.

ar̂'senal *n.* State establishment where weapons and ammunition are made and stored. [Arab. *dār aṣ-ṣināʻa* factory, place where fighting ships are equipped]

ar̂'senĭc *n.* (chem.) Brittle steel-grey semi-metallic element, symbol As, at. no. 33, at. wt 74·9216; (pop.) white mineral substance (~ *trioxide*), a violent poison. **ar̂'senĭc** (*or* -sĕ'n-) *adj.* Of arsenic; (chem.) applied to compounds in which arsenic is pentavalent. **ar̂sĕ'nĭcal** *adj.* [Gk *arsenikon*, f. Arab. *az-zirnīḵ* orpiment, arsenic]

ar̂sē'nĭous *adj.* Containing arsenic in trivalent form.

ar̂'sine (-ēn) *n.* Colourless inflammable poisonous gas (AsH_3)

having an odour like garlic; any of a group of poisonous gases derived from this.

ar'sis *n.* (pl. *-sēs*). (pros.) Accented syllable in a metrical foot (opp. THESIS).

ar'son *n.* Wilful setting on fire of houses or other property.

art *n.* Skill, esp. applied to design, representation, or imaginative creation; human skill as opp. to nature; cunning, stratagem; subject in which skill may be exercised; (pl.) certain branches of learning (*liberal ~s*) traditionally serving as preparation for more advanced studies or for life (*Bachelor, Master, of Arts*, one who has obtained a standard of proficiency in these at a university); *applied, decorative ~s*, those concerned with the design and decoration of objects in practical use, handicrafts; *fine ~s*, (usu.) painting, architecture, sculpture, music, poetry; *Arts Council of Great Britain*, organization (incorporated 1946) for promotion of the fine arts.

Artaxer'xes (artazerksēz). Name of two kings of ancient Persia: *Artaxerxes I*, son of Xerxes, reigned 464–424 B.C.; *Artaxerxes* II, son of Darius II, reigned 404–358 B.C.

ar'tėfăct, ar'ti- *n.* 1. (archaeol.) Object, as palaeolithic flint, made by human workmanship. 2. (biol.) Something not present in the natural state of an organism but produced while it is being prepared for examination.

Ar'tėmĭs (ar-). (Gk myth.) Goddess of chastity and of hunting; daughter of Leto; twin sister of Apollo, identified with Selene and DIANA.

arter'ial *adj.* Belonging to, of the nature of, an artery; *~ road*, important main road.

arter'ialize *v.t.* Convert (venous blood) into arterial blood by impregnating it with oxygen in lungs; furnish with arterial system. **arterializā'tion** *n.*

arter'iōle *n.* Small artery.

arteriŏsclerō'sis *n.* Hardening of the walls of arteries.

ar'terў *n.* Muscular-walled blood-vessel conveying the blood impelled by the heart to the small vessels which supply the tissues; something serving as channel of supplies, e.g. main road.

artē'sian (-zhan) *adj.* *~ well*, perpendicular bore into a curved or slanting water-saturated stratum, penetrating it at a level lower than the source of the water, which rises spontaneously to the surface in a continuous flow. [f. *Artois*, Fr. province]

ar'tful *adj.* Cunning, crafty.

arthrī'tis *n.* Inflammation of joint. **arthrĭ'tĭc** *adj.*

ar'thrŏpŏd *n.* One of the Arthropoda, the largest animal phylum, comprising insects, arachnids, myriapods, crustaceans, and trilobites, and characterized by jointed limbs and a hard jointed external skeleton.

Ar'thur[1] (ar-). King of Britain; historically perh. a 5th- or 6th-c. chieftain or general; acc. to legend he was the son of Uther Pendragon and Igerne, wife of Gorlois of Cornwall; became king of Britain at age of 15; married Guinevere; held court at Caerleon-on-Usk and established there a company of knights whose seats were at a Round Table so that none had precedence; was mortally wounded at Camelford in battle against his usurping nephew Modred; was then borne off in a magic boat to Avalon whence he will one day return; *~'s Seat*, saddle-backed hill on E. side of Edinburgh, dominating the city. **Arthur'ian** *adj.*

Ar'thur[2] (ar-), Prince, Duke of Brittany (1187–1203). Grandson of Henry II of England; declared by his uncle, Richard I, to be heir to the throne, to which his other uncle, John, also laid claim; but during the war between France and Britain he was captured and, prob. by John's orders, murdered at Rouen.

Ar'thur[3] (ar-), Chester Alan (1830–86). American politician, lawyer, and soldier (in Civil War); 21st president of U.S., 1881–5.

ar′tic *n.* (colloq.) Articulated vehicle.

ar′tichōke *n.* 1. Plant, *Cynara scolymus* (of which bottom of flower and bases of its scales are edible), allied to thistle. 2. *Jerusalem* ~, species of sunflower with edible tuberous roots. [It. *articiocco*, f. Arab. *alkaršūfa*; Jerusalem, corrupt. of It. *girasole* sunflower]

ar′ticle *n.* Separate portion of anything written; separate clause, literary composition forming part of magazine etc.; particular; particular thing; (gram.) either of the adjectives 'a, an' (*indefinite* ~) and 'the' (*definite* ~), or their equivalents in other languages. ~ *v.t.* Bind by articles of apprenticeship; set forth in articles.

artĭ′cūlar *adj.* Of the joints.

artĭ′cūlate *adj.* Having joints; distinctly jointed, distinguishable; able to express oneself well; (of speech) clearly defined. **artĭ′cūlāte** *v.* Connect by joints; divide into words, pronounce distinctly; speak distinctly; *articulated vehicle*, one with flexibly connected sections. **artĭ′cūlatorȳ** *adj.*

artĭcūlā′tion *n.* Articulate utterance, speech; jointing.

artifact: see ARTEFACT.

ar′tĭfĭce *n.* Device; cunning; skill. **artĭ′fĭcer** *n.* Craftsman; (in Royal Navy) mechanic.

artĭfĭ′cial (-shal) *adj.* Produced by art; not natural; not real; ~ *horizon*, (i) level reflector used in determining altitudes of stars etc.; (ii) instrument in aircraft indicating attitude of the aircraft to the horizon; ~ *insemination*, injection of semen into uterus by artificial means; ~ *language*, invented language, esp. one designed for international use; ~ *rain*, rain made by dispersal of solid carbon dioxide or other chemical material in suitable cloud, causing the cloud to cool and condense; ~ *respiration*: see RESPIRATION; ~ *silk*: see RAYON. **artĭfĭ′ciallȳ** *adv.* **artĭfĭcĭă′lĭtȳ** *n.*

artĭ′llerȳ *n.* Large mounted firearms of calibre greater than small arms; cannon; ordnance; branch of army that uses these; *art′illeryman*, one belonging to the artillery, gunner. **artĭ′llerĭst** *n.* Artilleryman.

artĭsă′n (-z-) *n.* Mechanic; handicraftsman.

ar′tĭst *n.* One who practises one of the fine arts, esp. painting; one who makes his craft a fine art; artiste. **artĭ′stĭc** *adj.* **ar′tĭstrȳ** *n.*

artĭ′ste (-ēst) *n.* Professional singer, dancer, etc.

ar′tlėss *adj.* Guileless, simple; lacking art, crude. **ar′tlėsslȳ** *adv.* **ar′tlėssnėss** *n.*

art nouveau (ar nōōvō). Decorative style (*c* 1880–*c* 1910) using flowing curves and naturalistic motifs. [Fr., = 'new art']

Artois (ar′twah). Ancient province of NE. France.

ar′tȳ *adj.* Having artistic pretensions.

ār′um *n.* Plant of genus *A*~ including cuckoo-pint (lords and ladies); ~ *lily*, inflorescence of

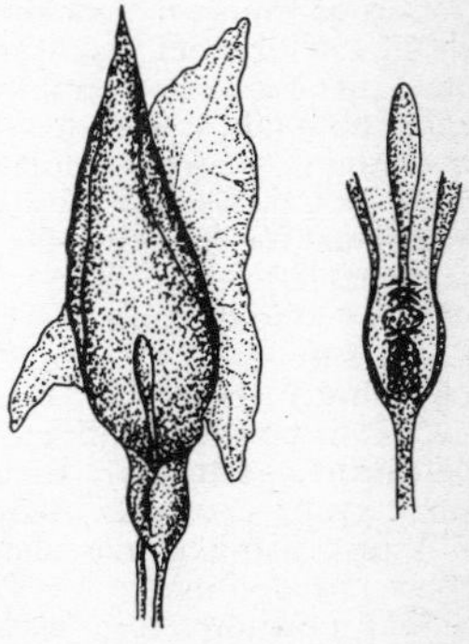

plant *Zantedeschia aethiopica*, used for decoration, esp. on altar.

A.R.W.S. *abbrev.* Associate of the Royal Society of Painters in Water-colours.

Ar′ȳan (ār-) *adj.* & *n.* 1. (archaic) Indo-European; (esp.) Indo-Iranian. 2. (loosely) (Member) of a people speaking an Indo-European language; in Nazi Germany esp. contrasted with SEMITE.

[Sansk. *ārya* noble (in earlier use a national name comprising worshippers of the gods of the Brahmans); the earlier *Arian* is f. L *Arianus*, = 'of Aria' (f. Gk *Areia* eastern Persia)]

ărўbă'llos (pl. *-oi*) *n.* (Gk antiq.) Globular oil-flask with narrow neck.

as[1] (ăz, unemphat. *az*) *adv.* In the same degree; similarly. ~ *conj.* While, when; since, seeing that. ~ *prep.* In the capacity or role of.

ăs[2] *n.* (pl. *ă'ssės*). Roman copper coin, orig. weighing 12 oz. but finally reduced to ½ oz.

A.S. *abbrev.* Anglo-Saxon.

ăsafoe'tĭda (-fēt-) *n.* Concreted resinous gum of various Persian plants of genus *Ferula* with strong smell of garlic and bitter taste, used in medicine. [Pers. *aza* mastic, L *foetida* stinking]

A'saph (ā- *or* ă-), St. (d. *c* 596). Welsh saint, prior of Llanelwy, and first bishop of St. Asaph; commemorated 1 May.

ăsbĕ'stos (*or* ăz-) *n.* White or grey fibrous mineral (consisting largely of calcium and magnesium silicates) that can be woven into an incombustible fabric used for fireproof clothing, thermal insulation of pipes, etc., or formed into light sheet material for roofing. [Gk, = 'unquenchable']

ascĕ'nd *v.* Go or come up; rise, mount, climb.

ascĕ'ndancў, -encў *n.* Dominant control, powerful influence.

ascĕ'ndant, -ent *adj.* Rising; (astron.) rising towards zenith; (astrol.) just rising above eastern horizon; predominant. ~ *n.* Ascendant position etc.; (astrol.) ascendant point of ecliptic or degree of zodiac.

ascĕ'nder *n.* (esp. printing) Limb of letter above x-height.

ascĕ'nsion *n.* Ascent; ascent of Christ into Heaven on fortieth day after resurrection; rising of a celestial body; *A~ Day*, day commemorating Christ's ascension, sixth Thursday after Easter.

Ascĕ'nsion I'sland (īl-). Small island in S. Atlantic, discovered by Portuguese on Ascension Day 1501, but uninhabited until a British garrison was placed there in 1815.

ascĕ'nt *n.* Ascending, rising; upward path or slope.

ăscertai'n *v.t.* Find out. **ăscertai'nable** *adj.* **ăscertai'nment** *n.*

ascĕ'tĭc *adj.* Severely abstinent, austere. ~ *n.* One who practises severe self-discipline, esp. (eccles. hist.) one who retired into solitude for this purpose. **ascĕ'tĭcal** *adj.* **ascĕ'tĭcallў** *adv.* **ascĕ'tĭcism** *n.*

Ascham (ă'skam), Roger (1515–68). English scholar and prose-writer, author of 'The Scholemaster', a treatise on the (private) education of boys.

ascĭ'dĭan *n.* Tunicate, esp. of the order Ascidiacea. [Gk *askidion* dim. of *askos* wine-skin]

asclē'pĭăd *n.* Verse of a spondee, two or three choriambs, and an iambus (said to have been invented by Asclepiades).

Asclē'pĭadēs (-z) (*c* 290 B.C.). Greek epigrammatic poet.

Asclē'pĭus. (Gk myth.) Hero and god of healing, freq. represented bearing staff with serpent coiled round it.

ăscomў'cēte *n.* Fungus producing ascospores, e.g. cup fungus

ascŏr'bĭc *adj.* ~ *acid*, Vitamin C, which occurs in fresh foods, esp. fruits and vegetables, and is necessary to obviate scurvy.

ă'scospŏre *n.* Spore developed in an ascus.

A'scot (ă-). (Used for) ~ *Heath*, race-course in Berkshire; ~ *Week*, annual race-meeting there in June, instituted by Queen Anne, 1711.

ascrī'be *v.t.* Attribute, impute; consider as belonging *to*. **ascrĭ'ption** *n.* Ascribing; formula ascribing praise to God at end of sermon.

ă'scus *n.* (pl. *-cī*). (bot.) Round or elongated sac-like body containing spores, in certain fungi.

ă'sdĭc (ăz-) *n.* Echo-sounding device for detecting under-water objects. [initials of *A*nti-*S*ubmarine *D*etection *I*nvestigation *C*ommittee]

A.S.E. *abbrev.* Associated Society (*or* Associate of the Society) of Engineers.

āsĕ'psĭs *n.* Absence of putrefactive matter or harmful bacteria; aseptic method in surgery.

āsĕ'ptĭc *adj.* Free from putrefaction or blood-poisoning; sterilized; seeking the absence, rather than counteraction, of septic matter.

āsĕ'xūal *adj.* Not sexual, without sex; ~ *generation*, (biol.) any form of reproduction not brought about by the union of gametes.

A'sgārd (ăz-). (Scand. myth.) Region in the centre of the universe, inhabited by the gods.

ăsh[1] *n.* Forest-tree of genus *Fraxinus* with silver-grey bark, pinnate leaves, and close-grained wood; wood of this; *mountain* ~, rowan tree; ~*-plant*, sapling of ash-tree used as walking-stick etc.

ăsh[2] *n.* (freq. pl.) Powdery residue left after combustion of any substance; (pl.) remains of human body after cremation; *the Ashes*, imaginary trophy claimed by winner of each series of cricket matches (Test Matches) between England and Australia (from epitaph in 'Sporting Times' on occasion of first match won by Australia, 1882, lamenting death of English cricket and stating that the ashes would be taken to Australia); ~ *blond*(*e*) (*adj.*) light blond; (*n.*) person with ash-blond hair; *A*~ *Wednesday*, first day of Lent (from early custom of sprinkling ashes on penitents' heads); *a'sh-tray*, receptacle for tobacco ash etc.

ashā'med (-md) *adj.* Abashed, upset, by consciousness of guilt.

Ashă'ntĭ *n.* (pl. *-s* or as sing.). Native of Ashanti, a division of Ghana.

ă'shen *adj.* Pertaining to an ash-tree; made of ash-wood; pale.

A'sher (ă-). Hebrew patriarch, son of Jacob (Gen. 30: 12, 13); tribe of Israel, traditionally descended from him.

Ashkĕna'zĭm (ă-, -ah-) *n.pl.* Polish-German Jews (as dist. from SEPHARDIM). [mod. Heb., f. *Ashkenaz* (Gen. 10: 3), typifying race identified in medieval times with Germans]

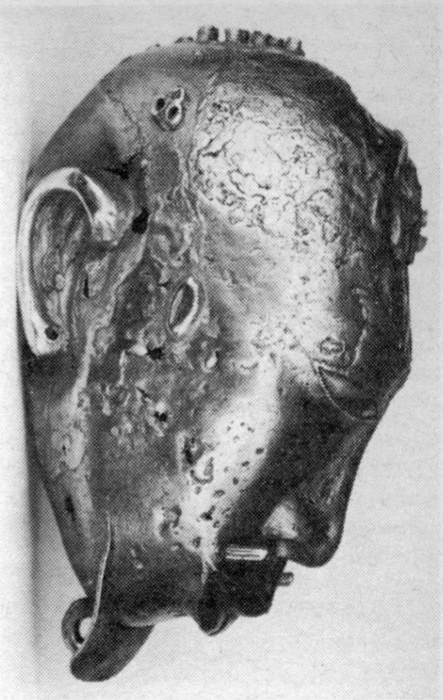

ă'shlar *n.* Squared hewn stone(s); masonry of this.

ă'shlarĭng *n.* Short upright wall in garrets, cutting off acute angle formed by rafters with floor.

A'shmōle (ă-), Elias (1617–92). English antiquary, founder of the Ashmolean Museum at Oxford.

ashōr'e *adv.* To or on shore.

A'shtorĕth, -arōth (ă-). = ASTARTE. [Heb.]

ă'shȳ *adj.* Of ashes; ash-coloured; pale.

Asia (ā'sha). Continent of N. hemisphere, E. part of the great land-mass formed by the Old World; separated from Europe by the Ural Mountains and the Caspian Sea; home of the oldest known civilizations; ~ *Minor*, westernmost part of Asia, a peninsula bounded by the Black Sea, the Aegean, and the Mediterranean, and comprising most of Turkey; Anatolia. **A'sian, Asiă'tĭc** (*or* -shĭ-) *adjs.* & *ns.*

asī'de *adv.* To or on one side; away, apart. ~ *n.* Words spoken by an actor and supposed not to be heard by other performers.

ă'sĭnīne *adj.* Of asses; stupid.

Asir (*azēr'*). Region of SW. Arabia, forming with Hejaz and Nejd the Kingdom of Saudi Arabia.

ask (ah-) *v.* Call for an answer (to); make a request (for); invite; demand, require.

A'skalon (ă-). Ancient Philistine city of the E. Mediterranean coast (near Majdal in modern Israel), destroyed *c* 1270 after several times changing hands in the Crusades.

askă'nce (*or* -ahns) *adv.* Sideways; *look ~ at*, view suspiciously.

ăskar'ĭ *n.* European-trained African native soldier. [Arab.]

askew' *adv.* Obliquely, awry.

asla'nt (-ahnt) *adv.* Obliquely.

aslee'p *adv.* In a state of sleep. ~ *pred. adj.* (of limbs) Benumbed; (of top) spinning without apparent motion.

A.S.L.E.F., A'slĕf (ăz-) *abbrev.* Associated Society of Locomotive Engineers and Firemen.

A.S.L.I.B., A'slĭb (ăz-) *abbrev.* Association of Special Libraries and Information Bureaux.

aslō'pe *adv.* & *pred. adj.* Sloping, crosswise.

Asmodē'us, -daeus (ăz-). (Jewish legend) Evil spirit (Tobit 3: 8).

āsō'cial (-sh*a*l) *adj.* Antagonistic to society or social order.

Asō'ka (*or* *a*sh-) (d. *c* 232 B.C.). Emperor of India from *c* 269 B.C.; ruled over the greater part of the peninsula; was converted to Buddhism, did much to propagate it, and is revered by Buddhists.

ăsp *n.* 1. Small viper of S. Europe (*Vipera aspis*). 2. Viper of N. Africa and Arabia (species of *Cerastes*).

aspă'ragus *n.* Liliaceous plant of genus *A~* with many-branched fine stems, and leaves reduced to scales; species of this (*A. officinalis*) whose vernal shoots are a table delicacy; ~ *fern*, the species *A. plumosus* used as decoration.

Aspā'sia (-zĭ*a* *or* -zhĭ*a*) (5th c. B.C.). Greek courtesan, mistress of Pericles.

ă'spĕct *n.* Way a thing presents itself to eye or mind; side (of building etc.) looking, fronting, in a given direction; appearance; (philol.) form of the verb expressing duration, completion, etc., of an action.

ă'spen *n.* Kind of poplar (*Populus tremula*) with leaves tremulous on account of long thin leaf-stalks.

Aspĕr'gēs (-z) *n.* (R.C. Ch.) Anthem beginning with this word (L, = 'Thou shalt sprinkle') sung before High Mass while altar, clergy, and people are sprinkled with holy water; the rite itself.

ăspĕ'rĭtȳ *n.* Roughness; severity; harshness.

aspĕr'se *v.t.* Attack the reputation of, calumniate. **aspĕr'sion** *n.*

ă'sphălt *n.* 1. Solid or plastic pitch derived from petroleum either naturally (as in asphalt lakes of Trinidad and Venezuela) or by distillation. 2. Mixture of this with sand etc. used for surfacing roads etc. ~ *v.t.* Lay (road) with asphalt.

ă'sphodĕl *n.* Any of various hardy liliaceous plants from Mediterranean and India, including classical *Asphodeline lutea* in Greece; (poet.) immortal flower in Elysium.

asphȳ'xĭa *n.* Defective aeration of blood, caused by blockage of air-passages or paralysis of respiratory muscles or collapse of the lungs, and resulting in death if air-flow fails completely. **asphȳ'xĭāte** *v.* Kill by asphyxia, suffocate. **asphȳxĭā'tion** *n.* [Gk *a-* not, *sphuxis* pulse]

ă'spĭc *n.* Savoury jelly, used as a garnish or for making moulds of cooked meat, fish, eggs, etc.

ăspĭdĭ'stra *n.* Plant of the lily family, with broad tapering leaves, freq. grown as a pot-plant, and often regarded as a symbol of dull middle-class respectability. [Gk *aspis* shield]

ă'spirant (*or* *a*spīr'-) *n.* One who aspires.

ă'spirate *adj.* Aspirated. ~ *n.* Aspirated consonant; the sound of *h.* **ă'spirāte** *v.t.* 1. Pronounce with a breathing, blended with sound of *h.* 2. Draw out (gas) from vessel.

ăspirā'tion *n.* Drawing of breath; desire; action, use of, aspirator.

ă'spirātor *n.* Apparatus for drawing gas through tube or through a liquid.

aspīr'e *v.i.* Feel earnest desire or ambition; (fig.) reach high.

ă'spirĭn (*or* -pr-) *n.* Compound of acetylsalicylic acid, used as an analgesic and febrifuge; tablet of this.

asquĭ'nt *adv.* & *pred. adj.* With a squint.

A'squĭth (ă-), Herbert Henry, first Earl of Oxford and Asquith (1852–1928). British Liberal statesman; prime minister 1908–16.

ăss (*or* ahs) *n.* 1. Quadruped (*Equus onager*, *E. hemippus*, *E. hemionus*, etc.) related to the horse but smaller, with tuft at end of tail and long ears, domesticated for draft and riding and descended from the *wild* ~ (*Equus asinus* or *E. taeniopus*) of Ethiopia; donkey. 2. (slang) Ignorant or stupid person.

ăssa'i (-ah-ē) *adv.* (mus.) Very. [It.]

assai'l *v.t.* Attack, assault. **assai'lant** *n.* One who assails.

Assă'm (*or* ă'-). State of NE. India; capital, Shillong. **Assamē'se** (-z) *adj.* & *n.*

assă'ssĭn *n.* One who undertakes to kill treacherously; *Assassins*, (hist.) fanatical sect of the Ismaili Muslims in time of Crusades, founded in the 11th c. by the 'Old Man of the Mountains' (Hasan-ben-Sabbah), and notorious for secret murders carried out at the order of their chief. [Arab. *ḥashshāshīn*, oblique pl. of *hashshàsh* hashish addict]

assă'ssināte *v.t.* Kill (person) for political or sectarian reasons. **assăssinā'tion** *n.*

assau'lt (*or* -ŏlt) *n.* Hostile attack; rush against walls of fortress etc.; (law) unlawful personal attack, menacing words. ~ *v.t.* Make attack upon.

assay' *n.* Testing of an alloy or ore to determine the proportion of a given metal; determination of strength of substance by testing on an organism; ~ *mark* (on gold and silver), hallmark indicating standard of fineness. ~ *v.* Try the purity or strength of; attempt.

ă'ssėgai (-gī) *n.* Slender spear of hard wood tipped with iron, used as missile by S. Afr. tribes. [Fr. *azagaye*, f. Arab.]

assĕ'mblage *n.* Collection, concourse.

assĕ'mble *v.* Bring or come together; collect; fit together parts of (machine etc.).

assĕ'mblў *n.* 1. Gathering of persons, esp. of deliberative body; ~*-room*, large room for social gatherings. 2. (eng.) Assembling of those parts of a machine etc. that form a unit; parts so assembled; ~*-line*, sequence of machines and workers for assembly of product.

assĕ'nt *v.i.* Agree (*to*), defer (*to*); express agreement; say yes. ~ *n.* Concurrence; sanction.

assẽr't *v.t.* Vindicate a claim to (rights); declare; ~ *oneself*, insist upon one's rights.

assẽr'tion *n.* Insistence upon a right; affirmation, positive statement.

assẽr'tĭve *adj.* Given to assertion; positive, dogmatic. **assẽr'tĭvelў** *adv.* **assẽr'tĭvenėss** *n.*

assĕ'ss *v.t.* Fix amount of (taxes, fine); fine, tax; estimate value of (esp. for taxation). **assĕ'ssment** *n.*

assĕ'ssor *n.* One who assesses taxes or estimates value of property for purpose of taxation; adviser to judge or magistrate.

ă'ssĕt *n.* 1. (pl., law) Enough goods to enable heir to discharge debts and legacies of testator; property liable to be so applied; effects of insolvent debtor; property that may be made liable for debts; (sing.) item of this in balance-sheet. 2. (loosely) Any possession; any useful quality. [med. L *ad satis* sufficiently]

assĕ'verāte *v.t.* Solemnly declare. **assĕverā'tion** *n.*

ăssĭdū'ĭtў *n.* Close attention, persistent application.

assĭ'dūous *adj.* Persevering, diligent. **assĭ'dūouslў** *adv.* **assĭ'dūousnėss** *n.*

assi'gn (-īn) *v.t.* Make over formally; allot; appoint; ascribe. ~ *n.* One to whom a property, right, etc., is legally transferred.

ăssĭgnā'tion *n.* Assigning; appointment (of time and place).

ăssignee' (-īnė) *n.* One appointed to act for another; assign.

assi'gnment (-īn-) *n.* Allotment; legal transference; document effecting this, attribution; task, commission.

assĭ'mĭlāte *v.* Make or become like; absorb, be absorbed into the sўstem. **assĭmĭlā'tion** *n.* **assĭ'mĭlatĭve, assĭ'mĭlatorў** *adjs.*

Assi'sĭ (-ēzĭ). Town of Umbria, central Italy; birth-place of St. Francis.

assĭ'st *v.* Help; be present at meeting etc. **assĭ'stance** *n.*

assĭ'stant *adj.* Helping. ~ *n.* Helper, subordinate worker.

assī'ze *n.* (usu. pl.) Periodical sessions in counties of England and Wales held (until 1971) by judges on circuit for administration of civil and criminal judgement; (hist.) statutory price (of bread and ale).

assoc. *abbrev.* Association.

assō'ciāte (*or* -shĭ-) *v.* Join; connect in idea; combine; have frequent dealings (*with*); *Associated State*, any of various States of the E. Caribbean regarded as forming part of the Commonwealth through their relationship with member States. **assō'ciate** (*or* -shĭat) *adj.* Joined, allied. ~ *n.* Partner, companion; subordinate member of an association; thing connected with another. **assō'ciatĭve, assō'ciatorў** *adjs.*

assōciā'tion *n.* Associating; organized body of persons; connection of ideas; intercourse; *free* ~: see FREE; ~ *football*, kind of football played by two teams of eleven players, with spherical ball, which must not be handled when in play except by the goalkeeper.

assoi'l *v.t.* (archaic) Absolve from sin, pardon.

ă'ssonance *n.* Resemblance of sound between two syllables; rhyming of one word with another in the accented vowel but not in the following consonants (e.g. *sonnet, porridge*). **ă'ssonant** *adj.*

assŏr't *v.* 1. (archaic) Arrange in sorts. 2. Suit, harmonize (*with*).

assŏr'tėd *adj.* Of various sorts.

assŏr'tment *n.* Assorting; mixture of various sorts.

A.S.S.R. *abbrev.* Autonomous Soviet Socialist Republic.

Asst *abbrev.* Assistant.

assuā'ge (-sw-) *v.t.* Calm, soothe; appease. **assuā'gement** *n.*

assū'me *v.t.* Take upon oneself; undertake; simulate; take to be true for purpose of argument or action. **assū'mĭng** *adj.* Taking much upon oneself, arrogant.

assŭ'mption *n.* Assuming; thing assumed; arrogance; *the A~*, the reception of the Virgin Mary into heaven; feast in honour of this, 15 Aug.

A'ssur, A'shur (ă-). Local god of the city of that name, the ancient capital of Assyria (on the Tigris at modern Sharqat in N. Iraq); he became the supreme god of the Assyrians, the god of war, and the protector of the people.

assur'ance (*a*shoor-) *n.* Positive assertion; self-confidence; impudence; (life) insurance.

assur'e (*a*shoor) *v.t.* Make safe; make certain, ensure; insure (life); make (person) sure (*of*); tell (person) confidently. **assur'ėdlў** *adv.*

Assў'rĭa. More northerly of the two ancient empires of Mesopotamia; capital, Assur; supremacy ended soon after the death of Assur-bani-pal (7th c. B.C.), who subdued rebellious Egypt and Elam but left the empire too exhausted to repel the Medes; these finally destroyed Nineveh, the last Assyrian stronghold, in 612 B.C.

Assў'rĭan *adj.* & *n.* 1. (Member)

ASSYRIAN

of the Assyrian people, a mixed Semitic race; (of) the Assyrian language, a dialect of Akkadian. 2. (Member) of the NESTORIAN community. [f. ASSUR]

Assўrĭŏ'logў *n.* Study of the civilization, language, etc., of Assyria. **Assўrĭŏ'logist** *n.*

Astar'tė (ă-). Goddess of love and fertility; Phoenician equivalent of Aphrodite.

ă'statine *n.* (chem.) Radioactive element of short life (symbol At, at. no. 85, principal isotope at. wt 211), which does not occur in nature but can be made artificially; the heaviest element of the halogen group. [Gk *astatos* unstable]

ă'ster *n.* Herbaceous plant of genus *A*~ including Michaelmas daisies, with showy radiated flowers of various colours. [Gk *aster* star]

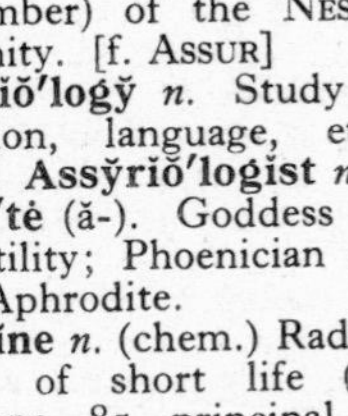

ă'sterisk *n.* Star * used to mark words for reference or distinction, to indicate a hypothetical form or fill up space in a line where something is omitted. ~ *v.t.* Mark with asterisk.

ă'sterism *n.* Cluster of stars; three asterisks ⁂ calling special attention to word or passage.

aster'n *adv.* In, at, the stern; behind.

aster'nal *adj.* ~ *rib*: see RIB.

ă'steroid *n.* 1. (astron.) Any of the small planets revolving round sun mainly between orbits of Mars and Jupiter. 2. (zool.) One of the class of Asteroidea or starfishes. **ăsteroi'dal** *adj.* [Gk *asteroeidēs* starlike]

ă'sthma (-sm-) *n.* Disorder, freq. of allergic origin, characterized by paroxysms of difficult breathing. **ăsthmă'tic** *adj.* & *n.* (Person) suffering from asthma. **ăsthmă'tically** *adv.*

A'sti (ă-). Town in Piedmont producing wines, sparkling (~ *spumante*) and still.

asti'gmatism *n.* Structural defect in eye or lens, preventing rays of light from being brought to a common focus, arising from unequal refraction at different points. **ăstĭgmă'tĭc** *adj.* **ăstĭgmă'tĭcallȳ** *adv.*

astīr' *adv.* In motion; out of bed.

Aston: see BIRMINGHAM.

astŏ'nĭsh *v.t.* Amaze, surprise. **astŏ'nĭshment** *n.*

astou'nd *v.t.* Shock with alarm or surprise; amaze.

ă'stragal *n.* 1. (archit.) Small moulding round top or bottom of column. 2. Ring round cannon near mouth.

astră'galus *n.* 1. Ball of ankle-joint. 2. Leguminous plant of genus *A~* which includes milk-vetch (*A. glycyophyllos*).

Astrakha'n[1] (ă-, -kăn). Province of R.S.F.S.R. on the lower Volga; town on Caspian Sea at head of Volga delta.

ăstrakhă'n[2] (-kăn) *n.* Caracul fur; cloth imitating this.

ă'stral *adj.* Connected with, consisting of, stars; ~ *body*, (theosophy) ethereal counterpart of the human body accompanying it in life and surviving its death.

astray' *adv.* Out of the right way.

astrī'de *adv.* & *prep.* With legs apart or on either side (*of*); extending across.

astrĭ'ngent (-j-) *adj.* Causing to contract, styptic; severe; austere. ~ *n.* Astringent substance.

ă'strodōme *n.* Dome-shaped window in aircraft used for aeronautical observations.

ă'strolābe *n.* Instrument used to take altitudes and solve other problems of practical astronomy, especially of stars; *prismatic* ~, surveying instrument for determining position by observations to stars at a fixed altitude (45° or 60°).

astrŏ'logȳ *n.* Art of understanding the reputed occult influence of the stars on human affairs. **astrŏ'loger** *n.* **ăstrolŏ'gĭcal** *adj.* **ăstrolŏ'gĭcallȳ** *adv.*

ă'stronaut *n.* One who travels in space.

ăstronau'tĭcs *n.* Science of navigation in space. **ăstronau'tĭc, -ĭcal** *adjs.*

astrŏ'nomer *n.* One who studies astronomy; *A~ Royal*, astronomer appointed by the Crown, the first holder being appointed by Charles II in 1675 when the Royal Observatory at Greenwich was founded.

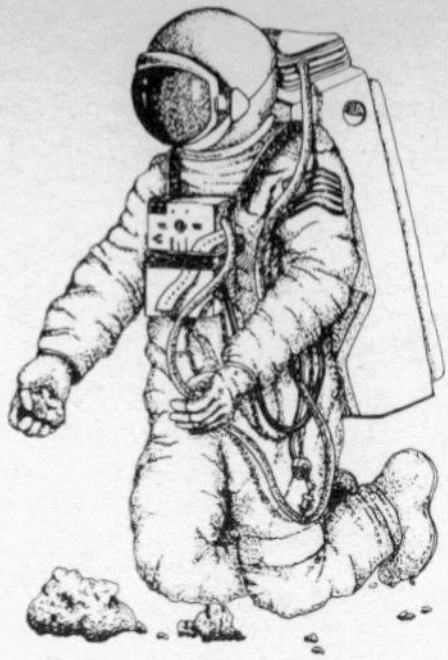

ASTRONAUT

ăstronŏ'mĭcal *adj.* Relating to, concerned with, astronomy; (of numbers, distances, etc.) very big, immense; ~ *unit*, (abbrev. a.u.) mean distance of the earth from the sun as unit of measurement, approx. 150 million kilometres (93 million miles). **ăstronŏ'mĭcallȳ** *adj.*

astrŏ'nomȳ *n.* Science of the heavenly bodies.

ă'strophȳ'sĭcs (-z-) *n.* That branch of physics which deals with the physical or chemical properties of heavenly bodies. **ăstrophȳ'sĭcal** *adj.* **ăstrophȳ'sĭcĭst** *n.*

Astūr'ĭas (ă-). Region of NW. Spain; *Prince of the* ~, former title of eldest son of the king of Spain. **Astūr'ĭan** *adj.* & *n.*

astū'te *adj.* Shrewd; crafty. **astū'telȳ** *adv.* **astū'teness** *n.*

Asunción (*a*sōōnsĭŏ'n *or* -thĭŏ'n). Capital city of Paraguay.

asŭ'nder *adv.* Apart; to pieces.

Asūr'a. (Hinduism) Evil demon, enemy of the gods; (in Veda) freq. a god.

Aswan Dăm (ă'swahn). Dam (1⅓ m. long) built on the Nile at Aswan in SE. Egypt for irrigation 1902, enlarged 1933; *Aswan High Dam*, larger dam, *c* 4 m. upstream, for hydro-electric power as well as irrigation, completed 1969.

asȳ'lum *n.* Sanctuary, place of

refuge;(formerly) institution for the care of the afflicted or destitute, esp. the insane; (also *political* ~) protection from arrest or extradition given by one nation to refugee from another.

asy̆′mmėtry (*or* ā-) *n.* Absence of symmetry. **ăsy̆mmĕ′trĭc, -ĭcal** *adjs.* **ăsy̆mmĕ′trĭcally̆** *adv.*

ă′symptōte *n.* Line which continually approaches a given curve, but does not meet it within a finite distance.

at[1] (ăt, unemphat. *a*t), *prep.* Particle expressing exact, approximate, or vague position (*at York, at school, at dinner*) or time of day (*at one o'clock*); ~ *that,* at that estimate, moreover.

ăt[2] (*or* aht) *n.* Small coin of Laos, $\frac{1}{100}$ of a kip.

A.T.A.(S.) *abbrev.* Air Transport Auxiliary (Service).

Atală′nta (ă-). (Gk legend) Huntress and athlete; she required all her suitors to run a race with her and killed them if they lost; but Milanion (or Hippomenes) won the race by throwing down three golden apples given to him by Aphrodite, which were so beautiful that Atalanta stopped to pick them up.

Atatürk (ă′t*a*tẽrk), Kemal (*c* 1880–1938). Turkish nationalist leader; first president of the republic 1923–38; known first as Mustapha Kemal, then as Kemal Pasha; took surname Atatürk in 1934. [Turk., = 'father-Turk']

ă′tavĭsm *n.* Resemblance to remote ancestors, reversion to earlier type. **ătavĭ′stĭc** *adj.* **ătavĭ′stĭcally̆** *adv.* [L *atavus* great-grandfather's grandfather]

ată′xĭa *n.* Irregularity of animal functions; *locomotor* ~, disease (*tabes dorsalis*) causing loss of control of co-ordinated movement by destruction of the sensory nerves concerned. **ată′xĭc** *adj.*

A.T.C. *abbrev.* Air Training Corps.

A′tė (ā- *or* ah-). (Gk myth.) Goddess of evil, who incites men to wickedness and strife.

ătĕ′lier (-yā) *n.* Workshop, studio.

a tĕ′mpō (ah). (mus.) In the previous tempo. [It., = 'in time']

A′ten, A′ton (ah-). Name by which the sun was worshipped in ancient Egypt, esp. in reign of AKHNATEN.

Athanā′sĭus (ă-), St. (*c* 296–373). Bishop of Alexandria. Doctor of the Church. **Athanā′sian** (-sh*a*n) *adj.* Of Athanasius; ~ *Creed,* that beginning 'Quicunque vult' (L, = 'Whosoever will'), prob. composed not by Athanasius but by Caesarius, bishop of Arles in 6th c.

ā′thėĭsm *n.* Disbelief in the existence of God or gods; godlessness. **ā′thėĭst** *n.* **āthėĭ′stĭc** *adj.*

A′thelstan (ă-) (*c* 894–939). King of the West Saxons 925–39; grandson of Alfred the Great.

Athėnae′um (ă-). 1. (Rom. antiq.) College of rhetoric and poetry, founded at Rome *c* A.D. 133 by the Emperor Hadrian. 2. (also ~ *Club*) London club, founded 1824 as an association of men of distinction in literature, art, and learning. [L, f. Gk *Athēnaion* temple of ATHENE]

Athē′nė. (Gk myth.) Goddess of wisdom, industry, and war, identified with the Roman Minerva; she sprang fully grown and armed from the brain of her father, Zeus; her emblem was an owl.

A′thėns (ă-, -z). (Gk *Athenai*) Leading city of ancient Greece; capital of modern Greece. **Athē′nĭan** *adj.* & *n.*

athĩr′st *pred. adj.* Thirsty; eager (*for*).

ă′thlēte *n.* One who competes or excels in physical exercises; ~'*s foot,* tinea of the foot, esp. attacking skin between toes.

ăthlĕ′tĭc *adj.* Pertaining to athletes; physically powerful. **ăthlĕ′tĭcs** *n.pl.* Physical exercises; athletic sports (comprising, in organized sport, running, jumping, throwing, walking, hurdling, and steeplechasing). **athlĕ′tĭcism** *n.*

A′thŏs (ă-), Mount. Peninsula projecting into the Aegean Sea from Macedonia, occupied since the Middle Ages by various com-

munities of monks. **Athō'an** *adj.* **A'thonīte** (ă-) *adj.* & *n.*

athwar't (-ort) *adv.* Across from side to side (usu. obliquely). ~ *prep.* Across; ~*-hawse*, (of ship) across stem of another ship at anchor.

Atlă'ntĭc *adj.* Of, adjoining the Atlantic Ocean; ~ *Ocean*, great ocean lying between Europe and Africa on E. and America on W.; (orig.) sea near the NW. coast of Africa. ~ *n.* Atlantic Ocean; *Battle of the* ~, German offensive against Allied Atlantic shipping during the war of 1939–45; ~ *Charter*, declaration of eight common principles in international relations, drawn up at a conference in mid-Atlantic in Aug. 1941 by Winston Churchill and President Franklin D. Roosevelt on behalf of U.K. and U.S. and endorsed by other nations at war with Germany, Italy, and Japan; ~ *Pact*, agreement (1949) to ensure defence of countries with sea-boards on N. Atlantic. [f. ATLAS[2]]

Atlă'ntĭs. (Gk legend) Fabled island in the ocean W. of the Pillars of Hercules; it was beautiful and prosperous, the seat of an empire which dominated part of Europe and Africa, but was overwhelmed by the sea because of the impiety of its inhabitants.

A'tlas[1] (ă-). (Gk legend) One of the Titans, who was punished for revolting against Zeus by being made to support the heavens with his head and hands; acc. to another legend Perseus, with the aid of Medusa's head, turned him into a mountain (the ~ *Mountains* of N. Africa).

ă'tlas[2] (ă-) *n.* 1. Collection of maps in a volume, so called from the use of a figure of ATLAS[1] supporting the heavens as a frontispiece. 2. Size of drawing-paper (26 × 33 in. (660 × 838 mm)). 3. Uppermost vertebra of backbone, supporting the skull.

ă'tmosphēre *n.* Gaseous envelope surrounding a heavenly body, esp. the envelope of air surrounding the earth, which consists of gases (nitrogen, oxygen, argon, carbon dioxide, helium, and others) and water vapour, and is rarer as distance from the earth increases; air (of a place); mental or moral environment.

ătmosphĕ'rĭc *adj.* ~ *pressure*, pressure of the column of air above a given point, equivalent on the earth's surface to about 760 mm of mercury, but decreasing with increasing height above the earth.

ătmosphĕ'rĭcs *n.pl.* Atmospheric disturbances of electrical origin causing interference in telecommunications; crackling or other interference so caused.

at. no. *abbrev.* Atomic number.

ă'toll (*or* atŏ'l) *n.* Ring-shaped coral reef enclosing lagoon. [Malay]

ă'tom *n.* 1. Body too small to be divided; minute portion, small thing. 2. (chem.) Smallest particle of an element that cannot be further subdivided without destroying its identity, regarded as consisting of a minute central positively charged nucleus in which almost all the mass is concentrated, and a number of negative electrons arranged round the nucleus; ~ *bomb*, = ATOMIC bomb.

atŏ'mĭc *adj.* Of atoms; of, using, concerned with, atomic energy or weapons; ~ *bomb*, bomb deriving its destructive power from ~ *energy*, energy

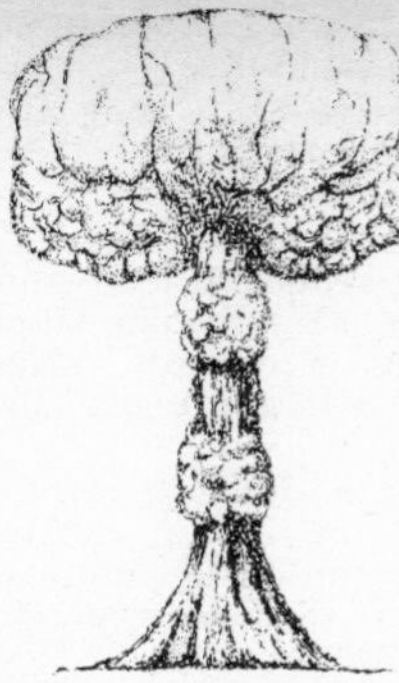

ATOM BOMB

released by fission of atomic nuclei of certain heavy elements such as uranium 235 or plutonium or by the fusion of light nuclei; ~ *mass*, mass of an atom measured in units based (since 1960) on one-twelfth of the mass of the carbon-12 atom; ~ *number*, (abbrev. at. no.) number of unit positive charges carried by the nucleus of an atom of an element, number determining the position of the element in the periodic table; ~ *theory*, theory that elements consist of atoms of definite relative weight and that atoms of different elements unite with one another in fixed proportions; (philos.) atomism; (*international*) ~ *time*, standard of time based on scale obtained by using continuously-running quartz clocks calibrated in terms of the caesium frequency standard; ~ *weight*, (abbrev. at. wt) = atomic mass (see above). **atŏ'mĭcallȳ** *adv.*

ă'tomĭsm *n.* (philos.) Theory that all matter consists of minute indivisible particles. **ă'tomĭst** *n.* **ătomĭ'stĭc** *adj.*

ă'tomīze *v.t.* Reduce to atoms. **ă'tomīzer** *n.* Instrument for reducing liquids to a fine spray.

ă'tomȳ *n.* (archaic) Atom, tiny being.

Aton: see ATEN.

atō'nal *adj.* (mus.) Not conforming to any system of key or mode. **ătonă'lĭtȳ** *n.*

atō'ne *v.i.* Make amends; ~ *for*, expiate. **atō'nement** *n.* *the A~*, expiation of man's sin by Christ; *Day of A~*: see YOM KIPPUR.

atŏ'nĭc *adj.* Unaccented; (path.) wanting tone. ~ *n.* Unaccented word (esp. in Gk gram.).

ătrabĭ'lĭous *adj.* Affected by black bile; melancholy; acrimonious. [L *atra bilis* black bile, transl. of Gk *melagkholia* MELANCHOLY]

A'trėūs (ā-). (Gk legend) King of Argos, who set the flesh of his brother Thyestes' children before their father at a banquet in revenge because Thyestes had seduced his wife; he was himself murdered by Aegisthus.

ā'trĭum *n.* (pl. *-ia*, *-iums*). 1. Central court of Roman house. 2. Covered portico, esp. before church door. 3. Either of the two upper cavities (*left* and *right* ~) of the heart into which the veins pour the blood.

atrō'cious (-sh*us*) *adj.* Extremely wicked; very bad. **atrō'ciouslȳ** *adv.*

atrŏ'cĭtȳ *n.* Atrocious deed; bad blunder; (colloq.) hideous object.

ă'trophȳ *n.* Wasting away through imperfect nourishment or lack of use. ~ *v.* Waste away.

ă'tropine (-ēn) *n.* White crystal-like alkaloid prepared from *Atropa belladonna* (deadly nightshade) and used to dilate the pupil of the eye or to relieve pain. [f. ATROPOS]

A'tropŏs (ă-). (Gk myth.) Eldest of the three Fates, who cut the thread of human life with her shears. [Gk, = 'inflexible']

A.T.S. *abbrev.* Auxiliary Territorial Service (now W.R.A.C.).

ă'tta *n.* Common wheaten flour or meal of India.

ă'ttaboy *int.* (orig. U.S.) Exclamation expressing encouragement or admiration.

attă'ch *v.* Fasten, join; attribute (importance etc. *to*); adhere, be incident *to*; seize by legal authority; bind in friendship, make devoted. **attă'chment** *n.* (esp.) ~ *of earnings*, court order by which employer is required to make deductions from employee's wages for the payment of certain debts etc.

attaché (-ă'shā) *n.* Junior official attached to ambassador's suite; military or naval officer connected with embassy in a foreign country in order to report on military or naval affairs; ~ *case*, small rectangular valise for carrying documents etc.

attă'ck *v.* Take the initiative in fighting; act destructively on; criticize adversely; (mus.) perform with precision and clarity. ~ *n.* Act of attacking; bout of illness etc.

attai'n *v.* Reach, gain, accomplish; ~ *to*, arrive at. **attai'nment** *n.* Attaining; thing attained; (pl.) personal accomplishments.

attai'nder *n.* (hist.) Consequences of sentence of death or outlawry (loss of civil rights, forfeiture of estate, etc.); *bill of* ~, legislative act inflicting attainder without judicial trial.

attai'nt *v.t.* Subject to attainder (hist.); affect; infect; sully.

ă'ttar *n.* Fragrant essential oil distilled from flowers, esp. roses. [ult. f. Arab. *'iṭr* perfume]

attĕ'mper *v.t.* Qualify by admixture; modify; temper.

attĕ'mpt *v.t.* Try; try to master. ~ *n.* Attempting; endeavour.

attĕ'nd *v.* 1. Turn the mind, apply oneself (*to*). 2. Be present (at); go regularly to (school, church, etc.). 3. Wait upon; serve; escort; accompany.

attĕ'ndance *n.* Attending (ATTEND *v.* 2, 3); number of persons present; ~ *centre*, centre at which boys under 17 are required to attend when found guilty of offences for which older persons could be sent to prison.

attĕ'ndant *adj.* & *n.* (Person) attending (another).

attĕ'ntion *n.* Act or faculty of attending (ATTEND *v.* 1); consideration, care; (pl.) ceremonious politeness; courtship, addresses; *at* ~, (mil.) formal attitude of troops standing on parade as dist. from *at* EASE or EASY; (as command) order to stand thus.

attĕ'ntĭve *adj.* Giving or paying attention. **attĕ'ntĭvelȳ** *adv.* **attĕ'ntĭvenėss** *n.*

attĕ'nūāte *v.t.* 1. Make slender or thin; reduce in force or value. 2. (radio etc.) Reduce amplitude of (signal or current). **attĕnūā'tion** *n.* **attĕ'nūate** *adj.* Slender; rarefied.

attĕ'st *v.* Testify, certify; put on oath or solemn declaration; *attested*, (of cattle) approved by authority as free from disease. **ăttėstā'tion** *n.*

A'ttĭc[1] (ă-) *adj.* Of Attica; ~ *dialect*, Greek spoken by ancient Athenians; ~ *order*, square column of any of the five orders (*see* ORDER); ~ *salt, wit*, refined wit. ~ *n.* Attic dialect.

ă'ttĭc[2] *n.* 1. (archit.) Structure consisting of small order placed above another of greater height. 2. (Room in) highest storey of building, usu. immediately under the roof and not having a flat ceiling. [Fr. *attique* upper part of house, so called from Attic order of architecture]

A'ttĭca (ă-). District of ancient Greece of which Athens was the capital.

ă'ttĭcism *n.* Style, idiom of Athens; extreme elegance of speech; attachment to Athens.

A'ttĭla (ă-) (d. A.D. 453). King of the Huns, known as the 'scourge of God'; ravaged the Eastern Roman Empire (445–50); after making peace with Theodosius invaded the Western Empire and was defeated at Châlons by Aëtius in 451.

attīr'e *v.t.* & *n.* Dress, array.

A'ttĭs, A'tȳs (ă-). (myth.) Youthful consort of CYBELE; his death was mourned for two days in the spring, and his recovery (when his spirit passed into a pine-tree and violets sprang up from his blood) then celebrated.

ă'ttĭtūde *n.* 1. Posture of body; settled behaviour, as indicating opinion; ~ *of mind*, settled mode of thinking. 2. Angular relation between aircraft's or spacecraft's axis and the wind, course, etc.

ăttĭtū'dĭnīze *v.i.* Practise attitudes; act, speak, etc., affectedly.

A'ttlee (ă-), Clement Richard, 1st Earl Attlee (1883–1967). British statesman; Labour prime minister 1945–51.

attor'ney (-têr-) *n.* One appointed to act for another in business in legal matters; *power of* ~, formal instrument of such appointment; *A~-General*, chief legal officer empowered to act in all cases in which the State is a party (in U.K. usu. a member of the House of Commons, appointed on advice of Government and resigning with it; in U.S. appointed by president).

attră'ct *v.t.* Draw to itself or oneself; excite pleasurable emotions of; draw forth and fix on oneself (attention etc.) **attră'ction** *n.* Attracting; thing that attracts. **attră'ctive** *adj.* **attră'ctĭvelў** *adv.* **attră'ctĭvenėss** *n.*

attrĭ'būte *v.t.* ~ *to*, consider as caused by, resulting or originating from, made or composed by; consider as belonging or appropriate *to*. **ăttrĭbū'tion** *n.* **ă'ttrĭbūte** *n.* Quality ascribed to anything; material object regarded as appropriate to person or office; characteristic quality; (gram.) attributive word.

attrĭ'bụtive *adj.* Assigning an attribute to a subject; (gram.) expressing an attribute, qualifying. ~ *n.* Word denoting an attribute. **attrĭ'būtĭvelў** *adv.*

attrĭ'tion *n.* Friction; abrasion; wearing out; weakening by harassment.

attū'ne *v.t.* Bring into musical accord; adapt; tune.

A'twōōd's machi'ne (ă-, -z, -shēn). Apparatus, consisting essentially of a nearly frictionless wheel which carries a cord with equal weights suspended from its ends, designed to demonstrate the mechanical law that a body which is not disturbed by force continues to move with uniform speed in a straight line. [named after George *Atwood* (1745–1807), English mathematician]

at. wt *abbrev.* Atomic weight.

ātў'pĭcal *adj.* Not typical.

aubade (ōbahd) *n.* Music for singing or playing at dawn; morning concert. [Fr.]

Auber (ōbar̄), Daniel François Esprit (1782–1871). French musician, composer of operas.

aubergine (ō'berzhēn) *n.* Elongated, usu. purple, fruit of the egg-plant (*Solanum melongena*), used as a vegetable.

aubrietia, erron. **-retia** (-rē'-sha) *n.* Spring-flowering dwarf perennial plant of genus *Aubrieta* of mustard family, with flowers of colours ranging through purple, red, and blue. [after Claude *Aubriet* (d. 1743) French painter of flowers and animals]

au'burn *adj.* Reddish brown (usu. of hair).

Aubusson (ōbūsawn). Town in central France, famous since the 16th c., and esp. in the 18th, for the manufacture of tapestries and carpets.

A.U.C. *abbrev. Ab urbe condita* or *anno urbis conditae* (L, = from, in the year of, the founding of the city, i.e. Rome).

Au'ckland. Largest city and chief seaport of New Zealand; also, the province comprising the northern part of North Island.

au courant (ō kōōrahn). Acquainted *with* what is going on, well informed. [Fr.]

au'ction *n.* Public sale at which articles are sold to person making the highest bid; *Dutch* ~, sale at which price is reduced until a buyer is found; ~ *bridge*: see BRIDGE². ~ *v.t.* Sell (*off*) by auction.

auctioneer' *n.* One who conducts auctions. ~ *v.i.* Conduct auctions.

audā'cious (-shus) *adj.* Daring, bold; impudent. **audā'ciouslў** *adv.* **audā'ciousnėss, audă'cĭtў** *ns.*

Au'den, Wystan Hugh (1907–73).

English-born poet and dramatist.

au'dĭble *adj.* That can be heard. **au'dĭblȳ** *adv.* **audĭbĭ'lĭtȳ** *n.*

au'dĭence *n.* Hearing; formal interview; persons within hearing; group of listeners or spectators.

au'dĭō *adj.* Of (the reproduction of) sound; ~ *frequency*, (abbrev. A.F.) FREQUENCY perceived aurally; ~ *typing*, *typist*, (one) typing direct from tape or other recording; ~-*visual*, of, involving, both hearing and sight. ~ *n.* Reproduction of sound.

audiŏ'logȳ *n.* Science of hearing. **audiŏ'logist** *n.*

audiŏ'meter *n.* Instrument for measuring the sensitivity of the ear to sounds.

au'dĭt *n.* Official examination of accounts; periodical settlement of accounts between landlord and tenant; ~ *ale*, strong ale brewed in some colleges of Oxford and Cambridge, orig. for use on day of audit. ~ *v.t.* Examine (accounts) officially.

audĭ'tion *n.* Hearing; trial hearing of actor, singer, etc., seeking employment. ~ *v.* Test, be tested, by an audition.

au'dĭtor *n.* One who audits accounts.

audĭtor'ium *n.* Part of building occupied by audience.

au'dĭtorȳ *adj.* Of hearing. ~ *n.* Hearers, audience; auditorium.

Au'drey, St. (630?–679). Etheldreda, first abbess of Ely.

Au'dūbon, John James (1785–1851). Amer. naturalist and painter; author of 'Birds of America', engraved in aquatint (1827–38).

A.U.E.W. *abbrev.* Amalgamated Union of Engineering Workers.

au fait (ō fā). Conversant, instructed. [Fr.]

au fond (ō fawṅ). At bottom; basically. [Fr.]

Aug. *abbrev.* August.

Augē'an *adj.* Abominably filthy; resembling the stables of Augeas, legendary king of Elis, which were uncleansed for many years until Hercules, as one of his labours, accomplished the cleansing by diverting the river Alpheus through them.

au'ger (-g-) *n.* Tool for boring holes in wood, having a long shank with cutting edge and screw point, and handle at right angles.

aught (awt) *n.* Anything.

au'gment *n.* (gram.) Vowel prefixed to past tenses in the older Indo-European languages. **augmĕ'nt** *v.* Increase; prefix augment to. **augmĕ'ntėd** *adj.* (esp., mus., of an interval) Widened by a semitone. **augmentā'tion** *n.* Enlargment; addition; (mus.) repetition of a passage in notes longer than those of the original

augmĕ'ntatĭve *adj.* & *n.* Increasing; (gram.) (word or affix) increasing in force the idea of the original word; (mus.) lengthening of phrase by increasing the values of the notes.

au grand sérieux (ō grahṅ sĕrēēr). Quite seriously. [Fr.]

Au'gsburg (ow-). City of Bavaria; ~ *Confession*, statement of the Protestant position drawn up by Melanchthon for the Diet of 1530.

au'gur *n.* 1. (Rom. antiq.) Religious official who foretold future events by observing flight or notes of birds etc. 2. Soothsayer. ~ *v.* Forebode, anticipate; ~ *well*, *ill*, have good (bad) implications or

AUGSBURG

expectations *of*, *for*. **au'gūrў** *n*. Divination; omen; promise.

augŭ'st[1] *adj*. Majestic, venerable. **augŭ'stlў** *adv*. **augŭ'stnėss** *n*. [L *augustus* consecrated, venerable]

Au'gust[2]. 8th month of Gregorian (5th of Julian) calendar, with 31 days. [named after Rom. emperor AUGUSTUS]

Augŭ'stan *adj*. Of AUGUSTUS; ~ *Age*, period of literary eminence in the life of a nation, so called because Virgil, Horace, Ovid, etc., all flourished during Augustus' reign; in English literary history, the period of Pope and Addison.

Augŭ'stīne[1], St. (354–430). Doctor of the Church; son of a pagan father and Christian mother (St. Monica); was for a time attracted by Manichaeism, but baptized as a Christian 387; became bishop of Hippo in N. Africa, 391; defended Christianity in numerous writings, of which the best known are the 'City of God' ('Civitas Dei') and the autobiographical 'Confessions'; commemorated 28 Aug.

Augŭ'stīne[2], St. (d. 604). First archbishop of Canterbury; led mission to England from Rome and founded a monastery at Canterbury; commemorated in England 26 May, elsewhere 28 May.

Augustĭ'nĭan *adj*. Of St. AUGUSTINE[1] of Hippo; ~ *Canons*, order of R.C. canons regular, who adopted the 'rule of St. Augustine' (based largely on Augustine's writings but not formulated by him) in the 11th c.; ~ (or *Austin*) *Friars*, mendicant order founded *c* 1250 and observing the Augustinian rule.

Augŭ'stus (63 B.C.–A.D. 14). Gaius Octavius ('Octavian'), named Gaius Julius Caesar Octavianus after his adoption by Julius Caesar, his great-uncle; member of the 2nd triumvirate and first Roman emperor; the title of Augustus was conferred on him by senate and people in 27 B.C. and was borne by all subsequent Roman emperors.

auk *n*. Any of the Alcidae, a family of sea-birds which includes the guillemot, puffin, razor-bill, little auk (*Plautus alle*), and the great auk (*Pinguinus impennis*),

AUKS

formerly inhabiting N. Atlantic but extinct since mid-19th c.

auld *adj.* & *n.* (Sc.) Old.

au'lĭc *adj.* Pertaining to a court; *A~ Council*, official council of the emperor in the Holy Roman Empire, established by Maximilian I in 1499.

Au'lĭs. Ancient Greek town on Boeotian coast, where (in legend) the Greek fleet was detained by contrary winds before the Trojan War, and where Iphigenia was offered for sacrifice.

au'mbry̆ *n.* Closed recess in wall of church; (hist.) small cupboard.

au naturel (ō nătūrĕl). (Cooked) in the simplest way; uncooked. [Fr.]

aunt (ahnt) *n.* Father's or mother's sister; uncle's wife; (children's colloq.) unrelated woman who is a family friend; *A~ Sally*, game in which sticks or balls are thrown at wooden dummy (orig. at pipe in mouth of wooden woman's head); (fig.) any person or institution which becomes a mark of popular attack.

au'ntĭe, -ty̆ (ahn-) *n.* (colloq.) Aunt.

au pair (ō pār). (Person, esp. young girl) performing domestic duties in foreign country in return for hospitality etc. ~ *adv. phr.* [Fr.]

au pied de la lettre (ō pyā de lah lĕtr). Literally. [Fr.]

au'ra *n.* 1. Subtle emanation; atmosphere diffused by or attending a person etc. (esp. in mystical use as definite envelope of body or spirit). 2. (path.) Sensation as of cold air rising from part of body to head, premonitory symptom in epilepsy and hysterics. **au'ral**[1] *adj.*

au'ral[2] *adj.* Of, received by, the ear. **au'rally̆** *adv.*

Au'rangzēb (1618–1707). Mogul emperor of India, 1658–1707, a period of great wealth and splendour for the empire.

aurar: see EYRIR.

Aurē'lĭan. Lucius Domitius Aurelianus (*c* A.D. 212–75). Roman emperor, 270–5.

aurē'ola, au'rėōle *ns.* Celestial crown worn by martyrs, saints, virgins, etc.; pictorial representation of this in form of golden ring or disc painted behind and round head of wearer; halo, esp. that of the sun seen in eclipses. [L *aureola* (*corona*) golden crown]

aurėomy̆'cĭn *n.* Yellow crystalline antibiotic substance produced by the micro-organism *Streptomyces aureofaciens.*

au revoir (ō revwâr). (Goodbye) till we meet again. [Fr.]

au'rĭcle *n.* 1. External ear of animals; process shaped like lobe of ear. 2. Small appendage of the ATRIUM, sense 3.

aurĭ'cūla *n.* Species of Alpine primula, with ear-shaped leaf. [L *auris* ear]

aurĭ'cūlar *adj.* Pertaining to the ear; pertaining to auricle of the heart; ~ *confession*, confession made privately (in the ear of the priest).

aurĭ'ferous *adj.* Yielding gold.

Aurī'ga. The Wagoner or Charioteer, a northern constellation between Perseus and Gemini. [L]

Aurĭgnā'cian (-shan) *adj.* & *n.* (Of) a palaeolithic culture believed to have existed in France *c* 11,500–10,000 B.C. [f. *Aurignac* in Haute-Garonne, SW. France, where flint implements were found]

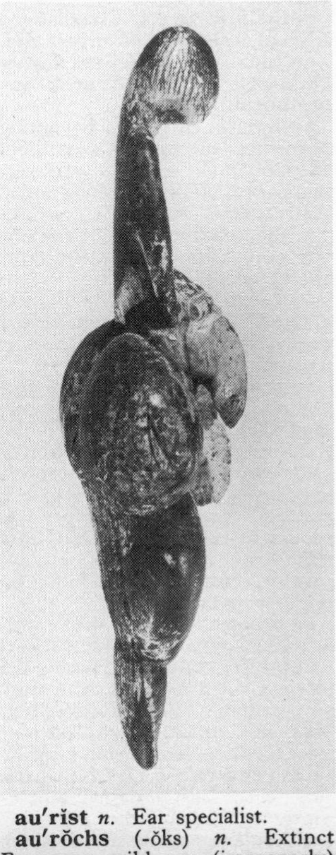

au'rĭst *n.* Ear specialist.

au'rŏchs (-ŏks) *n.* Extinct European wild ox; (improperly) European bison.

Aurōr'a[1]. (Rom. myth.) Goddess of the dawn, corresponding to the Greek Eos.

aurōr'a[2] *n.* (poet.) Dawn; ~ *australis*, phenomenon similar to aurora borealis, seen in southern latitudes; ~ *borealis*, luminous phenomenon, popularly called the *northern lights*, seen in northern latitudes esp. at night, usu. appearing as streamers of many colours ascending from above the northern horizon and supposed to be of electrical origin.

auscultā'tion *n.* Act of listening, esp. (med.) to movement of heart, lungs, etc. **auscŭ'ltatorў** *adj.*

au'spĭce *n.* Observation of birds for purpose of taking omens; (pl.) patronage. **auspĭ'cious** (-shus) *adj.* Of good omen; favourable; prosperous. **auspĭ'ciouslў** *adv.* **auspĭ'ciousnėss** *n.*

Au'ssĭe (*or* ŏ'zĭ) *n.* Australian, orig. of Australian troops in the war of 1914–18.

Au'stėn, Jane (1775–1817). English author of six novels: 'Pride and Prejudice', 'Northanger Abbey', 'Sense and Sensibility', 'Mansfield Park', 'Emma', and 'Persuasion'.

austēr'e *adj.* Harsh; stern; stringently moral; severely simple. **austēr'elў** *adv.* **austēr'enėss** *n.* **austĕ'rĭtў** *n.* Quality of being austere; severity, austere or ascetic practice; applied esp. during the war of 1939–45 to clothes etc. in which non-essentials were reduced to a minimum as a war-time measure of economy.

Au'sterlĭtz (ow-). (Czech *Slavkov*) town in Moravia, scene in 1805 of Napoleon's defeat of the Austrians and Russians.

Au'stĭn (*or* ŏ-), Alfred (1835–1913). English minor poet, poet laureate from 1896.

Au'stĭn Frī'ars (-z; *or* ŏ-): see AUGUSTINIAN Friars.

au'stral *adj.* Southern; of Australia or Australasia. [L *Auster*, the south wind]

Australā'sia (-zha; *or* ŏ-). Term used loosely to include Australia and the islands scattered over the

SW. Pacific. **Australā'sian** *adj.* & *n.*

Austrā'lia (*or* ŏ-). Continent of S. hemisphere in the SW. Pacific; federal commonwealth, member State of the British Commonwealth. The existence of a *Terra Australis* ('southern land') was known in Europe in the 16th c.; from 1606 onwards its W. coast was explored by the Dutch and in 1642 Tasman proved that it was an island; it was visited by an Englishman, William Dampier, in 1699; in 1770 Capt. James Cook, on the first of his three voyages, landed at Botany Bay on the E. side and formally took possession of New South Wales; British colonization began in 1788 (also the settling of convicts at Port Jackson, discontinued in 1840); in 1901 the six colonies (New South Wales, Victoria, Queensland, South Australia, Western Australia, and Tasmania) federated as sovereign states of the *Commonwealth of* ~, which also administers Northern Territory, Capital Territory (site of the federal capital, Canberra), and certain areas outside the continent.

Austrā'lian (*or* ŏ-) *adj.* Of Australia; ~ *Capital Territory*, federal territory in New South Wales consisting of two enclaves ceded by New South Wales, one in 1911 to contain Canberra, the other in 1915 containing Jervis Bay. ~ *n.* Australian person.

Au'strĭa (*or* ŏ-). German-speaking country of central Europe, which became a republic in 1918; formerly it was the nucleus of the Austro-Hungarian Empire; for much of its earlier history it was a mark (the Ostmark or eastern mark) of the German Empire, an outpost of defence against Slavs and Magyars; it became a duchy in 1156 and later the seat of the Habsburg emperors; in 1918 the empire was divided between Hungary, Poland, Czechoslovakia, Italy, Rumania, Yugoslavia, and Austria itself; in March 1938 Austria was forcibly annexed to the Third Reich; it was liberated from Nazi rule in 1945; capital, Vienna. **Au'strĭan** *adj.* & *n.* (Native) of Austria.

au'tarchy̆[1] (-k-) *n.* Absolute sovereignty, despotism. [Gk *autarkhia* (*arkho* rule)]

au'tarchy̆[2] (-k-), **au'tarky̆** *ns.* Economic self-sufficiency of a political unit. [Gk *autarkeia* (*arkeō* suffice)]

authĕ'ntĭc *adj.* Reliable, trustworthy; of undisputed origin; ~ *mode*, (mus., of eccles. modes) having their sounds comprised within an octave from the final. **authĕ'ntĭcally̆** *adv.* **authĕntĭ'cĭty̆** *n.*

authĕ'ntĭcāte *v.t.* Establish the truth or authorship of: make valid.

au'thor *n.* (fem. *au'thorĕss*) Originator; writer of book etc. **au'thorshĭp** *n.*

authorĭtār'ian *adj.* Favouring obedience to authority as opp. to individual liberty; of, pertaining to, a dictatorship. ~ *n.* Authoritarian person.

authŏ'rĭtatĭve *adj.* Possessing or claiming authority. **authŏ'rĭtatĭvely̆** *adv.*

authŏ'rĭty̆ *n.* Power or right to enforce obedience; delegated power; person etc. having authority; personal influence; expert.

au'thorīze *v.t.* Sanction; give ground for; give authority to; *Authorized Version*, (of the Bible) the English translation of 1611.

au'tĭsm *n.* Morbid absorption in fantasy; condition, esp. in children, preventing proper response to environment. **autĭ'stĭc** *adj.*

auto-, aut- *prefix.* Self-, by one's or its own agency.

au'tobahn *n.* (pl. *-nen*, *-ns*). In Germany, a motorway. [Ger.]

autobīŏ'graphy̆ *n.* Writing the story of one's own life; the story so written. **autobīogră'phĭc, -ĭcal** *adjs.* **autobīŏ'grapher** *n.*

au'tocar *n.* (rare) Motor-car.

autŏ'chthon (-k-) *n.* (usu. pl.; *-ones*, *-ons*) Original inhabitants. **autŏ'chthonous** *adj.*

au'toclāve *n.* Vessel in which chemical reactions take place at high temperatures under pressure;

apparatus for sterilizing by steam at high pressure. ~ *v.*

autŏ'cracy̆ *n.* Absolute government.

au'tocrăt *n.* Absolute ruler; dictatorial overbearing person; *A~ of all the Russias*, (hist.) title of the Tsar. **autocră'tic** *adj.* **autocră'tically̆** *adv.*

au'tocrŏss *n.* Cross-country racing in motor vehicles.

au'to-da-fé' (-dah-fā) *n.* Sentence of the Inquisition; execution of this, esp. burning of a heretic. [Port., = 'act of faith']

autogīr'ō *n.* Type of aeroplane, or gyroplane, deriving its lift mainly from a system of freely rotating horizontal wings and capable of landing in a very small space. [trade-name]

au'togrăph (*or* -ahf) *n.* Author's own manuscript; person's own handwriting, esp. signature; document signed by its author, as dist. from HOLOGRAPH, one wholly written in his hand (freq. attrib., as ~ *letter*). ~ *v.t.* Write one's signature on or in; sign. **autogră'phic, -ical** *adjs.* **autogră'phically̆** *adv.*

auto-immū'nity̆ *n.* (med.) Allergy of the body to its own secretions of antibodies or lymphoid cells. **auto-immū'ne** *adj.*

au'tomāte *v.* Apply automation (to).

automă'tic *adj.* Working of itself, without direct human actuation; mechanical; unconscious; necessary, inevitable; ~ *control*, device enabling machine to maintain a predetermined temperature, pressure, speed, etc., without intervention of operator; ~ *pilot*, similar device in aircraft for maintaining a set course or height; ~ *pistol*, *rifle*, firearm which, after each shot is exploded, by gas pressure or force of recoil automatically ejects the empty case, loads another into the chamber, and fires, repeating this movement until the ammunition in the mechanism is exhausted or pressure on the trigger is released; ~ *transmission*, system in motor vehicle in which gears engage automatically according to the speed of the vehicle or by means of a torque converter. ~ *n.* Automatic pistol; machine, tool, etc., operated automatically. **automă'tically̆** *adv.*

automā'tion *n.* (eng., orig. U.S.) Completely automatic control of a manufactured product through a number of successive stages; use of automatic mechanical or electronic devices.

autŏ'matism *n.* 1. Involuntary action; (psychol.) action performed unconsciously or subconsciously. 2. Doctrine that movements or actions of organic beings are mechanical, not resulting from volition.

autŏ'maton *n.* Mechanical device with concealed motive power; person whose actions are mechanical, following a customary routine.

au'tomobile (-ēl; *or* -ē'l) *n.* (chiefly U.S.) Motor-car.

autonŏ'mic *adj.* (physiol.) Of that part of the nervous system (~ or *involuntary nervous system*) which functions more or less independently of the will, comprising the sympathetic and parasympathetic nervous systems.

autŏ'nomous *adj.* 1. Self-governing. 2. (physiol., path.) Independent of the usual processes which regulate the growth of an organism. **autŏ'nomously̆** *adv.*

autŏ'nomy̆ *n.* Right of self-government; freedom of the will; self-governing community.

au'topista *n.* In Spain and Spanish-speaking countries, a motorway. [Span.]

autŏ'psy̆ (*or* aw'-) *n.* Personal inspection; post-mortem examination. **autŏ'ptic, -ical** *adjs.*

au'toroute (-rōōt) *n.* In France, a motorway. [Fr.]

autostra'da (-ah-) *n.* (pl. *-dė*, *-das*). In Italy, a motorway. [It.]

auto-suggĕ'stion *n.* Hypnotic suggestion proceeding from the subject himself.

au'toty̆pe *n.* Photographic printing process for reproducing in monochrome. ~ *v.t.* Reproduce by autotype.

au'tumn (-m) *n.* Season of year between summer and winter, popularly reckoned in N. hemisphere as comprising the months September, October, and November, but astronomically as lasting from autumnal equinox (22 or 23 Sept.) to winter solstice (21 or 22 Dec.); (fig.) season of incipient decay. **autŭ'mnal** (-m-n-) *adj.* Of autumn.

Auvergne (ōvārn). Ancient province of S. central France.

auxĭ'liarў (awgzĭlya-) *adj.* Helpful; subsidiary; (gram., of verbs) serving to form tenses, moods, voices, of other verbs. ~ *n.* Assistant; (esp. pl.) foreign troops serving with another country in war; (naval) vessel auxiliary to fighting vessels, as tanker, supply ship, etc.

A.V. *abbrev.* Authorized Version (of the Bible).

avai'l *v.* Be of use or assistance (to); help, benefit. ~ *n.* Use, profit.

avai'lable *adj.* At one's disposal, at hand; capable of being used. **availabĭ'lĭtў** *n.*

ă'valanche (-ahnsh) *n.* Mass of snow, rock, and ice, falling down mountain (also fig.); ~ *cone*, pile of material deposited by an avalanche; ~ *wind*, wind produced by avalanche, freq. causing further destruction.

A'valon (ă-). In the Arthurian legend, the place to which ARTHUR[1] was conveyed after death; (Welsh myth.) kingdom of the dead.

avant-garde (ăvahn-) *n.* Pioneers or innovators, esp. in any art in a particular period (freq. attrib.) [Fr.]

A'var (ah- *or* ā-) *n.* Member of a Turkic people prominent in SE. Europe in 6th–9th centuries; in the 7th c. their kingdom extended from the Black Sea to the Adriatic; finally subdued by Charlemagne. ~ *adj.*

ă'varice *n.* Greed for gain, cupidity. **ăvarĭ'cious** (-shus) *adj.* **ăvarĭ'ciouslў** *adv.*

ava'st (-ahst) *int.* (naut.) Stop, cease. [Du. *houd vast* hold fast]

ă'vatar *n.* (Hinduism) Descent to earth and incarnation of a deity.

avau'nt *int.* (archaic, joc.) Begone.

avdp. *abbrev.* Avoirdupois.

a'vė (ah-; *or* -vā) *int.* Hail, welcome; *A~ Maria, A~ Mary* (= Hail, Mary!), the angelic salutation to the Virgin (Luke 1 : 28), combined with that of Elizabeth (1 : 42), used as a devotional recitation, together with a prayer to the Virgin. ~ *n.* Utterance of 'ave'. [L]

A'veburў (āvb-). Village in Wiltshire, site of a very large prehistoric stone circle.

avĕ'nge (-j) *v.t.* Inflict retribution on behalf of; exact retribution for.

A'ventīne (ă-). Most southerly of the seven hills of Rome.

avĕ'nturine *n.* Brownish glass with copper crystals, first manufactured near Venice; quartz, spangled with mica or haematite, resembling this. [It. *avventura* chance (from its accidental discovery)]

ă'vėnūe *n.* Way of approach; approach to house bordered by trees; roadway with trees etc. at regular intervals; wide street.

aver' *v.t.* Assert, affirm.

ă'verage *n.* 1. Arithmetical mean; ordinary standard; generally prevailing degree etc.; (cricket) mean number of runs per completed innings of batsman; mean cost in runs per wicket of bowler. 2. Damage to or loss of insured ship or cargo; ~ *adjustment*, apportionment of liability resulting from this. ~ *adj.* Estimated by average; of usual standard. ~ *v.t.* Estimate average or general standard of; amount on an average to. [Arab. *'awārīya* damaged goods]

Aver'nus. Lake in Campania, Italy, filling crater of an extinct volcano, and regarded by the ancients as the entrance to the infernal regions.

Avĕ'rroës (-rōĕz). Abul Walid Muhammad ben Ahmed ibn Rushd (1126–98), Muslim doctor born at Cordova, philosopher, and author of a famous commentary on Aristotle.

avẽr'se *adj.* Opposed, disinclined (*to, from*); unwilling.

avẽr'sion *n.* Dislike, unwillingness; object of dislike.

avẽr't *v.t.* Turn away; ward off.

Avĕ'sta *n.* Collection of sacred Zoroastrian writings. **Avĕ'stan, Avĕ'stic** *adjs.* & *ns.* (Of) the ancient E. Iranian language in which the Avesta is written.

ā'viarў *n.* Large cage or building for keeping birds.

āviā'tion *n.* Operation of heavier-than-air aircraft. **ā'viātor** *n.*

Avĭcĕ'nna (ă-). Abu ibn Sina (980–1037), Persian physician, philosopher, and commentator on Aristotle.

ă'vĭd *adj.* Eager, greedy. **ă'vĭdlў** *adv.* **avĭ'dĭtў** *n.*

Avignon (ăvēnyawṅ). City on river Rhône, in S. France, to which Clement V removed the papal seat in 1308; it remained there until 1377, and after the papal schism in 1378 two anti-popes, Clement VII and Benedict XIII, resided there; the latter was expelled in 1408, but the city remained in papal possession until 1791.

avo (ah'vōō) *n.* $\frac{1}{100}$ of a pataca.

ăvoca'dō (-kah-) *n.* (also ~ *pear*) Succulent pear-shaped fruit, a drupe with soft-coated seed, borne by the tropical Amer. and W. Indian tree *Persea gratissima.* [Span. *avocado* advocate, corrupt. of Mex. name]

ăvocā'tion *n.* Minor occupation; vocation, calling.

ă'vocėt *n.* Wading bird with long upturned beak (*Recurvirostra avosetta*).

Avoga'drō (ă-, -gah-), Amadeo (1776–1856). Italian physicist; *~'s law*, hypothesis that equal volumes of all gases at the same temperature and pressure contain equal numbers of molecules; *~'s number*, number of molecules in the gramme-molecular weight of any gas; value, $6{\cdot}02 \times 10^{23}$.

avoi'd *v.t.* Shun, refrain from; evade, escape; (law) quash. **avoi'dable** *adj.* **avoi'dablў** *adv.* **avoi'dance** *n.*

avoirdupois (ăverdūpoi'z), *n.* System of weights used for all goods except precious metals and stones, and medicine; weight, heaviness. [corrupt. of Fr. *avoir de pois* goods of weight]

A'von[1] (ā-). River, flowing through Warwickshire, a tributary of the Severn (*Swan of ~*, Ben Jonson's sobriquet for Shakespeare, who was born at Stratford-upon-Avon); also, one of several other English rivers.

A'von[2] (ā-). County of SW. England (since April 1974), comprising Bath and Bristol and parts

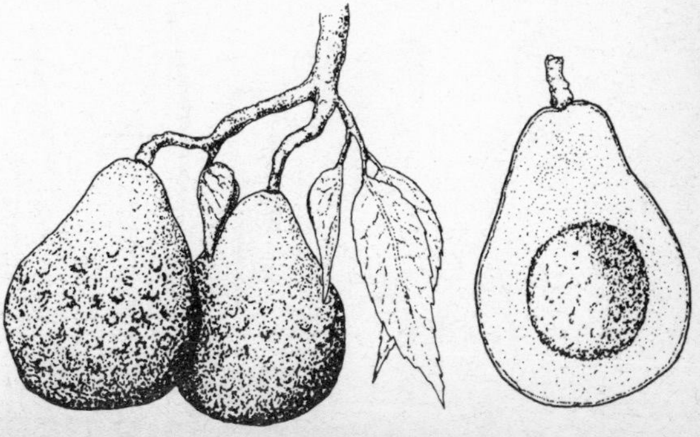

AVOCADO

of the former counties of Gloucester and Somerset.

avou'ch *v.* Guarantee; affirm; confess.

avow' *v.t.* Admit, confess. **avow'al** *n.* **avow'ėdlў** *adv.*

avŭ'ncūlar *adj.* Of, resembling, an uncle.

awai't (*a-*) *v.t.* Wait for.

awā'ke (*a-*) *v.* (past t. *awōke*; past part. *awōke*, *awāked*). Cease to sleep; rouse from sleep. ~ *pred. adj.* Not asleep; vigilant. **awā'ken** *v.* Awake.

awar'd (*aw*ôrd) *v.t.* Order to be given as payment, prize, etc.; grant, assign. ~ *n.* Judicial decision; payment, penalty, assigned by this; prize; grant.

awār'e (*a-*) *pred. adj.* Conscious, not ignorant (*of*, *that*). **awār'eness** *n.*

awa'sh (*awŏ-*) *pred. adj.* Flush with or washed by the waves.

away' (*a-*) *adv.* To or at a distance; on opponent's ground; constantly, continuously. ~ *adj.* (of game) Played on opponent's ground. ~ *n.* (football pools) Win in an away match.

awe *n.* Reverential fear. ~ *v.t.* Inspire with awe. **aw'esome** *adj.* **aw'estrĭcken, aw'estrŭck** *adjs.* Struck with awe.

aweigh (*awā'*) *adv.* (of anchor) Just raised from bottom in weighing.

aw'ful *adj.* Inspiring awe; solemnly impressive; (colloq.) notable in its kind (usu. of thing or person disliked). **aw'fullў** *adv.* (esp. colloq.) Extremely. **aw'fulnėss** *n.*

awhee'l (*a-*) *adv.* On wheels, riding (esp. cycle).

awhī'le (*a-*) *adv.* For a short time.

aw'kward *adj.* Ill-adapted for use; hard to deal with; clumsy. **aw'kwardlў** *adv.* **aw'kwardnėss** *n.*

awl *n.* Small pointed tool for piercing holes in leather, wood, etc., esp. that used by shoemakers.

awn *n.* Stiff bristle-like process terminating grain-sheath of barley, oats, etc. **awned** (-nd) *adj.*

aw'nĭng *n.* Sheet of canvas etc. stretched on framework as protection from sun etc.

A.W.O.L. *abbrev.* Absent without leave.

awry (*arī'*) *adv.* & *pred. adj.* Crookedly; amiss.

ăxe *n.* Metal tool for chopping, cleaving, etc., with wooden handle; drastic reduction of public expenditure. ~ *v.t.* Cut down (personnel, expenses, etc.); put an end to (project).

ă'xĭal *adj.* Forming, belonging to, an axis. **ă'xĭallў** *adv.*

ă'xĭl *n.* Upper angle between leaf and stem it springs from, or between branch and trunk.

ăxĭ'llarў *adj.* 1. Of the armpit. 2. (bot.) In, growing from, the axil (~ *bud*).

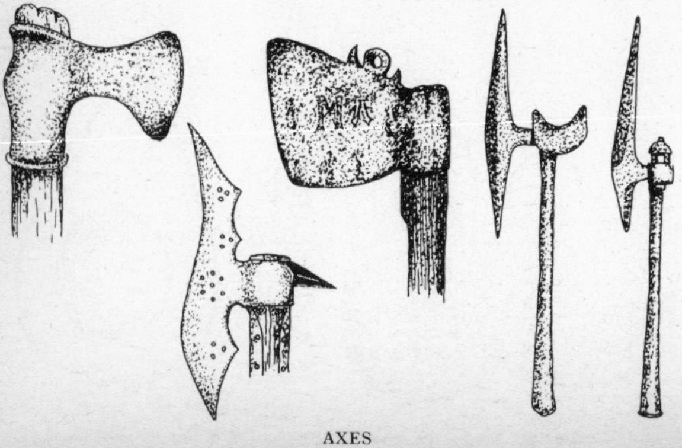

AXES

ă'xiom *n.* Self-evident truth; established principle; maxim; (geom.) self-evident theorem. **ăxiomă'tic** *adj.* **ăxiomă'ticallў** *adv.*

ă'xis *n.* (pl. *axēs*). 1. Line about which a body rotates (~ *of equator*, that between N. and S. Poles, round which the earth turns daily); straight line from end to end of a body. 2. (math.) Line dividing a regular figure symmetrically; line by revolution about which a plane figure is conceived as generating a solid. 3. (bot.) Stem or shoot; *floral* ~, that part of a shoot which bears the floral organs, receptacle 4. (anat.) Second cervical vertebra, on which the head turns 5. (optics) Ray passing through centre of eye or lens or falling perpendicularly on it. 6. *Rome–Berlin A*~, alliance between Germany and Italy, May 1939, later joined by Japan (*Rome–Berlin–Tokyo–A*~); *A*~ *Powers*, these nations.

a'xle *n.* Spindle on or with which wheel revolves. end of axle-tree; axle-tree; ~*-box*, box closed by detachable cap, in nave of wheel, through which the ends of axle-tree pass; ~*-tree*, bar connecting wheels of carriage etc.

A'xminster (ă-). Small town in Devon; ~ *carpet*, carpet of cut pile made by various methods, first made at Axminster, orig. in imitation of hand-knotted oriental carpets.

ă'xolŏtl *n.* Salamander of genus *Amblystoma* of mountain lakes of Mexico and south-western U.S., usu. retaining larval form throughout life. [Aztec]

ă'xon *n.* That part of the nerve which is its conducting element or nerve fibre.

ay (ī) *adv.* = AYE[1].

ayah (ī'*a*) *n.* Hindu nurse. [Port. *aia* fem. of *aio* tutor]

aye[1] (ī) *adv.* (esp. Sc. & dial.) Yes. ~ *n.* Affirmative answer or vote.

aye[2] (ā) *adv.* Always; *for* ~, for ever.

aye-aye (ī'ī) *n.* Small tree-climbing animal (genus *Daubentonia*) found in Madagascar, a primate related to the lemurs.

Aylesburў (ā'lz-). County town of Buckinghamshire; ~ *duck*, duck of white domestic breed.

Ayrshire (ār'-). Former county of SW. Scotland, since May 1975 part of the region of Strathclyde; hence, breed of dairy cattle, mostly white with reddish or black markings, orig. raised there; kind of bacon cured in Ayrshire.

azā'lėa *n.* Flowering shrubby plant of the genus *Rhododendron*, chiefly native of N. America and China. [mod. L, f. Gk *azaleos* parched, because Linnaeus believed them to grow in dry situations]

Azerbaijan (ăzerbījah'n). 1. One of the constituent republics of the U.S.S.R., lying between the Black and Caspian Seas; capital, Baku. 2. Province of NW. Iran. **Azerbaija'n, -a'nĭ** *adjs.* & *ns.* (Native, inhabitant, language) of Azerbaijan.

Azĭ'lĭan *adj.* & *n.* (Of) a mesolithic culture of S. France. [f. Mas d'*Azil* in Fr. Pyrenees, where remains were found]

ă'zĭmuth *n.* Arc of the heavens extending from the zenith to the horizon, which it cuts at right angles; (in full, *true* ~ of a heavenly body) arc of horizon intercepted between north (in S. hemisphere, south) point of horizon and the point where the vertical circle passing through the body cuts the horizon; *magnetic* ~, arc intercepted between this circle and the magnetic meridian; ~ *circle*, circle of which this is a quadrant, passing through zenith and nadir. **ăzĭmū'thal** *adj.* ~*projection:* see ZENITHAL projection. **ăzĭmū'thallў** *adv.* [Arab. *al samt* the way, road, used in astron. for azimuth]

ă'zō *adj.* (chem.) Containing the *azo group*, —N = N—, where both bonds are attached to carbon atoms; ~ *dye*, dye containing this.

Azores (-ōr'z). Group of islands in N. Atlantic, some 800 miles

W. of Portugal; in Portuguese possession.

Azov (ā'zŏf), Sea of. Inland sea of southern U.S.S.R., separated from the Black Sea by the Crimea and communicating with it by a narrow strait.

A'zrāel (ă-). (Jewish & Muslim myth.) Angel who at death severs the soul from the body.

A'ztĕc (ă-) *n.* Member of a native Amer. people first known (*c* A.D. 1100) as inhabitants of the valley of Mexico; they built their capital (on the same site as modern Mexico City) in 1324 and extended their conquests in the 15th c., their most successful leader being Montezuma I (reigned 1440–69); they were conquered by the invading Spaniards under Cortez, early in the 16th c. ~ *adj.*

ă'zure (-zh*er*, -zhy*er*) *adj.* & *n.* Sky-blue; blue of unclouded sky; lapis lazuli; (heraldry) blue [Arab *al lāzuward* lapis lazuli, cerulean blue, f. Pers. *lazhward*]

AZTEC

B

B, b (bē). 1. 2nd letter of modern English and ancient Roman alphabet, representing a voiced bilabial stop, and derived from the Greek *beta* (β) and Phoenician and Hebrew *beth* (𐤁, ב). 2. 2nd in series, order, or class. 3. *B*, (mus.) 7th note in the natural scale (C major); scale or key with this note for tonic.

b. *abbrev.* Born; (in cricket) bowled, bye.

B. *abbrev.* *Beatus*, *-a* (L, = 'blessed'); *B*, black (of pencil-lead); (phot.) bulb-release.

B.A. *abbrev.* Bachelor of Arts; British Academy.

baa (bah) *n.* & *v.* (of sheep) Bleat.

Bā'al (pl. *-ĭm*). God of the ancient Phoenicians and Canaanites; false god. **Bā'alism** *n.* Worship of Baal, idolatry. [Heb. *ba'al* lord, master]

Baalbĕ'k (bahl-). Site in Lebanon of the Roman colony of Heliopolis (1st–3rd centuries A.D.), a centre of worship of the sun-god Helios, identified with BAAL.

baas (bahs) *n.* Boss, master; S. Afr. form of address, esp. of non-European to white man. [Du., = 'master', 'uncle']

baba (bah'bah) *n.* (also ~ *au rhum*, pr. ō ro͝om) Small rich sponge-cake soaked in rum syrup.

bă'bbĭtt *n.* Soft alloy of tin, copper, and antimony, used for machine bearings (also *Babbitt's metal*); bearing made of this. ~ *v.* Line with babbitt. [I. *Babbitt* (1799–1862), Amer. inventor]

Bă'bbĭtt. Hero of a novel (1922) by Sinclair Lewis; hence, typical business man of U.S. Middle West. **Bă'bbĭttism, Bă'bbĭttrў** *ns.*

bă'bble *v.* Talk half-articulately, incoherently, foolishly or excessively; murmur (of stream etc.). ~ *n.* Foolish or childish talk. **bă'bbler** *n.* Chatterer; teller of secrets; any of a group of Old World passerines with loud babbling cry, related to warblers.

bābe *n.* Baby.

Bā'bel[1]. (Heb. myth.) = BABYLON; its people (Gen. 11) tried to build a tower which would reach heaven, but God prevented them by 'confounding' their language (so that they could not understand one another) and scattering them abroad; hence, *tower of* ~, visionary scheme.

bā'bel[2] *n.* Scene of confusion and uproar; noisy assembly. [f. BABEL[1]]

Ba'bĭ (bah-) *n.* (Member of) sect whose doctrines combined Muslim, Christian, Jewish, and Zoroastrian elements, founded in 1844 by a Persian, Mirza Ali Muhammad, who became known as the *Bab* (pr. bahb; Arab. *bāb ad-dīn* gate of the faith). **Ba'bĭsm, Ba'bīte, Ba'bĭst** *ns.*

Bă'bĭngton, Anthony (1561–86). Page to Mary Queen of Scots; executed for conspiring to murder Elizabeth and release Mary from imprisonment.

băbĭru'sa, -r(o)ussa (-ro͞o-) *n.* Wild hog (*Babirusa babyrussa*), male of which has long upper canine teeth which pierce the lip and grow upward like horns; found only in islands of Celebes and Buru. [Malagasy, = 'hog deer']

babo͞o'n *n.* Medium-sized monkey (several species in genus *Papio*) of Arabia and Africa S. and E. of Sahara, living in bands in open rocky country, occas. tree-climbing, characterized by dog-like snout, cheek-prominences, and coloured bare patches on the buttocks; *sacred* ~, species living on Red Sea coasts and formerly in Egypt (*P. hamadryas*).

TOWER OF BABEL

babu (bah'bōō) *n.* Hindu gentleman; Indian clerk or official who writes English; (contempt.) Hindu, esp. Bengali, with superficial English education.

Babur (bah'boor) (1483–1530). First Mogul emperor, descended from Tamburlaine; he invaded India *c* 1525 and conquered the territory from the Oxus to Patna.

bā'bȳ *n.* Infant, very young child; childish person; very young animal; thing small of its kind; (fig.) one's responsibility; one's particular interest; *~-farmer*, person who keeps babies for payment; *~ grand*: see GRAND; *~-sitter*, (colloq.) person who looks after young child when parents go out. **bā'bȳhōōd** *n.* **bā'bȳish** *adj.*

Bă'bȳlon. Capital city, on the Euphrates, of the ancient Chaldean Empire; the Jews were brought there in captivity by Nebuchadnezzar (597 and 586 B.C.); its *hanging* (i.e. terraced) *gardens* were one of the Seven Wonders of the ancient world; it was sacked by Cyrus of Persia in 538 B.C.; *Whore of ~*: see WHORE. **Băbȳlō'nĭa.** Empire of Babylon. **Băbȳlō'nĭan** *adj.* & *n.*

băccalau'rėate *n.* University degree of bachelor.

bă'ccarat (-ah) *n.* Gambling card-game, played against banker by punters staking that their hand will total nine.

bă'ccāte *adj.* (bot.) 1. Bearing berries. 2. Berry-shaped.

bă'cchanal (-k-) *adj.* Of Bacchus or his rites. *~ n.* Priest or votary of Bacchus; reveller.

Băcchanā'lĭa (-k-) *n.pl.* Festival held in honour of Bacchus; drunken revelry, orgy.

Bă'cchant (-k-), **Bacchă'ntė** (*or* -kă'nt) *ns.* Priest or priestess of Bacchus, often represented with loose hair garlanded with ivy, and dressed in a leopard-skin; (drunken or noisy) reveller.

bă'cchĭc (-k-) *adj.* Of Bacchus or his worship; riotous, drunken.

Bă'cchus (-k-). (Gk & Rom. myth.) God of wine: see DIONYSUS.

băcci'ferous, bă'cciform, băcci'vorous (băks-) *adjs.* Berry-bearing, -shaped, -eating.

bă'ccy (-k-) *n.* (colloq.) Tobacco.

Bach (bahχ), Johann Sebastian (1685–1750). German musical composer, the great master of contrapuntal music; author of many fugues and other works for organ and other keyboard instruments, a

great Mass, and much other choral church-music. Of his eleven sons, several distinguished in music, two of the better-known are *Carl Philipp Emanuel* ~ (1714–88), who contributed much to the development of the sonata form, and *Johann Christian* ~ (the 'English Bach', 1735–82), who spent some time in England.

bă'chelor *n.* Unmarried man; (hist.) knight serving under another's banner; *B~ of Arts* (B.A.), *of Science* (B.Sc.), etc., holder of university degree below master; *~'s button*, any of various flowers of round or button-like form, orig. the double variety of *Ranunculus acris*; *~ girl*, young unmarried woman living independently.

baci'llary *adj.* Consisting of little rods; connected with bacilli.

baci'lliform *adj.* Rod-shaped.

baci'llus *n.* (pl. *-llī*). Any straight rod-shaped bacterium; (loosely and usu. pl.) disease-producing bacteria. [L dim. of *baculus* stick]

băck *n.* Hinder surface of human body, part of this between shoulders and hips; corresponding part of animal's body; side or part normally more remote or away from spectator or direction of motion; side of hand opposite palm; edge of book, opposite openings of pages, where sections are joined together; (footb. etc.) player positioned behind forwards; *Backs,* gardens behind colleges bordering on the river Cam at Cambridge. ~ *adj.* Situated behind or at rear; remote; inferior; belonging to past period. ~ *adv.* To the rear; in (to) an earlier position; to or in remote or retired position. ~ *v.* Put, or be, a back, lining, support, or background to; support with money, argument, etc. (also ~ *up*); bet on; endorse (cheque etc.); ride (horse); (cause to) move back; lay (sail) against the wind; (of wind) change anti-clockwise (cf. VEER); ~ *out of*, withdraw from. **bă'cker** *n.* One who backs or supports. **bă'cking** *n.* Support, assistance.

băck- in comb.: *~-bench, ~-bencher*: see BENCH *n.* 3; *ba'ckbite* (*v.*) slander; *ba'ckbiter* (*n.*); *ba'ckblocks,* (Austral.) the remotest fringe of settlement; *ba'ckboard,* (esp.) board worn to support or straighten the back; (basket ball) board or surface behind the basket; *ba'ckbone,* spine; main support; firmness of character; *~-chat,* (slang) impudent retort(s); *~-cloth,* painted cloth hung at the back of scene or stage; *~-comb* (*v.*) comb underlying hairs of a strand towards scalp; *~-date* (*v.t.*) affix earlier date to (document etc.); make (agreement etc.) valid retroactively; *~-door* (*adj.*) using underhand or secret approach; *backfire,* (of internal combustion engine) premature ignition in the cylinder during suction stroke; explosion in hot exhaust-pipe of gases escaping when a cylinder has misfired; (*v.i.*) ignite, explode, thus; (fig. of plan etc.) go wrong; have adverse effect on instigator; ~ *formation*, making from a supposed derivative (as *burglar*) of the non-existent word (*burgle*) from which it might have come; word so formed; *ba'ckground* (*n.*) back part of scene or picture; social surroundings, environment; obscurity, retirement; (*adj.*) in, providing, a background; *ba'ckhand*(*ed*) (*adjs.*) delivered with the back of the hand, or with the back of hand turned in the direction of the stroke; (fig.) ambiguous, equivocal; *backha'nder* (*n.*) backhand blow; indirect attack: *backlash*(*ing*), irregular recoil of wheels in machinery due to defect or sudden pressure (also fig.); *ba'cklog*, arrears of uncompleted work etc.; ~ *number*, out-of-date issue of magazine etc., (slang) out-of-date person or thing; ~-*pedal* (*v.i.*) check movement of wheel when bicycling by pressing rising pedal down; also fig. (*v.*); ~-*projection*, (cinemat.) projection of a film on to a translucent screen from behind, as background for action taking place in front of the screen; ~-*scattering*, (phys.) scattering of radiation in a reverse direction from an irradiated substance; ~ *seat*, humble or obscure position; ~-*seat driver*, one who gives unsolicited advice while taking no responsibility; *ba'ckside*, buttocks; *ba'cksight*, (of gun) that nearer the stock; (surveying) sight taken backwards; ~ *slang*, slang in which words are pronounced backwards; *backsli'de*, relapse into sin, error, etc.; ~ *spacer*, typewriter key that moves the carriage one space backward; ~ *stage*, (part of theatre) behind the scenes; also fig.; ~-*stairs* (*adj.*) underhand, secret; *ba'ckstays*, ropes from the upper mast-heads to the sides of a ship, supporting the masts under sail; *ba'ckstitch*, sew by inserting the needle each time behind the place where it has just been brought out; (*n.*) stitch made thus; *ba'ckstroke*, stroke made whilst swimmer is lying on his back; *ba'ckwash*, motion of receding wave; motion of water caused by passage of vessel; *ba'ckwater*, stretch of still water parallel with a stream and fed from it at the lower end; (fig.) place or condition of intellectual stagnation; *ba'ckwoods*, remote, only partially cleared forest-land; *ba'ckwoodsman*, settler in backwoods, uncivilized person; peer who rarely attends House of Lords.

băckgă'mmon *n.* Game for two persons, played by moving pieces like draughtsmen, according to the

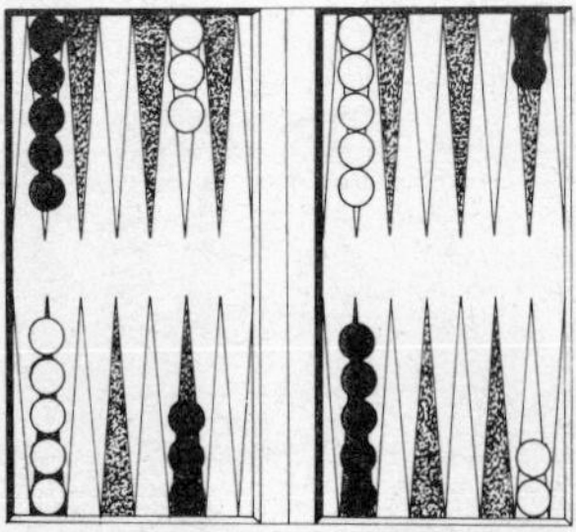

throw of dice, on a board of two tables, each marked off into twelve spaces of alternating colours.

bă'cklėss *adj.* Having no back; (of dress etc.) cut low at the back.

bă'ckward *adv.* Back foremost; back towards the starting-point; the reverse way; ~ *and forward*, to and fro. ~ *adj.* Directed to rear or starting-point; reversed; slow in learning or developing. **bă'ckwardnėss** *n.* **bă'ckwards** (-z) *adv.* Backward.

băckwardā'tion *n.* (Stock Exch.) Percentage paid by seller of stock for right of delaying delivery (cf. CONTANGO).

bā'con[1] *n.* Cured back and sides of a pig; piece of this.

Bā'con[2], Francis, Baron Verulam and Viscount St. Albans (1561–1626). Lord Chancellor of England (1618–20), philosopher who introduced the inductive method into science, and author of 'Essays'. **Bācō'nĭan** *adj.* & *n.* (Advocate) of the theory that Bacon wrote the plays of Shakespeare.

Bā'con[3], Roger (1214?–94). English Franciscan, philosopher and student of experimental science (esp. optics) at Paris and Oxford; credited, then and later, with magical powers.

băctĕr'icīde *n.* Substance that destroys bacteria. **băctĕrĭcī'dal** *adj.*

băctĕrĭŏ'logȳ *n.* Study of bacteria, esp. as a branch of medicine. **băctĕrĭolŏ'gĭcal** *adj.* ~ *warfare*, use of bacteria to spread disease in the enemy. **băctĕrĭŏ'logist** *n.*

băctĕr'iophāge (*or* -fahzh) *n.* Virus capable of destroying bacteria. **băctĕrĭophā'gal, -phā'gic** *adjs.*

băctĕr'ium *n.* (pl. *-rĭa*) Any of several types of microscopic or ultra-microscopic single-celled organisms occurring in enormous numbers everywhere in nature, not only in land, sea, and air, but also on or in many parts of the tissues

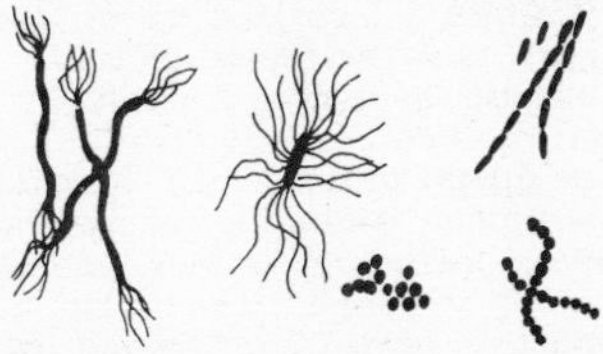

of plants and animals, and forming one of the main biologically interdependent groups of organisms in virtue of the chemical changes which many of them bring about, e.g. many forms of decay, certain diseases, and the building up of nitrogen compounds in the soil. **băctĕr'ial** *adj.* Of or caused by bacteria. [Gk, dim. of *baktron* stick]

Bă'ctrĭa. Ancient country of central Asia (now *Balkh* in N. Afghanistan), lying between the Hindu Kush and the Oxus.

Bă'ctrĭan *adj.* Of Bactria or its people; ~ *camel*, two-humped camel of central Asia, *Camelus bactrianus*. ~ *n.* Native or inhabitant of Bactria.

băd *adj.* (comp. *worse*, superl. *worst*). 1. Worthless, inferior, defective, inefficient; not valid; unpleasant; (of coinage) counterfeit; (of weather) unpleasant; *go* ~, decay; *not* ~, (colloq.) rather good; ~ *debt*, one not recoverable; *B~ Lands*, arid rocky regions (esp. those in S. Dakota, U.S.), seamed with deep vertical gullies by occasional heavy rain and thus uncultivable. 2. Wicked, vicious. 3. Painful; harmful; ~ *blood*, ill feeling. 4. Ill, in pain. ~ *n.* Ill fortune, ruin; *go to the* ~, go to ruin, degenerate. **bă'ddish** *adj.* **bă'dlȳ** *adv.* **bă'dnėss** *n.*

Badar'ian *adj.* & *n.* (Member) of a predynastic culture of Upper Egypt using stone tools and pottery. [f. *Badari*, village in Upper Egypt]

Bă'ddėley (*or* -dlĭ), Robert (1732?–94). English actor, who left money to provide wine and cake (the ~ *cake*) on Twelfth Night in the green-room of Drury Lane Theatre, London.

Ba'den (bah-). Former State of SW. Germany; now part of the Federal Republic.

Ba'den-Ba'den (bah-). Health resort, with mineral springs, in Baden, Germany.

Bā'den-Powell (pō'*el*), Robert Stephenson Smyth, 1st Baron Baden-Powell of Gilwell (1857–1941). English soldier; defended Mafeking, 1900; founded the Boy SCOUT organization, 1908.

bădge *n.* Distinctive emblem or mark as a sign of office, membership, etc.

bă'dger *n.* Nocturnal plantigrade quadruped (*Meles vulgaris*), intermediate between weasel and bear, with coarse dark-coloured fur and a white blaze on the forehead, which digs a burrow, hibernates, and defends itself fiercely against attack; *honey* ~, ratel; ~ *game*, extortion scheme in which a man is lured into a compromising situation and then surprised and blackmailed. ~ *v.* Pester as dogs worry a badger; tease, torment.

bă'dĭnage (-ahzh) *n.* Banter.

bă'dmĭnton *n.* Game like lawn tennis played with shuttlecocks

SHUTTLECOCK

and rackets over a net 1·5 m high. [name of Gloucestershire seat of Duke of Beaufort]

Bae'dėker (bād-) *n.* Any of the guide-books issued by Karl ~ (1801–59), German publisher, and his successors; ~ *raids*, reprisal raids undertaken by German air force in April and May 1942 on places of cultural and historical importance in Britain.

Baer (bar̄), Karl Ernst von (1792–1876). Estonian biologist; discovered human ovum and made important contributions to embryology.

Baeyer (bī'yer), Johann Friedrich Wilhelm Adolf, Ritter von (1835–1917). German chemist; discovered synthetic indigo; exerted profound influence on development of organic chemistry.

Bă'ffin, William (1584?–1622). English navigator and explorer; discovered ~ *Land*, large island off the NE. coast of Canada, and ~ *Bay*, sea between it and Greenland.

bă'ffle *v.t.* Foil, frustrate, perplex. **bă'ffling** *adj.* Bewildering.
bă'ffle *n.* Shielding device or structure; esp. (also ~*-board*) one checking or deflecting sound-waves, improving tone of loud-speaker by hindering return of sound-waves to back of speaker; (also ~*-plate*) one hindering or regulating passage of gases or fluids; one in exhaust-pipe of an internal combustion engine to reduce noise; (photog.) one that screens light; ~*-wall*, wall parallel with doorway to stop draughts, blast from air-raids, etc.

bă'ffy *n.* Short wooden golf-club for lofting the ball.

baft (-ah-) *adv.* & *prep.* Abaft.

băg *n.* Receptacle of flexible material with an opening usu. at the top; sac in animal body for storing honey, poison, etc.; all a sportsman has shot in one expedition; (esp. pl.) folds of loose skin beneath the eyes; (pl.) (slang) trousers; large number or amount; ~*-wig*, wig with the back hair tied in a bag. ~ *v.* Put in a bag; secure (game); (colloq.) take possession of, steal; buldge, hang loosely.

Bagă'nda *n.* (Member of) a Negroid Bantu-speaking people inhabiting Buganda.

băgatĕ'lle *n.* 1. Mere trifle; short unpretentious piece of music. 2. Game played on a table with a semicircular end, the object being to strike balls into numbered holes with a cue.

bă'ggage *n.* Portable equipment of an army; luggage; (joc.) saucy girl.

bă'ggy̆ (-gĭ) *adj.* That bags or hangs loosely.

Băghdă'd (-gd-). City on the Tigris, now the capital of Iraq.

bagnio (bă'nyō) *n.* Oriental prison; brothel.

bă'gpīpe *n.* (freq. pl.) Musical instrument consisting of several pipes, including drones and a chanter through which air is forced by pressure on a wind-bag held under the arm; now associated chiefly with Scotland and Ireland, but once popular in England and

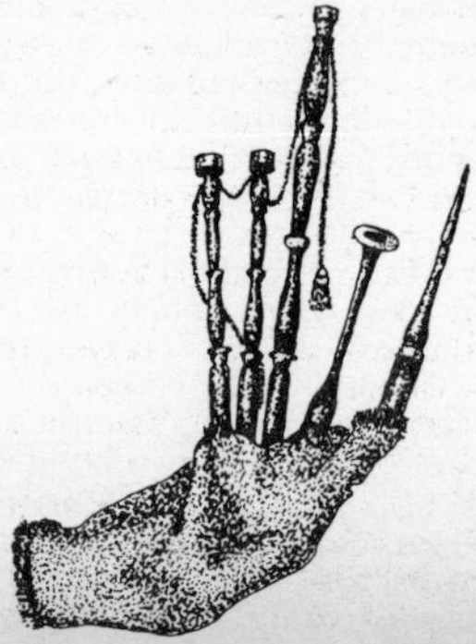

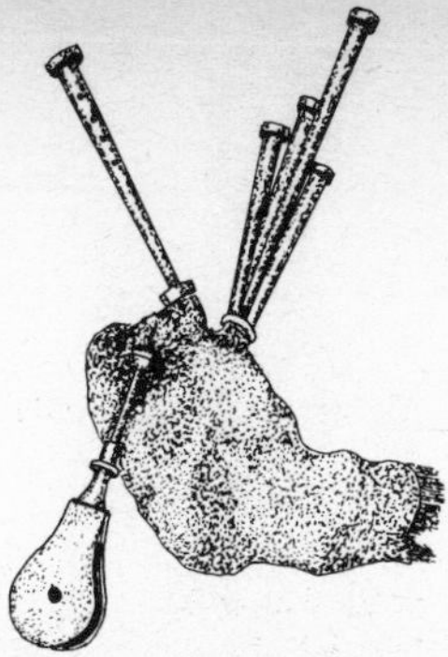

still played in some places on the Continent, notably Brittany.

B.Agr., B.Agric. *abbrevs.* Bachelor of Agriculture.

Baha'dur (b*a*hah-). Title of respect appended in India to person's name.

Baha'ism (b*a*hah-) *n.* Religion, based on Babism, founded by the Babist leader Mirza Hosain Ali (1817–92), known as *Baha-ullah* (Pers. *bahā'u-'l-lāh* 'splendour of God'). **Baha'ĭ, Baha'ĭst** *ns.* & *adjs.*

Baha'mas (b*a*hahm*az*). (also *Bahama Islands*) Archipelago of British W. Indies, the first land touched by Columbus in 1492; first colonized by Spaniards and later (in 17th c.) by the English; British colony 1783–1973; independent 1973; capital, Nassau. **Bahā'mian** *adj.* & *n.*

Bahrai'n, -ei'n (-ān *or* -īn). Independent sheikdom consisting of a group of islands, the largest being Bahrain Island, in the Persian Gulf; capital, Manama.

Bahram V (b*a*rah'm) (d. 439). Sassanid king and national hero of Persia, known as *Bahrām Gūr*, 'the Wild Ass'.

baht *n.* Principal monetary unit of Thailand, = 100 stangs.

Baikal (bīkah'l), Lake. Large lake in S. Siberia.

bail[1] *n.* 1. Security for a prisoner's appearance for trial. 2. Person who becomes surety. ~ *v.t.* 1. Become bail for, secure the liberation of on bail. 2. Deliver (goods) in trust.

bail[2] *n.* 1. Bar separating horses in an open stable. 2. (cricket) Either of the crosspieces resting on top of the stumps. 3. (also ~ *bar*) Hinged bar holding paper against platen of typewriter. **bai'ler**[1] *n.* Ball that hits the bails.

bail[3], **bāle** *v.t.* Scoop water out of (boat etc.). **bai'ler**[2] *n.* Utensil for bailing.

bailēē' *n.* Person to whom goods are entrusted.

bai'ley *n.* Open space enclosed by a fortification; *Old B~*: see OLD.

Bai'ley brĭdge. Bridge of lattice steel designed for rapid assembly from standard parts. [f. Sir Donald *Bailey* (1901–) designer]

bai'lĭe *n.* Senior burgh councillor in Scotland (corresp. to former English alderman) serving also as magistrate.

bai'liff *n.* 1. King's representative in district (now chiefly hist.), esp. chief officer of a hundred. 2. Sheriff's officer who executes writs and processes, distrains, and arrests. 3. Lord of the manor's agent; steward.

bai'lĭwick *n.* District, jurisdiction, of bailie or bailiff.

bai'lment *n.* Delivery of goods in trust; bailing of prisoner.

bai'lor *n.* One who entrusts goods to another.

Bain, Alexander (1818–1903). Scottish philosopher: exponent of a system of psychology which traces psychological phenomena to the nerves and brain.

bain-marie (băṅ-mărē') *n.* Vessel of hot water in which pans of food are placed for slow cooking; double boiler.

Bairam (bīrah'm). Each of the two principal festivals of the Muslim year, *Lesser* ~ (lasting 3 days) following the fast of Ramadan, and *Greater* ~ (lasting 4 days) 70 days later.

bairn *n.* (Sc.) Child.

bait *v.* 1. Worry (animal) by setting dogs at it; worry (person) by jeers. 2. Give (horse etc.) food, esp. on a journey; (of horse) take food thus. 3. Put bait on or in (fish-hook, trap, etc.). ~ *n.* 1. Food etc. used to entice prey; allurement. 2. (obs.) Halt for refreshment.

bai'za (bī-) *n.* One thousandth of a rial saidi.

baize *n.* Coarse woollen usu. green stuff used chiefly for coverings, linings, etc.

bāke *v.* Cook by dry heat, as in an oven; harden by heat; be or become baked; *baked beans*, haricot beans so cooked (esp. as a tinned food, in tomato sauce); *baked meats*, (obs.) pastry; *ba'kehouse*, place for baking bread etc.; *ba'king-powder*, powder consisting of bicarbonate of soda and cream of tartar with a filling of starch or flour, used instead of yeast to make cakes etc. rise.

bā'kelīte *n.* Synthetic plastic material used for insulating, to make moulded articles etc. [trade-name, f. L. H. *Baekeland* (1863–1944), Belgian-American inventor]

bā'ker *n.* One who bakes and sells bread; ~'*s dozen*, 13 objects of any kind. **bā'kerў** *n.* Bakehouse; trade of baking.

Bā'kewĕll (-kw-). Town in Derbyshire; ~ *tart*, pastry case, lined with a layer of jam, with rich almond paste filling.

bă'kshēēsh *n.* Small gift of money. [Pers. *bakhshish* gift, munificence]

Băkst, Leon (1866–1924). Russian stage-designer who worked in Paris for Diaghilev's Russian ballet company.

bă'kū[1] *n.* Fine kind of straw grown in the Philippines and woven in China, and used for hats; hat woven of this.

Băku'[2] (-ōō). Capital of Azerbaijan, on the shore of the Caspian Sea; a centre of the petroleum industry.

Bakunin (-kōō'nĭn), Mikhail Alexandrovich (1814–76). Russian anarchist, revolutionary leader, and founder of NIHILISM.

BAL *abbrev.* British Anti-Lewisite, drug (*dimercaprol*) used

BAKST

to neutralize metallic poisons, e.g. arsenic.

Bā'laam (-l*a*m). Gentile prophet (see Num. 22–4).

Bălacla'va (-klah-). Crimean village near Sebastopol, scene of battle (1854) of the Crimean War during which occurred the Charge of the Light Brigade; ~ *helmet*, knitted woollen cap covering the whole head and neck, with an opening for the face, worn esp. by soldiers on active service.

bălalai'ka (-līk*a*) *n.* Russian stringed instrument played by plucking, resembling guitar but with triangular body and 2, 3, or 4 strings.

bă'lance *n.* 1. Weighing apparatus consisting of a beam moving freely on a central pivot with a scale-pan at either end; spring or lever substitute for this. 2. Regulating gear of a clock, watch, etc. 3. (State of) even distribution of weight or amount. 4. Preponderating weight or amount. 5. Excess of assets over liabilities or vice versa. 6. Remainder. 7. ~ *of payments*,

difference of value between payments into and out of a country, including invisible exports and imports; ~ *of power*, equilibrium of military and political power between several States; ~ *of trade*, difference between total exports and total imports of a country, *favourable* if exports exceed imports, and *adverse* if there is an excess of imports; ~*-sheet*, statement of assets and liabilities, esp. of public company. ~ *v.* 1. Weigh. 2. Equalize, match; bring or come into equilibrium. 3. Find the balance of assets and liabilities in (an account-book). **bă'lanced** (-st) *adj.* (esp., of diet) Containing essential nutriments in suitable proportions.

bă'las *n.* Rose-red kind of spinel ruby. [med. L *balascus*, f. Pers. *Badakshān*, district of origin, near Samarkand]

bă'lata (*or* balah'-) *n.* Dried milky juice of tropical Amer. tree, used as substitute for gutta-percha.

Bălbō'a[1], Vasco Nuñez de (1475–1517). Spanish explorer, esp. of Central America; first sighted the Pacific Ocean in 1513.

bălbō'a[2] *n.* Principal monetary unit of Panama = U.S. dollar.

bă'lconў *n.* 1. Balustraded or railed platform on the outside of a building with access from an upper-floor window. 2. In a theatre, the seats above the dress or upper circle usu. = GALLERY in other public buildings, (seats in) a gallery above ground-floor seats.

bald (bawld) *adj.* 1. Having the scalp wholly or partly hairless; (of animal, bird) without fur, feathers, etc. 2. Bare; meagre; dull. **ba'ldlў** *adv.* **ba'ldnėss** *n.*

baldachin, -quin (baw'ld*a*kĭn) *n.* Canopy over an altar, throne, etc., dependent from a ceiling or projecting from a wall. [It. *baldacchino* silk material exported by *Baldacco* Baghdad]

ba'ld-coot, ba'ldĭcoot (bawl-) *n.* = COOT.

Ba'lder, -dur (bawl-). (Scand. myth.) God of the summer sun, invulnerable to all things except mistletoe, with which Loki by a trick induced the blind god Hödur to kill him.

ba'lderdăsh (bawl-) *n.* Jumble of words; nonsense, rubbish.

ba'ldĭng (bawl-) *adj.* Becoming bald.

ba'ldrĭc (bawl-) *n.* Belt for supporting a sword, bugle, etc., worn over shoulder and across body to opposite hip.

Ba'ldwĭn[1] (bawl-) (1058–1118). First Christian king of Jerusalem, a leader in the 1st Crusade, and brother and successor of Godfrey of Bouillon.

Ba'ldwĭn[2] (bawl-), Stanley (1867–1947), 1st Earl Baldwin of Bewdley. British Conservative statesman; prime minister 1923–4, 1924–9, 1935–7.

bāle[1] *n.* (archaic) Evil, destruction, woe.

bāle[2] *n.* Large bundle or package, esp. of merchandise, usu. wrapped and corded or looped. ~ *v.t.* Make up into bales.

bāle[3] *v.* Erroneous but more usual spelling of BAIL[3] *v.*; ~ *out*, make emergency descent by parachute from aircraft.

Bāle[4], John (1495–1563). English priest, author of the first English historical play, 'King John'.

Băleă'rĭc I'slands (īl*a*ndz). Group of islands, including Majorca and Minorca, off E. coast of Spain; a province of Spain.

bale͞e'n *n.* Whalebone.

bā'lefīre (-lf-) *n.* (archaic) Great fire in the open, beacon fire.

bā'leful (-lf-) *adj.* Pernicious, destructive, malignant. **bā'lefullў** *adv.* **bā'lefulnėss** *n.*

Bă'lfour (-foor), Arthur James, 1st Earl of Balfour (1848–1930). British Conservative statesman and philosopher; prime minister 1902–5; author of 'A Defence of Philosophic Doubt' (1879).

bălĭbŭ'ntal *n.* Fine straw of very close weave, used for hats.

Balĭnē'se (bah-, -z) *adj.* & *n.* (Native, language, people) of the island of Bali in Indonesia.

Bā'lĭol. Surname of several kings of Scotland: John de Baliol (1249–1315) was that claimant to the Scottish throne in 1290 in whose favour Edward I of England decided.

balk, baulk (bawk; *or* -lk) *n.* 1. Roughly squared beam of timber; tie-beam. 2. Stumbling-block. 3. (usu. *baulk*) Area on billiard table where ball may be exempt from direct hit by another ball. 4. Ridge left unploughed between two furrows. *v.* 1. Thwart hinder; discourage. 2. Jib, shy.

Ba'lkan (bawl- *or* bŏl-) *adj.* Of the Balkan Peninsula or States; ~ *Peninsula*, peninsula of Europe south of the Danube and Sava rivers; home of various peoples (Albanians, Vlachs, Greeks, Serbs, Bulgars, and Turks) with differing cultures. From the 3rd to the 7th centuries the peninsula, nominally ruled by the Byzantine emperors, was invaded by successive migrations of Slavs; later, parts of it were conquered by Venice and other States; in 1356 began the Ottoman invasion; Constantinople fell to the Turks in 1453, and by 1478 most of the peninsula was in their power; the subject nations, though largely retaining their languages and religions, did not recover independence until the 19th c.; in 1912–13 Turkey was attacked and defeated by other Balkan peoples in alliance; during the war of 1914–18 (the immediate cause of which was the assassination of the Austrian Archduke Franz Ferdinand in Serbia) Turkey and Bulgaria sided with Austria and Germany and the other Balkan States with the Allies; after the war the peninsula was divided between Greece, Bulgaria, Albania, and Yugoslavia, with Turkey retaining only Constantinople and the surrounding land; ~ *States*, countries of the Balkan Peninsula. **Ba'lkans** (-z) *n.pl.* Balkan States.

Ba'lkĭs (bawl- *or* bŏl-). Name of the Queen of Sheba in Arabic literature.

ball[1] (bawl) *n.* 1. Solid or hollow sphere, esp. one used in a game; rounded mass (as of snow, string, etc.); ~ *of foot, thumb*, rounded

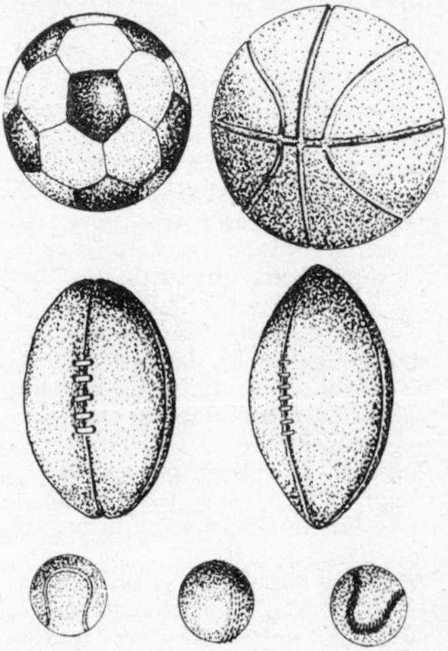

base of great toe, thumb. 2. (cricket) Single delivery of the ball by a bowler. 3. Missile for cannon, rifles, etc. 4. ~ *bearing*, bearing in which revolving parts of a machine turn upon a number of hard balls running in grooves, which diminish friction; one of these balls; ~ *cartidge,* cartridge containing bullet; ~- *cock* device for regulating inflow of water, esp. in cisterns, consisting of a floating ball which rises or falls with the height of the water, thereby shutting or opening a valve through which the water flows in ; ~- *flower*, ornament resembling a round bud, carved in hollow of moulding in Gothic architecture ; ~- *point* (*pen*), writing instrument having for point a small ball-bearing moistened from a reservoir of semi-liquid ink; ~-*turret*, turret protecting underside of a bomber. ~ *v.* (of snow etc.) Form lumps.

ball² (bawl) *n.* Social assembly for dancing; *ba'llroom*, large room suitable for this.

Ball³ (bawl), John (d. 1381). English priest, one of the leaders of Wat TYLER's rebellion, for his share in which he was executed.

bă'llad *n.* 1. Narrative poem (esp. traditional) designed to be sung, with the same melody for each verse. 2. Any poem in similar style. 3. ~ *metre*: see COMMON metre; ~-*monger*, (contempt.) dealer in ballads. **bă'lladrÿ** *n.* Ballad poetry. [Provençal *ballada* dancing-song]

bălla'de (-ahd) *n.* 1. Poem of one or more triplets of 7- or 8-lined stanzas, each ending with the same line as refrain, followed by an envoy freq. of 4 lines. 2. Piece of esp. lyrical or romantic instrumental music.

bă'llast *n.* 1. Heavy material, as sand or water, placed in a ship's hold or carried in a balloon or airship for stability. 2. Coarse stone, clinker, etc., forming bed of railway or substratum of road. 3. (elect.) Device for stabilizing current. 4. (fig.) Elements of character which give stability. ~ *v.t.* Furnish with ballast.

bălleri'na (-ēna) *n.* Female ballet-dancer (strictly, dancer who takes one or more of certain classical roles).

bă'llet (-lā) *n.* Stage entertainment in which a story is enacted or a dramatic idea expressed by means of dancing to music with the aid of costume and scenery, dating from the late 16th c. and developed principally in France, Italy, and Russia; members of company performing this.

băllėtomā'nia *n.* Enthusiasm for ballet. **bă'llėtomāne** *n.*

balli'sta *n.* (pl. *-ae*). Ancient military engine for hurling stones etc.

balli'stic *adj.* Of projectiles; ~ *missile*, *rocket*, one that is powered and sometimes guided in the initial stage of its flight but falls freely. **balli'stics** *n.* Science of projectiles.

ballon d'essai (bălawṅ dĕsā). Experiment to see how a policy etc. will be received. [Fr., = 'trial balloon']

bă'llonĕt *n.* Secondary envelope in a balloon designed to be inflated with air as the buoyant gas is released from the envelope proper.

balloo'n *n.* Large air-tight envelope of silk or other light material inflated with gas lighter than air so as to rise in the air, sometimes provided with a basket or car slung beneath from a net enclosing the envelope, used for making observations and as an anti-aircraft

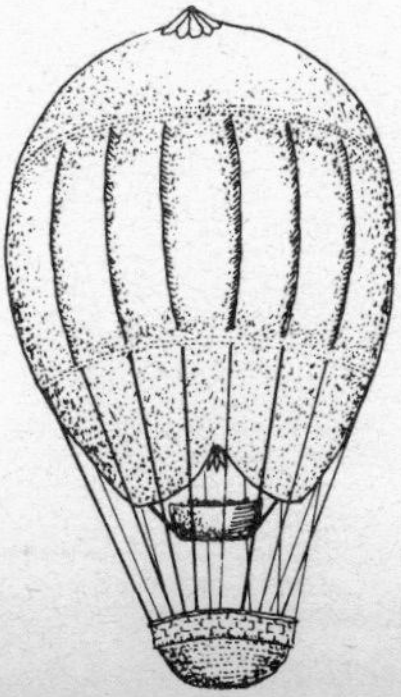

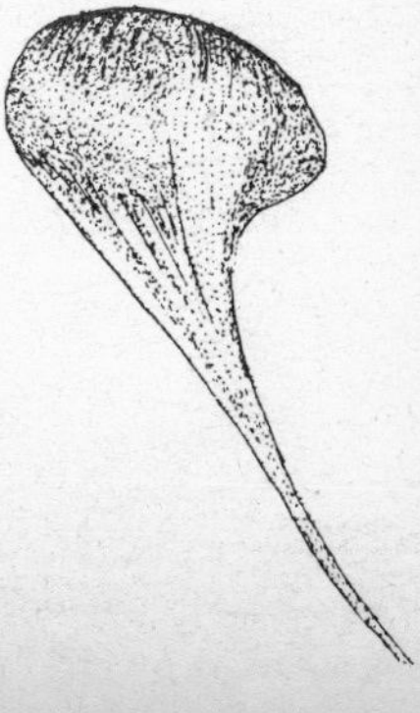

defence; small usu. rubber envelope inflated with air as toy; (colloq.) balloon-shaped outline enclosing speech or thought of character in strip cartoon etc. or added matter for printing etc.; ~ *tyre*, low-pressure motor tyre of large section. ~ *v.t.* Swell out like a balloon (of sails, tyres, etc.).

bă'llot *n.* 1. Secret voting (usu. by placing a voting-paper etc. in a closed ~-*box*). 2. Ball, ticket, or paper used in this. 3. Drawing of lots. ~ *v.i.* Vote by ballot (*for*); draw lots. [It. *ballotta* little ball]

bă'llȳ *adj.* & *adv.* (slang) Euphemism for *bloody*, used as a vague intensive.

băllȳhōō' *n.* (orig. U.S.) Advance publicity of vulgar or misleading kind; vulgar advertisement; 'eyewash'.

bă'llȳrăg *v.* Play practical jokes on; indulge in horse-play.

balm (bahm) *n.* 1. Aromatic substance consisting of resin mixed with volatile oils, exuding naturally from various trees; tree yielding this; ~ *of Gilead*, plant or tree of genus *Commiphora* yielding fragrant resinous substance; this substance. 2. Aromatic herb *Melissa officinalis*. 3. Aromatic oil or ointment. 4. Healing or soothing influence.

Bălmŏ'ral[1]. Scottish residence in upper Deeside, Grampian, of the British sovereign.

bălmŏ'ral[2] *n.* 1. Kind of round cap worn by some Scottish regiments. 2. (obs.) Laced walking shoe or boot. 3. (obs.) Kind of striped woollen petticoat.

ba'lmȳ (bahmĭ) *adj.* 1. Of or like balm; fragrant, mild, soothing. 2. (slang) Crazy, silly. **ba'lmĭlȳ** *adj.* **ba'lmĭnėss** *n.*

bă'lnėarȳ *adj.* Of baths or bathing.

ba'lsa (bawl- *or* bŏl-) *n.* Tropical American tree, *Ochroma lagopus*; its wood (~ *wood*, *corkwood*), used for life-belts, model aeroplanes, etc., because of its extreme lightness.

ba'lsam (bawl- *or* bŏl-) *n.* 1. = BALM 1; balm of Gilead; *Canada* ~: see CANADA. 2. Aromatic ointment, of various substances dissolved in oil or turpentine. 3. Tree yielding balm. 4. Flowering plant of genus *Impatiens*, with hooded and spurred coloured sepals and thick succulent stem.

Balt (bawlt *or* bŏlt) *n.* Native or inhabitant of one of the Baltic States of Lithuania, Latvia, and Estonia, esp. a German inhabitant. ~ *adj.*

Bălthă'zar[1]. 1. = BELSHAZZAR[1]. 2. Traditional name of one of the three MAGI, represented as king of Chaldea.

Bălthă'zar[2] *n.* = BELSHAZZAR[2].

Ba'ltĭc (bawl- *or* bŏl-) *adj.* Of the Baltic Sea, States, or languages; ~ *Exchange*, world market, in

BALMORAL CASTLE

London, for the chartering of cargo ships; ~ *languages*, branch of Indo-European languages containing Lithuanian, Lettish, and Old Prussian; ~ *Sea*, almost land-locked sea in N. Europe, bordered by Sweden, U.S.S.R., Germany, Denmark, etc.; ~ *States*, former independent republics of Estonia, Latvia, and Lithuania. ~ *n.* Baltic Sea.

Ba'ltimore (bawl- *or* bŏl-). Seaport in N. Maryland; ~ *oriole*, bird of the starling family (*Icterus galbula*) found throughout N. America whose colours, black and orange, are like the coat of arms of Lord Baltimore. [Lord *Baltimore* (d. 1632), English proprietor of territory which later became Maryland]

Balto-Slă'vic, -Slavŏ'nic (bawl- *or* bŏl-) *adjs.* & *ns.* (Of) the group of languages including the Baltic and Slavonic branches.

Balu'chi (-ōō-) *n.* Native or inhabitant of, the Iranian language of, Baluchistan. **Baluchista'n** (-ahn). Mountainous region of southern Asia, forming part of Iran and Pakistan.

bă'luster *n.* Short pillar of circular section and carving outline. [Gk *balaustion* wild-pomegranate flower]

bălustrā'de *n.* Row of balusters with a rail or coping as the parapet of a balcony etc.

Bălzăc, Honoré de (1799–1850). French realistic novelist, whose

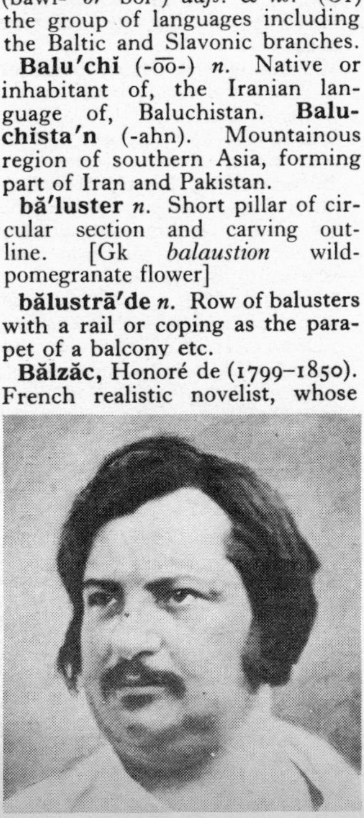

'Comédie Humaine' is a long series of novels intended to depict the whole of contemporary French society.

bămbōō' *n.* Tropical giant grass of genus *Bambusa*, with hollow

jointed stem; stem of this as a stick, as material etc.

bămbōō'zle *v.t.* Hoax, mystify.

băn[1] *v.t.* Prohibit, interdict. ~ *n.* Curse, formal prohibition.

ban[2] (bahn) *n.* (pl. *-i* pr. -ē). $\frac{1}{100}$ of a leu.

bana'l (-ahl; *or* bă-; *or* bā'n*a*l) *adj.* Commonplace, trite. **bană'lĭtў** *n.*

bana'na (-ahn*a*) *n.* Tropical fruit-tree, *Musa sapientum*; finger-shaped yellow pulpy fruit of this, growing in clusters or bunches; ~ *republic*, (esp. derog.) any small country whose economy depends on export of fruit. [Port. or Span., f. native name in Guinea]

Banaras: see BENARES.

Bă'nburў. Town in Oxfordshire, formerly noted for the number and zeal of its Puritan inhabitants; ~ *cake*, pastry filled with a currant mixture, orig. made at Banbury.

bănd *n.* 1. Thing that binds, bond (archaic). 2. Strip or hoop of material for supporting or holding things together or for decoration etc.; belt connecting wheels, pulleys, etc.; strip forming part of garment, esp. binding the neck or waist; (pl.) pair of white linen strips worn at neck as part of legal, ecclesiastical, or academic dress. 3. Body of musicians playing together, esp. wind-instrument performers (*brass, dance, military* ~); organized company or group of persons; *B~ of Hope*, association of people pledged to total abstinence from alcoholic drinks. 4. (elect.) Range of frequencies or wavelengths falling between two limits (also *wave-~*). 5. (phys.) Group of closely spaced lines in a molecular spectrum. 6. (sound-recording) One of several separately recorded sections of a record. 7. *ba'ndbox*, box for hats (orig. for neckbands); (*adj.*) conspicuously neat and clean; *ba'ndmaster*, conductor of a band of musicians; *~-saw*, endless saw running over wheels *ba'ndsman* member of a military or brass band; *ba'ndstand*, (covered, open-air) platform for musicians; *ba'ndwagon*, (orig. U.S.) wagon carrying the band at the head of a procession; *climb, jump, on the bandwagon*, join an enterprise that is likely to be successful. ~ *v.* Form into band or league; put a band on; *ba'ndĕd*, (bot., zool.) marked with coloured bands or bars.

BANDSMAN

bă'ndage *n.* Strip or band of textile material used to bind a wound, sore, etc., or for blindfolding the eyes. ~ *v.t.* Bind up with a bandage.

băndă'nna *n.* Coloured handkerchief with yellow or white spots. [prob. from Hind. *bāndhnū*, a method of dyeing in different colours]

bă'ndeau (-ō) *n.* Band of ribbon etc. round the head; band inside a woman's hat.

Bănde'llō, Matteo (1480–1562). Italian writer of short stories.

bă'nderōle *n.* Long narrow flag with cleft end flying from a ship, lance, etc.; ribbon-like scroll; (archit.) feature resembling this and bearing inscription.

Bă'ndersnătch *n.* Fleet furious creature of dangerous propensities in Lewis Carroll's 'Through the Looking-Glass' and 'Hunting of the Snark'.

bă'ndicōōt *n.* 1. Insectivorous and herbivorous Australian marsupial of genus *Perameles*, somewhat rat-like in appearance. 2. (also ~ *rat*) Large rat (*Nesocia bandicota*), up to 1 m in length, found in India. [Telugu]

bă'ndit *n.* (pl. *-s, banditti*). Outlaw, brigand; lawless and violent robber, esp. member of an organized gang.

băndoleer', -lier' *n.* Shoulder-belt with loops or pockets for cartridges.

băndolēr'ō *n.* Highwayman, robber.

bă'ndy̆ *v.t.* Throw or pass to and fro; discuss; exchange. ~ *n.*

(obs.) Hockey; hockey-stick. ~ *adj.* (of legs) Curving outwards at the knees; so *~-legged.*

bāne *n*, Ruin; poison. **bā'neful** *adj.* Poisonous; pernicious; injurious. **bā'nefullȳ** *adv.* **bā'nefulnėss** *n.*

Bă'nffshire. Former county of NE. Scotland, since May 1975 part of the region of Grampian.

băng[1] *v.* Strike or shut noisily; make sound as of a blow or explosion; thrash. ~ *n.* Sharp blow; loud noise. ~ *adv.* (colloq.) Right, exactly.

bang[2]: see BHANG.

băng[3] *n.* & *v.t.* (Cut *hair* in) a fringe.

bă'nger *n.* (esp., slang) Sausage; noisy old car.

Băngkŏ'k. Capital city of Thailand.

Bangladĕ'sh (bŭ- *or* bŭngg-). Muslim country in SE. Asia, formerly East Pakistan; member State of the Commonwealth, independent since 1971; capital, Dacca. [Bengali, = 'land of Bengal']

bă'ngle (-nggl) *n.* Ring bracelet or anklet.

bani: see BAN[2].

bă'nian, bă'nyan *n.* 1. Hindu trader; (Bengal) native broker to European business house. 2. Indian flannel jacket. 3. (also ~ *tree*) E. Indian fig tree, *Ficus bengalensis*, whose branches root themselves like new trees over a large area (first applied to a particular tree under which banians had built a pagoda).

bă'nish *v.t.* Compel (person) to leave his country; dismiss from one's presence or mind. **bă'nishment** *n.*

bă'nister, bă'nn- *n.* Post supporting hand-rail of a staircase; (pl.) posts and handrail together. [corrupt. of BALUSTER]

bă'njō *n.* (pl. *-os* or *-oes*). Musical instrument having 4, 5, 6, or 7 strings, head and neck like guitar, and body like tambourine, played with fingers or with plectrum; introduced into Europe by Amer. Negroes. **bă'njōist** *n.* [Gk *pandoura* 3-stringed mus. instrument]

bănjule'le (-lālĭ) *n.* Musical instrument combining features of banjo and ukulele.

bănk[1] *n.* 1. Raised shelf of ground; artificial slope. 2. Ground at edge of river. 3. (Flat-topped) mass of cloud. ~ *v.* 1. Contain or confine as or with bank(s). 2. Make (road, track) higher at outer edge of a bend to facilitate cornering at high speeds; (aeronaut.) incline (aircraft) laterally in turning so as to avoid a side-slip; ~ *up*, heap or rise into banks; pack tightly (fire, for slow burning).

bănk[2] *n.* 1. Establishment for custody of money, which it pays out on customer's order; building housing this; *central* ~: see CENTRAL; *savings* ~: see SAVING; *~-bill*, bill drawn by one bank on another; (U.S.) bank-note; *~-book*, book showing the state of a customer's account at a bank; ~ *holiday*, day on which banks (and therefore most places of business) are closed by statute; *B~ of England*, London corporation nationalized in 1946, the central bank of England and Wales; ~ *manager*, superintendent of local branch of bank; *~-note*, banker's promissory note payable to the bearer on demand, used as currency as a substitue for coinage; ~ *rate*, rate at which the Bank of England would discount for its customers approved bills of exchange, regarded as an important indicator of money conditions and used as a basis for fixing certain interest rates in other banks (abolished Oct. 1972). 2. Money-box; *piggy-~*: see PIGGY. 3. Money before keeper of a gaming-table. 4. Store, reserve supply (of blood, tissue, etc.). ~ *v.* Keep a bank; deposit money at a bank; ~ *on*, count or rely on.

bank[3] *n.* Galley-rowers' bench; tier (of oars) in galley; row of organ keys; group of similar objects connected in line.

bă'nker *n.* 1. Proprietor or director of a BANK[2]; keeper of money. 2. Keeper of money staked at gaming-table. 3. Card-game in which punters bet that the bottom card of their pile will have a higher value than the bottom card of the banker's pile.

bănkĕ′t *n.* Conglomerate rock containing gold, found in Witwatersrand area of S. Africa. [Du., = kind of hardbake (BANQUET)]

bă′nking *n.* Business of a banker or commercial BANK².

bă′nkrŭpt *n.* (law) Insolvent person whose effects, on his own or his creditors' petition to the Bankruptcy Court, are administered and distributed for the benefit of all his creditors; (pop.) any insolvent person; ~*'s certificate,* one stating that he has satisfied legal requirements and may re-commence business. ~ *v.t.* Make bankrupt. ~ *adj.* That is a bankrupt; insolvent. **bă′nkruptcy̌** *n.* [It. *banca rotta* broken bank]

Bănks, Sir Joseph (1743–1820). English explorer and natural historian who accompanied James Cook in his voyage round the world in the *Endeavour,* 1768–71.

bă′nksia *n.* Australian shrub of genus *B*~ with spicate flowers; ~ (or *banksian*) *rose,* Chinese species of climbing rose bearing small white or yellow flowers in clusters. [f. BANKS]

bă′nner *n.* Rectangular flag of a king, country, army, etc.; strip or piece of fabric bearing emblem or slogan etc.; (also ~ *headline*) newspaper headline in large type, esp. running across whole page.

bă′nnerėt *n.* Knight with vassals under his banner; one knighted on the field for valour.

bannister: see BANISTER.

bă′nnock *n.* (Sc. & north.) Round flattish loaf usu. of unleavened bread.

Bă′nnockburn. Town in Stirlingshire where the Scots under Robert Bruce defeated Edward II and the English coming to the relief of Stirling in 1314.

bănns (-z) *n.pl.* Notice of intended marriage, read three times in church, in order that any objections may be lodged.

bă′nquėt *n.* Sumptuous feast; dinner with speeches. ~ *v.* Regale with, take part in, banquet. [Fr., f. It. *banchetto,* dim. of *banco* bench]

bănquĕ′tte (-kĕt) *n.* Firing-step in trenches.

bă′nshee *n.* Spirit supposed by Irish and Highland superstition to wail under the windows of a house in which one of the inmates is about to die. [Ir., = 'fairy woman']

bă′ntam *n.* 1. Small variety of domestic fowl, of which the cock is a spirited fighter. 2. Small but spirited person. 3. *ba′ntamweight,* boxer of weight between flyweight and featherweight (see BOXING). [f. *Bantam,* seaport in W. Java]

bă′nter *n.* Humorous ridicule. ~ *v.* Make good-humoured fun of, rally; jest.

Bă′nting¹, William (1797–1878). English undertaker who advocated a method of reducing weight by dieting.

Bă′nting², Sir Frederick Grant (1891–1941). Canadian physiologist, co-discoverer of insulin 1922; Nobel Prize for medicine 1923.

bă′ntling *n.* Brat, young child.

Bă′ntu (-ōō) *n.* (Member of) an extensive group of Negroid peoples inhabiting the equatorial and southern region of Africa; language(s) spoken by them.

Băntusta′n (-ōōstahn) *n.* Any of several reservations for Bantus in S. Africa.

Banville (bahṅvēl), Theodore Faullain de (1823–91). French poet of the Parnassian school.

banyan: see BANIAN (used esp. for the tree).

bā′obăb *n.* African tree, *Adansonia digitata,* naturalized also in Australia, India and Ceylon, having extremely thick stem and large woody fruit with edible pulp, known as 'monkey-bread'.

B.A.O.R. *abbrev.* British Army of the Rhine.

bă′ptism *n.* Religious rite of immersing in or sprinkling with water in sign of moral or spiritual purification or regeneration, and initiation into the (Christian) church; ~ *of fire,* soldier's first experience of battle. **băpti′smal** (-z-) *adj.*

bă'ptist *n.* One who baptizes; *the B~, St. John the B~*: see JOHN[2]; *B~*, member of a Protestant Christian sect, founded early in the 17th c., which holds that baptism should be administered only to believers, not to infants, and by immersion.

bă'ptisterў, -trў *n.* Part of church (or in early times separate building) used for baptism.

băptī'ze *v.t.* Administer baptism to; christen; name.

bâr[1] *n.* 1. Long piece of rigid material; straight strip; heating element of electric fire; ~ *tracery*: see TRACERY. 2. Rectangular piece (of soap, chocolate, etc.). 3. Strip of silver below clasp of medal as additional distinction. 4. (mus.) Vertical line across stave dividing composition into sections of equal time-value (also ~ *line*); such a section. 5. (her.) Stripe across shield, narrower than fesse ; ~ *sinister*, erron. for BEND[1] sinister. 6. Rod or pole used to confine or obstruct; bolt or beam for fastening door etc.; = BARRE. 7. Barrier of any shape; bank of sand across mouth of harbour. 8. Barrier limiting access etc.; place in law-court where prisoner stands; (parl.) rail dividing off space to which non-members may be admitted on business; *the B~*, the profession of advocate, barristers in general (from bar in Inns of Court seperating benchers' seats from rest of hall); *be called to the ~*, be admitted a barrister; *be called within the ~* (i.e. that in courts within which Q.C.s plead), be appointed Queen's Counsel. 9. Plea arresting action or claim at law; obstacle; restriction. 10. Counter in inn etc. across which alcoholic drinks or other refreshments are served directly to customers; space behind this or room containing it; place serving refreshments across a counter; *bar'maid, bar'man, bar'tender*, attendant at bar of inn etc. ~ *v.t.* 1. Fasten with bars, keep in or out thus; obstruct, prevent; stay (process or party) by legal objection; exclude from consideration; object to, dislike (person etc.). 2. Mark with stripes.

bâr[2] *n.* Unit of barometric pressure, = 10^5 newtons per square metre.

bâr[3] *prep.* Except, excluding.

Bară'bbas. Robber released instead of Jesus Christ (Matt. 27: 16–26).

bărathē'a *n.* Fine cloth of wool or wool and silk or cotton.

bârb[1] *n.* Beard-like feelers of barbel etc.; chin-piece of nun's head-dress; lateral filament branching from shaft of feather; subordinate recurved point of arrow, fish-hook, etc. ~ *v.t.* Furnish with barb; *barbed wire*, wire used in fencing and as an obstruction in war, with short

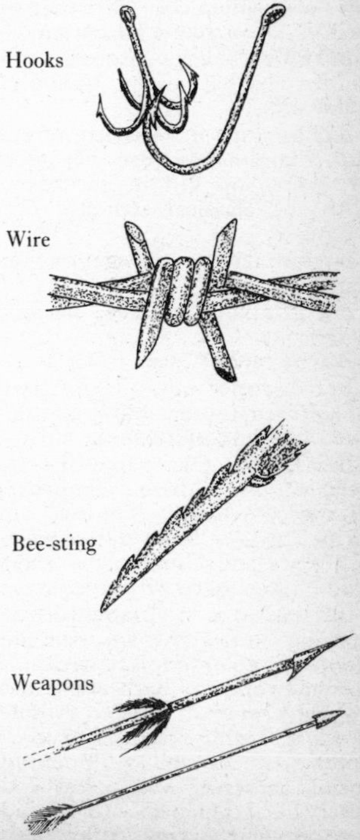

BARB

pointed pieces of wire twisted in at intervals. [L *barba* beard]

bar̂b[2] *n.* 1. Horse of the breed imported from Barbary, noted for speed and endurance. 2. Fancy black or dun-coloured pigeon, orig. introduced from Barbary.

Bar̂bā'dos (-ōz). Island in W. Indies settled by the British 1627, crown colony 1652; member State of the Commonwealth 1966; capital, Bridgetown. **Bar̂bā'dian** *adj.* & *n.*

bar̂'bara *n.* (logic) First word of the scholastic mnemonic lines for figures and moods of the syllogism.

bar̂bar̄'ian *n.* 1. Rough, wild, uncultured or uncivilized person (orig. foreigner, one differing in language and customs). 2. (hist.) Non-Greek; person outside the Roman Empire; person outside the civilization of Christendom. ~ *adj.* Of or like a barbarian.

bar̂bă'ric *adj.* Rough, uncultured; of barbarians. **bar̂bă'rically** *adv.*

bar̂'barism *n.* Absence of culture; ignorance; (use of) word or expression not in accordance with the classical standard of a language.

bar̂bă'rity *n.* Savage or barbarous cruelty.

bar̂'barīze *v.* Make, become, barbarous.

Barbarossa: see FREDERICK[1].

bar̂'barous *adj.* Uncivilized, uncultured, savage. **bar̂'barously** *adv.* **bar̂'barousness** *n.*

Bar̂'bary. Old name for the part of N. Africa comprising Morocco, Algeria, Tunisia, and Tripoli; ~ *ape*, large tailless ape of N. Africa and Gibraltar; ~ *sheep*, wild N. Afr. sheep with large horns.

bar̂'bėcūe *n.* 1. Framework for cooking meat above an open fire; (freq. portable) fireplace with such a framework. 2. Barbecued meat or fish; animal roasted whole; ~ *sauce*, highly seasoned sauce of vinegar, spices, etc. 3. (Open-air) social gathering where barbecue is served. 4. Open floor for spreading out and drying coffee-beans etc. ~ *v.t.* Cook on barbecue or with barbecue sauce. [Haitian *barbacòa* crate on posts]

bar̂'bel *n.* Large European freshwater fish of genus *Barbus* with fleshy filaments hanging from mouth; such a filament.

bar̂'ber *n.* Men's hairdresser; ~*'s itch*, skin disease affecting face and neck caused by a fungoid organism and communicated by (unsterilized) shaving apparatus; ~*'s pole*, pole painted spirally with red and white stripes, used as barber's sign.

bar̂'berry *n.* European shrub of genus *Berberis* with spiny shoots and small yellow flowers; oblong, red, sharply acid fruit of this.

bar̂bĕ'tte *n.* Platform or mound for mounting guns in a fortification; circular armoured platform with hood protecting heavy guns in warship.

bar̂'bican *n.* Outer defence to city or castle, esp. double tower over gate or bridge.

bar̂bi'tūrate *n.* (chem.) Salt of barbituric acid; (pharmac.) any of various hypnotic substances derived from barbituric acid. **bar̂bitūr'ic** *adj.* ~ *acid*, white crystalline substance ($C_4H_4O_3N_2$) from which barbiturates are derived.

Bar̂'bizon (-zawn). Village near Fontainebleau, near Paris, frequented in mid-19th c. by the ~ *School*, a colony of painters (T. Rousseau, Millet, Daubigny, and others) who produced naturalistic pictures of landscapes and peasant life.

bar̂bō'la *n.* Decorative work of flowers etc. modelled in a plastic paste and coloured.

Bar̂'bour (-*ber*), John (1316–95). Author of 'The Bruce' (*c* 1375), a long historical poem; regarded as father of Scottish poetry.

bar̂'carōle, -ŏlle *n.* Gondolier's song; imitation of this.

Bar̂cėlō'na. City and province of Catalonia, NE. Spain; ~ *nuts*, hazel-nuts imported from France and Portugal.

Bar̂'chėster: see TROLLOPE.

bârd[1] *n.* Celtic minstrel, (in Wales) poet recognized at the Eisteddfod; poet. **bâr'dĭc** *adj.*

bârd[2] *v.t.* Cover (meat) with slices of bacon before cooking.

bāre *adj.* Unclothed, uncovered; exposed; unadorned; scanty; mere; unarmed; *bar'eback* (*adj.* & *adv.*) on unsaddled horse; *ba'refaced*, shameless, impudent; *ba'refoot* (*adj.* & *adv.*) with bare feet; *bareha'nded* (*adj.* & *adv.*) unarmed. **bār'elȳ** *adv.* Scarcely; only just. **bār'enėss** *n.* **bāre** *v.t.* Make bare, strip, expose.

Barebones Pâr'liament (bār'-bōnz, -lam-). Nickname of Cromwell's 'Little' Parliament (1653), from one of its members, Praise-God Barbon, an Anabaptist leather-seller in Fleet Street.

Bār'ėnts, Willem (d. 1597). Dutch Arctic explorer, after whom is named the ~ *Sea*, the extreme NE. part of the Atlantic Ocean.

bâr'gain (-gĭn) *n.* Agreement on terms of transaction between two parties, compact; thing acquired by bargaining; advantageous purchase; *into the* ~, moreover; *strike a* ~, come to terms. ~ *v.i.* Haggle over terms of transaction; stipulate; ~ *for*, be prepared for, expect.

bârge *n.* Flat-bottomed freight-boat for canals and rivers; large oared vessel for State occasions; house-boat; ~*-pole*, pole with which a barge is propelled. ~ *v.i.* (colloq.) Lurch or rush heavily *into*, *against*.

bârge- *prefix.* (archit.) Gable: ~*-board*, board or ornamental screen under edge of gable; ~*- couple*, two beams which meet at the point of a gable; ~*-course*, that part of the roof which projects beyond them; ~*-stones*, those forming the sloping or stepped line of a gable. [med. L *bargus* gallows]

bârgee' *n.* Man in charge of barge; *swear like a* ~, swear fluently and forcibly.

barite: see BARYTES.

bărĭtōne *n.* Male voice between tenor and bass; singer with this voice. ~ *adj.*

bār'ium *n.* (chem.) White metallic element, first separated by Sir Humphry Davy in 1808, occurring as the basis of baryta; symbol Ba, at. no. 56, at. wt 137·34; ~ *sulphate*, white, very insoluble heavy powder ($BaSO_4$), opaque to X-rays, used in a mixture (~ *meal* etc.) in radiological examination of the alimentary tract.

bârk[1] *n.* Rind or outer sheath of the trunk and branches of trees; bark used in tanning. ~*v.t.* Strip bark from (tree); abrade (shins etc.).

bârk[2], **bârque** (-k) *n.* Three-masted vessel with fore- and main-masts square-rigged, and mizen fore-and-aft rigged; (poet.) ship, boat.

bârk[3] *v.* (of dogs etc.) Utter sharp explosive cry; make sound like this; speak sharply or petu-

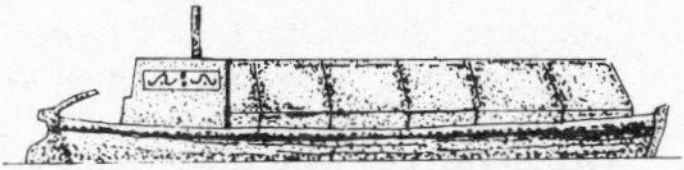

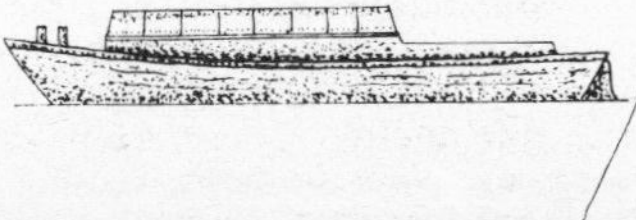

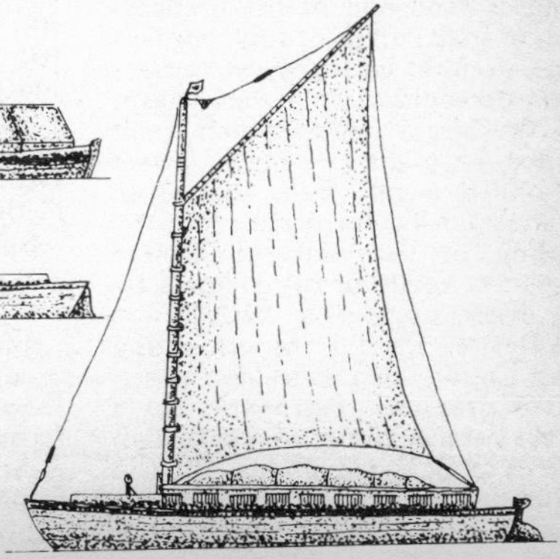

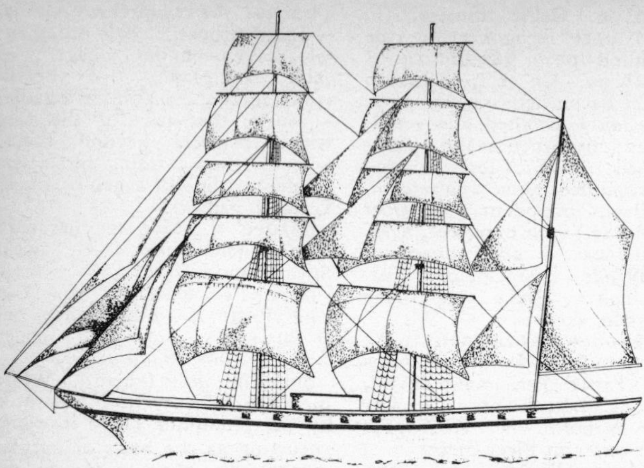

BARK

lantly; (slang) cough; *barking deer*, Indian muntjak, *Cervulus muntjak*, so named from its call. ~ *n.* Sharp explosive cry of dogs, foxes, squirrels, etc.; sound of gunfire; cough.

bar'ker[1] *n.* (esp.) 1. Pistol, gun. 2. Auction-room or side-show tout.

Bar'ker[2], Harley Granville (1877–1946). English dramatic critic, producer, and playwright, author of 'Waste', 'The Madras House', etc.

bar'ley *n.* Awned cereal (*Hordeum distichon* and *H. vulgare*), used as food and in the preparation of malt; grain of this; *bar'leycorn*, grain of barley; *John Barleycorn*, personification of barley, esp. as the grain from which malt liquor is made; ~*-sugar*, sweet of boiled sugar, freq. shaped in twisted sticks, formerly made by boiling in decoction of barley; ~*-water*, soothing drink made by the decoction of pearl barley.

barm *n.* Froth from fermenting malt liquor, used as leaven; yeast.

Bar'mècide. Patronymic of a noble Persian family who held high offices at Baghdad under Abbasid caliphs; acc. to the 'Arabian Nights', one of them set a number of empty dishes before a beggar, pretending that they contained a sumptuous banquet; hence, ~*'s feast*, imaginary or illusory benefits.

bar'mў *adj.* (slang) = BALMY, 2.

barn *n.* Covered building for storing grain (or hay, straw, etc.); ~*-door*, large door of this; target too big to be easily missed; ~*-door fowls*, domestic poultry; ~*-owl*, screech-owl, *Strix flammea*; *bar'nstormer*, strolling player; ~*-yard*, farmyard.

Bar'nabas, St. Joseph, surnamed Barnabas, an early leader of the Christian Church and companion of St. Paul on his missionary journeys (see Acts 4, 9, 11, etc.).

Bar'nabў. ~ *bright, long* ~, St. Barnabas's Day, 11 June, in the Old Style reckoned the longest day of the year.

bar'nacle[1] *n.* (usu. pl.) Pincers put on a horse's nose to keep him still for shoeing etc.

bar'nacle[2] *n.* 1. Arctic wild goose, *Anas leucopsis*, visiting the British coasts in winter. 2. Crustacean of the sub-class Cirripedia, either with a footstalk (*goose* ~), found attached to ships' bottoms etc., or without a footstalk (*acorn*

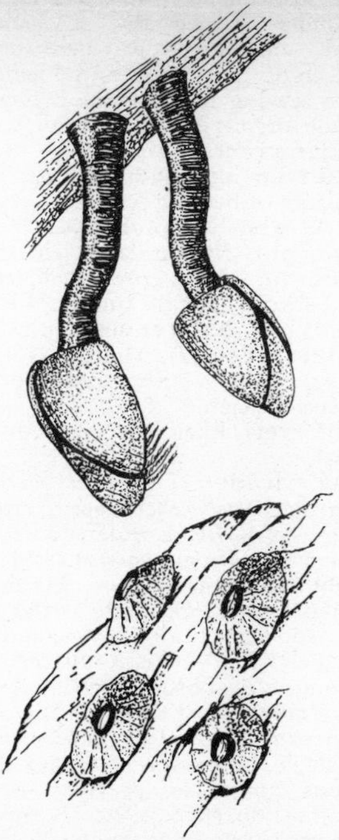

or *rock* ~), found attached to rocks.

Barnar'dō, Thomas John (1845–1905). British philanthropist, founder of homes (named after him) for destitute children.

Barnes (-nz), William (1801–86). Dorsetshire dialect poet.

bă'rogrăm *n.* Record of variations in atmospheric pressure.

bă'rogrăph (*or* -ahf) *n.* Barometer with apparatus (usu. paper roll on drum rotated by clockwork) for making a barogram.

barŏ'mėter *n.* Instrument for measuring atmospheric pressure (and hence for predicting changes in the weather) by means of a tube containing a column of mercury (which rises and falls according to the weight of the atmosphere) or of a vacuum box (see ANEROID ~). **bărométric, -ical** *adjs.* **bărome'trically** *adv.*

bă'ron *n.* 1. (hist.) Great noble, noble holding directly from the king by military service; *Barons' War*, revolt (1263–5) of English barons under Simon de Montfort against Henry III. 2. Member of lowest order of nobility in British peerage; holder of foreign title; (orig. U.S.) important financier or merchant (as *beef* ~). 3. ~ *of beef*, joint consisting of two sirloins left uncut at backbone. **bă'roness** *n.* Wife, widow, of baron; woman with baronial title in her own right.

bă'ronage *n.* Barons collectively; book with list of barons etc.

bă'ronet *n.* Member of the lowest hereditary titled order, ranking as a commoner.

bă'ronetage *n.* List of baronets.

bă'ronetcy *n.* Baronet's rank or patent.

barō'nial *adj.* 1. Of, belonging to, befitting, a baron. 2. *Scotch* or *Scottish B*~, applied to a style of architecture in Scotland in which the upper stories are decorated with corbelled turrets etc.

bă'rony *n.* Baron's rank, domain, or tenure; division of Irish county; large manor in Scotland.

barŏ'que (-k) *adj.* 1. Irregularly shaped (of jewels, esp. pearls); grotesque, odd. 2. Of the style of art which, evolved in Italy *c* 1600 out of that of the Renaissance, prevailed in Europe (chiefly in Catholic countries) until *c* 1720, being characterized by massive and complex design in which architecture was combined with painting, sculpture, etc., and esp. by vigorous, restless or violent movement; of the music or literature of this period. 3. Applied loosely to any style which is held to have similar characteristics. ~ *n.* Baroque style. [Fr., f. Span. *barrueco* rough pearl]

Barŏ'tsė *n.* Negroid people of Zambia; their language. **Barŏ'tsėlănd.** Region of W. Zambia.

bărou'che (-ōōsh) *n.* Four-wheeled horse-drawn carriage with a seat in front for the driver, and seats inside for two couples facing each other.

barque: see BARK[2], *n.*

barquentine (bar̂′kentēn) *n.* Three-masted vessel with foremast square-rigged and main and mizen fore-and-aft rigged.

bă′rrack *n.* (usu. pl.) Building(s) for lodging soldiers; large building of severely plain, dull, or dreary appearance. ~ *v.* Jeer (at), cheer ironically.

bărracou′ta (-ōōt*a*) *n.* Long narrow edible fish, *Thyrsites atun*, found in waters of S. Australia, New Zealand, and S. Africa (where it is called *snoek*).

bărracu′da (-ōōd*a*) *n.* Voracious fish of family Sphyraenidae, 2–3 m long, found in warm seas.

bă′rrage (-ahzh) *n.* 1. Artificial bar in river or watercourse. 2. (mil.) Obstacle to offensive or defensive action on part of an enemy, usu. in form of a line, area, or volume into which high-explosive shells are fired from a large number of guns either continuously or for pre-arranged periods; ~ *balloon*, large balloon supporting steel cable in an almost vertical position, esp. as one of a series forming anti-aircraft defence; *creeping* ~, one laid down in front of an advance of one's own troops and moving with them.

bă′rrator *n.* One who vexatiously incites to litigation or raises discord.

bă′rratry̆ *n.* 1. Purchase or sale of ecclesiastical preferments or offices of State. 2. Vexatious persistence in or incitement to litigation. 3. Fraud or gross and criminal negligence of ship's master or crew to the prejudice of the owners and without their consent. **bă′rratrous** *adj.*

bar̂re *n.* Hand-rail at waist level used by dancers to maintain balance while exercising.

bă′rrel *n.* 1. Wooden vessel of curved staves bound by hoops, with flat ends; contents or capacity of such a vessel. 2. Revolving cylinder in capstan watch, etc. 3. Cylindrical body of object; belly and loins of horse. 4. Metal tube of firearm, through which the missile is projected. 5. ~*-organ*, musical instrument with pinstudded cylinder turned by a handle and operating a mechanism which opens the pipes, the handle also serving to work the bellows; piano organ; ~ *vault*, vault with uniform concave roof.

bă′rren *adj.* Not bearing, incapable of bearing (children, fruit, etc.); waste; unprofitable. ~ *n.* (usu. pl.) Barren land; elevated plains on which grow small trees and shrubs, but no timber. **bă′rrenly̆** *adv.* **bă′rrenness** (-n-n-) *n.*

Barrès (bārĕz), Maurice (1862–1923). French author and Nationalist politician.

Bă′rrett, Elizabeth: see BROWNING[1].

bă′rricāde *n.* (Defensive) barrier, esp. one hastily erected across street etc. ~ *v.t.* Block or defend with a barricade. [Span. *barrica* cask]

Bă′rrie, Sir James Matthew (1860–1937). Scottish writer of comedies and short stories, author of 'Peter Pan', 'Quality Street', 'A Window in Thrums', etc.

bă′rrier *n.* Fence barring advance or preventing access; any obstacle, boundary, or agency that keeps apart, or prevents communication, success, etc.; ~ *cream*, cream that protects the skin against dirt, corrosive substances, etc.; ~ *reef*, high wall of coral rock separated from land by a broad deep channel and with a precipitous face on the seaward side, esp. the *Great B~ Reef*, off E. coast of Australia, some 1,100 miles long and 30 broad.

bă′rrister *n.* Student of law, who, having been called to the Bar (see BAR[1] *n.* 8), has the privilege of practising as advocate in the superior courts of law.

bă′rrow[1] (-ō) *n.* Prehistoric grave-mound, tumulus.

bă′rrow[2] (-ō) *n.* Rectangular frame with short shafts for carrying loads; shallow box with two shafts and one wheel, small two-wheeled handcart; ~ *boy*, costermonger.

bar̂′ry̆[1] *adj.* (her.) Divided horizontally by bars.

Bă′rry̆[2], Sir Charles (1795–1860).

Architect (with A. W. Pugin) of the English Houses of Parliament.

Bar'săc *n.* White wine, less sweet than most Sauternes, produced at Barsac, adjoining the district of Sauternes, in the Gironde.

Bar'sėt, Bar'sėtshire. Imaginary county in novels of Anthony Trollope, containing Barchester.

Bart *abbrev.* Baronet (commonly written after the name of one who holds that rank, to distinguish him from a knight).

bar'ter *v.* Exchange (goods, rights, etc.) *for* things of like kind. ~ *n.* Traffic by exchange.

Barth (-t), Karl (1886–1968). Swiss Protestant theologian.

Barthŏ'lomew, St. One of the 12 Apostles, commemorated on 24 Aug.; *Massacre of St.* ~, massacre of Huguenots throughout France ordered by Charles IX at the instigation of his mother Catherine de Médicis and begun without warning on the feast of St. Bartholomew, 1572; *St.* ~*'s Hospital,* (colloq. *Bart's*) London hospital founded 1123 by the English monk Rahere, prebendary of St. Paul's.

bartiză'n *n.* Battlemented parapet, or overhanging battlemented corner turret, at top of castle or church tower. [Coined by Sir W. Scott from misunderstanding of an illiterate Sc. spelling of *bratticing* parapet]

Bar'tŏk, Béla (1881–1945). Hungarian composer and collector of Hungarian folk-music.

Bartolommeo (-mā'ō) di Pagholo, Fra (1475–1517). Florentine painter.

Bartolŏ'zzi (-tsĭ), Francesco (1727–1815). Italian engraver (after Holbein etc.), active chiefly in England.

bar'ton *n.* (archaic) Farmyard.

Bart's. (colloq.) St. Bartholomew's Hospital, London.

Bar'uch (-ōōk). Book of the Apocrypha, attributed in the text to Baruch, the scribe of Jeremiah (Jer. 36).

bă'rȳon *n.* (phys.) Elementary particle whose mass is equal to or greater than that of a proton.

bă'rȳsphēre *n.* Core of the earth, consisting of a very heavy substance, prob. nickel iron.

barȳ'ta *n.* Barium monoxide, an alkaline earth distinguished by its great density.

barȳ'tēs (-z) *n.* (also *bar'īte*) Barium sulphate, heavy spar, used as a white paint.

bă'rȳtōne *n.* 1. = BARITONE. 2. Brass wind instrument of saxhorn family, used in military bands. 3. (hist.) Stringed instrument resembling viola da gamba. 4. (Gk gram.) Barytone word. ~ *adj.* 1. = BARITONE. 2. (Gk gram.) With no or grave accent on last syllable.

bā'sal *adj.* Of or at the base. **bā'sallȳ** *adv.*

bă'salt (-awlt *or* b*a*saw'lt) *n.* Dark-coloured fine-grained rock occurring as a lava or as an intrusion, often showing columnar structure, as at the Giant's Causeway in N. Ireland. **basa'ltĭc** *adj.*

bă'sanīte *n.* Smooth fine-grained black variety of quartz; touchstone.

bă'scūle *n.* Lever apparatus used in ~ *bridge*, kind of drawbridge balanced by a counterpoise which rises or falls as the bridge is lowered or raised, as the Tower Bridge, London.

bāse[1] *adj.* Morally low, mean, ignoble, debased; menial; ~*-born*, of low birth; illegitimate; ~ *metals*, those which quickly corrode or tarnish (opp. NOBLE OF PRECIOUS *metals*). **bā'selȳ** *adv.* **bā'senėss** *n.*

bāse[2] *n.* 1. That on which anything stands or depends; support, foundation, principle, groundwork, starting-point, principal element; substance used as first layer (of paint, make-up, etc.). 2. (biol.) End at which an organ is attached to trunk. 3. (geom.) Line or surface on which a plane or solid figure is held to stand. 4. (surv., also ~*-line*) Known line used as geometrical base for trigonometry. 5. (math.) Starting-number for system of numeration or logarithms (as 10 in decimal counting). 6. (chem.) Antithesis of ACID, substance capable of combining with an acid to form a salt (including, but wider than, ALKALI). 7. (archit.) Part of column between shaft or pedestal and pavement. 8. (mil.) Town or other area in rear of any army where drafts, stores, hospital, etc., are concentrated. 9. (gram.) Form of a word to which suffixes are attached. 10. One of the four corners of the diamond in baseball. 11. *~-line*, (surv.) see sense 4; line at end of court in lawn tennis; *ba'seman*, fielder at base in baseball. ~ *v.t.* Found or establish *on*.

bā'seball (-sbawl) *n.* National field-game of U.S., played between two teams of nine players on a diamond-shaped field with four bases round which the batter runs in order to score; ball used in this game.

bā'selėss (-sl-) *adj.* Groundless, unfounded.

bā'sement (-sm-) *n.* Lowest part of a structure; inhabited storey partly or wholly below ground-level.

basĕ'nji *n.* Small hunting dog of African breed which rarely barks.

băsh *v.t.* Strike heavily so as to smash *in*. ~ *n.* Heavy blow; *have a* ~ (*at*), (slang) attempt.

Bā'shan. Ancient kingdom beyond Jordan, conquered by Israelites under Moses (Num. 21: 33), and famous for its cattle (Ps. 22: 12, Amos 4: 1).

bă'shful *adj.* Shy, sheepish. **bă'shfullỹ** *adv.* **bă'shfulnėss** *n.*

băshi-bazou'k (-o͞ok) *n.* (hist.) Mercenary soldier of Turkish irregular troops, notorious for lawlessness, plundering, and brutality. [Turk. *başıbozuk* irregular soldier, not in uniform]

bā'sĭc *adj.* 1. Of, forming, or serving as a base or basis, fundamental; ellipt. (as *n.*) basic allowance, pay, etc. 2. (chem.) Having the chemical properties of a base. 3. (min., of igneous rocks) Having little silica in proportion to the amount of lime, potash, etc. 4. Applied to processes of steel manufacture from phosphoric pig-irons and to the steel thus produced; ~ *slag*, slag from this process, used finely ground as a fertilizer because of its phosphorus and manganese content. 5. *B~ English*, system of English comprising a select vocabulary of 850 words, devised by C. K. Ogden of Cambridge as a medium of international communication. **bā'sĭcallỹ** *adv.*

bāsĭ'cĭtỹ *n.* (chem.) Number of equivalents of a base with which one molecule of an acid can react.

basĭdĭomȳ'cēte *n.* Fungus producing basidiospores, e.g. mushroom and toadstool.

basĭ'dĭospōre *n.* (bot.) Spore borne at the extremity of a basidium.

basĭ'dĭum *n.* (pl. *-dia*). Spore-bearing structure in some fungi.

bă'sĭl[1] (-z-) *n.* Aromatic herb of the genus *Ocimum*, esp. *sweet* ~ (*O. basilicum*) and the dwarf *bush* ~ (*O. minimum*), the leaves of which are used for flavouring soups, salads, etc. [L *basilisca* the plant (supposed antidote to basilisk's bite)]

Bă'sĭl[2] (-z-), St. (*c* 330–79). Doctor of the Church, founder of a monastic rule which is still the basis of monasticism in the Orthodox Church.

basĭ'lĭc (-z-) *adj.* ~ *vein*, large vein of the upper arm.

basĭ'lĭca (-z-) *n.* 1. (in ancient Rome) Large oblong building used as exchange or law-court, having an apse at one or each end and freq. side-aisles; colonnaded hall, resembling this, in Roman house. 2. Church of similar shape, having a wide nave with aisles, and an apse at one (orig. western) end. **basĭ'lĭcan** *adj.* [Gk *basilika* (*oikia*) royal (house), f. *basileus* king]

bă'sĭlĭsk (băz-) *n.* 1. Cockatrice, fabulous reptile hatched by a serpent from a cock's egg, said to kill by its breath or glance. 2. Small Amer. lizard of the family Iguanidae, with a hollow crest that can be inflated at will. [L *basilicus* kind of lizard, f. Gk *basiliskos* little king]

bā'sin (-sn) *n.* 1. Circular or oval vessel of greater width than depth and with sloping or curving sides, for holding water etc.; contents of a basin. 2. Hollow depression; circular or oval valley; tract of country drained by river and its tributaries. 3. = DOCK³ 1, 2; land-locked harbour. **bā'sinful** *n.*

bā'sĭs *n.* (pl. *basēs*). Base; foundation, beginning, determining principle; main ingredient; common ground for negotiation etc.

bask (-ah-) *v.i.* Revel in warmth and light (*in* the sun, firelight, etc.); *basking shark*, one of the largest species of shark, *Cetorhinus maximus*, found in northern seas, so called from its habit of lying near surface of water.

ba'skėt (bah-) *n.* Receptacle of plaited or interwoven canes, osiers, etc.; contents of this; ~ *ball*, ball game played with inflated ball which is tossed into baskets suspended from posts; ~ *chair*, chair made from wickerwork; *B~ Maker*, member of an ancient Amer. Indian culture of southwestern U.S., preceding the Pueblo; *ba'sketwork*, interlaced osiers, twigs, etc.

Basle (bahl). (Ger. *Basel*, Fr. *Bâle*) Town and canton of Switzerland.

basque¹ (bahsk) *n.* Short continuation of bodice below waist; bodice having this.

Basque² (bahsk) *adj.* & *n.* (Member) of a people inhabiting both slopes of the W. Pyrenees and speaking a non-Indo-European language; (of) this language.

băs-rėlie'f (-lēf; *or* bah-) *n.* Low relief, carving or modelling in which figures project less than one half of their true proportions from the background.

băss¹ *n.* (pl. *bass* or *-es*). Any of a large group of perch-like fishes in sea or fresh water including *sea-~* (family Serranidae), *white ~* (*Roccus chrysops*), *yellow ~* (*Morone interrupta*), etc.

bāss² *adj.* Deep-sounding; of, suited to, lowest part in harmonized music; having a voice extending 1½ octaves or more below middle C; ~ CLARINET, DRUM, FLUTE, see these words; ~ *clef*: see CLEF; ~ *viol*, viola da gamba. ~ *n.* Bass part; music for, singer with, bass voice.

bass³: see BAST.

bă'ssėt *n.* (also *~-hound*) Short-legged dog of breed originating in France, used in hunting hares or badgers, followed on foot.

bă'ssėt-hôrn *n.* Tenor clarinet, of somewhat greater compass than the ordinary clarinet.

băssinĕ't *n.* Hooded wicker cradle or perambulator.

bă'ssō *adj.* & *n.* (mus.) Bass; ~ *profundo*, (singer having) deep bass voice.

bassōō'n *n.* Double-reed musical instrument, the bass of the wood-wind family, having an 8-ft pipe turned back so that the whole instrument measures only 4 ft; organ or harmonium stop of similar quality.

Băss Rŏck. Rock 350 ft (106 m) high, off coast of E. Lothian; in 17th c. the site of a prison; now a bird sanctuary.

băst, băss³ *ns.* Inner bark of lime or linden-tree, which, cut into strips and coarsely plaited, is used for matting etc.; similar fibre obtained from leaf-bases or leaf-stalks of certain palms and used for ropes, brooms, etc.; any flexible or fibrous bark.

bă'stard (*or* bah-) *n.* Person born out of wedlock; hybrid, counterfeit thing; used as term of abuse, or sometimes merely = fellow. ~ *adj.* **bă'stardȳ** *n.*

bă'stardīze (*or* bah-) *v.t.* Declare or render bastard.

bāste¹ *v.t.* Sew together loosely, sew with long loose stitches, tack.

bāste² *v.t.* 1. Moisten (roasting meat etc.) by pouring over it melted fat, gravy, etc. 2. (colloq.) Thrash, cudgel.

Băsti'lle (-tēl). (hist.) 14th-c. prison-fortress in Paris, used for political and other prisoners, stormed and destroyed by the mob on 14 July 1789; the anniversary

of its fall, as marking the end of absolute monarchy in France and the beginning of the French Revolution, is the national holiday of republican France.

băstĭnā'dō *n.* & *v.t.* (Punish with) caning or cudgelling on the soles of the feet.

bă'stĭon *n.* Mass of masonry or brick- or stone-faced earthwork projecting from fortification in the form of an irregular pentagon; (fig.) stronghold.

Basu'to (-ōō-) *n.* (Member of) a S. African people of Bantu stock.

băt[1] *n.* Small nocturnal mammal of the order Chiroptera, resembling a mouse, with leather-like wings consisting of a membrane stretched from neck over forearms and elongated fingers, and along sides of body to hind-limbs and (usu.) tail; *have* ~*s in the belfry*, (slang) be insane; hence *bats*, (slang) insane.

băt[2] *n.* Wooden implement with handle and striking surface, esp. that used in cricket; long, round stick with handle at one end used in baseball and other games; signalling object resembling table-tennis bat used for guiding landing aircraft; (slang) blow, knock; *ba'tsman*, player with bat in cricket etc.; man who signals with bats held in the hands. ~ *v.* Use bat, have innings (in cricket etc.).

băt[3] *v.t.* (colloq.) Blink; *not to* ~ *an eye(lid)*, (fig.) be unperturbed.

băt[4] *n.* (slang) Pace.

batā'ta (*or* -aht*a*) *n.* Sweet potato.

Batā'vĭa. 1. Former name of DJAKARTA. 2. (hist.) Region between Rhine and Waal, inhabited in Roman times by a Celtic tribe, the Batavi. 3. (literary, poet.) The Netherlands. **Batā'vĭan** *adj.* & *n.*

bătch *n.* Quantity of loaves etc. baked at one time; quantity, number, or set of people or things associated together, esp. in time.

bāte[1] *v.* Let down; restrain (breath); deduct; fall off in force.

bāte[2] *n.* (school slang) Rage.

bă'teau (-tō) *n.* (pl. *bateaux* pr. -ōz). Light river-boat, esp. the long, tapering, flat-bottomed boat used by French Canadians.

bath[1] (-ah-) *n.* 1. Immersion in liquid for cleansing or therapy; exposure to air etc. for therapy; water etc., for bathing. 2. Vessel, room (also *ba'throom*), or (usu. pl.) building for bathing in; (usu. pl.) swimming-bath. 3. Spa re-

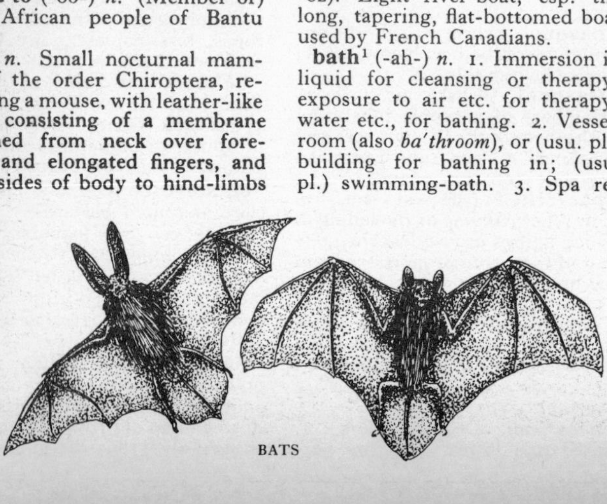

BATS

sorted to for medical treatment by bathing etc. 4. *Order of the B~*, high order of British knighthood, founded 1725 as revival of the 'Knights of the Bath' first created 1399 at coronation of Henry IV and so named from the ceremonial bath which preceded installation. ~ *v.* Wash in bath.

Bath[2] (-ah-). City in county of Avon (since 1974), noted for its hot springs; site of a Roman city (Aquae Sulis) and baths; a medicinal spa since 17th c., in 18th c. a fashionable resort; university, 1966; *~-brick*, calcareous earth moulded into a brick, used for cleaning metal; ~ *bun*, round, spiced currant-bun with sugar-icing; ~ *chair*, wheeled chair for invalids; ~ *chap*, pickled lower half of pig's cheek; ~ *Oliver*, unsweetened biscuit said to have been invented by William Oliver (1695–1764) a physician of Bath; ~ *stone*, oolite building-stone.

Bath: et Well: *abbrev.* (Bishop) of Bath and Wells (replacing surname in his signature).

bāthe (-dh) *v.* Immerse (in liquid, air, etc.); moisten all over; envelop; go swimming; *ba'thing-costume, -dress*, etc., garment for bathing or swimming in; *ba'thing-machine*, small hut on wheels, formerly used by sea-bathers for undressing and dressing. ~ *n.* Taking of bath, esp. in sea, river, or swimming-bath. **bā'ther** *n.*

bă'tholĭth *n.* Large body of intrusive rock (e.g. granite) such as is found esp. along Pacific coast of America.

bā'thŏs *n.* Fall from sublime to ridiculous; anticlimax. **bathĕ'tĭc** *adj.*

Băthshē'ba. Wife of Uriah the Hittite (2 Sam. 11); she became one of the wives of David and the mother of Solomon.

bă'thȳscăphe, -scăph *n.* Vessel for deep-sea diving and exploration. [Fr., f. Gk *bathus* deep+

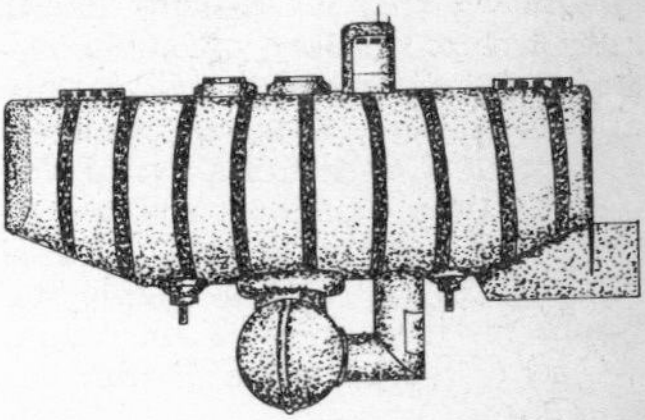

skaphos ship; coined by A. Piccard (1884–1962), Swiss physicist]

bă'thȳsphēre *n.* Spherical diving apparatus for deep-sea observation.

bă'tĭk *n.* Javanese method, practised also in the West, of executing designs on textiles by

BATH

painting parts of the pattern in wax, dyeing the parts left exposed, and then removing the wax; material dyed thus. [Javanese = 'drawing']

bati'ste (-ēst) *n.* Fine light cotton fabric of same texture as cambric, but differently finished; fine smooth woollen fabric. [Fr., f. *Baptiste* of Cambrai, first maker]

bă'tman *n.* (fem. *bă'twoman*). Member of army or air force acting as officer's servant. [orig. man who carried officer's baggage (Fr. *bât* pack-saddle)]

bă'ton *n.* 1. Staff of office, esp. *Marshal's* ~; constable's truncheon. 2. (her.) Ordinary like a narrow bend broken off at the extremities, in English heraldry only as ~ *sinister*, = BEND[1] sinister. 3. (mus.) Conductor's wand for beating time. 4. Short rod passed from one runner to another in a relay race. 5. Stroke replacing figure on face of clock or watch. ~ *v.t.* Strike with baton or truncheon.

batrā'chĭan (-k-) *adj.* & *n.* = ANURAN.

battă'lĭon *n.* Large body of men in battle array; unit of infantry, consisting of four companies and an H.Q. company and forming part of a brigade.

bă'ttels (-z) *n.pl.* College account at Oxford for board and provisions supplied, or for all college expenses.

bă'tten[1] *n.* 1. Long thin piece of squared timber used for flooring, hanging roof-tiles, etc. 2. (naut.) Strip of wood, esp. used to fasten down edges of hatchway tarpaulin in bad weather. ~ *v.t.* Strengthen, fasten *down*, with battens.

bă'tten[2] *v.i.* Feed gluttonously *on*; grow fat, (fig.) thrive at another's expense.

bă'tter[1] *v.* Strike repeatedly so as to bruise or break; beat out of shape; handle severely; *battered baby*, young child with injuries which appear to have been inflicted by a parent; *battering-ram*, heavy beam anciently used for breaching walls, sometimes with ram's-head end. ~ *n.* 1. Mixture of flour and eggs beaten up with liquid for cooking. 2. Defect in printing type or stereotype plate.

bă'tter[2] *v.i.* (of walls etc.) Incline from perpendicular so as to have a receding slope. ~ *n.* Slope of wall etc. from the perpendicular.

bă'tter[3] *n.* Batsman, esp. in baseball.

bă'tterў *n.* 1. (law) Infliction of blows or the least menacing touch to clothes or person. 2. (mil.) Set of guns with their men, horses, and vehicles; group of guns on a warship; unit of artillery consisting of two troops and forming part of an artillery regiment. 3. Set of similar or connected instruments, utensils, etc.; cell or set of cells supplying electricity; series of individual cages in which laying hens, cattle, etc., are confined.

bă'ttle *n.* Combat, esp. between large organized forces; *line of* ~, troops or ships drawn up to fight; *line-of-~ ship*, (obs.) battleship of 74 or more guns; *~-axe*, kind of long-handled axe used as a medieval weapon; prehistoric stone weapon; (fig.) formidable or domineering woman; *~-cruiser*, large, fast, and heavily armed cruiser; *~-cry*, war-cry; slogan; *ba'ttledress*, (formerly) soldier's etc. everyday uniform of blouse and trousers; *ba'ttlefield*, scene of battle; *ba'ttleship*, warship of the largest and most powerfully armed class. ~ *v.i.* Struggle *with* or *against*.

Bă'ttle A'bbey (ă-) Abbey founded by William the Conqueror (1069) on site of battle of Hastings; ~ *Roll*, document, prob. compiled in 14th c., which purports to show the names of families which came over to England with William; extant versions date from the 16th c.

bă'ttledōre *n.* Wooden, stringed, or parchment bat like a small racket for striking shuttlecock; ~ (*and shuttlecock*), game played with this by two persons who strike the shuttlecock to and fro between them. [prob. f. Span. *batallador* champion]

bă'ttlement (-lm-) *n.* Indented parapet at top of wall etc., orig. for purposes of defence against assailants.

băttū'e (*or* -ōō) *n.* Driving of game from cover towards point where sportsmen are stationed to shoot them; wholesale slaughter, esp. of unresisting crowds.

bă'ttȳ *adj.* (slang.) Crazy.

bau'ble *n.* 1. Showy trinket. 2. Baton surmounted by fantastic head with asses' ears carried by Court fool or jester.

Baudelaire (bōdlār), Charles Pierre (1821–67). French lyric poet, author of 'Les Fleurs du Mal' (1857).

Bauhaus (bow'hows). School of design founded by Walter Gropius (1883–1969) in Weimar in 1919; closed in 1933.

baulk: see BALK.

Baumé (bōmā), Antoine (1728–1804). French chemist; inventor of a hydrometer and two scales for use in measuring the specific gravity of liquids.

bau'xīte (bŏks-) *n.* Hydroxide of alumina, one of the chief sources of aluminium. [originally found at *Les Baux* near Arles, France]

Bavār'ia. Former State of S. Germany, now a province of the Federal Republic; capital, Munich.

Bavār'ian *adj.* & *n.*

baw'bee *n.* (Sc.) Halfpenny.

bawd *n.* (archaic) Procuress.

baw'dȳ *adj.* Humorously vulgar or indecent; ~-*house*, brothel. ~ *n.* Bawdy language; bawdiness.

baw'dĭlȳ *adv.* **baw'dĭnėss** *n.*

bawl *v.* Shout at the top of one's voice; ~ *out*, (slang) reprimand severely.

Băx, Sir Arnold Edward Trevor (1883–1953). English composer.

bay[1] *n.* 1. Kind of laurel, esp. the sweet bay or bay laurel, *Laurus nobilis*, with deep-green leaves (used to flavour soups etc.) and many dark-purple berries. 2. (usu. pl.) Wreath of bay leaves as a garland for a conqueror or poet. 3. (also *bay'berry*) West-Indian tree, *Pimenta acris*; ~ *rum*, aromatic liquid made from its leaves, used as an astringent.

bay[2] *n.* Part of sea filling wide-mouthed opening of land; ~ *salt*, salt obtained from sea-water by evaporation.

bay[3] *n.* 1. Division of wall between columns or buttresses. 2. Recess; compartment; *sick-*~, part of main deck used as hospital; part of building similary used. 3. Space added to room by advancing window from wall line; ~ *window*, window in a bay. 4. Railway platform having a cul-de-sac and serving as terminus for a sideline; the cul-de-sac itself; ~ *-line*, side-line starting from this.

bay[4] *n.* Bark of large dog or of hounds in pursuit, esp. as they draw near the quarry; *at* ~, in great straits; *stand, be, at* ~, show fight, turn against pursuers. ~ *v.* (of large dog) Bark, bark at.

bay[5] *adj.* (of horse) Having body of light to dark brown, with black mane and tail. ~ *n.* Bay horse; *the Bays*, the 2nd Dragoon Guards, who were mounted on bay horses *c* 1767.

bayadère (-ār') *n.* Hindu dancing-girl.

Bay'ārd, Pierre du Terrail, Seigneur de (1473–1524). French soldier of great valour and generosity, known as the knight 'sans peur et sans reproche'; hence (also *b*~), gentleman of high courage and honour.

Bayeux tă'pėstrȳ (bāyer̄). Long strip of embroidered linen at Bayeux Cathedral, containing scenes representing the Norman Conquest of England, with which it is usu. held to be nearly contemporary.

Bayle, Pierre (1647–1706). French philosopher and sceptic, author of a 'Dictionnaire historique et critique' (1695–7), which had great influence on Voltaire and other 18th-c. French sceptics.

bay'onėt *n.* 1. Stabbing blade which may be attached to rifle muzzle. 2. Cap on base of electric lamp etc. which engages with a

BAYEUX TAPESTRY

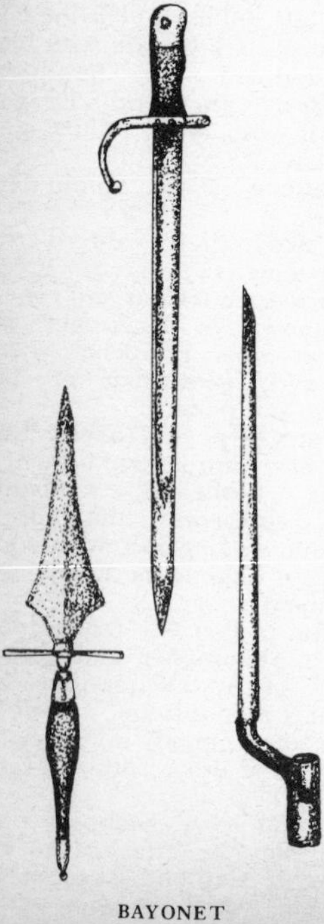

BAYONET

shaped slot in a corresponding socket. ~ *v.t.* Stab with bayonet.

bayou (bī′o͞o) *n.* (U.S.) Marshy inlet or creek of river or sea in southern states of U.S.

Bayreuth (bī′roit *or* bīroi′t). Bavarian town in which Wagner festivals are held in a theatre specially built for the production of his operas.

bazaar′ (-zâr) *n.* Oriental market-place or permanent market; fancy shop; fancy fair, esp. sale of goods for charities. [Pers. *bāzār* street of shops]

bazo͞o′ka *n.* (U.S.) 1. Crude, pipe-shaped musical instrument. 2. Amer. infantry light tubular projector for armour-piercing (esp. anti-tank) rockets.

BB, BBB *abbrevs.* Double-, treble-, black (of pencil-lead).

B.B. *abbrev.* Boys' Brigade.

B.B.C. *abbrev.* British Broadcasting Corporation.

B.C. *abbrev.* Battery Commander; before Christ; British Columbia.

B.C.E. *abbrev.* Before the Common Era.

B.Ch. *abbrev.*: see CH.B.

B.C.L. *abbrev.* Bachelor of Civil Law.

B.Com. *abbrev.* Bachelor of Commerce.

B.D. *abbrev.* Bachelor of Divinity.

bdĕ'llium (d-) *n.* Any of several trees or shrubs, chiefly of the genus *Commiphora*, yielding a gum-resin resembling impure myrrh, of bitter or acrid taste and more or less agreeable smell; the resin itself.

Bdr *abbrev.* Bombardier.

bds *abbrev.* Boards (in book-binding).

bē (*unstressed* bĭ) *v.i.* (past t. *was, were*, past part. *bēen*). Exist, occur; remain, continue; have a certain state or quality (specified by following noun, adj., etc.); *~-all* (*n.*) whole being, essence; esp. in *be-all and end-all*, absolutely everything, the whole *of*; *~ off*, go away.

B.E.A. *abbrev.* British Epilepsy Association.

beach *n.* Sandy or pebbly shore of the sea (or lake or large river); *~-comber*, (orig. U.S.) long wave rolling up from the sea; white man in Pacific Islands who lives by pearl-fishing, collecting jetsam, etc.; *~-head*, fortified position of troops landed on a beach. *~ v.t.* Run (ship etc.) ashore, haul up.

beach-la-mâr *n.* Jargon English used in the W. Pacific. [Port. *bicho do mar* sea-worm]

bea'con *n.* 1. Signal, signal-fire on hill or on pole raised above building. 2. Conspicuous hill suitable for the lighting of beacons. 3. Lighthouse; conspicuous object; (also *Belisha ~*) one of a pair of amber-coloured globes on poles marking certain crossing-places on highways. 4. Radio station enabling ship or aircraft to fix position.

Bea'consfield (bĕkonz-). Town in Buckinghamshire, England; *Earl of ~* (bēk-): see DISRAELI.

bead *n.* 1. Small perforated ball etc. for threading with others on a string or for sewing on to fabric; small bubble or drop of liquid; (pl.) rosary. 2. Small metal knob forming front sight of gun (*draw a ~ on*, take aim at). 3. (archit., also *beading*) Narrow cylindrical moulding sometimes carved to resemble a row of beads; so *~-and-reel*. 4. *~-roll* list or string of names, catalogue. *~ v.* Furnish or adorn with beads or a beading. [OE, 'prayer' from the use of strings of beads for keeping count of the number of prayers said]

bea'dĭng *n.* see BEAD *n.* 3.

bea'dle *n.* 1. (hist.) Inferior parish officer appointed to keep order in church, punish petty offences, and carry messages, etc. 2. Apparitor or precursor who walks officially in front of dignitaries, mace-bearer (in the Engl. universities usu. spelt *bedel*(*l*)).

bea'dledom *n.* Stupid officiousness.

bea'dsman (-z-) *n.* (hist.) One who prays for the soul or spiritual welfare of another, one paid to do this; hence, pensioner or almsman, inmate of alms-house. [see BEAD etym.]

bea'dў *adj.* (of eyes) Small and bright like beads.

bea'gle *n.* Small hound for hunting hares, followed on foot.

bea'glĭng *n.* Hunting with beagles.

beak[1] *n.* Horny projecting mandibles of bird; extremities, often horny in structure, of mandibles of other animals; hooked nose; projection at prow of ancient ships, esp. war-galleys; spout; *bea'khead*, one of a series of grotesque beaked heads carved as ornament on moulding in Romanesque architecture.

beak[2] *n.* (slang) Magistrate; master at public school.

bea'ker *n.* 1. Large drinking-cup. 2. (archaeol.) Wide-mouthed vessel found in graves of a neolithic people (*~ folk, ~ people*) who came to Britain from Europe in the second millennium B.C. 3. Straight-sided lipped glass for scientific experiments.

beam *n.* 1. Long piece of squared timber such as is used in house- or ship-building; horizontal support in building. 2. Great timber of plough, to which all other parts of plough-tail are fixed. 3. Wooden cylinder in loom on which the warp is wound 4. Transverse bar of balance; *~ compass*, compasses with transverse bar. 5. Transverse horizontal timber of a ship; hence, the greatest breadth of a ship; *on the* ~, at right angle to direction of ship. *on her* ~*-ends*, (of ship) lying on its side and in danger of capsizing; *on one's* ~*-ends*, (fig.) extremely hard-up. 6. Ray or pencil of light, or of electric radiation, etc.; (also *radio*, *wireless* ~) radio waves sent as a beam (i.e. not dispersed or broadcast) by a special aerial system, part of which acts as a reflector; (aeron.) directional radio signal used to guide aircraft or missiles; course indicated by this; (phys.) directional flow of radiation or particles. 7. Radiance, bright look, smile. ~ *v.* Emit (light, affection, etc.); direct, aim (radio signals etc.); shine, smile radiantly.

bean *n.* 1. Kidney-shaped non-endospermic seed borne in pods of the family Leguminosae. 2. Similar seed of other plants, as coffee. 3. (slang) *not a* ~, no money; *old* ~, familiar form of address; *full of* ~*s.* in high spirits; *give a person* ~*s*, deal severely with him; *spill the* ~*s*, give away information. 4. ~*-feast*, annual dinner given by employers to their workpeople; fête, merry time; *bea'nstalk*, stem of the bean-plant. ~ *v.t.* (U.S. slang) Hit on the head.

bea'nō *n.* (slang) Bean-feast.

bear[1] (bār) *n.* 1. Heavily-built, thick-furred plantigrade quadruped of family Ursidae; child's toy in shape of this, Teddy bear. 2. Rough, unmannerly or uncouth person. 3. (Stock Exch.) Speculator for a fall, one who sells stock for future delivery hoping to buy it cheaper in the interval; ~ *market*, one with falling prices. 4. *Great*, *Little B*~: see URSA. 5. ~ *animalcule*: see TARDIGRADE; ~*-garden*, orig. place for baiting bears; scene of strife and tumult; *bear'skin*, Guards'tall furry cap; ~ *leader*, travelling tutor to a rich young man. **bear'ish** *adj.* Rough-mannered, surly; (of stock market or prices) tending to fall. **bear** *v.* (Stock Exch.) Speculate for, cause, a fall in price of stocks etc.

bear[2] (bār) *v.* (past t. *bōre*, past part. *bōrne* exc. as below). 1. Carry, support; ~ *out*, confirm. 2. Endure, tolerate; ~ *up*, keep up one's courage; ~ *with*, be patient with. 3. (past part. usu. *born* in passive) Give birth to. 4. Produce, yield. 5. Apply weight; tend, incline; *bring to* ~, apply; ~ *down*, press downwards; (naut.) sail to leeward; ~ *down on*, move towards; ~ *hard on*, oppress, ~ *on*, relate to.

beard *n.* Hair upon lower part of man's face (now usu. excluding moustache and whiskers); chin tuft of animals; gills of oyster; awn of grasses; (print.) part of type above and below face which allows for ascending and descending letters. **bear'dless** *adj.* Youthful, immature. **beard** *v.t.* Oppose openly, defy.

Bear'dsley (-dzlĭ), Aubrey Vincent (1872–98). English artist and illustrator, chiefly in black and white; art editor of the 'Yellow Book'.

bear'er (bār-) *n.* 1. Bringer of letter etc., presenter of cheque; one who helps to carry coffin; ~ *bond*, *security*, etc., one not registered, the title to which is vested in its possessor. 2. (eng.) Plate or beam supporting load.

bear'ing (bār-) *n.* (esp.) 1. Behaviour. 2. Heraldic charge or device. 3. Relation, reference, aspect; tendency to exert influence *on*. 4. Part of machine that bears the movement. 5. Situation or direction of one point, object, etc., with respect to another; determination of this; (pl.) relative position (also fig.). 6. ~*-rein*, fixed rein from bit to saddle forcing horse to arch its neck.

beast *n.* 1. Animal; quadruped as dist. from birds, man, insects, etc.; bovine animal; animal used for riding, driving, etc. 2. Human being acting like an animal; brutal, savage man; person one dislikes.

bea'stlȳ *adj.* Like a beast or its

ways; unfit for human use, dirty; (colloq.) undesirable, unpleasant, annoying. **bea′stlĭnėss** *n.*

beat *v.* (past. t. *beat*, past part. *beaten* and occas. *beat*). 1. Strike repeatedly; (of sun etc.) strike *upon*. 2. Overcome, surpass; be too hard for, perplex; *dead* ~, (slang) utterly exhausted. 3. (of wings etc.) Move up and down; (of heart etc.) pulsate, throb; ~ *it*, (slang) go away; ~ *time*, mark the time of music by the beat of a wand, tapping with the foot, etc. 4. Shift, drive, alter, deform, or shape by blows; (also ~ *up*) mix to a froth or paste by turning (mixture etc.) over and over with a circular motion. 5. Strike bushes etc. to rouse game. 6. ~ *up*, (naut.) strive or tack against the wind; ~ (person) *up*, (colloq.) attack and injure him by blows and kicks. ~ *n.* 1. Stroke on drum; signal so given; movement of conductor's baton; measured sequence of strokes or sounds; throbbing. 2. Sentinel's or constable's appointed course; habitual round. 3. Idle worthless fellow (U.S.); (colloq.) = BEATNIK.

bea′ten *adj.*: see BEAT; (esp.) ~ *gold* etc., gold etc. hammered into foil, shaped by the hammer; ~ *track*, *way*, well-trodden way (also fig.).

bea′ter *n.* (esp.) Man employed to rouse game; man who beats gold etc.; implement which beats, as *carpet-*~, *egg-*~, etc.

beat gĕnerā′tion. Young people (esp. after 1939–45 war) adopting unconventional dress, manners, habits, etc., as a means of self-expression and social protest. [Prob. f. *beat* = 'exhausted'; perh. infl. by *beat* = 'rhythm'; but coined by J. Kerouac (b. 1922), U.S. novelist, connecting *beat* with *beatitude*]

bēatĭ′fĭc *adj.* Making blessed, imparting supreme happiness; blissful.

bėă′tĭfȳ *v.t.* Make supremely happy or blessed; (R.C. Ch.) declare to be in enjoyment of heavenly bliss (as the first step towards canonization). **bėătĭfĭcā′tion** *n.*

bėă′tĭtūde *n.* 1. Supreme blessedness; declaration of blessedness, esp. (pl.) those pronounced by Jesus Christ in the Sermon on the Mount (Matt. 5: 3–11). 2. (*B*~) Title of clergy of Orthodox Church of patriarchal rank.

bea′tnĭk *n.* Member of the beat generation.

Bē′atrĭce. Dante's name for a lady whom he loved, although he never spoke to her; he tells of his few meetings with her in the 'Vita Nuova', and in the 'Divina Commedia' she is his guide through Paradise; she represents for him the type of ideal love.

Bea′ttȳ, David, Earl (1871–1936). Naval officer, commander of the British battle-cruiser fleet at the battle of Jutland, 1916.

beau (bō) *n.* Fop; lady's-man, woman's male escort; *B*~ *Brummell*, *B*~ *Nash*: see these names.

Beau′fort scāle (bōf-). Series of numbers used by meteorologists to indicate force of wind (measured at 10 m above level ground), thus:

Force	*m.p.h.*		*knots*
0	less than 1	calm	less than 1
1	1–3	light air	1–3
2	4–7	light breeze	4–6
3	8–12	gentle breeze	7–10
4	13–18	moderate breeze	11–16
5	19–24	fresh breeze	17–21
6	25–31	strong breeze	22–27
7	32–38	near gale	28–33
8	39–46	gale	34–40
9	47–54	strong gale	41–47
10	55–63	storm	48–55
11	64–72	violent storm	56–63
12	73 or more	hurricane	64 or more

[devised by Admiral Sir F. *Beaufort* (1774–1857)]

beau geste (bō zhĕst). Display of magnanimity. [Fr., = 'beautiful (or splendid) gesture']

beau īdė′al (bō; *or* -ē′*al*). One's highest type of excellence or beauty. [Fr. (*idéal*), = 'the ideal Beautiful', often misconceived in English as a beautiful ideal]

Beaujolais (bō′zholā *or* -ōlā) *n.* Red or white Burgundy from the Beaujolais district in the Rhône department of France.

Beaumarchais (bōmărshā), Pierre Auguste Caron de (1732–90). French dramatist, author of two famous comedies, 'Le Barbier de Séville' (1775), 'Le Mariage de Figaro' (1778).

beau monde (bō mawṅd). Fashionable society.

Beau'mont (bōm-), Francis (1584–1616). English playwright, collaborator with John FLETCHER from *c* 1606 to 1616.

Beaune (bōn) *n.* Red wine produced near Beaune in the Côte d'Or district of France.

beau'tėous (būt-) *adj.* (archaic & poet.) Endowed with beauty.

beautician (būtĭ'shan) *n.* (U.S.) One who runs a beauty parlour; specialist in beauty treatment.

beau'tĭful (būt-) *adj.* Having beauty; capital, excellent. **beau'tĭfullȳ** *adv.* **beau'tĭful** *n. the* ~, beauty in the abstract.

beau'tĭfȳ (būt-) *v.t.* Make beautiful.

beauty (bū'tĭ) *n.* Combination of qualities (as form, colour, etc.) that delights the eye; combined qualities delighting the other senses, the moral sense, or the mind; beautiful trait or feature; person or thing possessing beauty; ~ *parlour*, place where the business of applying cosmetics, face-massage, and other beauty treatment is carried on; ~ *sleep*, sleep obtained before midnight; ~*-spot*, small patch placed on woman's face as foil to a beautiful complexion; beautiful scene; ~ *treatment*, use of massage, cosmetics, exercise, etc., in order to improve personal beauty.

bea'ver[1] *n.* 1. Amphibious rodent of genus *Castor* with broad, oval, horizontally flattened tail, webbed hind feet, soft fur, and hard incisor teeth with which it cuts down trees, remarkable for its industry esp. in constructing dams of wood and mud; *eager* ~, (colloq.) zealous person. 2. Soft, short, rather woolly light-brown fur of this animal; hat made from this.

Bea'verbrŏŏk, William Max-

BEAUNE

well Aitken, 1st Baron (1879–1964). British newspaper proprietor and Conservative politician.

bē'bŏp *n.* Kind of jazz music.

bėca'lm (-kahm) *v.t.* Make calm; deprive (ship) of wind.

bėcau'se (-ŏz) *adv.* By reason *of* ~ *conj.* For the reason that.

Béchamel sauce (bā'shaměl). Rich white sauce. [f. its inventor, Marquis de *Béchamel*, steward of Louis XIV]

bêche-de-mer (běsh, mār) *n.* = TREPANG.

Běchūa'na (-k-, -ahn*a*; *or* -ch-). *n.* = TSWANA.

běck[1] *n.* (north.) Brook, mountain stream.

běck[2] *n.* Significant gesture, nod, etc.; *at the* ~ *and call of*, entirely dominated by, completely at the service of. ~ *v.* (poet.) Make beck (to).

bě'ckėt[1] *n.* (naut.) Loop of rope or other simple contrivance for securing loose ropes, tackle, or spars, and for holding or securing the tacks or sheets of sails etc.

Bě'ckėt[2], St. Thomas à (1117–70). Archbishop of Canterbury (1162) and Chancellor of England (1158) under Henry II; he successfully opposed Henry's policy in taxation and other matters, and was murdered by Henry's orders, in Canterbury Cathedral; he was canonized in 1173, and his shrine became the most famous in Christendom; it was destroyed in 1538.

Bě'ckėtt, Samuel (1906–). Irish novelist and dramatist, many of whose works are written in French; author of the play 'En attendant Godot' (1952, transl. 'Waiting for Godot', 1954); Nobel Prize for literature 1969.

Bě'ckford, William (1759–1844). English eccentric; author of 'Vathek', an Oriental novel in French (1787).

bě'ckon *v.* Summon, call attention of, by gesture; make mute signal *to*.

bėclou'd *v.t.* Cover with clouds, obscure.

bėco'me (-ŭm) *v.* (past t. *became*, past part. *become*). 1. Come into being; begin to be; ~ *of*, (past t. & fut.) happen to (as in *what has, will, become of him?*). 2. Suit, befit, look well on. **bėco'ming** *adj.* Suitable; (of clothes etc.) giving pleasing appearance. **bėco'minglȳ** *adv.*

Becquerel (běkerěl), Antoine Henri (1852–1908). French physicist; discoverer of radioactivity; Nobel Prize for physics 1903; ~ *rays*, rays emitted by a radioactive substance.

běd *n.* 1. Thing to sleep or rest on; mattress; framework with mattress and coverings; animal's resting-place, litter; *go to* ~ *with*, (esp.) have sexual intercourse with. 2. Flat base on which anything rests; foundation of road or railway; garden-plot for plants; bottom of sea, river etc.; stratum. 3. ~*-bug*: see BUG; *be'dchamber*, (archaic) bedroom; *be'dclothes*, sheets, pillows, blankets, etc., of bed; *be'dfellow*, sharer of bed; (fig.) associate; *be'dgoer*, (formerly) one who accompanied monarch to his bedchamber as protection against assassins, (now) title of an official; *be'dlinen*, sheets and pillow-cases; *be'dpan*, shallow pan for containing excreta, used by persons confined to bed; ~*-plate*, metal plate forming base of machine. *be'dpost*, upright support of bedstead; ~*-ridden* (*adj.*) confined to bed by infirmity; ~*-rock*, solid rock underlying alluvial deposits etc.; also fig.; *be'droom*, room for sleeping in; *be'dside*, side esp. of invalid's bed; ~*-si'tting-room*, (colloq. ~*-si'tter*) combined bed-room and sitting-room; *be'dsore*, sore developed by long lying in bed; *be'dspread*, coverlet; *be'dstead*, framework of bed; *be'dstraw*, plant of genus *Galium* with slender stem and small clustered flowers; *be'dtime*, hour for going to bed. ~ *v.* 1. Put or go to bed; provide bedding for horses etc. 2. Plant *out* in a garden bed. 3. Cover up or fix firmly in something; (eng.) fit accurately. 4. Arrange as, be or form, a layer.

B.Ed. *abbrev.* Bachelor of Education.

bėdă'bble *v.t.* Splash with liquid.

bėdau'b *v.t.* Smear or daub with paint, mud, etc.

bĕ'dding *n.* (esp.) 1. Mattress and bedclothes; litter for horses etc. to sleep on. 2. (geol). Layered structure visible in some rocks resulting from their deposition in water in layers or beds.

Bēde, St. (*c* 673–735). English historian and scholar, a monk of Jarrow; author of a Latin history of the English Church and many other works in Latin; known since 9th c. as 'the Venerable ~'.

bėdĕ'ck *v.t.* Adorn.

bĕ'dėguar (-gar) *n.* Kind of gall caused by the puncture of an insect, *Cynips rosae*, and forming a moss-like excrescence on rose-bushes. [Pers. *badawar* brought by the wind]

bedel(l): see BEADLE.

bėdĕ'vil *v.t.* Torment diabolically, bewitch. **bėdĕ'vilment** *n.* Possession by devil; maddening trouble, confusion.

bėdew' *v.t.* Cover with drops of or like dew.

Bĕ'dfordshire. E. midland county of England.

bėdi'm *v.t.* Make dim, obscure.

bėdi'zen *v.t.* Deck out gaudily.

Bĕ'dlam[1]. (hist.) Popular name for the hospital of St. Mary of Bethlehem, founded as a priory in 1247 in Bishopsgate, and used as a hospital for lunatics; it was removed to Moorfields, then to Lambeth, and finally to Beckenham.

bĕ'dlam[2] *n.* 1. (hist.) Lunatic asylum. 2. Scene of uproar.

bĕ'dlamīte *n.* (hist.) Lunatic.

Bĕ'dlington *n.* (also ~ *terrier*) Curly-haired, grey terrier with narnow head, short body, and longish legs. [*Bedlington* in Northumberland]

Bĕ'douin, bĕ'douin (-ōō-) *n.* (pl. same). Arab of the desert. [Arab. *badawiyyūn*, oblique case *badawiyyīn* desert-dwellers]

bėdră'ggle *v.t.* Wet (dress etc.) by trailing it, or so that it trails or hangs limp.

Beds. *abbrev.* Bedfordshire.

bee *n.* 1. Hymenopterous four-winged stinging insect living in societies composed of one queen, a small number of drones, and a number of workers, who produce wax and collect honey, which they store up in wax cells for winter food. 2. Any of a large group of allied insects. 3. (chiefly U.S.) Meeting of neighbours to unite their labours for the benefit of one of them; gathering or meeting for some object, esp. for a competition in spelling (*spelling-* ~). 4. ~ *in one's bonnet*, eccentric whim, craze on some point; ~*-bread*, honey and pollen eaten by nurse-bees; *bee'hive*, HIVE; domed structure resembling one type of hive; ~*-line*, straight line between two points, such as a bee is supposed to make returning to the hive; *bee'swax* (*n.* & *v.t.*) (polish with) wax secreted by bees (see WAX[1], 1); *bee'swing*, crust of shiny filmy scales of tartar formed on port and some other wines after long keeping.

beech *n.* Forest-tree of Europe and W. Asia (genus *Fagus*) with fine thin smooth bark, glossy oval leaves, boughs and foliage which form a dense canopy, and three-sided nuts borne in pairs in a rough or prickly involucre; its wood; any of various other trees more or less resembling this; ~*-marten*, marten (*Martes foina*) of Europe and Asia, with white patch on breast and throat, stone-marten; ~*-mast*, beech nuts collectively. **bee'chen** *adj.* Of beech or beechwood.

beef *n.* Flesh of ox, bull, or cow used as food; ox, any animal of the ox kind; (slang) complaint, ground for this; *bee'featers*, (f. obs. sense of 'dependants') pop. name of Yeomen of the Guard and of warders of the Tower of London, who wear the same uniform; ~*-steak*, slice of beef cut from hind-quarters and suitable for grilling, frying, etc. ~ *tea* ,stewed beef juice for invalids.

bee'fȳ *adj.* Solid, muscular;

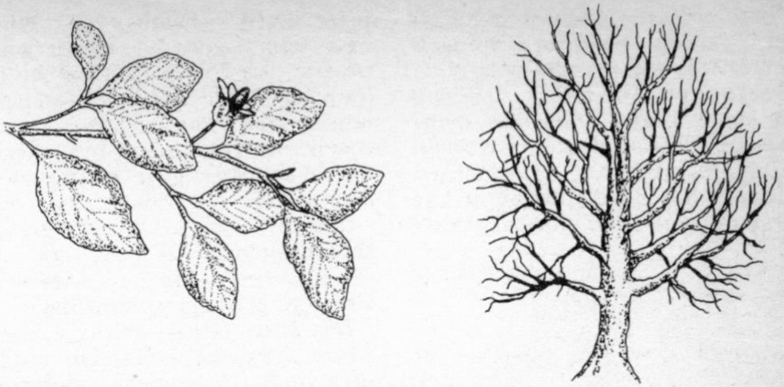

BEECH

stolid. **beef** *v.i.* (slang) Complain, grumble.

Bēē'lzėbŭb. Canaanite god, mentioned in 2 Kings 1: 2 as the 'god of Ekron', and in the N.T. as 'prince of demons'; the Devil. [Heb. *ba'al-z^{e}b̲ûb̲* fly-lord]

been: see BE.

beer *n.* Alcoholic liquor made from fermented malt flavoured with hops, ale; (in trade usage) any of the liquors brewed from malt, as ale, stout, porter, lager; (pop.) ale as distinct from the others; *small* ~, weak beer; (fig.) trifling matter or person; ~*-engine*, apparatus for drawing beer from the barrel in the cellar to the tap in the bar of a public house.

Beer'bohm (-bōm), Sir Max (1872–1956). English author and caricaturist.

beer'ȳ *adj.* Of or like beer; betraying its influence.

bee'stings (-z) *n.pl.* First milk drawn from a cow after parturition.

beet *n.* (pl. same). **Any of several plants with edible roots (varieties**

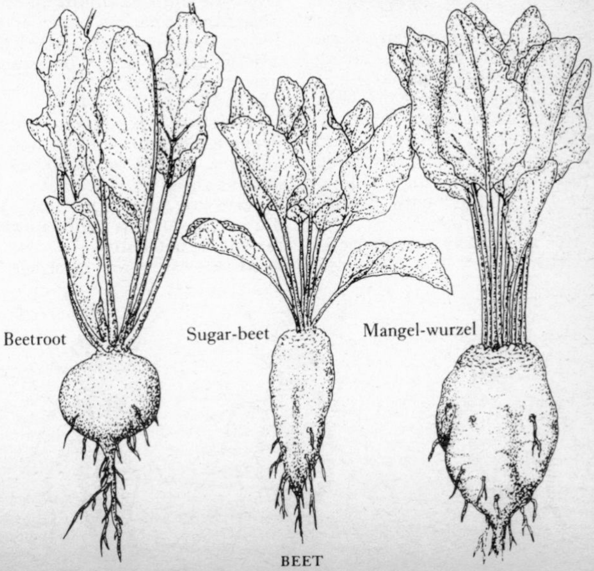

BEET

of *Beta vulgaris*), including sugar-beet, garden beetroot, spinach beet, chard, and mangel-wurzel.

Beethoven (bā'tōvn), Ludwig van (1770–1827). German composer of Flemish descent; worked mainly in Vienna; contributed much to the development of the symphony and other musical forms;

wrote nine symphonies, an opera, many pianoforte sonatas, string quartets, and other orchestral and chamber music; during his later years he was stone-deaf.

bee'tle[1] *n.* Tool with handle and heavy head for crushing, ramming, etc., mallet; machine for finishing cloth. ~ *v.t.* Beat with beetle; finish (cloth) with beetle.

bee'tle[2] *n.* 1. Any coleopterous insect with front wings converted into hard sheaths or wing-cases which close over the back and protect the lower or true wings; (pop.) insect resembling these, esp. largish black one; *black-~*, cockroach. 2. Dice-game in which a beetle-shaped figure is drawn or assembled.

bee'tle[3] *v.i.* 1. Overhang threateningly. 2. Go *off* etc. ~ *adj.* (in ~ *brows*, *~-browed*) Projecting, shaggy, scowling.

Bee'ton (-tn), Mrs. Isabella Mary (1836–65). English author of a book of cookery and household management, first published serially 1859–61.

bee'troot *n.* (pl. same). Crimson root of garden beet, used in salads etc.

B.E.F. *abbrev.* British Expeditionary Force.

bėfa'll (-awl) *v.* Happen, happen to.

bėfĭ't *v.t.* Be suited to, become.

bėfŏ'g *v.t.* Envelop in fog; confuse, obscure.

bėfōō'l *v.t.* Make a fool of, dupe.

bėfōr'e *adv.* Ahead; in front; at an earlier time, already. ~ *prep.* In front of, ahead of; in the presence of; earlier than. ~ *conj.* Before the time when; rather than.

bėfōr'ehănd *adv.* In anticipation, in readiness.

bėfou'l *v.t.* Make foul.

bėfrie'nd (-rĕnd) *v.t.* Act as friend to, help.

bĕg *v.* 1. Ask for (food, money, etc.) as alms; live by alms. 2. Ask earnestly or humbly, entreat. 3. (of dog etc.) Sit up with forepaws raised expectantly. 4. ~ *the question*, take for granted the

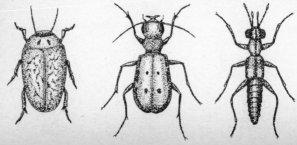

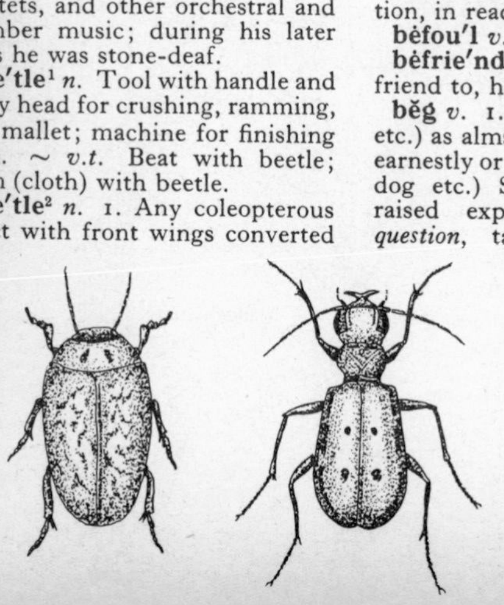

matter in dispute, assume by implication what one is trying to prove.

bėgĕ't *v.t.* (past t. *begŏ't*, past part. *begŏ'tten*). Procreate (usu. of father); give rise to, occasion. **bėgĕ'tter** *n.*

bĕ'ggar *n.* One who begs, esp. one who lives by begging; poor person; (colloq.) fellow. ~ *v.t.* Reduce to poverty; exhaust resources of; *~-my-neighbour*, simple card-game in which the object of each player is to acquire all the cards.

bĕ'ggarlȳ *adj.* Needy, poverty-stricken; mean, sordid, intellectually poor.

bĕ'ggarȳ *n.* Extreme poverty.

Bĕ'ghard (-gerd) *n.* Member of lay brotherhoods which arose (in imitation of the BÉGUINES) in the Low Countries in 13th c.; the name was soon adopted by many who were simply idle mendicants, and from the 14th c. the brotherhoods were denounced by Popes and Councils and persecuted by the Inquisition; in the 17th c. those which survived were absorbed in the Tertiarii of the Franciscans.

bėgi'n *v.* (past t. *begă'n*, past part. *begŭ'n*). Start, perform first part of, set about; be the first; originate; come into being, arise. **bėgi'nner** *n.* (esp.) Tiro, learner. **bėgi'nning** *n.* (esp.) Time at which anything begins; source, origin; first part.

bėgir'd *v.t.* (past part. *begirt*) Gird, encircle.

bėgŏ'ne *v.imp.* Be off, away with you (also occas. as infin.).

bėgō'nia *n.* Tropical plant of genus *B~*, having flowers with brightly coloured perianths (but no petals) and often richly coloured foliage; often cultivated as an ornamental plant. [Michel *Bégon*, Fr. patron of science (1638–1710)]

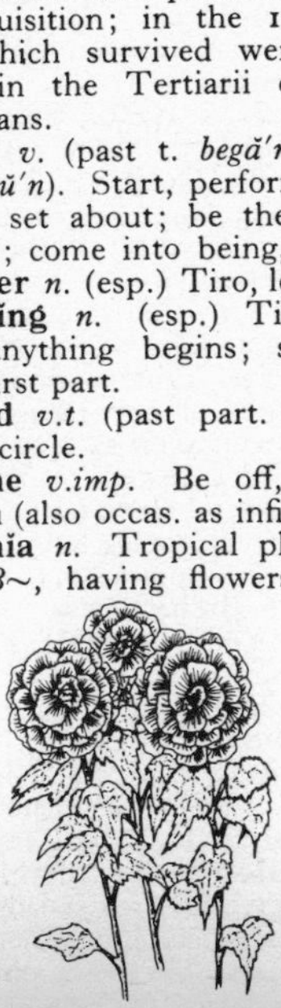

begotten: see BEGET.

bėgrī'me *v.t.* Make grimy.

bėgrŭ'dge *v.t.* Grudge.

bėgui'le (-gīl) *v.t.* Delude; cheat; charm, amuse; divert attention from (passage of time etc.). **bėgui'lement, bėgui'ler** *ns.*

Béguine[1] (bāgē'n) *n.* Member of certain lay sisterhoods, small communities of which still exist esp. in Belgium, first founded in the Netherlands in the 12th c., who devoted themselves to a religious life but did not bind themselves by strict vows. [f. Lambert *Bègue* (or *le bègue* the stammerer), the founder]

bėgui'ne[2] (-gēn) *n.* S. Amer. dance; kind of syncopated dance rhythm.

bē'gum *n.* Indian Muslim woman of high rank. [Turk. *bīgam*, fem. of *beg* lord]

begun: see BEGIN.

bėha'lf (-ahf) *n.* Part, account, or interest *of*.

bėhā've *v.i.* & *refl.* Act in a particular way (~ *well*, *badly*, etc.); show good manners.

bėhā'viour (-yer) *n.* Manners, conduct, way of behaving. **bėhā'vioural** *adj.*

bėhā'viourism (-yer-) *n.* Psychological doctrine, based on the objective study of behaviour, that all human actions admit of analysis into stimulus and response. **bėhā'viourist** *n.*

bėhea'd (-hĕd) *v.t.* Cut off the head of.

beheld: see BEHOLD.

bėhē'moth *n.* Enormous creature; in Job 40: 15, prob. the hippopotamus.

bėhĕ'st *n.* Command.

bėhī'nd *adv.* In or to the rear; past, too late; in concealment; in arrear. ~ *prep.* In or to the rear of; hidden by; supporting. ~ *n.* The buttocks.

bėhī'ndhănd *adv.* & *pred. adj.* Late; backward, out of date.

Behn (bān), Mrs Aphra (1640–89). English dramatist and novelist, author of 'Oroonoko'.

bėhō'ld *v.t.* (past t. & past part. *behĕ'ld*). (archaic & rhet.) See; take notice, attend. **bėhō'lder** *n.*

bėhō'lden *pred. adj.* Under obligation *to.*

bėhōō'f *n.* (archaic) Benefit, advantage.

bėhō've, bėhōō've *v.t. impers.* Be incumbent on; befit.

Behring: see BERING.

beige (bāzh) *n.* Yellowish-grey colour of unbleached wool. ~ *adj.* Of colour of beige.

bē'ing *n.* (esp.) Existence; constitution, nature, essence; anything that exists; person.

bĕl[1] *n.* Unit, = 10 decibels. [A. G. BELL[2]]

Bĕl[2]. (Babylonian & Assyrian myth.) = BAAL; ~ *and the Dragon,* book of the Apocrypha, included as part of Daniel in the Vulgate.

bėlā'bour (-ber) *v.t.* Thrash.

Bela Kun: see KUN.

bėlā'tėd *adj.* Coming late. **bėlā'tėdlў** *adv.*

bėlau'd *v.t.* Load with praise.

bėlay' *v.t.* Coil (running rope) round cleat etc., to secure it; *imp.* (naut.) stop!; *belaying pin,* fixed wooden or iron pin for belaying on.

bĕl că'ntō. Singing in the Italian manner, characterized by full rich tone and accomplished technique. [It.]

bĕlch *v.* Emit wind noisily from stomach through mouth; utter noisily or drunkenly; (of gun or volcano) emit (fire, smoke, etc.). ~ *n.* Belching.

bĕ'lcher *n.* Neckerchief with blue ground and large white spots having a dark-blue spot in the centre. [James *Belcher* (1781–1811), English prize-fighter]

bĕ'ldam, -dame *n.* Old woman, hag; virago.

bėlea'guer (-ger) *v.t.* Besiege.

bĕ'lemnīte *n.* Common fossil, occurring in Mesozoic rocks, consisting of the hard part of an extinct marine animal similar to the squid, freq. torpedo-shaped and up to 304 mm long. [Gk *belemnon* dart]

Bĕlfa'st (-ahst). Seaport in Ulster, capital city of N. Ireland; centre of the Irish linen industry; university, 1908.

bĕ'lfrў *n.* Bell tower; room or storey in which the bells are hung

Bĕ'lgian (-jan) *adj.* & *n.* (Native or inhabitant) of Belgium.

Bĕ'lgic *adj.* Of the Belgae, an ancient people of N. Gaul.

Bĕ'lgium (-jum). Small kingdom of N. Europe, the S. part of the Low Countries (see NETHERLANDS, 2), inhabited by people of French and Flemish stock speaking both languages; established in 1831, its independence and neutrality were guaranteed by the European powers and Russia in 1839 and violated by the German invasion in 1914; capital, Brussels. [L, territory occupied by the *Belgae*]

Bĕlgrā'de. (Serbo-Croatian *Beograd*) City on the Danube, capital of Yugoslavia and formerly of Serbia.

Bĕlgrā'vĭa. Fashionable residential district of London, S. of Knightsbridge. [f. *Belgrave* Square, named after Belgrave in Leicestershire]

Bē'lĭal. 1. (O.T.) Spirit of evil personified (as *sons of* ~); (2 Cor. 6: 15) the Devil. 2. (in Milton) Fallen angel representing impurity. [Heb. *b*[e]*līyya'al* without use, without avail]

bėlī'e *v.t.* Fail to justify or act up to; give false notion of.

bėlie'f *n.* Trust, confidence (*in*); acceptance of any received theology; acceptance as true or existing; thing believed.

bėlie've *v.* Have faith (*in*), trust word of; accept as true; suppose, think; be of opinion *that.* **bėlie'vable** *adj.* **bėlie'ver** *n.*

bėlī'ke *adv.* (archaic) Probably; perhaps.

Bĕlisār'ĭus (?505–65). General under JUSTINIAN I.

Beli'sha bea'con (-lē-): see BEACON 3. [Leslie Hore-*Belisha,* Minister of Transport 1931–7]

bėlī'ttle *v.t.* Disparage, dwarf.

Bĕli'ze (-ēz): see HONDURAS 2.

bĕll[1] *n.* 1. Hollow object of cast metal esp. in deep cup shape

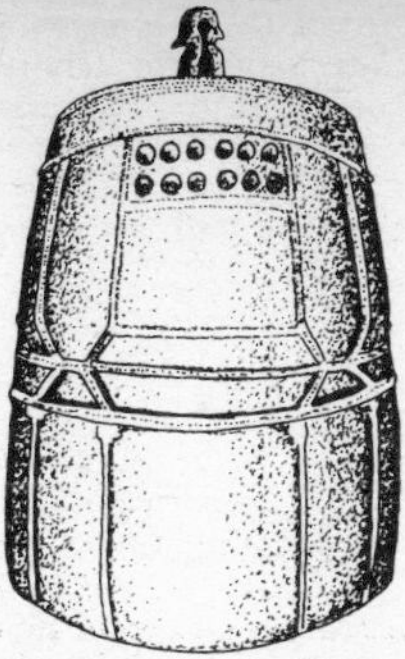

Japanese Temple

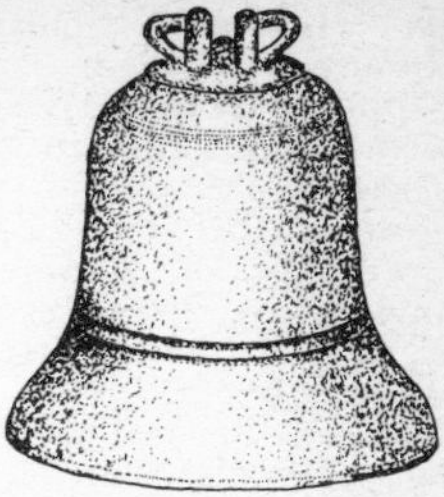

Christian Church

BELL

widening at lip, made to emit clear musical sound when struck by a tongue or clapper suspended inside it or by a hammer impelled by a spring or by electricity etc. 2. Sound of this, esp. as signal; (naut.) *one* to *eight* ~*s*, half-hours of watch, indicated by strokes of bell. 3. Bell-shaped object or part. 4. ~*-bottomed*, (of trousers) widening from below knee to bottom of leg; ~*-boy*, (U.S.) hotel page-boy; ~*-buoy*, buoy with a bell rung by the motion of the sea; ~*-founder*, caster of bells; ~*-foundry*, place where bells are cast; ~*-glass*, bell-jar; ~*-hop*, (U.S. slang) bell-boy; ~*-jar*, bell-shaped glass used to protect instruments or contain gases etc. in a laboratory; ~*-man*, crier, town-crier (who attracted attention to his announcements by ringing a bell); ~*-metal*, alloy of copper and tin, with more tin than in ordinary bronze, used for bells; ~*-ringer*, one who rings church-bells, campanologist; ~*-ringing*, art of ringing church-bells, campanology; ~*-tent*, conical tent; ~*-wether*, leading sheep of flock, with bell on neck (also fig.).

Bĕll², Alexander Graham (1847–1922). Scottish-American inventor of the telephone.

Bĕll³, Currer, Ellis, and Acton. Pen-names of Charlotte, Emily, and Anne Brontë.

bĕlladŏ'nna *n.* Specific name of the deadly nightshade, *Atropa belladonna*, with dark purple flowers and poisonous black berries; dried parts of this, containing atropine and related alkaloids, used as a drug which causes marked dilatation of the pupils; ~*-lily*, amaryllis. [It., = 'fair lady']

Bĕ'llay, Joachim du (*c* 1524–60). French poet and critic, a member of the Pleiad and author of its

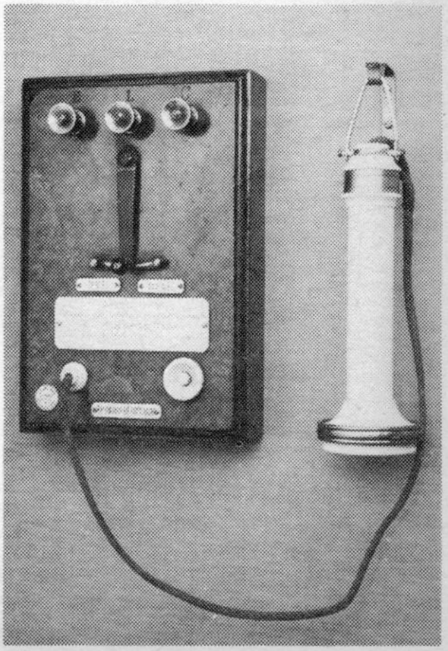

BELL TELEPHONE

manifesto, 'Deffence et Illustration de la Langue Françoyse' (1549).

bĕlle *n.* Handsome woman; reigning beauty.

Bėllĕ'rophon. (Gk legend) Hero who slew the Chimaera with the help of Pegasus.

belles-lettres (bĕl lĕtr) *n.pl.* Studies, writings, of a purely literary kind; essays, literary criticism, etc., as a division of literature. **bĕllėtrĭ'stic** *adj.*

bĕ'llĭcōse *adj.* Inclined to war or fighting. **bĕllĭcŏ'sitȳ** *n.*

bėllĭ'gerent *adj.* Waging war, bellicose. ~ *n.* Belligerent State, party, or person. **bėllĭ'gerencȳ** *n.*

Bĕlli'nĭ[1] (-lē-), Giovanni (*c* 1435–1516). Italian painter of the Venetian School; his father Jacopo (*c* 1400–70) and brother Gentile (1429?–1507) were also painters.

Bĕlli'nĭ[2] (-lē-), Vincenzo (1801–35). Italian composer of operas.

Bĕ'llŏc, Joseph Hilaire Pierre (1870–1953). English essayist, novelist, and poet, born in France.

Bĕllō'na. (Rom. myth.) Goddess of war.

bĕ'llow (-ō) *v.* Roar as a bull; shout, roar with pain; shout loudly and angrily; reverberate, roar. ~ *n.* Bellowing sound.

bĕ'llows (-ōz) *n.pl.* 1. Instrument or machine for driving strong blast of air into fire, organ, etc., in its simplest form consisting of a pair of boards joined by flexible leather sides, with a valve through

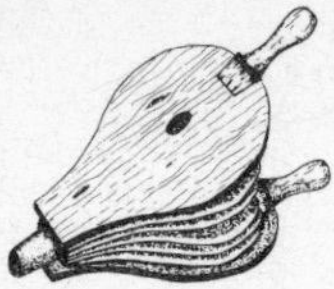

which air enters when the boards are moved apart, and a nozzle or tube through which air is forced as they are brought together. 2. Expansible portion of folding camera.

bĕ'llȳ *n.* Abdomen; stomach; underpart of animal as cut of meat; cavity or bulging part of anything; *be'llyache* (*v.i.*, slang) complain; ~ *dance*, erotic oriental dance involving movements of the abdominal muscles; so ~ *dancer*; *be'llyflop* (*n.*, slang) dive in which abdomen hits the water (also *be'llyflopper*); (of aircraft) belly landing; (*v.i.*) dive, land, thus; *be'llyful*, (colloq.) surfeit; ~ *landing*, (of aircraft) crash-landing on underside of fuselage; ~*-laugh,*

BELLINI

(colloq.) deep unrestrained laugh. ~ *v.* Swell out.

bėlŏ'ng *v.i.* Have a rightful or appropriate place or position; fit an environment etc.; ~ *to*, (esp.) be a member or adherent etc. of; be a possession of. **bėlŏ'ngings** (-z) *n.pl.* Person's movable property etc.

Bĕlōrŭ'ssia (-sh*a*). White Russia, one of the constituent republics of the U.S.S.R., including the former provinces of Minsk, Vitebsk, and Mogilov; capital, Minsk. **Bĕlorŭ'ssian** *adj.* & *n.* (Native, language) of Belorussia; White Russian.

bėlo'vėd (-lŭ-; *or* -vd) *adj.* Dearly loved; ~ *disciple*, St. John the Apostle. ~ *n.* Beloved person.

bėlow' (-ō) *adv.* At or to a lower level; in a lower position or rank. ~ *prep.* Lower in position, amount, degree, rank, etc., than; unworthy of, beneath.

Bĕlshă'zzar[1]. (also *Balthazar*) Acc. to O.T. (Dan. 5), son of Nebuchadnezzar and last king of Babylon, who was killed in the sack of the city by Cyrus (538 B.C.); his doom was foretold by writing which appeared on the walls of his palace at a great banquet; but in inscriptions and documents from Ur, Belshazzar was the son of the last king of Babylon, Nabonidos, and did not himself reign.

Bĕlshă'zzar[2] *n.* (also *Balthazar*) Very large wine-bottle. [f. BELSHAZZAR[1]]

bĕlt *n.* 1. Broadish flat strip of leather etc., used to gird or encircle the person, confine some part of the dress, or support various articles; such an article awarded to boxing champion or worn as a mark of rank by knight or earl. 2. Strip of colour etc., line of trees, round or on anything; zone or district; endless strap connecting pulleys in machinery. flexible strip holding machine-gun cartridges and carrying them to firing chamber. ~ *v.* Put belt round, fasten with belt; thrash with belt; (slang) rush.

Bĕ'ltāne. Celtic name for 1 May (Old Style), formerly a quarter-day in Scotland, and of the ancient Celtic May Day celebrations, in which bonfires were kindled on the hills.

bĕ'lvėdēre *n.* Raised turret or lantern, summer-house, to view scenery from. [It., = 'fine view']

B.E.M. *abbrev.* British Empire Medal.

bėmea'n *v.t.* Render mean or base.

bėmīr'e *v.t.* Besmirch, befoul.

bėmoa'n *v.t.* Lament.

bėmū'se (-z) *v.t.* Make confused or muddled; stupefy.

bĕn[1] *n.* (Sc.) Inner room (usu. of two-roomed cottage); *but and* ~, outer and inner room, i.e. the whole house.

bĕn[2] *n.* (Sc.) Mountain peak.

Bėnar̂'ės (-z). = VARANASI.

bĕnch *n.* 1. Long seat of wood or stone; thwart of boat. 2. Judge's or magistrate's seat; office of judge, law-court (*King's*, *Queen's*, *B*~, a division of the High Court of Justice); judges, magistrates; *on the* ~, serving as judge or magistrate. 3. (parl.) Seats in Houses of Parliament traditionally appropriated to certain groups, as *back benches*, for members who have never held office (*back benchers*), *front benches*, for members of Government and leaders of Opposition, *Treasury* ~, front bench on Government side, i.e. on Speaker's right, occupied by First Lord of the TREASURY, Chancellor of the Exchequer, and other members of the Government. 4. Working-table in carpenter's shop, laboratory, etc. 5. Level ledge or terrace in masonry, earthwork, hillside, etc.; ~*-mark*, surveyor's mark, consisting of a broad arrow with a horizontal line through its apex, cut in stone etc. to indicate a point in a line of levels. ~ *v.t.* Exhibit (dog) at show.

bĕ'ncher *n.* (esp.) One of the senior members of the Inns of Court, who form for each Inn a self-elective body managing its affairs; *back* ~: see BENCH *n.* 3.

bĕnd[1] *n.* 1. (naut.) Knot. 2.

(her.) Diagonal band from dexter chief to sinister base of shield; ~ *sinister*, bend in the opposite direction, a mark of bastardy. 3. Shape in which hides are tanned.

bĕnd² *v.* (past t. & past part. *bent*). 1. Force into, receive, curved or angular shape. 2. Tighten up; bring to bear; (pass.) be determined. 3. Attach (sail etc.) with bend or knot. 4. Turn in new direction. 5. Incline from perpendicular; bow, stoop, submit, force to submit. 6. Direct, apply (oneself) *to*. 7. Modify (law, rule, etc.) for one's own purposes. ~ *n.* 1. Bending, curve; bent part. 2. (pl.) Caisson disease. 3. *round the* ~, (slang) insane.

bĕ'ndėd *adj.* (of knee) Bent.

bĕ'nder *n.* (slang) Drinking spree.

bĕ'ndy̆ *adj.* 1. (colloq.) That bends. 2. (her.) Divided diagonally into equal fields.

bėnea'th *adv.* & *prep.* Below, under, underneath.

bĕnėdī'cĭtė *n.* 1. Blessing invoked; grace at table. 2. *B*~, One of the canticles, from the opening words, *Benedicite omnia opera* (L, = 'O all ye works (of the Lord), bless ye (the Lord)'). [L, = 'bless ye']

Bĕ'nėdĭck. Character in Shakespeare's 'Much Ado about Nothing'; hence, a newly married man.

Bĕ'nėdĭct, St. (*c* 480–543). Italian monk, founder (529) of the first of the monastic orders of the Western Church, for which he built the abbey of Monte Cassino.

Bĕnėdĭ'ctĭne *adj.* Of the order of St. Benedict; ~ *Rule*, rule written for it by St. Benedict, later adopted by other monastic communities. ~ *n.* 1. Benedictine monk. 2. (-ēn) Liqueur of brandy flavoured with herbs etc., made at Fécamp in Normandy, orig. by the monks of the Benedictine abbey there.

bĕnėdĭ'ction *n.* Utterance of blessing, at end of church service, or at table; *B*~, R.C. service; a blessing, blessedness. **bĕnėdĭ'ctory̆** *adj.*

Bĕnėdĭ'ctus. 1. Fifth movement in the service of Mass, beginning *Benedictus qui venit* (L, = 'blessed is he that cometh'). 2. Hymn of Zacharias (Luke 1: 68) used as a canticle in the Church of England. [L, = 'blessed']

bĕnėfă'ction (*or* bĕ'-) *n.* Doing good; charitable gift.

bĕ'nėfăctor *n.* (fem. *bĕ'nėfăctrėss*) Person who has given friendly aid; patron of, or donor to, cause or charity.

bĕ'nėfĭce *n.* (C. of E.) Material livelihood of incumbent of a parish; rectory, vicarage, or perpetual curacy. **bĕ'nėficed** (-ĭst) *adj.*

bėnĕ'fĭcent *adj.* Doing good, showing active kindness. **bėnĕ'fĭcence** *n.*

bĕnėfĭ'cial (-sh*a*l) *adj.* 1. Advantageous. 2. (law) Of, having, the usufruct of property. **bĕnėfĭ'cially̆** *adv.*

bĕnėfĭ'ciary̆ (-sh*a*-) *adj.* Holding or held by feudal tenure. ~ *n.* Holder by feudal tenure; holder of living; receiver of benefits.

bĕ'nėfĭt *n.* 1. Advantage. 2. Allowance, pension, etc. to which person is entitled; *sickness*, *unemployment*, etc. ~, allowance payable under National Insurance Acts to person who is sick, unemployed, etc. 3. ~ *of clergy*, (hist.) exemption from ordinary courts by the privilege of one's order. 4. Theatre performance, game, etc., of which proceeds go to particular players or charity. ~ *v.* Do good to; receive benefit.

Bĕ'nėlŭx. Collective name for *Bel*gium, the *Ne*therlands, and *Lux*emburg, esp. with reference to their economic collaboration.

Beneš (bĕ'nĕsh), Eduard (1884–1948). President of Czechoslovakia 1935–8 and 1946–8.

bėnĕ'volent *adj.* Desirous of doing good; charitable. **bėnĕ'volently̆** *adv.* **bėnĕ'volence** *n.*

B.Eng. *abbrev.* Bachelor of Engineering.

Bĕnga'l (-nggawl). District of the Ganges delta, formerly a province of British India, divided into *West* ~, a state of India (capital,

Calcutta), and BANGLADESH; *Bay of ~*, part of Indian Ocean lying between Indian peninsula and Burma; *~ light*, firework with steady vivid light, used as a signal; *~ tiger*, the tiger proper, so called from its abundance in lower Bengal.

Bĕnga'lĭ (-nggaw-) *adj.* & *n.* (Of) the Indo-European language spoken in Bengal; (native) of Bengal.

bėni'ghtėd (-nīt-) *adj.* Overtaken by night; involved in moral or intellectual darkness; ignorant.

bėni'gn (-īn) *adj.* Gracious, gentle; fortunate, salutary; (path., of disease) mild, not malignant; (of tumour) not cancerous, displacing but not destroying surrounding tissue (opp. MALIGNANT).

benĭ'gnant *adj.* Kind, kindly, to inferiors; gracious; salutary. **benĭ'gnancy̆, benĭ'gnity̆** *ns.*

Benin. See DAHOMEY.

bĕ'nĭson (-zn) *n.* (archaic) Blessing.

Bĕ'njamĭn. Hebrew patriarch, youngest and favourite son of Jacob (Gen. 35: 8, 42, etc.); smallest tribe of Israel, traditionally descended from him.

Bĕ'nnėtt, Enoch Arnold (1867–1931). English novelist; author of novels of life in the Potteries, including 'The Old Wives' Tale' (1908), 'Clayhanger' (1910), 'Riceyman Steps' (1923), etc.

Bĕn Nĕ'vĭs. Mountain in the region of Grampian, the highest peak (4,406 ft, 1343 m.) in the British Isles.

bĕnt[1] *n.* Reedy or rush-like stiff-stemmed grass of various kinds; grass of genus *Agrostis*; stiff flower-stalk, old stalk, of grasses; heath, unenclosed pasture.

bĕnt[2] *n.* Inclination, bias.

bĕnt[3] *adj.*: see BEND[2] *v.*; (esp.) curved, crooked; (slang) dishonest, perverted, homosexual.

Bĕ'ntham (-t*a*m), Jeremy (1748–1832). English Utilitarian philosopher, and writer on ethics, jurisprudence, and political economy; prison and poor-law reformer; he believed that the end of life is happiness (which he identified with pleasure) and that the highest morality is the pursuit of the greatest happiness of the greatest number. **Bĕ'nthamĭsm, Bĕ'nthamīte** *ns.*

bĕn trova'tō (-ah-). Well invented, characteristic if not true. [It.]

bėnŭ'mb (-m) *v.t.* Make torpid; paralyse.

bĕ'nzėdrine (-ēn) *n.* Preparation of amphetamine. [trade-name]

bĕ'nzēne *n.* (chem.) Aromatic hydrocarbon (C_6H_6), a colourless, volatile, and highly inflammable liquid obtained from coal-tar etc., used as a solvent and in the chemical industry; *~ ring*, ring-like arrangement of the six carbon atoms in the benzene molecule.

bĕ'nzine (-ēn) *n.* Mixture of

BEN NEVIS

hydrocarbons obtained from petroleum and used as a solvent, for removing grease stains etc.

bĕ'nzōin *n.* 1. (also *gum-~*) Fragrant aromatic resin obtained from various trees of the genus *Styrax* from Sumatra and Thailand, and used in perfumery, medicine, etc. 2. (chem.) Constituent of gum-benzoin. **bĕnzō'ĭc** *adj.* (chem.) Of or derived from benzoin; ~ *acid*, benzene carboxylic acid (C_6H_5COOH). [Fr. *benjoin* f. Arab. *lubān jāwī* Java frankincense]

bĕ'nzŏl *n.* 1. (obs.) Benzene. 2. (in trade use) Unrefined benzene, used as a motor spirit.

Be'owulf (bā'owŏŏ-). Legendary Swedish hero celebrated in the Old English epic poem 'Beowulf'.

bėquea'th (-dh), *v.t.* Leave by will.

bėquĕ'st *n.* Bequeathing; thing bequeathed.

Béranger (bārahṅzhā), Pierre Jean de (1780–1857). French poet, author of many satirical and political songs of great contemporary influence.

bėrā'te *v.t.* (now chiefly U.S.) Scold.

Bẽr'ber *adj.* & *n.* (Member) of a fair-skinned aboriginal people of N. Africa.

berceuse (bārsẽr'z) *n.* Cradle-song; composition in style of this.

bėrea've *v.t.* 1. (past t. & past part. *bereaved* or *berĕft*) Rob, dispossess *of*. 2. Leave desolate; deprive of relation, wife, etc. **bėrea'vement** *n.*

Bĕrėnī'cė[1] (3rd c. B.C.). Egyptian queen, wife of Ptolemy III Euergetes; during his absence on a warlike expedition in Syria, she dedicated her hair as votive offering for his safe return; the hair was stolen, and legend said that it was carried to the heavens, where it became the constellation *Coma Berenices*.

Bĕrėnī'cė[2] (b. *c* A.D. 28). Jewish princess, called Bernice in Acts 25; daughter of Agrippa I and wife of her uncle Herod, king of Chalcis; after his death she lived with her brother Agrippa II.

beret (bĕ'rā) *n.* Round flat woollen cap, worn by Basque peasantry; similar cap worn esp. as part of sports or holiday costume or as a military cap.

bẽrg *n.* = ICEBERG.

bẽr'gamŏt[1] *n.* 1. Tree of the lemon kind, *Citrus bergamia*; fragrant oil extracted from its fruit. 2. Any of various plants of the family Labiatae, esp. *Monarda* species. [f. *Bergamo* in Italy]

bẽr'gamŏt[2] *n.* Fine kind of pear. [Turk. *beg* prince, *armūdī* pear]

Bergerăc (bārzh-), Cyrano de (1619–55). French soldier and author of comedies.

bergschrund (bār'kshrŏŏnt) *n.* Crevasse or gap at junction of steep upper slope with glacier or nevé.

Bergson (bārgsawṅ), Henri (1859–1941). French philosopher who regarded reality as change and movement, 'becoming' rather than 'being'. **Bẽrgsō'nian** *adj.* & *n.*

bĕ'rĭbĕrĭ *n.* Disease, with symptoms including polyneuritis, oedema, heart failure, etc., caused by deficiency of vitamin B_1 in diet and affecting chiefly tropical and sub-tropical populations whose staple food is rice from which the outer layer of the grain (containing the vitamin) has been polished away. [Sinhalese *beri* weakness]

Bĕ'ring, Behr'- (bār-), Vitus Jonassen (1680–1741). Danish navigator and explorer of Arctic Asia; sailed along coast of Siberia from Kamchatka and reached America from the E.; died on an island near Kamchatka subsequently called ~ *Island*; ~ *Sea*, northernmost part of Pacific; ~ *Strait*, strait between Asia and America, connecting Bering Sea with Arctic Ocean.

Berkeley (bâr'klĭ), George (1685–1753). Irish bishop and idealist philosopher. **Berkelei'an** (-lēan) *adj.* & *n.*

bẽrkē'lium *n.* (chem.) Metallic radioactive transuranic element; symbol Bk, at. no. 97, principal isotope at. wt 243. [*Berkeley*, Calif., where first made]

Berks. *abbrev.* Berkshire.

Ber'kshire (bârk-). Southern inland county of England, on right bank of Thames; hence, one of a breed of black pigs with occas. white markings.

Berli'n[1]**.** Chief city of Germany, on river Spree; formerly capital of Prussia; capital of Germany from 1871; since 1945 divided into *East* ~, capital of East Germany, and *West* ~, an isolated part of West Germany; ~ *wall*, wall dividing Berlin; ~ *wool*, fine wool used for knitting or tapestry. **Berli'ner** *n.* Native, inhabitant, of Berlin.

berli'n[2] *n.* Four-wheeled covered carriage with hooded seat behind, invented in Berlin in 17th c., popular in France and England in the 18th c.

Berlioz (bār-), Hector (1803–69). French composer of operas, symphonic works, etc.

berm *n.* Narrow space or ledge; (esp., fort.) space between ditch and parapet.

Bermū'da. (also ~ *Islands*, *Bermudas*) Group of islands, a British colony, in W. Atlantic, discovered early in 16th c. by Juan Bermudez, a Spaniard; ~ *rig*, rig for yacht, carrying a very high tapering sail (*Bermudian mainsail*); ~ *shorts*, (also *Bermudas*) knee-length shorts. **Bermū'dian** *adj.* & *n.*

Bernadŏtte (bār-), Jean Baptiste (1763–1844). French soldier; one of Napoleon's marshals; was adopted by Charles XIII of Sweden in 1810 and himself became king (as Charles XIV) in 1818, thus founding the present royal house.

Ber'nard[1], St. (923–1008). Priest of Menthon; founder of the Alpine hospices of the Great and Little St. Bernard; *St.* ~ (*dog*), dog of large and very intelligent breed, of the mastiff type, usu. light brown and white, orig. bred by the monks of the St. Bernard hospices and trained to search for travellers lost in the snowdrifts of the Alpine passes.

Ber'nard[2], St. (1090–1153). French churchman, first abbot of Clairvaux; he reformed the Cistercian Order and preached the 2nd Crusade.

Bernard[3] (bārnâr), Claude (1813–78). French physiologist; famous for his research on the pancreas and the glycogenic function of the liver, and his discovery of the vaso-motor system.

Bernardin de Saint-Pierre (bārnârdăṅ, săṅ pyār), Jacques Henri (1737–1814). French naturalist; author of the novel 'Paul et Virginie'.

Berne (*or* bārn). Canton and capital city of Switzerland. **Bernē'se** (-z) *adj.* & *n.*

Ber'nhardt (bārnhârt), Sarah. Name adopted by the French romantic and tragic actress Rosine Bernard (1845–1923).

Bernini (bārnē'nĭ), Giovanni Lorenzo (1598–1680). Italian baroque architect and sculptor; designer of the colonnade of St. Peter's in Rome.

Bernou'lli (-ōō-). Surname of Swiss family including several eminent mathematicians and scientists, including Jacob or James (1654–1705) and Daniel (1700–82).

bĕ'rrȳ *n.* 1. Any small round or oval juicy fruit without a stone; grain (of wheat etc.). 2. (bot.) Fruit of any size with seed(s) enclosed in pulp. 3. Egg of lobster, crayfish, etc.

ber'serk *n.* (also *ber'serker*) Wild Norse warrior fighting with mad frenzy; *go* ~ (berzer'k), behave thus. [Icel., prob. = 'bear-coat']

berth *n.* 1. Convenient sea-room; room for ship to swing at anchor; ship's place at wharf; *give a wide* ~ *to*, avoid. 2. Sleeping-place in ship, railway-carriage, etc. 3. Situation, appointment. ~ *v.* Moor (ship); reach moorings.

ber'tha[1], **berthe** *n.* Deep falling collar or small cape on dress.

Ber'tha[2]. In the war of 1914–18, a German gun of large bore, esp. (*Big* ~) a long-range gun used to bombard Paris in 1918. [Frau *Berta* Krupp von Bohlen und Halbach, head of the Krupp steel works in Germany]

Bertillon (bārtēyawṅ), Alphonse (1853–1914). French inventor and general anthropologist; advocate of a system of anthropometric measurements for the identification of criminals, and esp. of the use of finger-prints for this purpose.

Berwickshire (bĕ′rĭk-). Former county of SE. Scotland, since May 1975 part of the region of Borders.

bĕ′rȳl *n.* Transparent precious stone of pale-green colour or of light-blue, yellow, or white, chemically a beryllium aluminium silicate; mineral species including also the emerald, which differs from the beryl only in its rich green colour, due to traces of chromium.

bėrȳ′llĭum *n.* (chem.) Very light metallic element obtained from beryl; symbol Be, at. no. 4, at. wt 9·01218.

Berzē′lĭus, Jons Jakob (1779–1848). Swedish chemist; discovered selenium and other elements, and invented the present system of representing chemical elements by symbols.

Bĕ′sant (-z-), Mrs Annie (1847–1933). English writer and ardent supporter of socialism and agnosticism; became a theosophist in 1887 and President of the Theosophical Society in 1907; was active in the cause of Indian self-government and in 1917 was President of the Indian National Congress.

bėsee′ch *v.t.* (past t. & past part. *besought*, pr. -awt). Ask earnestly for; entreat.

bėsee′m *v.t.* Suit, be fitting or suitable to.

bėsĕ′t *v.t.* Hem in; assail, encompass.

bėshrew′ (-ōō) *v.t.* (archaic, only in imprecations) Plague take.

bėsī′de *prep.* At the side of, close to; compared with; wide of; ~ *oneself*, strongly moved by emotion.

bėsī′des (-dz) *adv.* In addition; otherwise, else. ~ *prep.* In addition to; except.

bėsie′ge *v.t.* Lay siege to; assail, crowd round.

bėslă′ver *v.t.* Slaver upon or over; flatter fulsomely.

bėsmear′ *v.t.* Smear, bedaub.

bėsmĭr′ch *v.t.* Soil, discolour; sully.

bē′som (-z-; *or* bĭ-) *n.* Bundle of twigs tied round stick for sweeping; (colloq., derog.) woman.

bėsŏ′ttėd *adj.* Stupefied (esp. with drink); infatuated; foolish.

besought: see BESEECH.

bėspă′tter *v.t.* Spatter; asperse.

bėspea′k *v.t.* (past t. *bespō′ke*, past part. *bespō′ken*). Engage beforehand; order; speak to (poet.); indicate, be evidence of. **bėspō′ke** *adj.* Ordered (now only in ~ *tailoring*, *footwear*, etc., opp. ready-made, or of tradesman making goods to order).

bėsprĭ′nkle *v.t.* Sprinkle.

Bĕ′ssėmer, Sir Henry (1813–98). English engineer; inventor of ~ *process*, process for making steel, in which iron is decarbonized by blowing a blast of air through the molten metal.

bĕst *adj.* (superl. of *good*) Of the most excellent kind; most advantageous, desirable, or serviceable; ~ *man*, bridegroom's supporter at wedding; *the* ~ *part*, most; ~ *seller*, (orig. U.S.) book wth large sale. ~ *adv.* (superl. of *well*) In the most excellent way etc.; *had* ~, would find it wisest. ~ *n.* That which is best; *for the* ~, with good intentions or outcome; (collect.) most excellent persons.

bĕ′stĭal *adj.* Of, like, a beast; brutish, barbarous; depraved, obscene. **bĕstĭă′lĭtȳ** *n.* (esp., law) Crime of person having sexual intercourse with animal. **bĕ′stĭalīze** *v.t.*

bĕ′stĭarȳ *n.* Medieval moralizing treatise on beasts.

bėstĭr′ *v.refl.* Exert, rouse.

bėstow′ (-ō) *v.t.* Confer as gift; deposit, lodge. **bėstow′al** *n.*

bėstrew′ (-ōō) *v.t.* (past part. *bestrewed* or *bestrewn*). Strew.

bėstrī′de *v.t.* (past t. *bestrōde*, past part. *bestrĭdden*). Get or sit upon with legs astride; stand astride over.

bĕt *v.* (past t. & past part. *bet*). Risk one's money etc. against another's on result of doubtful event; (loosely) think, reckon (something to be true etc.); *betting shop*, bookmaker's shop or office. ~ *n.* Act of betting; money etc. so risked.

bē'ta *n.* 2nd letter of Gk alphabet (Β, β), corresponding to *b*, used of the 2nd star in a constellation, and in other classifications; examiner's second-class mark; ~ *brass*, compound of zinc and copper with special metallurgical properties; ~ *particles, rays*, fast-moving electrons emitted by radioactive substances, orig. regarded as rays, and having greater penetrating power than alpha particles and less than gamma rays.

bėtā'ke *v.refl.* (past t. *betook*, past part. *betaken*). Commit (oneself) *to* some cause or means; turn one's course, go.

bē'tatron *n.* (phys.) Apparatus for accelerating electrons.

bē'tel *n.* Leaf of a shrubby evergreen plant, *Piper betle*, which is wrapped round a few parings of areca nut and chewed by people of India etc.; hence (erron.) ~ *nut*, areca nut. [Malayalam *veṭṭila*]

Bĕ'telgeuse (-zhêrz *or* -jōōz). Yellowish-red variable star, the brightest in the constellation of Orion.

bête noire (bāt nwâr). Person or thing one particularly dislikes. [Fr.]

bĕ'thel *n.* Hallowed spot; Nonconformist, esp. Methodist or Baptist, chapel; seamen's church (ashore or floating). [Heb., = 'house of God'; see Gen. 28: 17–19]

bėthi'nk *v.refl.* (past t. & past part. *bethou'ght*, pr. -awt). Reflect, stop to think; remind oneself.

Bĕ'thlėhĕm. Town near Jerusalem; birthplace of Jesus Christ.

bėti'de *v.* Happen, befall.

bėtī'mes (-mz) *adv.* Early; in good time.

bêtise (bātēz) *n.* Foolish remark; folly. [Fr.]

Bĕ'tjeman (-tch-), Sir John (1906–). English poet, admirer of Victorian architecture; poet laureate 1972.

bėtō'ken *v.t.* Be token of; presage; indicate.

bĕ'tonў *n.* Labiate plant, *Stachys officinalis*, with spike of reddish-purple flowers; *water* ~, plant, *Scrophularia aquatica*, common beside streams.

bėtray' *v.t.* Give up or reveal treacherously; be disloyal to; lead astray; reveal involuntarily; be evidence or symptom of. **bėtray'al, bėtray'er** *ns.*

bėtrō'th (-dh) *v.t.* Bind with a promise to marry. **betrō'thal** *n.* **betrō'thed** (-dhd) *adj.* & *n.*

bĕ'tter *adj.* (comp. of *good*) Of a more excellent kind; ~ *half*, (joc.) wife; ~ *part*, greater part; ~ *world*: see WORLD. ~ *adv.* (comp. of *well*) In a more excellent way; (of person) (partially) recovered from illness; *had* ~, would find it wiser; *think* ~ *of it*, reconsider, decide more wisely. ~ *n.* Person of higher rank (usu. pl.); *get the* ~ *of*, defeat, outwit. ~ *v.* Improve; surpass. **bĕ'tterment** *n.* Improvement.

bė'tween *prep.* In, into, along, or across, a space or interval bounded by (*lies* ~ *Paris and Rouen*; *happened* ~ *Monday and Friday*); separating; connecting; intermediately in time, place or order (to); shared by, confined to; to and from; reciprocally on the part of; ~*-maid*, servant helping two others, as cook and housemaid; ~ *whiles*, in the intervals. ~ *adv.* Between two points.

bėtwi'xt *prep.* & *adv.* 1. (archaic) Between. 2. ~ *and between*, in position intermediate between; neither one thing nor the other.

BeV *abbrev.* (U.S.) Billion (= 1,000 million) electron volts.

bĕ'vel *n.* 1. Joiner's and mason's tool, a flat rule with movable

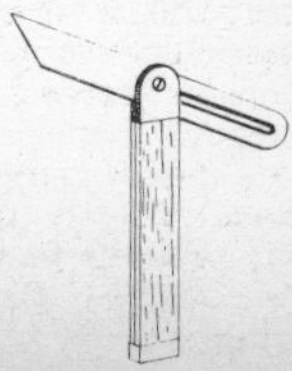

tongue or arm stiffly jointed to one end for setting off angles. 2. Slope from right angle, or from horizontal or vertical, surface so sloped; ~ *gear*, gear with toothed surface oblique with the axis usu. meshing with another set at right angles. ~ *v*. Impart bevel to, slant.

bĕ′verage *n*. Drink.

bĕ′vȳ *n*. Flock (of birds, esp. larks or quails); group (of women or girls); group (of roebucks).

bėwai′l *v.t.* Wail over, mourn for.

bėwār′e *v*. (used without inflexions). Be cautious (of), take heed (*of*, *lest*, *how*).

bėwĭ′lder *v.t.* Lead astray, confuse, perplex. **bėwĭ′lderment** *n*.

bėwĭ′tch *v.t.* Affect by magic; charm, enchant.

bey (bā) *n*. Turkish governor of province or district. **bey′lĭc** *n*. District or jurisdiction of bey. [Turk., = 'lord']

Beyle, Henri: see STENDHAL.

bėyŏ′nd *adv*. & *prep*. At, to, the further side (of), past, besides; out of reach, comprehension or range (of). ~ *n*. Future life, the unknown; *back of* ~, very remote or out-of-the-way place.

Bĕ′zaleel. Maker of the Ark of the Covenant (Exod. 31: 2, 35: 30, etc.).

bĕ′zant (*or* bĭză′nt) *n*. 1. (hist.) Gold coin current in England in 9th and 10th centuries; later, silver coin. 2. (her.) Roundel or [f. *Byzantium*, where orig. struck]

bĕ′zel *n*. Sloped edge or face of chisel etc; oblique side or face of cut gem; groove holding gem or watch-glass in setting.

bezi′que (-ēk) *n*. Card-game for two players who score chiefly by holding various sequences and combinations of cards; combination of queen of spades and knave of diamonds in this game.

b.f. *abbrev*. Bloody fool; bold face (type); brought forward.

B.F.B.S. *abbrev*. British and Foreign Bible Society.

bhăng (bă-), **băng**[2] *n*. Leaves of Indian hemp mixed with resin used as intoxicant and narcotic.

b.h.p. *abbrev*. Brake horse-power.

Bhutan (bōōtăh′n). Independent kingdom, a protectorate of the Republic of India, lying on the SE. of the Himalayas; capital, Punakha.

bi- *prefix*. Twice-, doubly, having two.

bī′as *n*. 1. (in bowls) Curving course in which bowl runs, shape of bowl causing it to do this. 2. Inclination, predisposition, prejudice, influence; (statistics) systematic distortion; (elect.) steady voltage or current applied to electronic device. 3. (dressmaking) Diagonal across material, direction in which material stretches; ~ *binding*, bias-cut binding; ~*-cut*, cut on the bias. ~ *v.t.* Give bias to, influence, prejudice.

bĭb[1] *v.i.* (archaic) Drink much or often, tipple. **bĭ′bber** *n*.

bĭb[2] *n*. Cloth etc. placed under child's chin to keep dress-front clean; apron-top.

bĭb[3] *n*. Sea-fish (*Trisopterus luscus*) which can inflate a membrane covering the eyes and other parts of the head.

bĭb-cŏck *n*. Cock or tap with turned-down nozzle (dist. from *stopcock*).

Bī′ble *n*. Sacred book of Christianity; edition or copy of this; sacred book, authoritative text-book; ~ *Belt*, those parts of the (Southern and Middle Western) U.S. reputed to be fanatically puritan or fundamentalist; ~ *Christians*, Protestant sect, existing chiefly in SW. England, founded 1816 by a Wesleyan preacher, William O'Bryan; ~ *oath*, solemn oath taken on the Bible.

bĭ′blĭcal *adj*. Of, in, concerning, the Bible; (of language) of the Authorized Version.

bĭblĭŏ′graphȳ *n*. History of books, their authorship, editions, etc.; book containing such details; list of books of any author, subject, printer, etc. **bĭblĭŏ′grapher** *n*. **bĭbliogră′phical** *adj*.

bĭbliŏ′later *n.* Worshipper of books. **bĭbliŏ′latrȳ** *n.* **bĭbliŏ′latrous** *adj.*

bĭbliomā′nia *n.* Mania for collecting books. **bĭbliomā′niăc** *n.* & *adj.*

bĭ′bliophĭle *n.* Book-lover.

bĭ′būlous *adj.* Addicted to drinking.

bīcă′meral *adj.* With two (legislative) chambers.

bīcar′bonate *n.* 1. Salt of carbonic acid in which only one hydrogen atom is replaced by a metal. 2. (pop.) Sodium bicarbonate ($NaHCO_3$) used in medicine and as constituent of baking-powder etc.

bīce *n.* Dullish blue pigment obtained from smalt; *green* ~, dull green pigment made by adding yellow orpiment to smalt; colour of either of these.

bīcĕntĕ′narȳ (*or* -sĕ′ntĭn-) *n.* 200th anniversary.

bīcĕntĕ′nnĭal *adj.* Occurring every, lasting for, 200 years. ~ *n.* (U.S.) Bicentenary.

bīcĕ′phalous *adj.* Two-headed.

bī′cĕps *n.* & *adj.* (Muscle) with 2 heads or attachments, esp. that on front of upper arm, which bends forearm.

bĭ′cker *v.i.* & *n.* Quarrel, wrangle.

bīcŭ′spĭd *adj.* & *n.* (Tooth) with two cusps.

bī′cȳcle *n.* Vehicle having two wheels and a seat on which the rider sits astride, driven either by two pedals operating a crank or by a motor. ~ *v.i.* Ride bicycle. **bī′cȳclist** *n.*

bĭd *v.* (past t. *băde*, *bid*, past part. *bi′dden*, *bid*). Command to; invite; salute with (greeting etc.); (past t. & past part. *bid*) offer (price) for a thing; (at bridge) made a bid. **bĭ′dder** *n.* **bĭd** *n.* Offer of price, esp. at an auction; (at bridge) announcement of the number of tricks that a player will undertake to win at no trumps or with a specified suit as trumps; attempt.

bĭ′ddable *adj.* Obedient; (of a suit in a hand at bridge) on which a bid can reasonably be made.

bīde *v.* Abide (archaic except in ~ *one's time*).

bidet (bē′dā) *n.* Shallow oval basin fitted in bathroom, for washing the genital region.

bīĕ′nnĭal *adj.* Lasting, recurring every, two years. **bīĕ′nnĭallȳ** *adv.* **bīĕ′nnĭal** *n.* Plant which springs from seed one year and flowers, fructifies, and dies the next.

bier *n.* Movable frame on which corpse or coffin is taken to grave.

B.I.F. *abbrev.* British Industries Fair.

biff *n.* (slang) Blow, whack. ~ *v.t.* Strike, hit.

bĭ′ffĭn *n.* Deep-red variety of cooking-apple. [= *beefing*, f. *beef* (with ref. to the colour)]

bī′fĭd *adj.* Divided by a deep cleft into two lobes.

bīfō′cal *adj.* (of spectacle lenses) Having two segments of different focal lengths, the upper for dis-

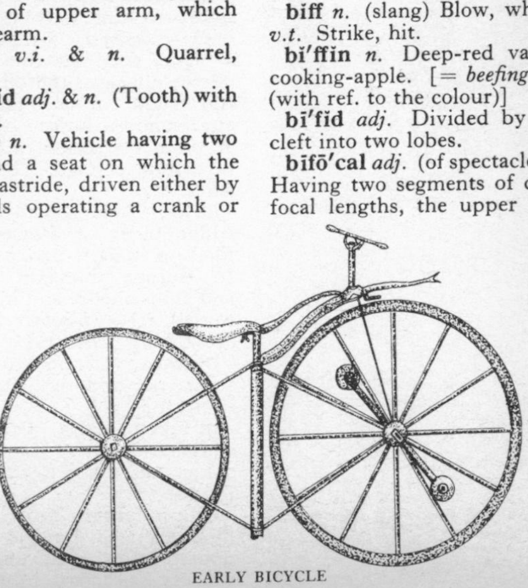

EARLY BICYCLE

tant, the lower for near, vision. **bīfō′cals** (-z) *n.pl.* Bifocal spectacles.

bīfō′lĭate *adj.* Of two leaves.

bī′furcāte (-fer-) *v.* Divide into two branches, fork. ~ *adj.* Forked. **bīfurcā′tion** *n.*

bĭg *adj.* Large; grown-up; important; boastful; (colloq., orig. U.S.) magnanimous; ~ *with child*, advanced in pregnancy (also fig. *with news* etc.); *B~ Ben*, great bell which strikes the hours in Houses of Parliament; *B~ Brother*, head of State in George Orwell's novel '1984'; hence, head of authoritarian organization exercising dictatorial pseudo-benevolent power; ~ *business*, commerce on grand scale; ~ *end*: see END *n.* 5; ~*-headed*, (colloq.) conceited; ~ *gun*, *noise*, (fig.) important person; ~ *money*, large amount of money; ~ *three*, *four*, etc., predominant few; ~ *toe*, innermost, largest toe; ~ *top*, circus marquee; *bi′gwig*, important person. ~ *adv.* **bĭ′gnėss** *n.*

bĭ′gamȳ *n.* Crime of going through a form of marriage while first marriage is still valid. **bĭ′gamous** *adj.* **bĭ′gamouslȳ** *adv.* **bĭ′gamĭst** *n.*

bĭgarade (-ahd) *n.* Spanish bitter orange. [Fr.]

bight (bīt) *n.* Loop of a rope; curve, recess, of coast, river, etc., bay.

bĭ′got *n.* Person obstinately and unreasonably holding some creed or view and intolerant towards others. **bĭ′gotėd** *adj.* **bĭ′gotrȳ** *n.*

Bĭhar′. State of NE. India; capital, Patna. **Bĭhar′ĭ** *n.*

bijou (bē′zhōō) *n.* Jewel, trinket. ~ *adj.* Small and elegant.

bīke *n.* & *v.i.* (colloq.) Bicycle, motor-cycle.

bĭki′nĭ (-kē-) *n.* Scanty two-piece beach-garment worn by women. [f. name of island in the Pacific]

bīlā′bĭal *adj.* & *n.* (phon.) (Consonant) produced by the junction or apposition of both lips. **bīlā′bĭallȳ** *adv.*

bīlă′teral *adj.* Of, on, with, two sides; affecting, between, two parties; ~ *symmetry*, symmetry about a plane, such that one half is a mirror-image of the other (as left and right in general outward appearance of human body and in all other vertebrate and many invertebrate animals). **bīlă′terallȳ** *adv.*

bĭ′lberrȳ *n.* Small blue-black edible berry of *Vaccinium myrtillus*, a dwarf hardy shrub of N. Europe abundant on heaths and stony moors and in mountain woods (also *blaeberry*, *whortleberry*, U.S. *blueberry*).

bĭ′lbō *n.* (hist.) Sword noted for its temper and elasticity. [*Bilbao* in Spain]

bĭ′lboes (-ōz) *n.* Iron bar with sliding shackles for prisoner's ankles, and a lock to fix one end of the bar to the floor or ground.

bīle *n.* Bitter, brownish-yellow fluid secreted by the liver and poured into the duodenum in the process of digestion; (hist.) one of the four humours; (fig.) anger, peevishness.

bilge *n.* Nearly horizontal part of ship's bottom; foulness that collects in bilge; (slang) nonsense, rot belly of a cask; *~-water*, foul water that collects in ship's bilge. *v.* Stave in the bilge of, spring a leak in the bilge; bulge, swell.

bilhar'zia *n.* Disease produced by trematode worm of genus *B~*, parasitic in veins of human pelvic region and urinary organs, esp. in Africa. [f. Theodor *Bilharz* (1825–62), German physician]

bi'liary *adj.* Of the bile.

bili'ngual (-nggw-) *adj.* Having, written in, speaking, etc., two languages. **bili'ngualism, bili'ngualist** *n.*

bi'lious *adj.* Arising from derangement of the bile; liable to, affected by, this. **bi'liously** *adv.* **bi'liousness** *n.*

bilk *v.t.* 1. (cribbage) Balk or spoil person's score in his crib. 2. Evade payment of (creditor, esp. taxi-driver, or bill); cheat, give the slip to. **bi'lker** *n.*

bill[1] *n.* 1. Obsolete weapon, varying from simple concave blade with long wooden handle, to kind of concave axe with spike at the back of shaft terminating in a spear-head; 2. (also *bi'llhook*) Implement used for pruning etc., having long blade with concave edge, often ending in a sharp hook, and a wooden handle in line with blade.

bill[2] *n.* 1. Bird's beak, esp. when slender or flattened; horny beak of platypus. 2. Narrow promontory. 3. (naut.) Point of anchor-fluke. ~ *v.i.* Stroke bill with bill (as doves); (also *~ and coo*) exchange caresses.

bill[3] *n.* 1. Draft of proposed Act of Parliament. 2. (obs., law) Written statement of (plaintiff's) case, proposed indictment submitted to grand jury. 3. Note of charges for goods delivered or services rendered. 4. Poster, placard; programme of entertainment; *fill the ~*, (orig. U.S.) suffice. 5. (also *~ of exchange*) Written order to pay sum on given date to drawer or named payee. 6. (U.S.) Bank-note. 7. *~ of fare*, list of dishes to be served; *~ of health*, certificate regarding infectious disease on ship or in port at time of sailing; *~ of lading*, ship-master's receipt for goods to consignor, undertaking to deliver them to a specified port; *~ of sale*, document transferring personal property or authorizing its seizure by lender of money if payment is delayed; *~s of mortality*, (hist.) weekly return of deaths in London and district, which began to be published in 1592; *within the ~s of mortality*, within the district covered by these bills; *B~ of Rights*: see RIGHT *n.* 2; *~-broker*, dealer in bills of exchange; *~-poster*, man who pastes up placards. ~ *v.t.* Announce, put in the programme; plaster with placards; send a bill to.

bi'llabong *n.* (Austral.) Branch or effluent of river forming back-water or stagnant pool.

bi'llet[1] *n.* Order requiring householder to board and lodge soldier etc. bearing it; place where such a person is lodged; appointment, situation. ~ *v.t.* Quarter (soldiers etc.) *on* town, householder, etc., *in*, *at*, place. **billetee'** *n.* Person billeted.

bi'llet[2] *n.* 1. Thick piece of firewood. 2. Small bar of metal. 3. (archit.) Short roll inserted at intervals in hollow moulding.

billet-doux (bĭlĭdōō') *n.* (pl. *billets-doux*). Love-letter (joc.).

bi'lliards (-lyardz) *n.pl.* Game played with three small solid balls, one red, one plain white, and one spot white, driven about by cues on a horizontal rectangular table covered with smooth green cloth, surrounded by a cushioned ledge, and provided with six pockets at the corners and in the middle of the long sides; *billiard ball, cue, table*, etc., one used in billiards; *billiard marker*, one (esp. attendant) who marks the score at billiards.

Bi'llingsgate (-z-; *or* -āt). Fish-market established at one of the old gates of London on the riverside; hence (also *b*~), foul language (for which the market was famous in 17th c.).

bĭ'llion (-yon) *n.* One million millions; (U.S.) one thousand millions. **bĭllionair'e** *n.* One whose wealth is a billion (dollars, pounds, etc.) or more.

bĭ'llon *n.* Alloy of gold or silver with a predominating amount of some base metal, used for coinage.

bĭ'llow (-ō) *n.* Great wave; anything that sweeps along, as sound etc. ~ *v.i.* Rise, move, in billows. **bĭ'llowy̆** *adj.*

bĭ'lly̆[1] *n.* (also *bi'llycan*; orig. Austral.) Tin can for boiling water etc. in camping.

bĭ'lly̆[2] *n.* = BILLY-GOAT.

bĭ'llycŏck *n.* Man's round, low-crowned, hard felt hat; bowler.

bĭ'lly̆-goat *n.* Male goat.

bīlō'bed (-bd) *adj.* Having, or divided into, two lobes.

bĭ'ltŏng *n.* Strips of sun-dried lean meat (antelope, buffalo, etc.).

bīmėtă'llĭc *adj.* 1. Of two metals; ~ *strip*, sensitive element in some thermostats, made of two bands of different metals, one of which expands more than the other when temperature rises, and so causes the strip to bend. 2. Using both gold and silver as currency, at fixed ratio to each other. **bīmĕ'tallĭsm, bīmĕ'tallĭst** *ns.*

bī-mo'nthly̆ (-mŭ-) *adj.* & *n.* (Periodical) produced or occurring every two months.

bĭn *n.* Receptacle for corn, coal, bottled wine, etc.; receptacle for household rubbish; canvas receptacle used in hop-picking.

bī'nary̆ *adj.* Dual, of or involving pairs; ~ *compound*, (chem.) one consisting of two elements; ~ *form*, (mus.) applied to a melody or composition having two sections, the 2nd of which is balanced against the 1st and seems to answer it; ~ *measure*, (mus.) having two beats to a bar; ~ *scale*, (math.) system of numbers etc. using only two elements, 0 and 1.

bīnd *v.* (past t. & past part. *bound*). 1. Tie, fasten; put in bonds, restrain; fasten or hold together; (cookery) cause to cohere. 2. Be obligatory, impose constraint or duty upŏn; (pass.) be required by duty; subject to legal obligation; indenture as apprentice; ~ *over*, (esp.) make person give recognizance not to commit a breach of the peace. 3. Make costive. 4. Bandage; wreath *with*; edge *with* braid, iron, etc.; fasten (sheets, book) into cover. 5. (slang) Complain. ~ *n.* 1. (mus.) = TIE *n.* 4. 2. (slang) Bore, nuisance.

bī'nder *n.* (esp.) 1. Book-binder. 2. Long broad band of material to bind round body. 3. Long stone extending through a wall 4. Reaping-and-binding machine.

bī'ndĭng *adj.* Obligatory (*on*). ~ *n.* (esp.) Book-cover; braid etc. for binding raw edges of textiles.

bī'ndweed *n.* Convolvulus.

bīne *n.* Flexible shoot; stem of climbing plant, esp. the hop.

Binet (bēnā), Alfred (1857–1911). French psychologist; experimented in the measurement of intelligence and was the first to devise intelligence-tests.

bĭnge (-j) *n.* (slang) Heavy drinking-bout; spree.

bĭ'ngō (-ngg-) *n.* Form of lotto in which the player who first covers all numbers on his card wins the money staked.

bĭ'nnacle *n.* Box for compass on a ship.

bĭnŏ'cūlar *adj.* Adapted for both eyes; ~ *vision*, type of vision, peculiar to man and some other primates, in which both eyes co-operate in observing the same object and receive a stereoscopic impression. **bĭnŏ'cūlars** (-z) *n.pl.* Binocular field- or opera-glasses.

bīnō'mĭal *adj.* Consisting of two terms; ~ *theorem*, general algebraic formula, discovered by Newton, by which any power of a binomial quantity may be found without performing the progressive multiplications. ~ *n.* Algebraic expression consisting of two terms joined by + or −.

bīnŏ'mĭnal *adj.* Of two names; ~ *system*, (biol.) system of nomenclature by genus and species.

bĭnt *n.* (colloq., usu. derog.) Girl, woman. [Arab., = 'daughter', girl]

bĭntur'ŏng (-oor-) *n.* Prehensile-tailed civet, *Arctictis binturong*, of S. Asia.

bīo- *prefix.* (Course of) life of, concerning, organic life; biological.

bīochĕ'mĭstrў (-k-) *n.* Science dealing with the chemical properties of the parts of living organisms. **bīochĕ'mĭcal** *adj.* **bīochĕ'mĭst** *n.*

bīoclīmatŏ'logў *n.* Study of climate in relation to life and esp. to human health.

bīogĕ'nėsĭs *n.* 1. (usu. hist.) T. H. Huxley's term for descent of living matter from living matter (opp. ABIOGENESIS). 2. Hypothetical development of living matter from complex but inanimate substances.

bīogėŏ'graphў *n.* Study of the distribution of animals and plants.

bīŏ'graphў *n.* Written life of a person, branch of literature dealing with such lives. **bīŏ'grapher** *n.* **bīogră'phĭcal** *adj.* **bīogră'phĭcallў** *adv.*

bīŏ'logў *n.* Science of life, dealing with the morphology, physiology, behaviour, origin, and distribution of animals and plants. **bīolŏ'gĭcal** *adj.* Of biology; ~ *control*, control of pests by the use of other organisms which devour or destroy them; ~ *warfare*, use of toxins to spread disease in the enemy. **bīolŏ'gĭcallў** *adv.* **bīŏ'logĭst** *n.*

bīolūmĭnĕ'scence (*or* -lōō-) *n.* Emission of light by living organisms. **bīolūmĭnĕ'scent** *adj.*

bī'ōme *n.* (ecol.) Biotic community of plants and animals.

bīŏ'mėtrў *n.* Application of mathematics to biology, esp. the study of resemblances between living things by statistical methods. **bīomĕ'trĭcal** *adj.* **bīomėtrĭ'cian** (-shan) *n.*

bīophў'sĭcs (-z-) *n.* Science dealing with the mechanical and electrical properties of the parts of living organisms. **bīophў'sĭcal** *adj.* **bīophў'sĭcĭst** *n.*

bī'opsў *n.* (med.) Examination of tissue removed from the living body.

bī'oscōpe *n.* Early form of cinematograph; (S. Afr.) cinema.

bī'osphēre *n.* Regions of earth's crust and atmosphere occupied by living organisms.

bīŏ'tĭc *adj.* (biol.) Relating to life; peculiar to living organisms.

bīpartĭsă'n (-z-) *adj.* Of or involving two (political) parties.

bīpar'tīte *adj.* Divided into or consisting of two parts; (law, of agreement etc.) drawn up in two corresponding parts, each party delivering a counterpart to the other.

bī'pĕd *n.* & *adj.* Two-footed (animal).

bīpĭ'nnate *adj.* (bot.) Having leaflets arranged in two rows on either side of leaf-stalk, the leaflets being themselves subdivided.

bī'plāne *n.* Aeroplane with two planes or main supporting surfaces, one above the other.

bīquadră'tĭc (-kwŏd-) *adj.* Of, raised to, the square of a square (or 4th power) of a number; ~ *equation*, one in which the unknown quantity is biquadratic. ~ *n.* Biquadratic equation; 4th power of a number.

bĭrch *n.* 1. Hardy northern forest-tree of genus *Betula* with smooth tough bark and slender graceful branches; wood of this;

~-*bark canoe*, one made of the bark of *B. papyrifera*. 2. Bundle of birch-twigs used for flogging. ~ *v.t.* Flog with birch. **bir'chen** *adj.* Made of birch.

bird *n.* 1. Any feathered vertebrate animal, member of a class nearly allied to reptiles but distinguished by warm blood, feathers, and adaptation of the fore-limbs as wings. 2. Game bird. 3. (slang) Young woman; (joc.) person, esp. *old* ~. 4. (slang) Prison (sentence). 5. *get the* ~, (slang, esp. theatr.) be hissed, booed, etc.; be dismissed; so *give the* ~; ~-*bath*, dish of water set in garden for birds' use; ~-*brain(ed)*, (person) with small brain; *bir'dcage*, wire cage for bird(s), object of similar design; ~-*call*, note of bird; instrument imitating this; ~-*cherry*, species of cherry tree (*Prunus padus*); ~-*lime*: see LIME[1]; ~ *of paradise*, bird of family Paradiseidae native to New Guinea and notable for its brilliant colours and elegant plumes; ~ *of passage*, migratory bird (also fig. of sojourner); ~-*sanctuary*, island or enclosed piece of land where birds are protected by law; ~-*seed*, any of various kinds of seed used esp. for feeding caged birds; ~'*s-eye*, any of several plants, esp. the speedwell, with small round bright flowers; ~'*s-eye maple*, wood of the sugar maple when full of little knots; ~'*s-eye view*, view of landscape from above; résumé of a subject; ~'*s nest*, (esp.) edible nest of certain swallows found in the China Sea; ~'*s nesting*, search for birds' nests usu. in order to collect eggs; ~-*table*, raised platform on which food for birds is placed; ~-*watching*, study of birds in their natural surroundings.

bī'rēme *n.* Ancient galley with two banks of oars.

birĕ'tta *n.* Square cap worn by R.C. and some Anglican clerics.

Birgitta, Birgittine: see BRIDGET[2].

Bir'mingham (-ng-*a*m). Midland city in West Midlands, 2nd largest in England, noted for its metal manufactures; university, 1900; university of Aston, 1966.

bir'ō. Ball-point pen. [trade-name]

birth *n.* 1. Emergence of child or animal from body of female parent; process of producing young; *give* ~ *to*, (of female parent) produce (young) from body (also fig.). 2. Origin, beginning. 3. Parentage, descent; noble lineage. 4. ~ *certificate*, form showing date and place etc. of birth; ~ *control*, regulation of birth by means of contraceptive methods or devices; *bir'thday*, (anniversary of) day of one's birth; *birthday honours*, titles of honour annually conferred by the British sovereign, announced on his or her official birthday; *birthday suit*, (slang) state of nakedness; *bir'thmark*, congenital mark on the body; ~-*place*, place at which one was born; *bir'thrate*, number of births per 1,000 of population per annum; *bir'thright*, rights, privilege, or position to which one is entitled by birth, esp. by being the eldest son.

bĭs *adv.* Twice; (mus.) repeat. [Fr. & It.]

Bi'scay, Bay of. Part of N. Atlantic between N. coast of Spain and W. coast of France, notorious for storms.

bĭ'scuit (-kĭt) *n.* 1. Kind of crisp, dry bread or cake more or less hard, variously flavoured, and usu. unleavened, prepared usu. in small flat thin pieces; (U.S.) kind of small leavened cakes resembling scones. 2. Porcelain and other pottery-ware after first firing and before being glazed or painted. 3. Characteristic light-brown colour of biscuit. 4. Small square army mattress, three of which form full-size mattress. ~ *adj.* Of the colour of biscuit.

bīsĕ'ct *v.t.* Cut or divide into two (usu. equal) parts. **bīsĕ'ction** *n.* **bīsĕ'ctor** *n.* Bisecting line.

bīsĕ'xūal (*or* -kshōō-) *adj.* Of two sexes; having both sexes in one individual, hermaphrodite. **bīsĕxūă'lĭtў** *n.*

bĭ'shop *n.* 1. Clergyman consecrated as ecclesiastical governor of a diocese; *Bishops' Bible*, English translation prepared by the bishops and printed 1568; ~ *sleeves*, very full sleeves like those worn by bishop, 2. Mitre-shaped chessman moved diagonally. 3. Mulled spiced wine. **bĭ'shopric** *n.* Diocese or office of a bishop.

Bĭ'sley (-z-). Village in Surrey where annual meeting of National Rifle Association is held.

Bĭ'smârck (-z-), Otto Eduard Leopold, Prince von (1815–98). German statesman; Prussian prime minister 1862; chancellor of N. German Federation 1867; after the

war with France, in which the S. German States co-operated, became first chancellor of the German Empire 1871; resigned, having displeased William II, 1890.

Bĭ'smârck Archĭpĕ'lagō (-z-, ârk-). Group of small islands in the Pacific, NE. of New Guinea, under Australian administration.

bĭ'smuth (-z-) *n.* (chem.) Reddish-white brittle metallic element melting at low temperatures; symbol Bi, at. no. 83, at. wt 208·9806; (pop.) salt of this, used to relieve digestive disorders.

bī'son *n.* 1. Species of wild ox (*Bison europaeus*) of heavy build with humped shoulders, formerly

prevalent in Europe and still existing in the Caucasus. 2. N. Amer. wild ox (*B. americanus*) formerly roaming in vast herds over the continent, now almost extinct except in protected areas.

bĭsque[1] (-k) *n.* Point given to opponent in certain games, which he may take at any stage, esp. in tennis and golf; (croquet) right of playing extra turn.

bĭsque[2] (-k) *n.* (pottery) Unglazed white porcelain used for statuettes etc., biscuit.

bĭsque[3] (-k) *n.* Soup made with shellfish etc.

bĭssĕ'xtīle *adj.* & *n.* Leap (-year). [L *bis sextilis* (*annus*) (year) containing the doubled sixth day (because in the Julian calendar the day repeated, 24 Feb., was acc. to the inclusive Roman method of reckoning the sixth before the Calends of March)]

bĭ'stôrt *n.* Plant (*Polygonum bistorta*) with large twisted rhizome and cylindrical spike of small flesh-coloured flowers, yielding an astringent medicinal drug.

bĭ'stoury (-orĭ) *n.* Surgeon's scalpel.

bĭ'stre (-t*er*) *n.* Brown pigment prepared from soot; colour of this.

bĭt[1] *n.* 1. Biting or cutting end or part of tool, as boring-piece of drill, cutting-iron of plane, etc.; part of key which engages with levers of lock. 2. Mouthpiece of horse's bridle. ~ *v.t.* Furnished (horse) with bit; restrain curb.

bĭt[2] *n.* 1. Morsel of food; something to eat. 2. Small piece of anything; small portion or quantity; small coin; *do one's* ~, play one's part; ~ *part, player*, (theatr.) (player of) very small part.

bĭtch *n.* 1. Female of dog, fox,

wolf. 2. (colloq.) Malicious or ill-tempered woman; difficult or unpleasant thing. **bĭ'tchȳ** *adj.* **bĭ'tchĭlȳ** *adv.* **bĭ'tchĭnėss** *n.*

bīte *v.* (past t. *bĭt*, past part. *bĭ'tten*). 1. Cut into or off, nip, with teeth; (of insects etc.) sting, suck; ~ *back*, restrain (speech) by biting lips. 2. (of fishes) Accept bait. 3. Cause glowing, smarting pain to. 4. Corrode. 5. (of wheels, screw, etc.) Grip. ~ *n.* Act of, wound made by, piece detached by, biting; occlusion; taking of bait by fish; snack; grip, hold.

Bĭthȳ'nia. Ancient region of NW. Asia Minor. **Bĭthȳ'nian** *adj.* & *n.*

bī'ting *adj.* (esp.) Pungent, stinging, sarcastic.

bĭ'tter *adj.* Tasting like wormwood, quinine, aloes, etc., obnoxious, irritating, or unfavourably stimulating to the gustatory nerve; unpalatable to the mind, full of affliction; virulent, relentless; biting, harsh; piercingly cold; ~*-apple*, colocynth; ~*-sweet*, sweet(ness) with bitter after-taste or element; woody nightshade. **bĭ'tterlȳ** *adv.* **bĭ'tternėss** *n.*

bĭ'tter *n.* 1. Bitterness. 2. Bitter beer; (pl.) liquors impregnated with wormwood etc. taken as stomachics.

bĭ'ttern *n.* Bird of genus *Botaurus*, allied to herons, but smaller; esp. *B. stellaris*, a European marsh-bird noted for its booming cry.

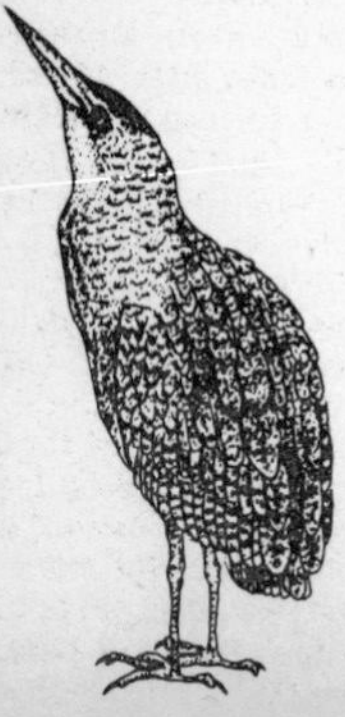

bĭ'ttȳ *adj.* Scrappy. **bĭ'ttĭnėss** *n.*

bĭ'tūmėn (*or* -tū'-) *n.* Mineral pitch, asphalt; any of various kinds of native oxygenated hydrocarbon, as naphtha, petroleum. **bĭtū'mĭnous** *adj.*

bĭ'tūmĭnīze *v.t.* Impregnate, cover, with bitumen.

bīvā'lent *adj.* (chem.) = DIVALENT.

bī'vălve *adj.* Having two valves, having two hinged shells. ~ *n.* Mollusc with shell consisting of two halves hinged together by elastic ligament.

bĭ'vouăc (-o͝o-) *n.* Temporary encampment without tents, etc.; improvised shelter, small tent. ~ *v.i.* Remain, esp. during the night, in open air without tents.

bĭ'vvȳ *n.* (army slang) Bivouac.

bĭzârre (-âr') *adj.* Eccentric, fantastic, grotesque, mixed in style, half barbaric. **bĭzarr'elȳ** *adv.* **bĭzarr'enėss** *n.* [Span. *bizarro* brave, handsome]

Bizet (bēzā), Georges (1838–75). French composer of 'Carmen' and other operas.

bīzō'nal *adj.* Of or concerning both of two zones.

Björnsen (byêr'-), Björnstjerne (1832–1910). Norwegian playwright, novelist, and poet.

B.L. *abbrev.* Bachelor of Law.

blăb *v.* Talk or tell foolishly or indiscreetly, reveal, let out; hence, **blă'bber** *n.* **blăb** *n.* Blabbing.

blăck *adj.* 1. Opposite to white, colourless from the absence or complete absorption of all light; so near this as to have no distinguishable colour; very dark-coloured. 2. Dark-skinned; dark-clothed; dusky, gloomy; dirty. 3. Deadly, sinister, wicked; dismal; angry, lowering; implying disgrace or condemnation (as ~ *mark* etc.); performed by blackleg labour; boycotted by trade unions during a dispute; existing, bought, sold, in contravention of economic regulations. 4. ~ *and blue*, discoloured with bruise(s); ~ *and tan*, (dog) of these two colours; *B~ and Tans* (from their black and khaki uniform, a mixture of con-

Clam

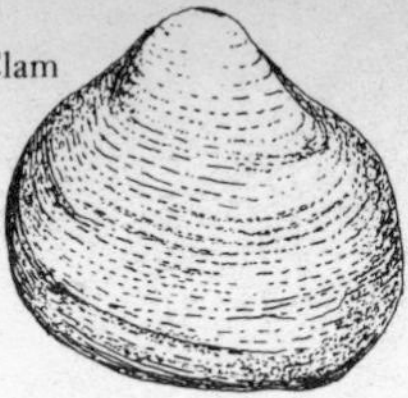

Mussel

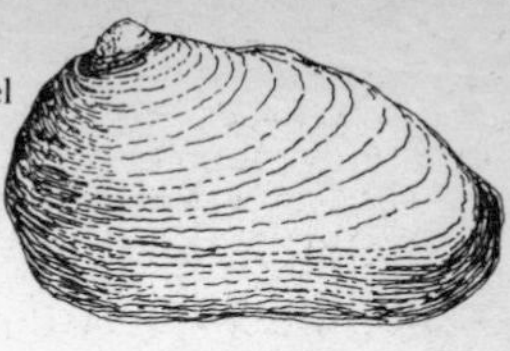

Side-view clam

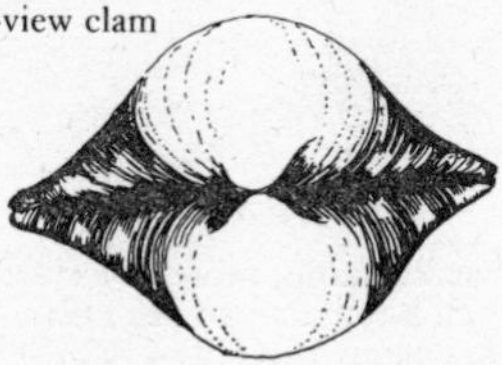

Scallop

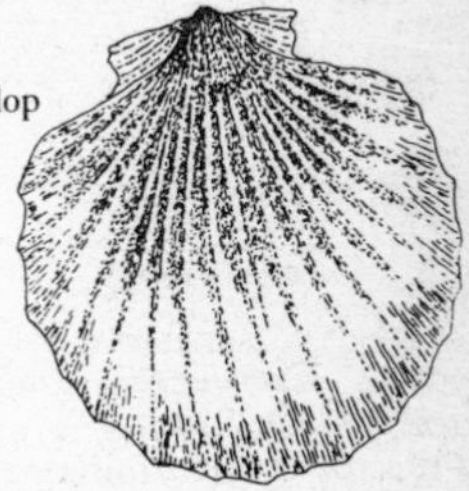

BIVALVES

stabulary and military uniforms), armed force specially recruited in 1921 to combat Sinn Fein in Ireland; ~ *art*, magic; *bla'ckball* (*v.t.*) exclude from club, society, etc. (orig. by putting black ball into urn or ballot box to express adverse vote); ~*-beetle*, domestic cockroach (*Blatta orientalis*); (slang) cleric, parson; ~ *belt*, (belt worn by) person who has attained a certain degree of proficiency in judo; *bla'ckberry*, bramble (*Rubus fruticosus*) or its fruit; *bla'ckberrying*, gathering blackberries; *bla'ckbird*, European song-bird (*Turdus merula*, one of the thrushes), the male being black with yellow bill, the female dark brown; (hist.) captive Negro on slave- or pirate-ship; *bla'ckboard*, large black board, panel, etc., used in schools and lecture-rooms for writing or drawing on in chalk; ~ *body*, (phys.) body or surface that absorbs all radiation falling upon it; ~ *box*, (esp.) device in aircraft recording details of flight; ~ *cap*, cap worn by English judges in full dress, formerly put on when passing sentence of death; *bla'ckcap*, bird, the warbler *Sylvia atricapilla*, which has the top of the head black; ~*-cock*, male of black grouse; ~ *coffee*, coffee without milk; *B~ Country*, parts of Staffordshire and Warwickshire grimed and blackened by the fumes and refuse of coal and iron-works; ~ *currant*, shrub *Ribes nigrum*; its small black fruit; ~ *damp*, choke-damp of coal-mines; *B~ Death*, outbreak of plague, mostly in bubonic form, which spread into Europe from Asia in the 14th c., its most lethal year in England being 1348–9, so called from the symptom of internal haemorrhages which blackened the skin of sufferers; ~ *earth*, dark soil rich in humus; ~*-earth zone*, belt of this in U.S.S.R. from Ukraine to S. Siberia; ~ *eye*, eye with black or very dark iris; (also) discoloration round eye due to bruise; ~*-eyed Susan*, flower with light usu. yellow petals and dark centre, esp. *Thunbergia alata* and *Rudbeckia hirta*; ~*-fellow*, Australian aboriginal; ~ *flag*, black flag used by pirates as ensign, as signal of execution etc.; *bla'ckfly*, kind of aphis; also collect.; *B~ Friar*, Dominican; ~ *frost*, hard frost without snow or rime; *blackguard* (blă'ga͡rd) (*adj.* & *n.*) scoundrel(ly),

BLACKBERRY BLACKBIRD

foul-mouthed (person); (*v.t.*) revile scurrilously; *blackguardly* (*adj.*); **bla'ckhead, black-headed greasy plug in mouth of hair follicle**; ~ *hole*, any dark hole or deep cell, esp. (hist.) punishment-cell or guard-room in barracks; *B~ Hole of Calcutta*, punishment-cell of the barracks in Fort William, Calcutta, in which 146 Europeans were confined for a night (1756) by order of Suraj ud Daula and only 23 survived until the morning; *~-house*, (Sc.) turf house; house built of unmortared stone, esp. in NW. Scotland and the Hebrides; ~ *jack*, pirate's black flag; ~ *jack*: see JACK[2]; *~-lead*, (pencil containing) graphite; (*v.t.*) colour or rub with (preparation of) graphite; *bla'ckleg*, swindler (esp. on turf); workman who breaks rules of a particular trade or group, works for employer whose men are on strike, etc.; (*v.*) act as blackleg; ~ *letter*, Gothic type, style of type used by early printers and still occas., esp. in Germany, as dist. from roman; ~ *list*, list of persons against whom charges are made, convictions recorded, etc.; *bla'cklist* (*v.t.*); *bla'ckmail*, (hist.) tribute exacted on Scottish and Highland borders by freebooters in return for protection and immunity; hence, payment extorted by threats or pressure, esp. by threatening to reveal discreditable secret; extortion of such payment; so *bla'ckmail* (*v.t.*); *bla'ckmailer* (*n.*); *B~ Maria*, prison van; during the war of 1914–18, large shell which on bursting emitted masses of black smoke; ~ *mark*: see sense 3; ~ *market*, illegitimate traffic in controlled goods or currencies or commodities in short supply; hence *blackmarketeer* (*n.* & *v.i.*); ~ *mass*, mass for the dead, at which vestments and drapings are black; travesty of this, used in the cult of Satanism; ~ *monk*, Benedictine (from the colour of his habit); *B~ Museum*, collection of objects connected with crime, at Scotland Yard; *B~ Prince*, 16th-c. name given, for unknown reasons, to Edward (1330–76), the eldest son of Edward III; ~ *pudding*, kind of sausage made of blood and suet; *B~ Rod*, gentleman usher to Lord Chamberlain's department, the House of Lords, and the Chapter of the Garter, so called from his ebony rod of office; *B~ Sea*, tideless sea between U.S.S.R. and Turkey; ~ *sheep*, scoundrel, unsatisfactory or disreputable member *of* (family etc.); *Bla'ckshirt*, Fascist (from black shirt in uniform of Fascist militia); *bla'cksmith*, smith working in iron (dist. from whitesmith, who works in tin etc.); ~ *spot*, place notorious for accidents, esp. on highway;

~ *tea*: see TEA; *bla'ckthorn*, sloe (*Prunus spinosa*), a thorny shrub bearing white flowers before the leaves and small dark-purple fruits; *blackthorn winter*, time when this thorn blossoms, usu. with cold weather and NE. winds; ~ *velvet*, mixture of stout and champagne; ~ *vomit*, (blackish matter vomited in severe cases of) yellow fever; *B~ Watch*: see WATCH; *bla'ckwater fever*, tropical fever, originating in malarial infection, characterized by brown or blue-black urine; ~ *widow*, female of venomous black spider *Latrodectus mactans*. **blă'ckish** *adj.* **blă'ckly̆** *adv.* **blă'ckness** *n.*

blăck *n.* 1. Black colour, paint, etc.; *in the* ~, (book-keeping) showing a credit balance. 2. Black substance, as soot etc.; fungus, smut, in wheat etc. 3. Black variety of anything; black cloth or clothing. 4. Negro. 5. (Player using) dark pieces in chess etc. 6. (slang) Blackmail (*put the* ~ *on*). ~ *v.t.* Make black, polish with blacking; declare to be 'black' (see *adj.*, 3); ~ *out*, obliterate (printed matter) with printer's ink; obscure (window, street, etc.) so that no light is visible from outside or from the air; extinguish lights during stage performance; become unconscious; *bla'ckout* (*n.*) (1) (period of) obscuration of artificial lights, esp. in war-time; material with which this is done; (2) failure or stoppage of electrical power, radio signal, etc.; (3) temporary loss of vision and consciousness, esp. in aviators when changing direction at high speeds, caused by blood being drawn away from the head; (4) temporary loss of memory.

blă'ckamoor *n.* (joc. or derog.) Negro; dark-skinned person.

blă'cken *v.* Make, grow, black or dark; speak evil of.

blă'cking *n.* (esp.) Paste or liquid for blacking or polishing boots.

Blă'ckmōre, Richard Doddridge (1825–1900). English novelist, author of 'Lorna Doone'.

Blă'ckstone, Sir William (1723–80). English jurist, author of 'Commentaries on the Laws of England' (1765–9).

Blă'ckwŏŏd, William (1776–1834). Scottish publisher; founded 'Blackwood's Magazine' (1817).

blă'dder *n.* 1. Membranous bag in human and other animal bodies esp, urinary bladder; animal's bladder or part of it prepared for various uses, inflated, etc. 2. Anything inflated and hollow, wordy man, windbag; inflated pericarp or vesicle in plants and seaweeds; *bla'dderwrack*, species of seaweed (*Fucus vesiculosus*) with air-bladders in substance of fronds

blāde *n.* 1. Flat lanceolate leaf of grass and cereals; (bot.) broad thin expanded part of leaf as opp. to petiole or leaf-stalk. 2. Broad flattened leaf-like part of instrument, as oar, paddle, spade, aircraft propeller, etc.; front flat part of tongue; broad flattened bone, esp. shoulder-blade; ~*-bone*, scapula; this part of animal as cut of meat. 3. Thin cutting part of edged tool or weapon; detachable usu. two-edged cutting part of safety razor. 4. Gallant, free-and-easy fellow.

blae'berry̆ (blāb-) *n.* = BILBERRY.

blague (-ahg) *n.* Humbug, claptrap.

blain *n.* Inflamed swelling or sore on skin.

Blair[1], Eric Arthur (1903–50). English novelist and essayist, born in Bengal; author, under his pseudonym George Orwell, of the political satires 'Animal Farm' (1945) and '1984' (1949), and writings on social themes.

Blair[2], Robert (1699–1746). Scottish poet, author of a melancholy and (in his own time) highly successful blank-verse poem, 'The Grave' (1743).

Blāke[1], Robert (1599–1657). English admiral; fought with distinction against the Dutch and Spanish fleets.

Blāke[2], William (1757–1827). English poet, painter, and mystic; engraved, and sometimes coloured by hand, many of his own works,

BLAKE: GOD CREATING THE UNIVERSE

which included the lyrical 'Songs of Innocence' (1789) and 'Songs of Experience' (1794), and the 'Prophetic Books' (1793–1804).

blāme *n.* Censure; responsibility for bad result. ~ *v.t.* Find fault with; fix responsibility on. **blā'melėss** *adj.* Innocent. **blā'melėsslў** *adv.* **blā'melėssnėss** *n.* **blā'meworthy** (-mwẽrdhĭ) *adj.*

Blanc (blahṅ), Jean Joseph Charles Louis (1811–82). French socialist and historian; was given by the revolution of 1848 an opportunity to put into practice his theories of the organization of labour; his experiment lasted less than two months and he was forced to flee to England, not returning to France until 1871.

blanch (-ah-) *v.* Make white by withdrawing colour, peeling (almonds), immersing in boiling water (raw meat), or depriving of light (plants); make or grow pale with fear, cold, etc.

blancmange (bl*a*mŏ′nzh) *n.* Opaque jelly of cornflour etc. and milk, usu. sweetened and flavoured.

blă′ncō *n.* White preparation for whitening accoutrements; similar preparation of khaki colour. ~ *v.t.* Treat with blanco. [trade-name]

blănd *adj.* Smooth and suave in manner, gentle; balmy, mild. **blă′ndlў** *adv.* **blă′ndnėss** *n.*

blă′ndĭsh *v.* Flatter, coax. **blă′ndĭshment** *n.*

blănk *adj.* 1. Not written or printed on; with spaces left for signature or details. 2. Empty, not filled. 3. Void of interest, incident, result, or expression; unrelieved, sheer. 4. ~ *cartridge*, one without a ball; ~ *cheque*, cheque signed by drawer, with amount left for payee to fill in; hence, full discretionary power; ~ *verse*, (esp.) English unrhymed verse of five-foot iambics; ~ *wall*, wall without opening; (fig.) impassable obstacle. **blă′nklў** *adv.* **blănk** *n.* 1. Void; space left to be filled up in document; dash (—) written in place of omitted letter or word(s); (parl.) provisional words printed in italics in bill. 2. Blank ticket in sweepstake (i.e. one not inscribed with the name of a runner); hence, *draw* ~, elicit no response, fail. 3. Piece of metal ready for stamping as coin, medal, etc.

blă′nkėt *n.* Rectangular piece of woollen etc. material used for warmth esp. as bed-covering, horse-cloth, etc.; (as *adj.*) covering or including all contingencies etc.; *born on the wrong side of the* ~, illegitimate; *wet* ~, (fig.) discouraging person; ~*-bath*, washing of sick person by stages while keeping him warm between coverings; ~ *stitch*, stitch for finishing raw edge, used on blankets. ~ *v.t.* Cover with blanket; stifle, keep quiet (scandal, question, etc.); toss in a blanket; take wind from sails of (yacht) by passing to windward of her.

Blănkėteer′s (-z) *n.pl.* (hist.) Body of workmen who met at the so-called Blanket Meeting in St. Peter's Field, Manchester, in March 1817, provided with blankets or rugs in order to march to London and put their grievances before the Government.

blă′nkėtĭng *n.* (esp.) Material for blankets.

blanquette (blahṅkĕ′t) *n.* Dish of meat etc. in white sauce.

blāre *v.* & *n.* (Make) sound of trumpet; utter loudly.

Blâr′ney[1]. Village near Cork in S. Ireland; ~ *stone*, inscribed stone, very difficult to reach, in the Castle of Blarney, supposed to confer upon anyone who kisses it a cajoling tongue and the art of flattery or of telling lies with unblushing effrontery.

blâr′ney[2] *n.* & *v.* (Use, assail with) cajoling talk or nonsense.

blasé (blah′zā) *adj.* Cloyed, exhausted, with pleasure.

blăsphē′me *v.* Talk impiously; utter profanity about, revile. **blăsphē′mer, blă′sphėmў** *ns.* **blă′sphėmous** *adj.* **blă′sphėmouslў** *adv.*

blast (-ah-) *n.* Strong gust of wind; violent gust of air caused by explosion of bomb etc.; blowing or sound of trumpet or other wind-instruments; strong current of air used in smelting etc.; quantity of explosive used in blasting; (colloq.) violent reprimand; (*at*) *full* ~, (colloq.) at maximum speed, capacity, etc.; ~*-furnace*, smelting-furnace into which a blast of compressed heated air is driven by a blowing-engine. ~ *v.t.* 1. Blow up, break, dislodge, with explosives. 2. Wither, shrivel, blight. 3. (of rocket or spacecraft, usu. ~ *off*) Take off, be launched into space; use power in flight; ~*-off*, (thrust used in) launching of rocket etc. ~ *int.* Exclamation of annoyance. **bla′stėd** *adj.* (esp., colloq.) Damnable.

blă'stoderm *n.* External layer of cells formed as a result of cleavage of a yolked egg, characteristic of eggs of reptiles, birds, and, in a different form, insects.

blă'stūla *n.* (pl. *-lae*). (biol.) Early embryonic stage, usu. a hollow ball of cells, produced by cleavage of an egg (cf. GASTRULA).

blā'tant *adj.* Noisy, vulgarly clamorous; palpably obvious. **blā'tantlў** *adv.* **blā'tancў** *n.*

blather: see BLETHER.

Blavă'tskў, Helena Petrovna (1831–91). Russian spiritualist, founder (in New York) of the Theosophical Society.

blāze[1] *v.i.* Burn with bright flame; be brilliantly lighted; burn with excitement etc.; show bright colours; emit light. ~ *n.* Bright flame or fire; glow of colour, bright display; *go to ~s*, (slang) go to hell.

blāze[2] *n.* White mark on face of horse or ox; white mark made on tree by chipping off bark, to indicate path, boundary, etc. ~ *v.t.* Mark (tree, path) with blaze; (fig.) ~ *a trail*, show a new way by pioneering activity.

blāze[3] *v.t.* Proclaim as with trumpet.

blā'zer *n.* (esp.) Unlined (orig. brightly coloured) jacket, usu. with badge on pocket, worn with

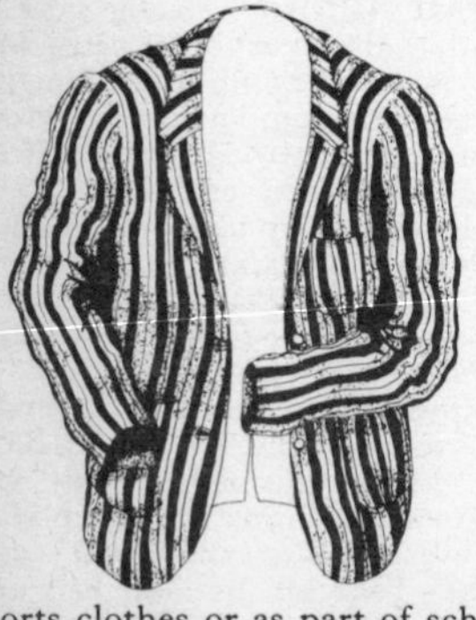

sports clothes or as part of school uniform.

blā'zon *n.* Heraldic shield, coat of arms, bearings, or banner; correct description of these; record, description, esp. of virtues etc. ~ *v.t.* Describe or paint (arms) heraldically; inscribe with arms etc. in colours; give lustre to; set forth in fitting words; proclaim. **blā'zonrў** *n.* (Art of describing or painting) heraldic devices, armorial bearings; brightly coloured display.

bleach *v.* Whiten by exposure to sunlight or chemical process; *bleaching powder*, chemical, such as chloride of lime, used for bleaching. ~ *n.* Bleaching process or substance.

bleak[1] *n.* Small European river-fish, *Alburnus lucidus*.

bleak[2] *adj.* Bare of vegetation; exposed, wind-swept; cold, chilly, dreary; (of person) depressed, lifeless. **blea'klў** *adv.* **blea'knėss** *n.*

blear *adj.* Dim, filmy, rheumy; misty, indistinct; *~-eyed* (*adj.*). ~ *v.t.* Dim (eyes) with tears, rheum, etc.; blur. **blear'ў** *adj.*

bleat *v.* (of sheep, goat, etc.) Utter characteristic tremulous cry; make sound resembling this, speak feebly or foolishly. ~ *n.* Cry of sheep, goat, etc.; any similar sound.

blĕb *n.* Small blister or bubble.

bleed *v.* (past t. & past part. *blĕd*). 1. Emit blood; suffer wounds or violent death; (of plants) emit sap; (of dyes) come out in water. 2. Draw blood surgically from; allow (liquid or gas) to escape from (a container). 3. Part with money, suffer extortion; extort money from. 4. (print.) Cut into print when trimming margin.

blee'der *n.* (esp.) Person suffering from haemophilia.

blee'dĭng *adj.* (esp., slang) Euphemism for 'bloody'.

bleep *n.* & *v.i.* (Emit) high-pitched intermittent sound.

blĕ'mĭsh *v.t.* Mar, spoil beauty or perfection of, sully. ~ *n.* Physical or moral defect, stain, flaw.

blĕnch *v.i.* Start aside, flinch, quail.

blĕnd *v.* (past part. occas. *blent*). Mix, mingle (esp. sorts of tea, tobacco, spirits, etc., to produce a certain quality); mingle intimately *with*; mix so as to be inseparable

BLENHEIM PALACE

and indistinguishable; pass imperceptibly into each other. ~ *n.* Blending; mixture made by blending.

blĕnde *n.* Zinc sulphide. [Ger. *blenden* deceive, because although it often resembled galena, it did not yield lead]

Blĕ'nheim (-nĭm). Village in Bavaria, scene of the victory (1704) of MARLBOROUGH and Prince Eugene over the French and Bavarians; ~ *Palace*, mansion near Woodstock, Oxfordshire, built by the nation for Marlborough after the battle, and designed by Sir John Vanbrugh; ~ *Orange*, variety of golden-coloured late-ripening eating apple, first grown at Blenheim Palace.

blĕ'nnȳ *n.* Small spiny-finned fish of genus *Blennius* of family Blenniidae, mostly shore-fishes found in shallow pools.

blent: see BLEND.

blĕpharī'tis *n.* Inflammation of the eyelids.

Blériot (blārĭō), Louis (1872–1936). French airman, first man to cross the English Channel in an aeroplane (1909).

blĕss *v.t.* (past part. *blessed*, sometimes *blest*). 1. Consecrate (esp. food); sanctify by making sign of cross. 2. Call holy, adore; glorify for benefits received. 3. Pronounce words (held) to confer supernatural favour and well-being upon; make happy or successful; make happy *with* some gift; *bless me!*, *bless you!*, (*God*) *bless my soul!*, *I'm blest!*, etc., exclamations of surprise or indignation.

blĕ'ssĕd (*or* -st) *adj.* 1. Consecrated; revered; fortunate; in paradise. 2. Blissful, bringing happiness. 3. (euphem.) Cursed etc. **blĕ'ssĕdlȳ** *adv.* **blĕ'ssĕdnĕss** *n.*

blĕ'ssĭng *n.* Declaration, invocation, or bestowal, of divine favour; grace before or after food; gift of God, nature, etc., that one is glad of; ~ *in disguise*, misfortune that works for eventual good.

blest: see BLESS.

blĕ'ther, blă'ther (-dh-) *n.* & *v.i.* (Talk) loquacious nonsense.

Bligh (blī), William (1754–1817). English vice-admiral, who as a lieutenant commanded the BOUNTY².

blight (-īt) *n.* 1. Disease of plants caused by fungoid parasites; kind of aphis destructive to fruit-trees. 2. Any obscure or mysterious malignant withering influence. ~ *v.t.* Affect with blight; exert baleful influence on; nip in the bud, mar, frustrate.

blī'ghter (-īt-) *n.* (esp., slang) Contemptible or annoying person or thing; fellow, thing.

Blī'ghtȳ (-ītĭ) *n.* (army slang) England, home, after foreign service. [Hind. *bilāyatī* foreign, European]

blī'mey *int.* (slang) Exclamation of surprise or contempt. [f. *Gorblimey* = God blind me!]

blĭmp¹ *n.* Small non-rigid type of airship.

Blĭmp², Colonel. Character invented by the cartoonist David Low (1891–1963) representing a muddle-headed, obese, elderly gentleman, pop. interpreted as type of diehard or reactionary. **blĭm'perȳ** *n.* **blĭ'mpish** *adj.*

blīnd *adj.* 1. Without sight; (aeronaut.) without direct observation of objects etc., relying on instruments. 2. Without foresight, discernment, or moral or intellectual light; reckless; not ruled by purpose. 3. Secret, obscure, concealed; without windows or openings; walled up; closed at one end; (of plant) failing to flower; (cookery, of pastry case) baked without filling. 4. (slang) Very drunk. 5. ~ *alley*, one closed at one end, not leading anywhere (also fig.); ~ *arcade*, series of arches attached to wall; ~ *corner*, corner of road round which a motorist etc. cannot see; ~ *date*, social engagement arranged between two persons of opposite sex who have not met; either of these persons; ~ *man's buff*, game in which blindfolded player tries to catch others; ~ *spot*, point in the retina not sensitive to light, where the optic nerve passes through the inner coat of the eyeball (also fig.); ~ *stamping, tooling*, (bookbinding), stamping, tooling, without the use of ink or gold-leaf; *bli'ndworm*, slow-worm. ~ *adv.* **blī'ndlў** *adv.* **blī'ndnėss** *n.*

blīnd *v.* Deprive of sight permanently or temporarily; take away power of judgement, deceive; (slang) go blindly or heedlessly; drive very fast. ~ *n.* Obstruction to sight or light; screen for windows etc., esp. on roller; pretext; legitimate business concealing an illegitimate one; stalking-horse; heavy drinking-bout.

blī'ndfōld *adj.* With eyes covered with cloth; without circumspection. ~ *v.t.* Deprive of sight by covering eyes with cloth.

blĭnk *v.* 1. Shut one's eyelids momentarily, esp. involuntarily; (of eyes) shut thus. 2. (fig.) Shut one's eyes to, evade. 3. Send (tears etc.) away by blinking. 4. Shine suddenly or momentarily. ~ *n.* Blinking; momentary gleam or glimpse; shining whiteness on horizon produced by reflection from distant masses of ice; *on the* ~, (slang) failing.

blĭ'nker *n.* Either of two leather screens on horse's bridle preventing him from seeing sideways; ~ *plate*, smoke deflector. ~*v.t.* Obscure with blinkers (freq. fig.).

blĭ'nkĭng *adj.* & *adv.* (slang) Damnable, damnably.

blĭp *v.* Strike with brisk rap; make quick popping sound. ~ *n.* Act, sound, of blipping; (radar) image of object as projected on to a screen.

blĭss[1] *n.* Gladness, enjoyment; perfect joy, blessedness; being in heaven. **blĭ'ssful** *adj.* **blĭ'ssfullў** *adv.* **blĭ'ssfulnėss** *n.*

Blĭss[2], Sir Arthur (1891–). British composer; Master of the Queen's Music 1953– .

blĭ'ster *n.* Thin vesicle on skin filled with serum, caused by friction, a burn, etc.; similar swelling on plant, metal, painted surface, etc.; rounded compartment protruding from body of aeroplane; anything applied to raise a blister; ~-*gas*, poison for causing blisters or intense irritation of the skin. ~ *v.* Raise blister on, be or become covered with blisters; (fig.) criticize scathingly.

B.Lit. *abbrev.* Bachelor of Literature.

blīthe (-dh) *adj.* (poet.) Gay, joyous. **blī'thelў** *adv.* **blī'thesome** *adj.*

blĭ'ther *v.i.* (-dh-) = BLETHER. **blĭ'therĭng** *adj.* (esp.) Consummate; contemptible.

B.Litt. *abbrev.* *Baccalaureus Literarum* (L, = Bachelor of Letters).

blĭtz *n.* Quick, violent campaign intended to bring speedy victory, intensive air-attack; (fig.) sudden violent attack. ~ *v.t.* Damage, destroy, by air-attack. [Ger. *Blitzkrieg* lightning war]

blĭ'zzard *n.* (orig. U.S.) Dense snow-storm, esp. one in which powdery snow is swept up from the ground by a high wind.

bloat[1] *v.t.* Cure (herring) by salting and smoking. **bloa'ter** *n.* Herring cured by bloating.

bloat[2] *v.* Inflate, swell. **bloa'tėd** *adj.* Inflated, swollen; (fig.) swollen with pride, excessive wealth, etc.

blŏb *n.* Drop of liquid; small

roundish mass; spot of colour; (cricket) score of nought.

blŏc *n.* Combination of political parties, or of governments, groups, etc., formed to forward some interest.

Blŏch (-χ), Ernest (1880–1959). Swiss-American composer.

blŏck *n.* 1. Log of wood; large piece of wood for chopping or hammering on, mounting horse from, etc., (hist.) on which condemned persons were beheaded. 2. Compact usu. solid piece of any substance; unhewn lump of rock; prepared piece of building-stone; mould or form on which something is shaped or displayed; piece of wood or metal engraved for printing; mech.) pulley, system of pulley mounted in case; (slang) head. 3. Section, compact set or group; large single building containing a number of flats, offices, etc.; group of buildings surrounded by (usu. four) streets; number of sheets of paper fastened together at edge; (Austral.) each large plot into which land for settlement is divided. 4. Obstruction; line of vehicles unable to proceed; (parl.) notice that bill will be opposed, which prevents its being taken at certain times; (psychol.) mental obstruction preventing a particular thought or expression; (path.) obstruction of a nervous or muscular impulse. 5. (cricket) Spot on which batsman blocks ball and rests bat before playing. 6. ~-*buster*, (slang) large high-explosive bomb; *blo'ckhead*, stupid person; *blo'ckhouse*, detached fort (orig. one blocking passage), occas. one of connected chain of posts; one-storeyed timber building with loopholes; reinforced concrete shelter; ~ *letters, writing*, (writing with) detached letters, as in printing, usu. capitals; ~ *printing*, hand-printing of fabrics with wooden blocks on which design is carved. ~ *v.t.* Obstruct (passage etc.); put obstacles in way of; restrict use or conversion of currency etc.; announce opposition to (bill); (cricket) stop (ball) with bat; shape on block; emboss (book cover); ~ *in, out*, sketch roughly, plan; *blocked*, (of ballet shoes) with stiffened toes.

blŏckā'de *n.* Surrounding of place, blocking of harbour, etc., by hostile forces to prevent goods etc. from reaching or leaving it; *raise, run the* ~, remove, evade, the blockading force. ~ *v.t.* Subject to blockade.

blŏ'ckage *n.* Obstruction.

Blŏk, Alexander (1880–1921). Russian poet, famous for his poem 'The Twelve', an apologia for the Russian Revolution.

blōke *n.* (slang) Man, fellow.

blŏnde *adj.* (also, esp. U.S., *blŏnd*; of hair) Light coloured, flaxen; (of complexion) fair. ~ *n.* Woman with blonde hair.

Blŏ'ndel de Nesle (nāl) (12th c.). Minstrel who, acc. to legend, discovered the place of captivity of his master Richard Cœur-de-Lion by singing under the window a song they had jointly composed.

blood (-ŭd) *n.* 1. Liquid circulating in the veins and arteries of vertebrates, carrying nourishment and oxygen to all parts of the body and bringing away waste products to be excreted, consisting of a serum or plasma in which corpuscles are suspended and usu. red because of their haemoglobin content; (hist.) one of the four humours (see HUMOUR, 4). 2. Analogous liquid in invertebrates performing (some of) the same functions. 3. (fig.) Sap, grape-juice, etc. 4. Taking of life, guilt of bloodshed; passion, temperament, mettle. 5. Race, relationship, kin, descent, parentage. 6. Dandy, man of fashion. 7. ~-*ally*, ally (marble) with red veins; ~-*bath*, massacre; ~-*brother*, brother by birth; one bound to another in solemn friendship by ceremonial mingling of blood; ~ *count*, (determination of) number of blood cells in a given volume of blood; ~-*donor*: see DONOR; ~-*feud*, feud between families of which one has spilt the other's blood; ~ *group*, one of several types into which human blood may

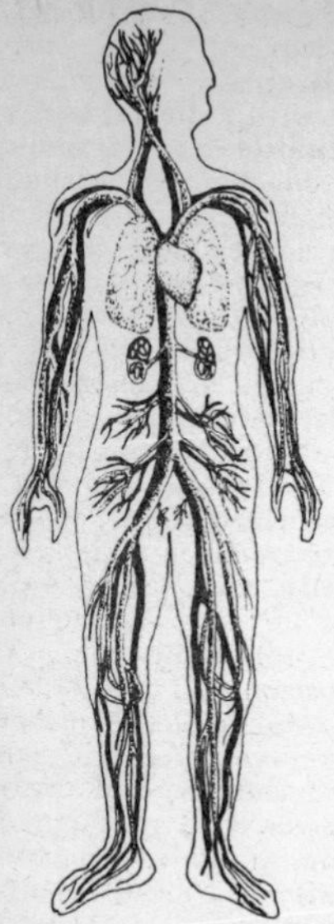

VENOUS and ARTERIAL SYSTEM

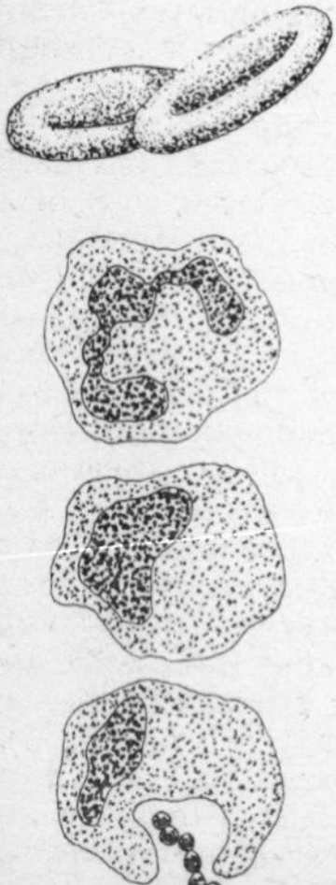

BLOOD CELLS

be divided on basis of its compatibility with that of other persons; ~*-heat*, normal heat of the blood, 37 °C (98·4 °F) in man; *bloo'dhound*, large keen-scented dog formerly used for tracking cattle, criminals, etc.; ~*-letting*, surgical removal of some of patient's blood; ~*-money*, reward to witness for securing capital sentence; compensation for slaughter of relative; ~ *orange*, orange with red-streaked pulp; ~ *poisoning*, condition caused by presence of pathogenic bacteria in the blood; ~*-pressure*, pressure of blood against walls of arteries as it is impelled along them, freq. measured in diagnosis because in certain conditions it may be higher (hypertension) or lower (hypotension) than normal; ~ *relation*, one related by virtue of common descent, not by marriage; *bloo'dshed*, spilling of blood, slaughter; *bloo'dshot*, (of eye) suffused, tinged, with blood; ~ *sport*, sport involving killing of animals, esp. hunting; *bloo'dstock*, thoroughbred horses collectively; *bloo'dstone*, green chalcedony with spots or veins of red jasper; helioptrope; *bloo'dstream*, circulating blood in human or animal system; ~*-sucker*, leech; extortioner; *bloo'dthirsty*, eager for bloodshed; ~*-vessel*, vein, artery, or capillary conveying blood; *bloo'dworm*, bright red larva of a midge, used as bait in fishing. ~ *v.t.* Remove surgically some of the blood of; allow first taste of blood to (hound); smear face of (novice at hunting) with blood of fox after kill. **bloo'dlėss** *adj.* Without blood; unfeeling; pale; without bloodshed.

bloo'dў (-ŭdĭ) *adj.* 1. Of, like, running or smeared with, blood. 2. Involving, loving, resulting from, bloodshed; cruel. 3. (slang) Damned. 4. *B~ Assizes*, those held in 1685 by Judge JEFFREYS; ~*-minded*, cruel; stubbornly intransigent or obstructive. ~ *adv.* (slang) Confoundedly, very. ~ *v.t.* Make bloody; stain with blood.

blōōm[1] *n.* Flower, esp. of plants grown or admired chiefly for the flower, florescence. 2.

Prime, perfection; flush, glow; delicate powdery deposit on grapes, plums, etc.; cloudiness on a shiny surface; freshness. ~ *v.* Bear flowers, be in flower; come into, be in, full beauty; flourish; (photog.) coat (lens) with metallic fluoride to reduce surface reflection. **blōō'mĭng** *adj.* (esp., slang) = BLOODY, 3.

blōōm[2] *n.* Mass of puddled iron hammered or squeezed into thick bar. ~ *v.t.* Make (puddled iron) into a bloom.

blōō'mer[1] *n.* (slang) Blunder.

Blōō'mer[2], Mrs. Amelia Jenks (1818–94). American advocate of 'rational dress' for women, invented by Mrs. E. S. Miller and consisting of a small jacket, a full skirt descending a little below the knee, and trousers down to the ankle.

blōō'mers (-z) *n.pl.* 1. (hist.) Costume advocated by Mrs. BLOOMER[2]; loose trousers reaching to the knee, knickerbockers, formerly worn by women for gymnastics, cycling, etc. 2. Undergarment of this shape, (colloq.) knickers.

Blōō'msbury̆ (-z-). District of west-central London containing British Museum and many buildings of London University, formerly a fashionable and later a literary quarter; (attrib.) intellectual, highbrow.

blŏ'ssom *v.i.* Open into flower (lit. & fig.). ~ *n.* Flower, mass of flowers on fruit-tree etc.; early stage of growth, promise. **blŏ'ssomy̆** *adj.*

blŏt[1] *n.* Spot or stain of ink etc., dark patch; disfigurement, blemish, defect; disgraceful act or quality in good character. ~ *v.* 1. Spot or stain with ink, etc.; make blots; smudge; sully, detract from; obliterate (writing etc.) with blot, destroy. 2. Dry with *blotting-paper*, absorbent paper for soaking up wet ink-marks.

blŏt[2] *n.* Exposed piece in backgammon.

blŏtch *n.* Discoloured or inflamed patch on skin; irregular patch of ink, colour, etc. **blŏ'tched** (-cht), **blŏ'tchy̆** *adjs.*

blŏ'tter *n.* Pad of blotting-paper.

blŏ'ttō *adj.* (slang) Very drunk.

blouse (-z) *n.* 1. (French) workman's or peasant's loose linen or cotton garment, usu. belted at waist. 2. Woman's or child's loose garment for upper part of body, usu. worn tucked into skirt or trousers. 3. Upper part of battledress, fitting closely at waist. ~ *v.* Arrange (material, bodice), be arranged, in loose light folds like a blouse.

blow[1] (-ō) *v.* (past t. *blew* pr. blōō, past part. *blown*). 1. Move as wind does, act as current of air; send current of air from mouth; pant, puff; (of whales etc.) eject water and air; cause to pant, put out of breath. 2. Drive, be driven, by blowing; sound (wind instrument, or note *on* or *with* this); direct air-current at; clear, empty, by air-current; break *in* or send flying *off, out, up,* by explosion; (of instrument) sound; ~ *in,* (colloq.) come in unexpectedly, drop in; ~ *up,* inflate, shatter or be shattered by explosion; reprove violently; (photog., colloq.) enlarge. 3. (of flies) Deposit eggs in. 4. (of electric fuse or lamp filament) Melt when overloaded; (of tin of food) swell or burst from internal pressure. 5. (slang) Curse, confound; squander. 6. *blow'fly,* bluebottle, flesh-fly; *blow'hole,* each of two holes (containing the nostrils) at top of head in whales etc. through which they blow; hole in ice through which seals etc. can breathe; *blow'lamp,* portable apparatus for directing intensely hot flame on a limited area; *blow'out,* bursting (of motor-tyre etc.); (slang) large meal, feast; *blow'pipe,* tube for heating flame by blowing air or other gas into it; tube through which arrows or darts are propelled by blowing; *~-up,* explosion; (colloq.) enlargement. ~ *n.* Blowing, taste of fresh air; blowing of flute, one's nose, etc.

blow[2] (-ō) *v.i.* (past t. *blew* pr. blōō, past part. *blown*). (archaic

& poet.) Burst into, be in, flower. ~ *n.* Blossoming.

blow[3] (-ō) *n.* Hard stroke with fist, hammer, etc.; disaster, shock; ~-*by*-~, (of narrative) giving all details in sequence.

blow′er (-ōer) *n.* (esp.) 1. Apparatus for increasing draught of fire, esp. sheet of iron held or fixed before grate. 2. (slang) Speaking-tube, telephone.

blown: see BLOW[1,2].

blow′y (-ōĭ) *adj.* Windy, wind-swept.

blowzed (-zd), **blow′zy̆** *adjs.* (of woman) Red-faced, coarse-looking; slatternly.

blŭb *v.i.* (colloq.) Cry, weep.

blŭ′bber *n.* 1. Fatty tissue of aquatic mammals, which keeps them warm, esp. *whale*-~, used as source of oil. 2. Weeping. ~ *adj.* (of lips) Swollen, protruding. ~ *v.* Utter with sobs, weep noisily.

Blü′cher (-ūχ-), Gebhard Lebe-recht von (1742–1819). Prussian soldier; led the Prussian army at the battle of WATERLOO.

blu′chers (-ōōkerz) *n.pl.* (19th-c.) Strong leather half-boots or high shoes. [f. BLÜCHER]

blŭ′dgeon (-jon) *n.* Short heavy-headed stick. ~ *v.t.* Strike heavily or repeatedly with or as with bludgeon.

blue (-ōō) *adj.* 1. Coloured like the cloudless sky, or with darker or paler shades of this colour; livid, leaden-coloured. 2. Affected with fear, discomfort, anxiety, low spirits, etc. 3. Dressed in blue; belonging to a political party (in Britain usu. Conservative) whose badge is blue; (of talk etc.) indecent, obscene. 4. ~ *baby*, infant suffering from congenital cyanosis; *blue′bell*, wild hyacinth, *Endymion non-scriptus*; (Sc. & north.) harebell; ~ *blood*, high birth; ~ *bonnet*, round flat blue woollen cap formerly generally worn in Scotland; (hist.) Scottish soldier wearing this; ~ *book*, parliamentary or Privy Council report, issued in blue paper cover; *blue′-bottle*, dipterous insect with blue body of genus *Calliphora* (esp. *C. vomitoria* and *C. erythroce-*

phala), which deposits eggs on meat, carrion, etc.; blue cornflower; (slang) policeman; ~ *cheese*, cheese with veins of blue mould; ~ *chip*, (Stock Exch.) share that is a fairly reliable investment, though less secure than gilt-edged (also attrib.); ~-*coat boy, school*, (pupil of) charity school, esp. of Christ's Hospital, whose uniform is a long dark-blue belted gown and yellow stockings; ~-*eyed boy*, (colloq.) favourite; ~ *grass*, species of *Poa*, esp. *P. pratensis* as found in Kentucky and Virginia; ~ *gum*, Australian variety of eucalyptus, *Eucalyptus globulus*, with bluish bark; *blue′-jacket*, seaman in Royal Navy; *B~ John*, blue fluorspar found in Derbyshire; ~ *law*, (U.S.) severely Puritanical law; ~ *mould*, fungus of genus *Penicillium* forming on food; *B~ Nile*: see NILE; ~ *pencil*, pencil making blue mark, used chiefly in making corrections, obliterations, etc.; ~-*pencil* (*v.t.*) make marks, cuts, or alterations in; censor; *B~ Peter*, blue flag with white square in centre, hoisted by ship before sailing; ~-*point*, (U.S.) small well-flavoured oyster from south shore of Long Island [f. name of headland]; ~-*print*, photographic print of white lines on blue ground or blue lines on white ground, used in copying plans, machine-drawings, etc.; (fig.) detailed plan, scheme; ~ *ribbon*, ribbon of the Garter; greatest honour or distinction in any sphere; badge of teetotalism; *blue′stocking*, woman having or affecting literary tastes and learning [f. *B~ Stocking Society*, name given in 18th c. to meetings for literary conversation etc. at the houses of Mrs Elizabeth Montagu (1720–1800) and her circle, from the fact that the men attending might wear the blue worsted stockings of ordinary day-time dress instead of the black silk of evening]; ~ *tit*: see TIT[1]; ~ *vitriol*, copper sulphate; ~ *water*, deep water, the open sea. **blū'ish** *adj.* **blue'nėss** *n.* **blue** *n.* 1. Blue colour or pigment; blue powder used in laundering; blue cloth etc. 2. Sky, sea (*the* ~); *out of the* ~, unexpectedly. 3. (Place in team etc. given to) one chosen to represent Oxford University (*dark* ~) or Cambridge (*light* ~) in athletic or sporting contests. 4. (pl.) Melancholy; (type of) melancholy song of Amer. Negro origin; *the Blues*, the Royal HORSE Guards. ~ *v.t.* (pres. part. *blueing* or *bluing*) Make blue; treat with laundering blue; (slang) squander (money).

Blue'beard (blo͞ob-). Hero of a popular tale, who killed several wives in turn because they showed undue curiosity about a locked room; ~'*s chamber*, repository of mysterious or horrible secrets.

blŭff[1] *adj.* Having prependicular broad front; abrupt, blunt, frank, hearty. **blŭ'fflȳ** *adv.* **blŭ'ffnėss** *n.* **blŭff** *n.* Headland with perpendicular broad face.

blŭff[2] *v.* Make pretence of strength to gain advantage etc. (orig. in poker); mislead thus. ~ *n.* Bluffing; *call person's* ~, challenge his attempted bluff.

blŭ'nder *v.* Move blindly, stumble; make gross mistake. ~ *n.* Stupid or careless mistake. **blŭ'nderer** *n.*

blŭ'nderbŭss *n.* Short flintlock gun with large bore, firing many balls or slugs, used esp. in 17th and 18th centuries. [Corupt of Du. *donderbus* lit. thundergun]

blŭnge (-j) *v.t.* (pottery) Mix (clay, powdered flint, etc.) with water.

blŭnt *adj.* Dull, not sensitive; without sharp edge or point; outspoken. **blŭ'ntlȳ** *adv.* **blŭ'ntnėss** *n.* **blŭnt** *v.t.* Make less sharp or sensitive.

blûr *n.* Smear of ink etc.; dimness, confused effect. ~ *v.* Smear with ink etc.; sully, disfigure; make indistinct; efface; dim.

blûrb *n.* (orig. U.S. slang) Publisher's eulogy or description of book printed on jacket etc.; descriptive or commendatory paragraph.

blûrt *v.t.* Burst *out* with, utter abruptly.

blŭsh *v.i.* Become red with shame or other emotion; be ashamed; be red or pink. ~ *n.* Glance, glimpse; reddening of face in shame etc.; rosy glow, flush of light.

blŭ'ster *v.* Storm boisterously; utter overbearingly. **blŭ'sterer** *n.* **blŭ'ster** *n.* Boisterous blowing, noisy self-assertive talk, threats. **blŭ'sterous, blŭ'sterȳ** *adjs.*

B.M. *abbrev.* Bachelor of Medicine; British Museum.

B.M.A. *abbrev.* British Medical Association.

B.Mus. *abbrev.* Bachelor of Music.

B.N.C. *abbrev.* Brasenose College, Oxford.

bō, boh (bō) *int.* Exclamation used to startle; *he cannot say bo to a goose*, he behaves meekly or timidly.

B.O. *abbrev.* Body odour.

bō'a *n.* 1. S. Amer. tropical non-poisonous snake of genus *B*~ that kills its prey by constriction or compression (pop. extended to pythons); ~ *constrictor*, large Brazilian species of boa; any great crushing snake. 2. Long round fur or feather wrap formerly worn round throat by women.

B.O.A.C. *abbrev.* British Overseas Airways Corporation.

Bōadĭcē'a: see BOUDICCA.

boar (bôr) *n.* Uncastrated male swine (wild or tame); flesh of this; *wild* ~, European wild swine, *Sus scrofa*.

board (bôrd) *n.* 1. Thin piece of timber, usu. rectangular, and of greater length than breadth; one or more pieces of this or similar substance, used in games, for posting notices, etc.; (pl.) the stage; thick stiff paper used in bookbinding etc.; *across the* ~, embracing all categories. 2. Table spread for meals; food served, daily meals provided at contract price or in return for services; council-table, councillors, committee. 3. Ship's side (only in certain phrases); (naut.) tack; *on* ~, aboard, in or into ship, train, etc. 4. ~ *school*, (hist.): see SCHOOL board; *B~ of Trade*, former British government department dealing with problems of trade; (U.S.) association of businessmen etc. to promote trade; *B~ of Trade unit*, (abbrev. B.T.U.) = KILOWATT-hour; ~ *wages*, wages paid to servants while their masters are away from home, including cost of food etc.; ~-*walk*, (U.S.) footway of boards or planks. ~ *v.* 1. Cover with boards. 2. Provide with, receive, stated meals at fixed rate; ~ *out*, place (children) in families where they are treated as members. 3. Go on board, enter (ship, train, etc.); (naut.) come alongside and force one's way on board (ship). 4. (naut.) Tack.

boar'der (bôr-) *n.* One who boards with someone; boy or girl at boarding-school; one who boards a ship to capture it.

boar'ding (bôr-) *n.* (esp.) ~-*house*, house in which persons are boarded and lodged for payment; ~-*school*, school in which pupils live during term-time, as dist. from day-school.

boast *n.* Exceedingly proud statement; cause of pride. ~ *v.* Praise oneself, make boast(s) (*of*, *about*); possess as thing to be proud of. **boa'ster** *n.* **boa'stful** *adj.* **boa'stfullў** *adv.* **boa'stfulnėss** *n.*

boat *n.* 1. Small open oared or sailing vessel; fishing-vessel, mail packet, small steamer; occas. large sea-going vessel; *in the same* ~, in the same predicament or circumstances. 2. Boat-shaped table-utensil for sauce etc. 3. ~-*axe*, boat-shaped battle-axe of the neolithic period in Scandinavia; ~-*hook*, long pole with hook and spike; ~-*house*, shed at water's edge for keeping boat; *boa'tman*, hirer, or rower or sailer of boat for hire; *B~ Race*, (esp.) race between crews of Oxford and Cambridge Universities, rowed annually on the Thames from Putney to Mortlake; *boatswain* (bō'sn), *bo'sun*, ship's officer in charge of sails, rigging, etc., and summoning men to duty with whistle; ~ *train*, train having connection with a steamer at a port. ~ *v.i.* Go in boat, esp. for pleasure.

boa'ter *n.* Straw hat with flat crown and brim.

Bō'ăz: see RUTH[2].

bŏb[1] *n.* 1. Weight on pendulum, plum-line , or kite tail. 2. Knot of hair, tassel-shaped curl; horse's docked tail bobbed hair. ~ *v.t.* Cut (hair) to hang short of the shoulders.

bŏb[2] *n.* 1. Jerk, bouncing movement; curtsy. 2. (bell-ringing) Kinds of change in long peals; *treble* ~, one in which the bells, esp. the treble, dodge; ~ *minor*, *triple*, *major*, *royal*, *maximus*, bobs on 6, 7, 8, 10, and 12 bells. ~ *v.i.* Move up and down, dance, rebound; curtsy; ~ *for*, try to catch (cherries, apples, etc., floating or hanging) with the mouth.

bŏb[3] *n.* (at Eton) *dry*-~, one who plays cricket, opp. *wet*-~, one who rows. [prob. pet-form of *Robert*]

bŏb[4] *n.* (slang) Shilling.

bŏb[5] *n.* & *v.i.* (Ride on) a bob-sled or -sleigh.

bŏ'bbĭn *n.* 1. Cylinder on which thread, wire, etc., may be wound, reel, spool; ~ *lace*: see LACE. 2. Rounded piece of wood attached to a string, for raising door-latch.

bŏ'bbĭnėt *n.* Machine-made net imitating bobbin lace.

bŏ'bbĭsh *adj.* (slang) Brisk, well.

bŏ'bble *n.* Small woolly ball used as ornament or trimming.

bŏ'bbў *n.* (slang) Policeman. [Pet-form of *Robert*, in allusion to Sir Robert Peel, who was Home Secretary when the Metropolitan Police Act was passed in 1828]

bŏ'bbў sŏcks. Socks reaching just above the ankle, worn esp. by teenage girls. **bŏ'bbў-sŏ'xer** *n.* (freq. derog.) Girl wearing bobby socks.

bŏ'bolink *n.* A N. Amer. song-bird, the rice-bunting (*Dolichonyx oryzivorus*). [orig. *Bob* (*o'*) *Lincoln*; imit. of its call]

bŏb-slĕd, bob-sleigh (-slā) *ns.* Sledge made of two short sledges coupled together.

bŏ'bstay *n.* (naut.) Rope holding bowsprit down.

bŏ'btail *n.* (Horse or dog with) docked tail; *tag, rag, and* ~, rabble.

boca'ge (-ahzh) *n.* Representation of sylvan scenery in ceramics.

Boccă'ccio (-chĭō), Giovanni (1313–75). Italian novelist, poet, and humanist, author of the 'Decameron'.

Bŏccheri'nĭ (-kerē-) Luigi (1740–1805). Italian composer, important chiefly for his works for violoncello.

Bŏche (-sh) *n.* & *adj.* (slang, esp. in 1914–18 war) German.

bŏck *n.* Strong dark-coloured German beer. [Ger., f. *Einbockbier*, beer from *Einbeck*, in Hanover]

bōde[1] *v.* Foresee, foretell (evil); portend, foreshow; promise *well, ill.* **bō'deful** *adj.* Ominous.

Bode[2] (bō'de), Johann Elert (1747–1826). German astronomer; gave currency to an empirical rule, previously formulated by J. D. Titius, but known as ~'*s law*, for determining the approximate distances of the planets from the sun.

bodē'ga *n.* Cellar or shop selling wine. [Sp., f. L, f. Gk *apothēkē* store]

Bŏdhĭsa'ttva (-dĭsah-) *n.* (Buddhism) Person who is entitled by his good deeds to enter Nirvana, but who delays doing so out of compassion for human suffering.

bŏ'dice *n.* Upper part of woman's dress, down to waist; undergarment for same part of body. [orig. (pair of) *bodies*, stays, corset]

bŏ'dĭlėss *adj.* Incorporeal, separated from the body.

bŏ'dĭlȳ *adj.* Of, affecting, the human body or physical nature (opp. *spiritual*). ~ *adv.* With the whole bulk, as a whole.

bŏ'dkĭn *n.* 1. Thick, blunt needle with large eye for threading tape etc. through hem. 2. Dagger (obs.); small pointed instrument for piercing holes in cloth etc.

Bŏ'dleian Lī'brarȳ (-lēan).

BODLEIAN LIBRARY

(also *the Bodlei'an*; colloq. *Bo'd-ley*) Library of Oxford University; founded by Humphrey, duke of Gloucester (1391–1447), and re-founded, 1603, by Sir Thomas Bodley (1545–1613), diplomat and scholar, one of the COPYRIGHT libraries.

bŏ'dȳ *n.* 1. Material frame of man or animal; corpse. 2. Trunk apart from head and limbs; main portion of anything; part of vehicle etc. fitted to receive the load; shank of piece of type. 3. Bulk, majority. 4. Person. 5. Aggregate of persons or things; collection; *in a* ~, in a group. 6. Piece of matter (*heavenly* ~); mass of tissue forming a structure; solidity, substance; (of wine) rich full flavour. 7. (pottery) Main substance. 8. ~ *carpet(ing)*, carpet(ing) manufactured in strips that are joined to form required size; *bo'dyguard*, guard for the person (esp. of sovereign or dignitary), retinue, escort; ~-*image*, (psychol.) mental image of one's own body; ~-*line bowling*, (cricket) fast bowling on the leg side directed or alleged to be directed at the person of the batsman; *the* ~ *politic*, the State; ~-*snatcher*, (hist.) one who secretly disinters corpses to sell them for dissection; ~ *stocking*, woman's undergarment covering trunk and legs; *bo'dywork*, (esp.) body of a vehicle. ~ *v.t.* (usu. with *forth*) Give mental shape to; exhibit in outward shape; typify.

Boehme (bẽr'me), Jakob (1575–1624). German mystic; held that will is the original force, that every manifestation involves opposition, and that existence is a process of conflict between pairs of contrasted principles, which are ultimately resolved into a new unity.

Boeotia (bēō'sha). Ancient country of central Greece, whose inhabitants were proverbial for slow-wittedness. **Boeo'tian** *adj.* & *n.*

Bō'er (*or* boor) *n.* S. Afr. farmer of Dutch origin; ~ *War*, each of two wars fought by Gt Britain: the 1st (1880–1) against Transvaal, which, annexed by Britain in 1877, had proclaimed its independence; the 2nd (1899–1902) against the Transvaal and Orange Free State, resulting in the annexation of these States by Gt Britain.

Bōē'thĭus, Anicius Manlius Severinus (*c* 475–525). Roman philosopher; consul under Theodoric the Ostrogoth; was suspected of treason and confined to prison, where he wrote 'De Consolatione Philosophiae'; the Neoplatonic and stoic ideas of this work had great influence throughout the Middle Ages.

bŏ'ffĭn *n.* (slang) One engaged in scientific esp. technical research.

Bō'fors (-z) *n.* (also ~ *gun*) Clip-fed, rapid-firing light anti-aircraft gun. [name of a munition works in Örebro Län, Sweden]

bŏg *n.* (Piece of) wet spongy ground, consisting chiefly of decayed or decaying moss or other vegetable matter; ~-*myrtle*, sweet gale, *Myrica gale*; ~ *oak*, oak-wood preserved in a black state in peat-bogs etc. **bŏ'ggȳ** *adj.* **bŏ'g-gĭnėss** *n.* **bŏg** *v.t.* Submerge in bog; ~ *down* (fig.).

bō'gey (-gĭ) *n.* 1. Bogy. 2. (golf) Number of strokes a good player is reckoned to need for the course or for a hole, freq. personified as *Colonel B*~. [app. jocular application of *bogy*, 'something to be afraid of']

bŏ'ggle *v.i.* Start with fright, shy; hesitate, demur. *at*.

bō'gie (-gĭ) *n.* Under-carriage with two or more pairs of wheels, pivoted below front part of railway-engine or ends of long railway-carriage, tram-car, etc., to facilitate travelling round curves.

bō'gus *adj.* (orig. U.S.) Sham, fictitious, spurious.

bō'gȳ (-gĭ) *n.* (also *bo'gey*) 1. (esp. *Old B*~) The Devil. 2. Goblin. 3. Bugbear.

bohea' (-hē) *n.* Black tea of lowest quality, the last crop of the season (in 18th c., the finest kinds of black tea). [Chin. *Wu-i* district]